Children's
Oral Communication Skills

DEVELOPMENTAL PSYCHOLOGY SERIES

SERIES EDITOR
Harry Beilin

Developmental Psychology Program
City University of New York Graduate School
New York, New York

LYNN S. LIBEN. *Deaf Children: Developmental Perspectives*

JONAS LANGER. *The Origins of Logic: Six to Twelve Months*

GILBERTE PIERAUT-LE BONNIEC. *The Development of Modal Reasoning: Genesis of Necessity and Possibility Notions*

TIFFANY MARTINI FIELD, SUSAN GOLDBERG, DANIEL STERN, and ANITA MILLER SOSTEK. (Editors). *High-Risk Infants and Children: Adult and Peer Interactions*

BARRY GHOLSON. *The Cognitive-Developmental Basis of Human Learning: Studies in Hypothesis Testing*

ROBERT L. SELMAN. *The Growth of Interpersonal Understanding: Developmental and Clinical Analyses*

RAINER H. KLUWE and HANS SPADA. (Editors). *Developmental Models of Thinking*

HARBEN BOUTOURLINE YOUNG and LUCY RAU FERGUSON. *Puberty to Manhood in Italy and America*

SARAH L. FRIEDMAN and MARIAN SIGMAN. (Editors). *Preterm Birth and Psychological Development*

LYNN S. LIBEN, ARTHUR H. PATTERSON, and NORA NEWCOMBE. (Editors). *Spatial Representation and Behavior Across the Life Span: Theory and Application*

W. PATRICK DICKSON. (Editor). *Children's Oral Communication Skills*

In Preparation

EUGENE S. GOLLIN. (Editor). *Developmental Plasticity: Behavioral and Biological Aspects of Variations in Development*

Children's Oral Communication Skills

Edited by

W. PATRICK DICKSON

*Wisconsin Research and Development Center
and Child and Family Studies Department
University of Wisconsin—Madison
Madison, Wisconsin*

ACADEMIC PRESS

A Subsidiary of Harcourt Brace Jovanovich, Publishers

New York   London   Toronto   Sydney   San Francisco

ACADEMIC PRESS, INC.
111 Fifth Avenue, New York, New York 10003

United Kingdom Edition published by
ACADEMIC PRESS, INC. (LONDON) LTD.
24/28 Oval Road, London NW1 7DX

Library of Congress Cataloging in Publication Data
Main entry under title:

Children's oral communication skills.

(Developmental psychology)
Papers presented at a conference held at the Wisconsin
Research and Development Center, Madison, Oct. 18–20,
1978.
Includes bibliographies and index.
1. Interpersonal communication in children––
Congresses. I. Dickson, W. Patrick. II. Series:
Developmental psychology series.
BF723.C57C48   155.4'13   80–1774
ISBN 0–12–215450–9

PRINTED IN THE UNITED STATES OF AMERICA

81 82 83 84   9 8 7 6 5 4 3 2 1

Contents

v

2
Cognitive Monitoring   35

JOHN H. FLAVELL

3
Comprehension Monitoring   61

ELLEN M. MARKMAN

4
The Role of Role-Taking in Children's Referential
Communication   85

CAROLYN UHLINGER SHANTZ

II
REFERENTIAL COMMUNICATION STUDIES

5
Training Referential Communication Skills   105

STEVEN R. ASHER AND ALLAN WIGFIELD

6
The Development of Informative Messages in Referential Communication: Knowing When versus Knowing How 127

GROVER J. WHITEHURST AND SUSAN SONNENSCHEIN

7
The Development of Listener Skills for Referential Communication 143

CHARLOTTE J. PATTERSON AND MARY C. KISTER

8
The Child's Understanding of Inadequate Messages and Communication Failure: A Problem of Ignorance or Egocentrism? 167

E. J. ROBINSON

16
Problem Solving Communication and Complex Information Transmission in Groups 357

JANINE BEAUDICHON

List of Contributors

Numbers in parentheses indicate the pages on which authors' contributions begin.

Vernon L. Allen (337), Department of Psychology, University of Wisconsin—Madison, Madison, Wisconsin 53706

Paul Ammon (13), School of Education, University of California, Berkeley, Berkeley, California 94720

Steven R. Asher (105), Bureau of Educational Research, University of Illinois, Urbana, Illinois 61801

Janine Beaudichon (357), Laboratoire de Psychologie Genetique, Rene Descartes University 75005 Paris 5e France

Mary Clevenger (207), Department of Sociology, University of Wisconsin—Madison, Madison, Wisconsin 53706

W. Patrick Dickson (1, 189), Wisconsin Research and Development Center, and Child and Family Studies Department, University of Wisconsin—Madison, Madison, Wisconsin 53706

Christine Dollaghan (207), Department of Communicative Disorders, University of Wisconsin—Madison, Madison, Wisconsin 53706

Frederick Erickson (241), Institute for Research on Teaching, College of Education, Michigan State University, East Lansing, Michigan 48824

John H. Flavell (35), Department of Psychology, Stanford University, Stanford, California 94305

Rocco Fondacaro (289), Department of Psychology, University of Western Ontario, London, Ontario, Canada N6A 5C2

Peg Griffin (271), The Laboratory of Comparative Human Cognition and Linguistics, University of California, San Diego, La Jolla, California 92093

E. Tory Higgins (289), Department of Psychology, University of Western Ontario, London, Ontario, Canada N6A 5C2

Angela Hildyard (313), Ontario Institute for Studies in Education, Toronto, Ontario, Canada M5S 1V6

Mary C. Kister (143), Department of Psychology, University of Virginia, Charlottesville, Virginia 22901

Ellen M. Markman (61), Department of Psychology, Stanford University, Stanford, California 94305

C. Douglas McCann (289), Department of Psychology, University of Western Ontario, London, Ontario, Canada N6A 5C2

David R. Olson (313), Department of Applied Psychology, Ontario Institute for Studies in Education, Toronto, Ontario, Canada M5S 1V6

Charlotte J. Patterson (143), Department of Psychology, University of Virginia, Charlottesville, Virginia 22901

E. J. Robinson (167), School of Education, University of Bristol, Bristol, BS8 1JA, England

Carolyn Uhlinger Shantz (85), Department of Psychology, Wayne State University, Detroit, Michigan 48202

Roger W. Shuy (271), Georgetown University and The Center for Applied Linguistics, Washington, D.C. 20057

Susan Sonnenschein (127), Department of Psychology, University of Maryland, Baltimore, Maryland 21228

Grover J. Whitehurst (127), The Merrill-Palmer Institute, Detroit, Michigan 48202

Allan Wigfield (105), Department of Educational Psychology, University of Illinois, Urbana, Illinois 61801

Louise Cherry Wilkinson (207), Department of Educational Psychology, University of Wisconsin—Madison, Wisconsin 53706

Preface

This book is an outgrowth of a conference held in October 1978 at the Wisconsin Research and Development Center in Madison. The purpose of the conference was to integrate the large body of research on children's communication skills deriving from two heretofore separate research perspectives: experimental research on referential communication skills and sociolinguistic approaches to research on children's communicative competence in natural settings. In addition, the participants in the conference were asked to consider the educational implications of this research and future directions for research and teaching of communication skills. The appearance of this book is especially timely in view of the attention now focused on oral communication. The recent inclusion of speaking and listening skills within the official definition of "basic skills" by the Office of Education has led to a great demand for information on children's oral communication skills, both how they can be measured and taught as well as how they affect children's participation in classroom activities.

The research brought together in this volume portrays an optimistic view of children's ability to communicate, both in the sense of specific communication skills such as speaking and listening and in broader aspects of communicative competence. Perhaps most exciting is the evidence emerging from recent research that children can be taught a number of speaking and listening skills. As recently as 1975, there was little in the reviews of research in this area to encourage the belief that communication skills were teachable. Indeed, the pervasive influence of the Piagetian concept of egocentrism had led to an inclination to accept the view that these skills would be rather impervious to training—a view that early studies seemed to support. The extensive body of research in recent years has dispelled this belief. Clearly, from the research reported in this volume, children can be taught to encode more informative messages and to ask for more information when given inadequate messages. And when children speak with children who ask effective questions, the speakers themselves appear to improve their messages. In addition, children can be taught that communication is a two-person activity, and that successful communication depends on the efforts of both the speaker and the listener—an insight that many children fail to achieve on their own.

A second encouraging theme underlying the present volume is that both the referential and sociolinguistic traditions have important contributions to make to our understanding of children's communication. In a sense, these two approaches are complementary. The referential tradition emphasizes experimental designs and has yielded valuable insights into specific communication skills and ways to teach them. The sociolinguistic tradition emphasizes observations of children's communication in natural settings and has yielded evidence of the richness of children's communication in such natural contexts as small reading groups and more extensive classroom activities. These two traditions have tended to remain isolated from each other, unable to surmount the communication barriers between them. The present volume is a step toward the kind of cross-disciplinary interchange that is needed for a full understanding of the development of communication skills.

The third major contribution of this volume is to offer broader theoretical perspectives on children's communication skills. Contained here is theoretical work that reflects the growing importance of cognitive models of the processes underlying children's communication performance. In addition, the processes involved in communication are shown to have much in common with other cognitive processes and to be applicable to processing written passages, as well as oral communication. Other aspects of communication are discussed, including the influence of nonverbal and social factors, which have all too often been neglected in research on children's communication.

This book is directed toward three major groups. First, for researchers in both the referential and sociolinguistic traditions, the book provides a summary of the state of the art in our efforts at understanding children's communication skills, coupled with theoretical perspectives to guide future research. Second, for educators concerned with the development of a curriculum for oral communication skills, the book indicates a number of skills that can be taught and describes techniques that have been successful in teaching these skills, thus providing a research base for curriculum development. Third, policymakers concerned with the role of communication skills in the curriculum at the local, state, and national levels should find the book useful, both as a comprehensive statement of what we know, as well as a demonstration that basic research can be brought to bear on a vital educational issue.

Acknowledgments

Earlier versions of the chapters contained in this volume were originally presented at a conference that was supported by funds from the National Institute of Education through the Wisconsin Research and Development Center for Individualized Schooling. Participants in the conference, along with the first authors of the chapters, were Sandor Brent, Robin Chapman, Barbara Foorman, Karen Fuson, Sam Glucksberg, Dean Hewes, Angela Hildyard, Marsha Ironsmith, Vinetta Johnson, Luis Moll, Scott Paris, Gary Price, Marcia Whiteman, Steve Yussen, and Courtney Cazden. These participants also served as reviewers for the chapters. Their valuable contributions are gratefully appreciated. Special thanks go to Lynn Sowle who handled the correspondence and typing for the conference and the book.

Children's
Oral Communication Skills

Introduction: Toward an Interdisciplinary Conception of Children's Communication Abilities

W. PATRICK DICKSON

This book seeks to integrate a large body of research on children's communication skills in a form that will not only be useful in guiding further research in this area, but that will also be useful to those concerned with the educational implications of the research. The research has implications both for explicitly teaching communication skills and for understanding the impact that children's communication skills have on classroom processes.

Communication, by its very nature, is a complex interaction between two or more people, and one that involves many different processes. For example, imagine a situation, as sketched in Figure I.1, where one person is trying to tell another person which of several trees in a forest he is looking at. He might describe the tree as an "oak tree." If the other person asks, "What's an oak tree?" he must look at the tree again and recode his description in other terms. Such recoding may be done several times before the two people arrive at a shared understanding. Even this simple example involves a large number of processes, some of which are tagged in Figure I.1. Discussions of many of these processes appear in later chapters of the book.

The point to be made here is that no single theory, no unitary measure of

1

Children's Oral Communication Skills

COMMUNICATION PROCESSES IN TELLING THE FOREST FROM THE TREES

① roletaking ② perceiving   ③ verbal processing ④ encoding
⑤ decoding   ⑥ comprehension monitoring ⑦ questioning   ⑧ comparing
⑨ recoding   ⑩ comprehending   ⑪ acknowledging   ⑫ metacommunication

Figure I.1. Communication processes in telling the forest from the trees.

communication skill or competence, is capable of encompassing all aspects of communication performance. All our theories and data can give but fragmentary glimpses of the phenomenon of human communication, rather like the tale of seven blind men describing an elephant. Two responses are possible when different perspectives lead to different viewpoints: One can seek to determine which is correct, or more profitably, one can call out in the dark and ask, "How does it look from where you stand?" The reader of this book is invited to ask the latter question. When the different viewpoints and insights are considered together, there emerge the outlines of a more comprehensive understanding of the nature and development of children's communication.

The need for multiple perspectives may be made clearer by an examination of two heretofore rather separate research traditions, which, for convenience, will be labeled the "referential" and the "sociolinguistic." A brief discussion of these two traditions may also help place the individual chapters in the book into a more meaningful context.

Referential and Sociolinguistic Research Traditions

The referential research tradition grew out of work by Piaget and began to receive attention in the United States in the late 1960s through the work of Flavell and associates and Glucksberg and Krauss and their associates. Reviewing this tradition, Flavell (1977, pp. 173–179) characterized it as focusing on referential communication in artificial tasks in laboratory settings and seeking to explain levels of performance in terms of underlying cognitive abilities, especially Piagetian notions of egocentrism and role-taking. Chapters in this book by Asher and Wigfield, Whitehurst and Sonnenschein, Patterson and Kister, Robinson, Shantz, and Beaudichon represent this work, and the chapter by Dickson examines in detail some other characteristics of this research tradition.

The sociolinguistic tradition has a more diversified ancestry, drawing from linguistics, anthropology, sociology, social psychology, and other disciplines. The sociolinguistic tradition is concerned with communicative competence in a broad sense, generally has observed children in natural settings, and has sought to explain children's communicative behavior in terms of social and contextual variables, rather than cognitive processes of the individual children. The chapters by Wilkinson, Clevenger, and Dollaghan, Shuy and Griffin, Erickson, and to a certain extent Olson and Hildyard, represent research in the sociolinguistic tradition.

Detailed discussions of these two traditions are given in the later chapters and will not be repeated here. Rather, the contrasts between these two traditions will be placed in the context of a more fundamental division in approaches to research which, again for convenience, will be labeled as "quantitative" and "qualitative" approaches. There are two risks in labeling and pointing out differences. First, labels rarely fit every case perfectly, and, second, the act of pointing out differences often is taken as invidious. Nevertheless, we will note some differences with a view of highlighting the complementarity of these two approaches and identifying specific contributions each research tradition might make to the other. The present discussion is influenced by a paper by Rist (1977) presented at a conference concerned with the qualitative versus quantitative contrast. (The proceedings of that conference, which was attended by many scholars in the sociolinguistic tradition, appeared in the May 1977 issue of *Anthropology and Education Quarterly*.)

A number of contrasts between research in the referential and sociolinguistic traditions are presented in Table I.1. The more qualitative approaches have tended toward a large number of observations and variables measured on small numbers of subjects. This approach has led to what Geertz (1973) calls "thick description," rather than the application of inferential statistics. The more quantitative approaches have tended toward large numbers of subjects with fewer observations. A second point of divergence is that the qualitative approach places greater emphasis on validity (hence the use of natural settings, ethnomethodologies, and participant observation from anthropology), with less attention to reliability. The quantitative approach has emphasized reliability considerably more than validity. Third, the qualitative approach tends to show little interest in individual differences. Indeed, some of the motivation behind the qualitative approach derives from an ethical stance that considerable harm has resulted from educational emphases on individual differences. In contrast, the more quantitative approaches have

TABLE I.1
Contrasts between the Referential and Sociolinguistic Traditions

	Referential	Sociolinguistic
1. Focus:	Referential skill	Broader communicative competence
2. Setting:	Experimental laboratory; children often communicating with experimenter	Naturalistic, realistic tasks; children communicating with other children or teachers
3. Explanation:	Cognitive processes: initially Piagetian, now moving toward information-processing models	Roles and situations
4. Finding:	Earlier, children seen as egocentric, incompetent; now egocentrism discounted as major factor	Children seen as not egocentric, highly competent
5. Numbers:	Few observations and variables, many subjects	Many observations and variables, few subjects
6. Data and analysis:	Statistical analysis of quantitative measures common; verbal protocols rare	Verbal protocols commonly presented and explicated; statistical analysis less often emphasized
7. Age of people studied:	Much research on ages 4–8	Much research either during infancy or in elementary school classrooms
8. Psychometrics:	Reliability emphasized; validity less emphasized	Validity emphasized; reliability less emphasized
9. Individual differences:	Correlations among measures on individuals common, but individuals as individuals rarely described	Individual cases described in detail, but correlations among measures on individuals rare
10. Analytic–Wholistic:	Analysis of subskills such as listening, speaking, questioning	Whole seen as more than sum of its parts
11. Training:	Training studies used to understand processes; recent success on training specific skills	Training studies rare
12. Philosophy of science:	Objectivity emphasized	Subjectivity seen as unavoidable and even valuable

measured individual performance and increasingly have looked at patterns of correlations in an attempt at understanding how these human abilities hang together.

Another dimension of difference lies in the level of analysis: The more quantitative approaches have tended to study components of communication, such as speaking, listening, or questioning skill, whereas the qualitative approach is more holistic, often arguing that so much is lost by analysis into subskills that the cost outweighs the benefit. The approaches tend to differ in the extent to which training studies are common: They are increasingly common in the quantitative approach, whereas the qualitative approach is less intervention oriented, believing that it is best to have a complete understanding of a situation before trying to intervene. And, in the rather more emotionally laden domain, the two approaches have differed in their level of self-scrutiny with respect to the objectivity–subjectivity dimension.

If one examines the contrasts outlined in Table I.1 without being diverted by the weary question of which approach is better, one can ask the more interesting question of what each approach has to offer to our understanding of children's communication. As is clear in the chapters in this book, each approach has much to contribute. The sociolinguistic approach, for example, has done the field a considerable service by emphasizing the importance of studying children in natural settings, and one outcome of this research has been to accentuate the positive communicative competencies of young children. The detailed study of a small number of children can be a fruitful source of hypotheses about factors influencing children's communication—as evidenced by Piaget's early clinical method. The rich verbal protocols and anecdotal evidence that researchers in the qualitative approaches present also serve to keep before our eyes the richness of natural communication and the individuality of the children whose communication is being studied. Finally, the sociolinguistic approach has given some attention to children communicating with other children and teachers in small groups and classrooms—work that is potentially useful in planning ways to enhance children's acquisition of communication skills in classrooms.

Research in the referential tradition has also made valuable contributions to our understanding of children's communication skills. Focusing on a single skill has made it possible to test specific hypotheses about basic processes underlying communication performance. In addition, the experimental approach makes it possible to disprove certain hypotheses that initially seemed plausible. For example, Piaget's hypothesis that egocentrism accounted in a substantial way for children's communicative failures has had considerable intuitive appeal. Only after a substantial number of carefully designed studies failed to confirm the hypothesized relationship between egocentrism and communicative performance was the hypothesized link revealed to be nonexistent, or at least much weaker than originally thought (see Chapter 4 by Shantz and Chapter 8 by Robinson). Research in the more quantitative referential tradition, by virtue of measuring the performance of relatively large numbers of children on specific tasks, has made us aware of the large individual differences in communication skills that exist among children of similar age and ability. This attention to measurement of individual performance is especially important for education, where teachers need ways of assessing individuals and monitoring their learning. The analytic approach used in referential communication research has also revealed the fact that communication ability does not consist of a single generalized skill but rather appears to include a number of fairly independent skills, such as skill in composing initial descriptions and skill in asking questions. Finally, the referential tradition has produced a number of ways of training communication skills.

Having highlighted some of the strengths of both the sociolinguistic and referential research traditions, let us now attempt the more difficult task of asking what techniques and insights each of the approaches might profitably adopt from the other. Sociolinguistic researchers might consider how the individual children they study in depth compare with their classmates on communication competencies analyzed. The demonstrations of instances of competent behavior in rich verbal protocols, which are common in ethnographic studies, might be supplemented by some quantitative data. In view of the fact that sociolinguistic research often involves relatively few subjects, exploratory data analysis techniques may be more appropriate in sociolinguistic analyses than parametric statistics. Figure 10.1 in Chapter 10 by Wilkinson, Clevinger, and Dollaghan is an example of displaying data in a way that includes both the qualitative and quantitative information. This display communicates not only the mean levels of behavior of small groups but also the means of individuals making up the groups. Further, although sociolinguistic studies have shown that even young children can demonstrate more competence in natural situations than referential research had led us to expect, this accentuation of the positive may lead us to the overly optimistic view that all children are sufficiently competent communicators early in their lives that no educational interventions are needed.

Reflecting perhaps the strong influence of anthropology upon its development, the sociolinguistic approach, in emphasizing natural settings, may overlook the possibility of actively intervening in educational settings to deliberately create new settings in order to achieve specific educational outcomes. It should be remembered that what is seen today as a natural setting (such as a reading circle) was once an intervention. Although experimental training studies may not appeal to many sociolinguists, other interventions involving the active participation of teachers and children may (see, for example, Chapter 12 by Shuy and Griffin).

At the same time, the referential research tradition could be considerably enriched by ideas developed in the sociolinguistic tradition. The laboratory tasks used in referential communication research have perhaps lacked validity less from the fact that they were laboratory tasks than from the fact that many of the tasks were not very representative of natural communication tasks. Dickson, in Chapter 9 in this volume, surveys changes in the types of tasks and experimental designs used in the referential tradition. He reaches the conclusion that referential research turned from rather complex communication tasks in which children were allowed to interact freely with other children to simpler tasks in which no interaction was allowed and typically the children interacted with an experimenter. Although this trend toward tighter experimental control has no doubt increased the reliability of the results, the validity of the measures appears to have suffered, along with the likelihood of the results being generalizable to natural contexts. The referential tradition has also tended to focus on a rather narrow age range, especially the age range of 4–8, primarily as a result of the Piagetian concerns. Yet, from the few studies done with elementary-school-age children and with adults, it is clear that communication skill continues to develop into adulthood and that large individual differences exist well beyond the age at which egocentrism in the Piagetian sense has any real meaning. Our understanding of the development of referential skill, and the applicability of our findings to education, would be increased by research on a broader age range. Finally, there has been relatively little attention to the generalizability of referential communication skill to natural settings. Studies of the relationship of referential communication skill to children's communicative behavior in classrooms and small groups are badly needed. At the same time, concern for the generalizability of communication skill should not obscure the fact that distinct types of competence exist, such as those involved in speaking to peers and those involved in speaking to teachers.

The detailed examination given to the referential and sociolinguistic research traditions should not obscure the fact that there are a number of other research perspectives. Cognitive psychology and information-processing theory are increasingly influential. The neo-Piagetian model discussed by Ammon in Chapter 1 represents this influence, as does Asher and Wigfield's discussion of a task-analytic approach in Chapter 5. Metacognitive theories concerned with the development of self-conscious monitoring of one's communicative performance appear in Chapters 2 and 3, by Flavell and Markman respectively. And there is a growing recognition of the influence of society and role upon communication behavior, which is manifest in Chapter 13 by Higgins, Fondacaro, and McCann, and Chapter 14 by Olson and Hildyard.

Overview of the Book

The book is divided into four parts. Part I, "Theoretical Perspectives on Communication," begins with an exposition by Ammon of Pascual-Leone's neo-Piagetian theory and the application of it to processes involved in children's communication. Ammon makes important distinctions between skills and other kinds of knowledge, as well as between knowledge relevant to only communication and other kinds of knowledge. The next chapter by Flavell places communication within a broader context of other cognitive processes and emphasizes the distinction between children's cognitive strategies and their metacognitive experiences, a distinction directly relevant to the training studies in Part II, where children taught strategies for communicating accurately also appear to gain some insights into reasons for communicative failure. Markman's chapter on comprehension monitoring points out the need for individuals to know what they know if they are to know when they know enough to act or seek more information when they do not. In Chapter 4, Shantz examines the concept of role-taking and its relationship to communication performance. Her review of this research reveals little support for the common belief that role-taking, as it has been defined in the past, plays a major role in communication performance.

Part II, "Referential Communication Studies," brings together the large body of research on the development of children's referential skills. Asher and Wigfield (Chapter 5) apply a task-analytic approach to the analysis of children's comparison activities in a word-pair communication task and find that young children in the speaker role fail to make necessary comparisons spontaneously but can learn to carry out comparisons when exposed to training that includes modeling and self-guidance statements. In Chapter 6, Whitehurst and Sonnenschein analyze children's encoding skills in a picture-describing communication task and find that children appear unaware of the need to describe differences when attempting to communicate; instructions to describe differences, coupled with specific feedback when descriptions were inadequate, led to major improvements in the children's messages. Patterson and Kister (Chapter 7) review research on listener behavior in referential tasks and conclude that even if young listeners realize that they do not have sufficient information to choose, they often fail to ask for more information because they have not learned to do so; training led to an increase in listener questions and a consequent increase in successful communication. In Chapter 8, Robinson explores one aspect of children's metacommunicative knowledge: the awareness that communication failures can be the fault of either the speaker or the listener. Robinson not only shows that children come to this awareness if exposed to specific feedback pointing out the source of the failure, but also reports observations of parents' and teachers' interactions with young children that suggest that adults may unconsciously keep children in their state of ignorance by failing to explicitly point out the inadequacy of children's descriptions. Dickson's chapter concludes Part II with a metaanalysis of research in the referential communication tradition, as well as an examination of referential communication activities for use in classrooms. He concludes with suggestions for future research and for curriculum development in the area of oral communication skills.

Part III, "Sociolinguistic Studies," contains three chapters that reflect different aspects of sociolinguistic research. Wilkinson, Clevenger, and Dollaghan (Chapter 10) analyze the pattern of interaction among children in three small reading groups. Their chapter illustrates the presentation of portions of verbal protocols and the display of data highlighting the large individual differences among these children in their tendency to ask questions of same-sex versus opposite-sex members of the groups. Erickson (Chapter 11) presents a detailed analysis of the way participants in a communication setting—in this case a screening test being given to a young child in a kindergarten class—interact in temporal sequence to jointly produce the communication event. Because the timing of tester and child are out of synchrony, the tester fails to understand the child, a failure that ends up being attributed to the child, not the adult. In Chapter 12, Shuy and Griffin discuss a major sociolinguistic study of language use in the early school years; they outline six major assumptions guiding the study and then present some of its results. The assumptions emphasize the importance of context, involvement of the participants in the research, and multidisciplinary perspectives.

Part IV, "Other Aspects of Communication," contains chapters that address several other influences upon communicative performance. In Chapter 13, Higgins, Fondacaro, and McCann suggest that speaking and listening differ in fundamental ways which have important implications for research on communication skill; although communication requires coorientation and interaction between speaker and listener, it also requires that they have the same goals—which may not always be the case. Thus, they conclude that communication failures often may result, not from lack of skill, but from divergent goals. Olson and Hildyard (Chapter 14) adopt a speech act orientation as a way of bringing together the referential and social aspects of language. They show how social relations influence the interpretation placed on any given message. Further, they find that young children appear to respond more to the social implications of statements, but that, with increasing age and education, children come to differentiate the truth value of propositions from their ellocutionary force to some extent. These rarely can be separated. In Chapter 15, Allen reviews research on nonverbal communication that is especially relevant to comprehension monitoring in oral communication; he shows that children evidence large individual differences in their sensitivity to nonverbal messages. Beaudichon (Chapter 16) reviews an extensive series of studies done in France. This research is of interest because it began with rather standard referential communication tasks and then moved to more natural referential tasks in which children, in groups of four, communicated about directions on a map. Beaudichon concludes with a description of the introduction of some referential tasks into classrooms.

Overall, the chapters in this book present a tapistry in which a rich, colorful picture of children's communication is woven from multidisciplinary threads. The different approaches and different theoretical conceptions each reveal unique facets of the complexity of children's communication. What is most satisfying is that these different perspectives are presented here in ways that accentuate the complementarity of these perspectives, in contrast to the more common tendency to attempt to bolster one disciplinary approach by denouncing another. The potential for collaboration between researchers bringing their views from different traditions to bear on research on children's communication is evident. The time is ripe for such interdisciplinary undertakings.

Finally, the attention given to the educational implications of the research discussed in each chapter should stimulate the exchange of ideas between research and practice. George Miller once described scientific journals as "catalogs of spare parts for a machine they never build [1956, p. 252]." Perhaps it is not too much to hope, however, that a more interesting oral communication curriculum might be built from the parts carefully assembled in this book.

References

Flavell, J. *Cognitive development*. Englewood Cliffs, N.J.: Prentice-Hall, 1977.

Geertz, C. *The interpretation of cultures*. New York: Basic Books, 1973.

Miller, G. A. Psychology's block of marble. *Contemporary Psychology*, 1956, *1*, 252.

Rist, R. C. On relations among educational research paradigms: From disdain to detente. *Anthropology and Education Quarterly*, 1977, *7*, 42–49.

1
Theoretical Perspectives on Communication

1
Communication Skills and Communicative Competence: A Neo-Piagetian Process–Structural View

PAUL AMMON

The phrase *communication skills* appears not only in the title of the present volume but also in numerous other books and articles in the recent literature of developmental psychology and education. It has become a catchall term for any of the psychological equipment that people use in communicating. Similarly, the term *communicative competence* often refers, in the literature of sociolinguistics and psycholinguistics, to the whole knowledge base underlying communicative performance. Because both of these terms are commonly used in very global and informal ways, they do have a certain convenience. But this global usage also tends to blur three distinctions which I regard as important:

1. The distinction between skills and other forms of knowledge
2. The distinction between knowledge that is relevant only to communication and knowledge that is relevant to communication, but not communication alone
3. The distinction between knowledge and psychological factors other than knowledge that influence communicative performance

13

None of these distinctions is especially new; each has already been discussed to some extent by others. Nevertheless, all three are still neglected in many current discussions about the development of communication skills or communicative competence. Because I believe this neglect impedes our progress in understanding and promoting communicative development, I will try here to explicate each of the three distinctions and to demonstrate their importance for research and practice regarding children's communication.

Perhaps these distinctions have been neglected, in part, because studies of language and communication generally have not been carried out within a theoretical framework that enables one to make them in an explicit and systematic fashion. The theory of constructive operators proposed by Pascual-Leone (1969, 1970, 1976a) offers this capability but is not widely known among those who are concerned with communicative development in children. In the sections that follow, I will draw heavily upon Pascual-Leone's neo-Piagetian approach (especially Pascual-Leone, 1976a), but I will not attempt to summarize the theory itself, as that would take too much space and would be redundant with summaries that are available elsewhere (Ammon, 1977; Case, 1974, 1978; Pascual-Leone, Goodman, Ammon, & Subelman, 1978).

Skills versus other Forms of Knowledge

In everyday usage, the word "skill" is usually reserved for a particular form of knowledge; it is practical knowledge, or knowing *how* as opposed to knowing *about* (see Cazden, 1972, for discussion of a similar distinction with reference to language). When a particular skill is applied, we expect that some sort of pragmatic action will ensue more or less automatically. Such is not the case with other forms of knowledge. A speaker may know, for example, that it is important to adapt messages to the perspective of one's audience in order to communicate effectively, yet lack the skills that are needed to put this knowledge about communication into practice. On the other hand, speakers may have certain practical skills and apply them successfully without knowing what general principles are involved. Knowledge of a principle, or plan, can of course influence performance by leading to the mobilization of appropriate skills, where this mobilization does not already happen more automatically (e.g., Cosgrove & Patterson, 1977), but the principle cannot itself bring about the performance without the application of one or more skills. Thus skills differ from other forms of knowledge in their immediate consequences or effects, specifically in the "directness" of their relationship to practical action (Pascual-Leone, 1976a). Another, related difference between skills and other forms of knowledge concerns their origins, or the conditions under which they are acquired. Knowledge *about* the performance of a communication task can be acquired from explanations or

demonstrations, but we usually expect that the *skills* involved in the performance can only be acquired through actual practice in performing the criterion task, in whole or in part.

Both of these intuitively familiar differences between skills and other
forms of knowledge seem potentially important from a pedagogical point of
view. On the one hand, it would be important not to mistake knowledge
about communication for communication skills in the strict sense. Assuming
that the goal of instruction vis-à-vis communication is effective *performance*,
it must be remembered that knowledge about communication does not
suffice, by itself, to produce communicative performance, nor does it
guarantee application of the necessary skills. On the other hand, acquisition
of knowledge about relevant aspects of communication may sometimes be a
useful basis for the subsequent development of appropriate skills, so long as
opportunities for the practice necessary in skill development are also provided. But in order for us to determine exactly what sorts of skills are
required in a given communication task, and what other sorts of knowledge
are relevant, we must be clearer as to how skills, in general, are structurally
different from, and functionally related to, other forms of knowledge.

Although we sometimes speak of "skill" as a continuous quantity which
someone can have more or less of, we are more likely to regard "skills" as
discrete modules or units of knowledge which can be combined or coordinated in various ways to produce complex performances. The latter view
seems the more promising one in that it leads to an analysis of the processes
underlying performance, whereas the former view treats skill as a purely
performatory construct, equivalent to a total score on a series of test items.
What is needed, then, is a theoretical explication of skills as units of knowledge.

From a Piagetian point of view, the basic structural unit of all knowledge, including skills, is a *scheme*. Pascual-Leone (1976a) has suggested that
it is possible to distinguish two fundamentally different kinds of schemes,
which he calls *predicative* and *transformational*. The primary difference between the two resides in their *effecting components*, that is, in the semantic or
pragmatic consequences that ensue when a given scheme has assimilated
some input, or "applied" to it, as Pascual-Leone would say. Predicative
schemes have the effect of *representing* objects and events, or their properties; they provide the mental objects that are the basic content of cognition.
Transformational schemes have the effect of *changing* the properties of mental objects, or of the physical objects they represent. The transformations
themselves can be represented through a special class of predicative
schemes called *fluents*, which are the structural basis for what Tolman called
expectancies. Given the representation of a particular transformation, the
subject also expects the result that the transformation entails. Such an expectancy may then lead the subject to apply one or more actual transformations which accord jointly with the expectancy and the subject's goals. Thus,

in general, cognitive processes involve a continual interplay between predicates and transformations: The application of predicative schemes to inputs gives rise to mental objects on which particular transformations are subsequently applied, resulting in new mental objects which can lead to further transformations, and so forth.

Given our intuitive understanding of what skills are, it seems consistent to suggest that skills may be defined more formally as transformational schemes (Pascual-Leone, 1976a). That is, skills are the direct psychological causes of the transformations that are involved in all cognitive processes, including the processes underlying communication. The transformations may be either physical, as in the overt production of speech, or entirely mental, as in the covert production or evaluation of a message. Accordingly, the other forms of knowledge involved in communication can be defined as predicative schemes, either ordinary predicates or transformation-representing predicates (fluents). Thus the principle that a message should be adapted to the audience to be effective may be regarded as a verbal description of a very general fluent. A person who has this fluent in his or her repertoire can have the expectancy that if certain adapting transformations are applied to a given message, then it will be correctly understood by the audience. It seems likely that such fluents comprise much of one's conscious knowledge about communication, or what has been called "metacommunicative" knowledge (Flavell, 1976, 1977).

This discussion of transformations and predicates as distinguishable aspects of communicative competence may resemble earlier discussions of "linguistic competence" by transformational grammarians. It is important to realize, however, that the resemblance is quite superficial and that the present view of competence differs in a fundamental way from the linguistic one. A brief comparison of the two approaches should help to make the difference between them clear. Although it has not always been understood as such, the linguistic view of competence entails a *purely structural* characterization of linguistic knowledge in terms of abstract rules—rules that describe certain regularities in language use from the *observer's* point of view, but which are not seen as the direct causes of the subject's performance. To indicate that this is a purely structural characterization of competence, it is often said that the speaker knows the rules "in some sense," or performs "as if" he knows them. Moreover, it is generally acknowledged that speakers sometimes do not perform in accordance with the rules they are supposed to know, but these irregularities are simply attributed to unanalyzed "performance factors."

In contrast, the present view of competence includes both skills, which *are* seen as the direct causes of performance, and other forms of knowledge, which guide the use of skills and provide mental objects for their application. Thus, instead of a *purely structural* characterization of competence, it is a *process–structural* characterization. Competence consists of certain functional structures that produce specific effects in the real-time process of performance. By explicating these structures in terms of Pascual-Leone's transformational and predicative schemes, we gain the possibility of using his theory to create models of the ways in which communication skills and knowledge about communication interact with each other, with other knowledge, and with other psychological factors that affect communicative performance. In this way, we also gain the possibility of accounting for all communicative performance—both the regular and the irregular (which, of course, will now be regarded as "regular," i.e., predictable, too). And, if one accepts the Piagetian view that knowledge is constructed from praxis, we therefore gain the added possibility of explaining how communicative competence is *acquired,* which cannot be done with a purely structural approach. Finally, it also becomes possible to account for individual differences in both competence and performance. However, in order to begin exploring these possibilities, we must go on to consider the other two distinctions that I mentioned at the outset.

Knowledge Relevant Only to Communication versus other Relevant Knowledge

So far I have suggested that the knowledge base underlying communicative performance, that is, communicative competence, includes both skills in the strict sense and other forms of knowledge as well, and that it is useful to distinguish between the two in terms of transformational versus predicative schemes. The question I want to address now is how to differentiate *communicative* competence from overall intellectual competence, or knowledge in general. Of all the schemes in a person's repertoire, there must be a subset that is of special interest to us because of its particular relevance to the person's performance as a communicator. In fact, we could simply define this subset to include all those schemes that might be applied at one time or another in communicative performance. But this purely *functional* definition of communicative competence is far too broad. It would include, among other things, all the schemes that might be involved in perceiving or thinking about the referent or topic of communication. Since the set of possible topics is limited only by an individual's knowledge of the world, it follows that the set of potentially relevant schemes would be proportionately large. Obviously some narrowing down is needed to give our field of study sharper focus.

The narrowing down may be easier if we treat the transformational and predicative aspects of communicative competence separately. To begin with the latter, it seems reasonable to include under communicative competence only those ordinary predicates and fluents that pertain to communication itself—the schemes that serve to represent messages, or message parts, and the transformations that involve them. (It should be stressed that we are concerned here with the *representation* of messages, as opposed to the production, comprehension, or evaluation of messages; the latter are caused most directly by transformational schemes, which I will discuss in what follows.) Thus the predicative component of communicative competence would include, for example, the means by which a speaker might represent the fact that a particular class of objects can be called *beagles,* but not the speaker's essentially nonlinguistic knowledge about beagles. Similarly, it would include the speaker's knowledge that a 3-year-old probably will not know the meaning of the word *beagle,* which is relevant only to communication, but it would not include the speaker's knowledge about the 3-year-old's capability of distinguishing beagles from nonbeagles, which is potentially relevant to other activities, as well as communication. In other words, communicative competence would not include knowledge about the topic or referent of a message—unless the topic were some aspect of language or communication itself, as in the present instance—nor would communicative competence include knowledge about people, except where people are considered *as communicators.* This is not to deny the obvious relevance of other knowledge about topics and people to communicative performance, but to argue that it is useful for us to ask what a given individual knows, or could learn, about communication per se.

The part of communicative competence that consists of skills might be said to include all the transformational schemes that could apply to production, comprehension, or evaluation of messages, independent of their particular content. But I would question whether all the schemes in this set ought properly to be called *communication* skills. Take, for example, the skills involved in comparing objects. Most referential communication tasks (at least of the laboratory variety) seem to require the use of comparison skills, as the speaker (or listener) must find attributes of the referent object that distinguish it from the immediate array of nonreferents. But the same sorts of skills could also be applied in a number of *non*communication tasks, such as classification or discrimination learning. Similarly, consider the skills involved in "people reading." They clearly are relevant to a variety of communication tasks, but they can be involved in other interpersonal tasks as well. Are we to say, then, that these skills are communication skills in some areas of application but not in others? We can, and often do, use the term "communication skills" in exactly this way, at least implicitly. In doing so, however, we ignore the possibility that, although some of the skills commonly involved in communication can also be applied in other contexts, there may be other skills that are actually peculiar to communication. The latter category would almost certainly include the transformational schemes that are the immediate causes of speech production, but it might include other, more interiorized transformations too.

The identification of skills that are communication-specific seems important from a practical standpoint, because those skills—by definition—can be acquired and assessed only through communicative performance. Other, more general skills present the possibility of being developed and assessed in other kinds of performance. Thus instructional activities that do not themselves entail communication may nonetheless be seen as contributing to the promotion of effective communication through the development of other, more general skills that can be used in communicative performances as well. Of course a danger in pursuing this last possibility is that we might be dealing in some instances with other skills that are actually less general than we assume and are, in fact, specific to particular kinds of *non*communication tasks. We should be able to avoid that pitfall, though, if we are sufficiently sensitive to the need for precision in specifying the contexts in which a given skill is applicable, from the *subject's* point of view. (Pascual-Leone would say "from the *meta*subject's point of view," to emphasize that the perspective we are taking is not that of the subject's phenomenal experience, but rather that of the psychological system underlying the subject's performance—or at least our model of that system.)

According to the theory of constructive operators, all skills (and all schemes in general) are in some way situation-specific. The degree of specificity may vary considerably from one scheme to another, but in all cases it should be possible, in principle, to identify a set of antecedent situational conditions, or *cues,* which must be present before a given scheme tries to apply. (I say "tries to apply" because schemes are seen as very active psychological constructs.) In Pascual-Leone's (1976a) terms, we are concerned here with the *releasing* component of a scheme, as opposed to its effecting component. If one or more of the cues represented in a scheme's releasing component are satisfied, then the scheme is activated, that is, it tries to apply. The greater the number of satisfied cues, the more strongly the scheme is activated (other things being equal) and the more likely it is actually to apply, that is, to produce the consequences specified in its effecting component. What I am suggesting, then, is that communication skills can be differentiated from other skills by their releasing components; they are transformational schemes that are activated only in communication situations. In this regard, the transformational part of communicative competence is delimited in essentially the same fashion as the predicative part.

Pascual-Leone's analysis of the releasing components of schemes immediately provides one way of explaining observed inconsistencies in an individual's performance across different tasks that appear to require the same skill. It is possible that the skill in question is released only by some task situations and not by others. The young child's comparison skills, for example, might be released by some kinds of object arrays but not by others, or by objects in one type of pragmatic context (e.g., a sorting task), but not by objects in another (e.g., referential communication). To borrow Flavell's (1970) terms from the study of memory development, the child's failure to perform comparisons in the context of communication reflects a *production* deficiency rather than a *mediation* deficiency. That is, the child possesses a comparison scheme (a *mediator*) which could produce desirable effects in a referential communication task but does not, because it is not activated sufficiently by input from the communication task environment. Perhaps in some situations the scheme is activated only weakly, due to a relatively small number of cues being satisfied, so that the scheme in question is easily overridden by some other, competing scheme which is more strongly activated. Any situation is likely to activate a large number of schemes in the subject's repertoire—more schemes than could actually apply at one time. Thus it is the relative activation of the pragmatically appropriate scheme and the competing alternatives that determines whether a production deficiency will occur with regard to that scheme or not. And the relative weighting of schemes depends, in part, on the fit between their respective releasing components and conditions in the situation at hand.

To illustrate further, suppose a young child possesses a comparison scheme and also a scheme for simply sampling the attributes of an individual object. Both schemes might be activated to some extent by any situation containing an array of visible objects. If the situation also contains cues indicating more or less explicitly that the child is to search for features of a target object that distinguish it from the others in the array, then the comparison scheme will be activated more strongly than the simple sampling scheme. On the other hand, if the situation contains cues indicating that the child is to select features that *describe* the target object, then the sampling scheme might be the one that is more strongly activated. If so, the higher activation weight of the sampling scheme could be explained as follows. First, some features of the referent object would probably be more salient or familiar to the child than others, so that the predicative schemes representing those features would immediately be activated more strongly than the schemes for other features of the same object. Such a state of affairs would be highly compatible with the sampling scheme, whose function is to select particular features from among those that are available, and this very compatibility could serve to increase the activation of the sampling scheme itself, which might then apply on one (or more) of the highly active feature schemes. In addition, the sampling scheme could receive further weighting in the communication task environment if object descriptions based on simple sampling have often sufficed to bring about effective communication in the past.

To the extent that a referential communication task requires attention to nonsalient features and resembles other situations in which comparisons are pragmatically unnecessary, it is a "misleading" task, very much like a Piagetian conservation task, for example. The more misleading a task, the more likely one is to find production deficiencies in performance. There is good reason to believe that such production deficiencies are, in fact, quite common in the referential communication performance of younger children. It has been found, for instance, that many children who would not spontaneously use distinctive features to describe a referent object nevertheless do so when explicitly asked how the referent differs from other objects in the same array (Whitehurst & Sonnenschein, this volume; Ammon, Tharinger, & Portnuff, in preparation).

From an instructional standpoint, it is clear that children who display the kind of production deficiency described do not need to learn *how* to make comparisons, but rather *when* to make them. In principle, this learning could be brought about through the sort of conditioning process that Pascual-Leone (1976a) calls *C-learning—C* for the "content" of schemes. That is, in the context of the standard communication task, the child could repeatedly be given explicit instructions to make comparisons, or to say how referents are different from nonreferents. Eventually it would become unnecessary to give these special instructions, as a variety of other cues from the standard task environment would be incorporated in the releasing component of a new comparison-for-communication scheme, and would be sufficient to activate the new scheme strongly under the standard task conditions.

In practice, however, it may be neither necessary nor desirable to use *C* learning as a means of overcoming the child's production deficiency with respect to the making of comparisons for communication. Stronger activation of the child's existing comparison scheme in communication situations might be brought about through the mediation of other schemes in the child's repertoire. According to the theory of constructive operators, the momentary activation weight of a given scheme often reflects the activity of other schemes, in addition to, or in lieu of, direct input from the environment. Of particular importance in this regard are those fluents that can function as *executives*, or "plans," which guide performance by bringing about the application of other schemes as needed.

The performance of comparisons in a referential communication task might be guided by an executive representing the rule that if the speaker says how the referents are different from the nonreferents, then the listener will be able to select the referents without error. The application of this fluent in the task situation would then lead to the strong activation and application of the subject's comparison scheme, even though the latter scheme might not be activated very strongly by direct input from the external situation. Some sort of mediated activation like this seems necessary to account for the effective performance of older subjects in the typical referential communication experiment, particularly when they succeed in selecting distinctive features despite the presence of misleading cues. In a sense, then, a production deficiency that is observed with regard to comparisons in the performance of younger subjects could still be attributed to a mediation deficiency, that is, to the absence of an appropriate executive scheme. But I will argue that the concept of mediation deficiency still does not suffice, in the end, to account for all failures in communicative performance.

It can be seen from the example of mediated comparisons that, even though the definition of communicative competence that has been suggested is relatively narrow, it will not result in the neglect of other knowledge in our attempts to explain communicative performance. The comparison scheme in the example is not, strictly speaking, a communication skill, but its contribution to communicative performance is nonetheless recognized, and it is brought about by another scheme which *is* part of communicative competence—namely, the fluent serving as the executive. The present approach forces us to ask not only *whether* comparison activity occurs in the subject's performance, but also *why* it occurs. Is there some communication-specific knowledge that brings the comparison activity about in the service of communication and, if so, what is it?

It seems worth mentioning that mediated comparison activity for referential communication could lead eventually to the construction of a new communication skill that would be functionally similar to the C-learned comparison-for-communication skill that has been described. If the subject had repeated practice in performing the same sort of task with mediated comparisons, the performance would probably take on a kind of automaticity after a while. We could explain this automaticity by saying that the subject had constructed a new skill—a complex transformational scheme that has in its releasing component a set of cues corresponding to the situation of the referential communication task, and that has in its effecting component the detection and labeling of attributes that distinguish referent objects from nonreferents. The entire process can now run off automatically once the new scheme applies, because the new scheme—by definition—functions as a single unit. Notice, also, that this more automatic comparison activity in referential communication is now a direct reflection of communicative competence, because the skill that causes this activity is specifically a communication skill. Thus the same kind of "competent" performance at different points in development, or by different individuals, does not necessarily indicate the same kind of communicative competence.

Let us return now to the fluent that I suggested might mediate comparison activity when such activity is not strongly activated by direct input from the external situation—the rule about saying how referents are different from nonreferents to ensure their correct selection by a listener. It is not enough simply to attribute this knowledge about communication to older children in order to explain their superior performance on referential communication tasks. We must also explain how the knowledge has been acquired by older children, and why it has not yet been acquired by children who are younger.

To touch just briefly on the first of these questions, it is entirely possible for some children to have been taught an appropriate referential communication fluent through modeling or didactic instruction. On the other hand, I certainly have the impression that many children construct such a scheme without any direct instruction, through a process of invention or discovery, just as they apparently construct their own solutions for other sorts of problems, such as Piagetian conservation tasks. In our research (Ammon *et al.*, in preparation), we have seen children in the midst of performing our experimental task suddenly experience an "Aha!" with respect to the need for comparisons, even in the absence of any feedback indicating that their prior performance was inadequate. Pascual-Leone's theory suggests that the fluent in question could be constructed through the process called *L learning* (*L* for "logical," structural learning), which entails the coordination and integration of other schemes already in the subject's repertoire—in this case, schemes for representing the goal of the task, the means available to the speaker, the listener's situation, and so on. I think it can be seen intuitively that some of these prerequisite schemes do not pertain specifically to communication, and therefore are not part of the individual's communicative competence per se. This, then, is another place where it becomes necessary to consider the role of "other knowledge": not only in the construction of communicative performance, but also in the construction of communicative competence. Exactly how this sort of insightful construction comes about is something I will discuss further in the following section, along with the question of why it is more likely to come about with older than with younger children.

To sum up the present section, we have been concerned primarily with the releasing components of schemes involved in the process of communication, that is, the antecedent conditions that activate the skills and other forms of knowledge that come into play. I have argued that communicative competence could be limited to those schemes—either transformational or predicative—that are activated specifically and exclusively in tasks having to do with communication. The value of this definition is that it gives more stability to the notion of communicative competence than a purely functional definition, and it gives us a focus for studying the competence underlying communicative performance, but without restricting our attention *only* to communicative competence. It also forces us to be precise in specifying the situations in which the subject's knowledge can apply.

In this last regard, it seems that behavioral scientists face a particularly tricky problem. On the one hand, they must look for regularities in the performance of their subjects, just as their subjects look for regularities in their own experience. In both cases, the schematized regularities provide a basis for prediction and explanation. On the other hand, though the scientists—with their well-developed powers of abstraction—also run the risk of overgeneralizing in their search for regularities, and of attributing the overgeneralizations to their subjects. In short, I suspect that a lot of the knowledge in communicative competence is more situation-specific than the rules that have been proposed by sophisticated observers would lead us to believe (see, for example, Maratsos, Kuczaj, & Fox, 1977; Kraus & Ammon, 1980). At the same time, it seems clear that many aspects of communicative performance are not at all peculiar to communication per se, and that a complete analysis of performance must go well beyond communicative competence to include other kinds of knowledge, some of which may be quite generaly in its applicability.

Knowledge versus other Psychological Factors

At this point I may appear to be taking the position that an accurate specification of an individual's repertoire of relevant schemes would be sufficient to explain his or her communicative performance at a given time in development, and hence to explain communicative development itself, once we knew what sorts of situations were provided by the individual's environment. It is a view that would be consistent with the strong bias toward empiricist epistemology that runs through much of American psychology. According to this view, present behavior results entirely from the application of knowledge gained through past experience, and intellectual development (including communicative development) results essentially from cumulative learning (e.g., Gagné, 1968). However, this is not the position I wish to convey in the present discussion.

An alternative epistemological position is that of constructive rationalism, as represented most notably in developmental psychology by Piaget, and as explicated in process–structural terms by Pascual-Leone in his theory of constructive operators. It should be clear by now that Pascual-Leone does treat situation-specific knowledge and cumulative learning as essential factors in behavior and development. But they are not seen as sufficient. Rather, Pascual-Leone maintains that an adequate theory of behavior and development must also include additional factors—factors that are independent of situation-specific knowledge, and that constrain the acquisition and use of such knowledge. I will not try to review all the philosophical and psychological arguments for this position (see Pascual-Leone, 1976a), nor will I discuss each of the additional factors identified in the theory of constructive operators to date (see Pascual-Leone et al., 1978). Instead, I will just comment briefly on one factor that seems especially important for explaining "mediated" communicative performance and communicative development.

Earlier discussions of the competence–performance distinction often cited as a "performance factor" the speaker's limited working memory, or capacity to process information. In fact, most process-oriented models of cognition have included such a factor. It is not surprising, then, that a similar construct is central in Pascual-Leone's theory too. In this case, the working memory factor is conceived as a reservoir of mental attentional energy, called M, which can boost the activation weights of selected schemes to the point where they apply. The selection of schemes to be mobilized in this way depends upon the particular executive scheme guiding the subject's current performance, in combination with the immediate situation. But, because the amount of mental energy in the subject's reservoir is limited, there is also a limit on the number of schemes that can be M-boosted at any one time. In fact, the maximum number of schemes that can be simultaneously M-boosted is the theoretical measure of a subject's M *power*. Independent of specific experiences, there appears to be a linear increase in M power from one scheme at about age 3 up to seven schemes by late adolescence.

It can be seen, then, that communicative performance mediated by the sort of executive fluent described earlier depends to a large extent on the availability of sufficient M power to boost the schemes that are needed for effective communication in a given situation. Even where the subject has in his or her repertoire a set of schemes that should suffice in principle, including an adequate task executive, performance may still suffer in practice if the M *demand* of the task exceeds the subject's M power (see Scardamalia, 1977, for a clear demonstration of this possibility in a noncommunication task). In other words, one might say in such a case that performance has underestimated competence (i.e., knowledge), or that a "pure" production deficiency has occurred.

An individual's limited M power also constrains his or her ability to construct new schemes through the integration of old ones, particularly by means of the process that Pascual-Leone calls *LM learning*—that is, logical, insightful learning that results when the subject "has in mind" all the essential elements of a problem, including those that require M boosting. Once a scheme has been constructed in this fashion, it functions as a single unit, like any other scheme, regardless of how many separate schemes went into its construction. Thus, even though *LM* structures may require considerable amounts of M energy for their construction, in the long run they are actually energy-saving devices, in that they eventually allow for the M-boosting of yet other schemes which can then be coordinated with them. First, however, the subject must have sufficient M power to make the initial integration of each structure. Taken together, M power itself plus the structures that result from *LM* learning account for much of the greater intellectual capability demonstrated in the performances of older children and adults.

It seems likely that many communication tasks, particularly those that discriminate between good and poor communicators, may have a relatively high M demand, at least for subjects who have not received special training on the tasks in question (see the final section for further discussion of training). Certainly the production of an unrehearsed narrative, for example, seems intuitively quite demanding: to be effective, the speaker must carefully select and order information, plan ways of expressing it in speech, and monitor what has been said and how it has been received by the audience. Even the typical referential communication task is not as simple as it might at first appear, since we know that performance continues to improve in some respects throughout childhood. The subject in such a task may first have to discover the necessity of making systematic comparisons between referents and nonreferents by seeing that this strategy is implied by the coordination of several aspects of the task situation. In addition the subject may, in some instances, need to compare several objects on several dimensions in order to produce an unambiguous message.

In spite of the limits M imposes on intellectual performance and learning, it is still possible at any age to bring about the performance of many tasks that initially seem well beyond the subject's spontaneous grasp (cf. Case, 1974, 1978; Pascual-Leone, 1976a; Pascual-Leone *et al.*, 1978). The general strategy for doing this is to minimize the M demand entailed in constructing a set of schemes that will suffice to produce the target performance within the limits set by the learner's M power. This can be accomplished, for example, by guiding the learner through the target performance, or parts thereof, over and over again, until the necessary schemes are constructed through the gradual process that Pascual-Leone calls *LC learning,* a more rote type of structural learning that does not require M-boosting of the individual schemes to be integrated. Or the learner may be led through an instructional sequence designed to produce cumulative *LM* learning by breaking the task down into parts that can be "chunked" together in a stepwise fashion with very little M demand at any one step (Case, 1975, 1978).

The possibility of facilitating learning by reducing its M demand may at first seem quite attractive, especially to the educator who is concerned with early childhood, where M power limitations are particularly severe. But there are certain costs to be balanced against the possible benefits that might accrue from instructional procedures that minimize M demand (Pascual-Leone *et al.*, 1978). For one thing, these procedures are likely to require a greater investment of instructional time and effort than would be necessary a few years later, when the learner has more M power to work with. Furthermore, the final products of low-M instruction may well leave something to be desired from the educator's point of view. Schemes acquired through *LC* learning tend to be highly context bound, because their releasing components need the satisfaction of many cues from the original learning situation before they are strongly activated. Cumulative *LM* learning may result in broader transfer, because activation of any of the constituent schemes in an *LM* structure will activate the entire structure. But the less *LM* learning requires the learner to use all of the M power at his or her disposal, the less it contributes to the development of certain *executive controls* that monitor the utilization of M. These controls are seen as general schemes acquired through all sorts of specific learning and problem-solving experiences, and they may account for the kinds of individual differences in performance that have been said to reflect differences in "cognitive style." In other words, some people learn to use their M energy more efficiently and effectively than others, and the types of instruction they receive can be a contributing factor. Instructional tasks that challenge learners to use all of the M power at their disposal, and then reward them for doing so by yielding to solution, should be more effective in promoting executive controls for high M arousal than tasks that provide solutions with lower M demands.

The executive controls just mentioned represent one more way in which "other knowledge" can combine with communicative competence in determining communicative performance. However, the main point I have tried to make here, through the example of M, is that the psychological resources underlying performance include more than just knowledge. Because other factors, like M, play a role in shaping performance, they also play a role in shaping the construction of new knowledge. One implication is that whenever we attribute a particular bit of knowledge (a scheme) to one of our subjects, we must ask ourselves whether there is some plausible way in which that knowledge could have been constructed by someone with the subject's M power.

It is perhaps obvious by now that the concepts discussed in this section—the concepts of M power and of LM and LC learning—provide a basis for formal definitions of such notions as the "complexity" or "familiarity" of a particular communication task. Both of these variables have been mentioned by others as possible explanations for evidence that young children do produce effectively "adapted" communications in some situations but not in others (e.g., Flavell, 1977). But they will have no real explanatory value until they are defined precisely enough to generate a priori predictions as to how a given subject will perform in a given situation.

Following Pascual-Leone's lead in the analysis of other cognitive tasks, the *complexity* of a communication task can be defined as its M demand, that is as the greatest number of schemes that must be simultaneously M-boosted at any one step in the performance of the task. In fact, Pascual-Leone and Smith (1969) have already presented such an analysis for one set of referential communication tasks. As they demonstrate, the determination of a task's M demand entails a step-by-step analysis of the subject's performance, with a specification of the executive, predicative, and transformational schemes involved in each step, and an accounting for the fact that just those schemes apply at that moment. The specific task analyses proposed by Pascual-Leone and Smith accounted for the different ages at which a majority of children were first observed to succeed on each of four tasks and, in another study, predicted the effects of training on the performance of these tasks by kindergarten children (Case, 1972).

The *familiarity* of a communication task might be defined by the extent to which the task situation activates LC and LM structures in the subject's repertoire, that is, complex schemes constructed through the process of L learning. When defined in this way, familiarity can be either an advantage or a disadvantage. It is helpful if the L structures activated by the situation lead to a pragmatically appropriate response, as in the case of frequent, naturally occurring situations. But if strongly activated L structures lead to an *in*appropriate response, then familiarity is more a hindrance than a help. Consider, for example, the experimental task in which children are asked to explain a board game to a blindfolded listener (Flavell, Botkin, Fry, Wright, & Jarvis, 1968). The game materials and the listener are both visible to the speaker and are in close proximity to one another. Because of past LC learning in situations with sighted listeners, these features of the experimental situation would tend to lead automatically to the use, for example, of deictic terms such as *that one* or *here,* which are clearly inappropriate for a blindfolded listener. Evidently some subjects quickly construct a new LM structure for overcoming the familiar but misleading aspects of this task, but presumably they can do so only if they have sufficient M power (and executive controls) to keep the listener's blindness in mind and to coordinate that fact with other aspects of the performance.

It is not easy to do the kind of task analysis that is required for assessing, from the (meta)subject's point of view, the complexity or familiarity of a given communication task. One of the main difficulties lies in deciding which schemes to assume the subject already has in his or her repertoire when the task is first presented. Such decisions must be informed by our knowledge about the way the subject (or other, similar subjects) would perform other relevant tasks. But that implies that we have already done analyses of the other tasks, which would require information about still *other* tasks, and so on and so on. However, we can escape this infinite regress by starting from intuition and by treating all old analyses as provisional while we test their implications with regard to new tasks. If an a priori analysis of a new task fails to predict performance, or if we cannot come up with a post hoc explanation of observed performance on the basis of our previous assumptions, then some of our previous assumptions must need revision. In other words, the whole enterprise is very much a "bootstraps" operation—a continual process of construction and reconstruction. In this regard, it is not unlike the process by which children appear to construct their knowledge of language and communication, or of the world in general. It seems fitting, then, that we should engage in the same kind of process to construct *our* knowledge of *their* knowledge.

Conclusions

In the course of this discussion, the concept of communication skills has shrunk from everything that underlies communicative performance, to just the transformational schemes that are the immediate causes of performance, and then still more specifically to those transformational schemes that are relevant only to communication. This progressive shrinking might provoke the criticism that it leaves us with a concept of communication skills that is far too narrow to account for the developmental and individual differences that are so striking in communicative performance. If so, I certainly would agree. My own guess is that many of the important differences in performance are due primarily to differences in general cognitive capacities and styles (cf. Shatz, 1978). Communication skills, in the narrow sense, are necessary for communicative performance, but they are not sufficient to explain all or even most of the observed variance in performance. When skills do account for some of the variance, their presence in some individuals or age groups and not in others still needs to be explained, and I suspect that differences in general cognitive capacities and styles would loom large in such an explanation, along with differences in specific communication experiences.

It follows from these considerations that instructional efforts aimed exclusively at the development of communication skills would not do much to increase children's overall communicative effectiveness. The same could be said more generally with regard to instruction aimed at the whole of communicative competence, as I have defined it. That is, even if a program of instruction addressed not only communication skills but also the simple predicative schemes and fluents that comprise one's knowledge about communication, it still would not provide a completely adequate basis for bringing about effective communication. So long as effective communication demands creativity—so long as the individual must produce solutions to *novel* communication problems—then the acquisition of specific communication skills or knowledge about communication will never be enough. Rather, the individual's effectiveness will vary directly with his or her mental power (M) and repertoire of executive controls for maximizing the efficient use of available M power to mobilize novel combinations of transformational and predicative schemes in solving a given problem.

Among investigators of communication, the creativity of language use has, in a sense, been emphasized most by those sociolinguists who stress the extent to which the meaning of an utterance depends on context (e.g., Erickson, this volume). Yet, ironically, the same investigators generally have not concerned themselves with the crucial role of psychological factors such as M power in the process of constructing "situated" meanings. Rather, they have focused on what language users must *know*—on communicative competence—which is certainly necessary, but not sufficient to account for the creative aspects of communication.

If mental power and executive controls are important determinants of effective communication, what are the implications for instruction? According to the theory of constructive operators, there is not much a teacher can do about the learner's M power per se, except wait for it to grow, because M power is seen essentially as a maturational factor. The theory suggests, however, that teachers can take steps to foster the development of executive controls. Pascual-Leone *et al.* (1978) discuss two general strategies, which they call the method of graded learning loops and the method of executive time sharing. Very briefly, the first of these methods attempts to promote high arousal of M through a kind of guided discovery learning in which the learner is given various versions of the same problem, ordered from difficult to easy, such that the learner will eventually succeed in solving some version of the problem spontaneously and, upon returning to more difficult versions, will experience the kind of cognitive conflict that can lead to *their* solution as well (see also Pascual-Leone, 1976b). The second method is intended to promote decentration in the deployment of M by requiring learners to shift their attention back and forth from one task or subtask to another.

If educators were able to promote efficient use of mental power by these or other means, then many more elements of communicative competence might be acquired spontaneously, without direct instruction. That is, if a particular type of communication problem were frequent enough to warrant the construction of specialized knowledge pertaining to it, individuals who had greater functional M powers would be more likely to construct that knowledge on their own, because they would initially be more likely to discover appropriate solutions on their own. On the other hand, the general controls that give one greater functional M power may well develop, in part, from communicative activity itself—particularly activity that presents the learner with problems that are challenging but solvable, given the learner's M power and repertoire of schemes. And, to insure that the learner does have the repertoire needed to engage in such activities, it may sometimes be desirable to teach selected aspects of communicative competence in a direct way.

Thus, the process–structural view I have outlined here argues for a balanced approach to instruction aimed at promoting communicative development. Such an approach would include some effort to teach specific communication skills and knowledge about communication, especially when the learner seems truly unable to engage in desired communicative activities without help. But plenty of attention would also be given to the development of general executive controls, by providing learners with ample opportunities to solve problems just barely within their grasp and to monitor the deployment of their attention while performing complex tasks. This learning to learn, or use of intelligence, could be promoted in all areas of the curriculum, in the language arts and in other areas as well.

These ideas regarding instruction for communicative development may seem very appealing (and perhaps very familiar) in the abstract, but how do we put them into concrete practice? How do we know when a novel communication problem is within a child's grasp? How do we know what sorts of knowledge are required, and how do we know if children usually have that knowledge at a particular age? These questions can be answered only through the kind of painstaking task analysis that attends to the three distinctions I have discussed. The challenge for researchers concerned with communicative development is to provide such analyses.

Acknowledgment

Preparation of this chapter was facilitated by support from the Roblee Foundation and from the Institute of Human Development, University of California, Berkeley. I am grateful to Sam Glucksberg, Gary Price, Veronica Fabian Kraus, and Irene Subelman for their comments on the first draft, to Barbara Nakakihara for her patient typing, and to Pat Dickson for his careful editing. The glossary was suggested and drafted by Gary Price.

Glossary

Scheme: The basic structural unit of all knowledge, as in Piagetian theory. In the process of solving a problem or performing a task, schemes assimilate input and relate specific antecedent conditions to specific consequences, which may be either semantic (representations) or pragmatic (transformations).

Effecting component of a scheme: The semantic or pragmatic consequences that ensue when a given scheme has assimilated or applied to some input.

Releasing component of a scheme: The set of cues corresponding to antecedent conditions in the input that are sufficient to activate a particular scheme, that is, to increase its assimilatory strength.

Activation of a scheme: The extent to which a scheme is likely to assimilate some input at a given moment, as determined by the match between conditions in the input and cues in the scheme's releasing component, and by the action of various scheme boosters, such as M.

Application of a scheme: The actual assimilation of some input by a highly activated scheme, such that the scheme brings about the consequences specified in its effecting component. For a scheme to apply, it must be more highly activated than other, competing schemes.

Predicative schemes: Schemes that have the effect of representing objects and events, or properties of objects and events.

Transformational schemes: Schemes that have the effect of changing mental or physical objects. Skills are transformational schemes.

Fluents: A special class of predicative schemes that have the effect of representing transformations. When a fluent applies, it gives rise to an *expectancy* about the changes that would ensue if the represented transformation were to occur.

Executive schemes: Fluents that guide performance toward its goal by bringing about the application of other schemes as needed.

C learning: The incorporation of new content into the effecting or releasing component of a scheme. As a person learns new cues that are relevant to the activation of a scheme, new content has been incorporated into the releasing component of that scheme. As a person learns to modify a transformation or a representation, new content has been incorporated into the effecting component of a scheme.

L learning: The coordination and integration of previously separate schemes into a single, consolidated scheme.

M: A finite reservoir of mental attentional energy. The application of a scheme sometimes requires its further activation through the use of mental attentional energy, which is referred to as *M-boosting.* The number of schemes that can be *M*-boosted simultaneously is limited by the amount of mental attentional energy.

M demand of a task: The complexity of the task as gauged by the greatest number of schemes that must be simultaneously *M*-boosted at any one step, in order to perform the task.

M power: The maximum number of schemes that an individual can simultaneously *M*-boost. *M* power increases with age, with an executive plus one scheme being the characteristic *M* power at age 3 and an executive plus seven schemes being the characteristic *M* power in late adolescence; increases occur in increments of one scheme at a time every two years. Individuals do not always use all of the *M* power at their disposal, which leads to within-age differences in effective *M* power.

LM learning: Insightful *L* learning, which requires *M*-boosting of the schemes that are to be integrated. Some persons—particularly young children—may lack sufficient *M* power to allow certain types of *LM* learning to occur. However, it is possible to design instructional sequences so that smaller, more manageable forms of *LM* learning can be incrementally coordinated by a process of *cumulative LM learning.*

LC learning: A gradual process, more rote than *LM* learning, which does not require simultaneous *M*-boosting of the individual schemes to be integrated. Schemes acquired through *LC* learning have releasing components that result in less broad transfer than with schemes acquired through *LM* learning, because the releasing components of *LC* schemes need the satisfaction of many cues from the original learning situation.

Executive controls: General schemes whose effect is to monitor and regulate the utilization of scheme boosters such as *M.* Some persons acquire executive controls that underutilize the *M* power at their disposal, whereas other persons acquire executive controls that favor full utilization of available *M* power. Executive controls are acquired through all sorts of specific learning and problem-solving experiences.

References

Ammon, P. Cognitive development and early childhood education: Piagetian and neo-Piagetian theories. In H. L. Hom and P. A. Robinson (Eds.), *Psychological processes in early education.* New York: Academic Press, 1977.

Ammon, P., Tharinger, D., & Portnuff, W. *Children's strategies in a referential communication task.* Manuscript in preparation.

Case, R. Learning and development: A neo-Piagetian interpretation. *Human Development,* 1972, *15,* 339–358.

Case, R. Structures and strictures: Some functional limitations on the course of cognitive growth. *Cognitive Psychology,* 1974, *6,* 544–573.

Case, R. Gearing the demands of instruction to the developmental capacities of the learner. *Review of Educational Research,* 1975, *45,* 59–87.

Case, R. A developmentally based theory and technology of instruction. *Review of Educational Research,* 1978, *48,* 439–463.

Cazden, C. B. *Child language and education.* New York: Holt, Rinehart & Winston, 1972.

Cosgrove, J. M., & Patterson, C. J. Plans and the development of listener skills. *Developmental Psychology,* 1977, *13,* 557–564.

Flavell, J. H. Developmental studies of mediated memory. In H. W. Reese & L. P. Lipsitt (Eds.), *Advances in child development and behavior* (Vol. 5). New York: Academic Press, 1970.

Flavell, J. H. *The development of metacommunication.* Paper presented at the Twenty-First International Congress of Psychology, Paris, July 1976.

Flavell, J. H. *Cognitive development*. Englewood Cliffs, N.J.: Prentice-Hall, 1977.

Flavell, J. H., Botkin, P. T., Fry, C. L., Wright, J. W., & Jarvis, P. E. *The development of role-taking and communication skills in children*. New York: Wiley, 1968.

Gagné, R. M. Contributions of learning to human development. *Psychological Review*, 1968, *75*, 177–191.

Kraus, V. F., & Ammon, P. Assessing linguistic competence: When are children hard to understand? *Journal of Child Language*, 1980, *7*, 401–412.

Maratsos, M., Kuczaj, S. A., & Fox, D. E. *Some empirical studies in the acquisition of transformational relations: Passives, negatives, and the past tense*. Paper presented at the Minnesota Symposium on Child Psychology, Minneapolis, 1977.

Pascual-Leone, J. *Cognitive development and cognitive style: A general psychological integration*. Unpublished doctoral dissertation, University of Geneva, 1969.

Pascual-Leone, J. A mathematical model for the transition rule in Piaget's developmental stages. *Acta Psychologica*, 1970, *32*, 301–345.

Pascual-Leone, J. Metasubjective problems of constructive cognition: Forms of knowing and their psychological mechanism. *Canadian Psychological Review*, 1976, *17*, 110–125. (a)

Pascual-Leone, J. On learning and development, Piagetian style: I. A reply to Lefebvre-Pinard. *Canadian Psychological Review*, 1976, *17*, 270–288. (b)

Pascual-Leone, J., Goodman, D., Ammon, P., & Subelman, I. Piagetian theory and neo-Piagetian analysis as psychological guides in education. In J. M. Gallagher & J. A. Easley (Eds.), *Knowledge and development: Vol. 2, Piaget and education*. New York: Plenum Press, 1978.

Pascual-Leone, J., & Smith, J. The encoding and decoding of symbols by children: A new experimental paradigm and a neo-Piagetian model. *Journal of Experimental Child Psychology*, 1969, *8*, 328–355.

Scardamalia, M. Information processing capacity and the problem of horizontal decalage: A demonstration using combinatorial reasoning tasks. *Child Development*, 1977, *48*, 28–37.

Shatz, M. The relationship between cognitive processes and the development of communication skills. In H. E. Howe and C. B. Keasey (Eds.), *Nebraska symposium on motivation, 1977*. Lincoln: University of Nebraska Press, 1978.

2
Cognitive Monitoring

JOHN H. FLAVELL

The principal aim of this chapter is to propose a model of how we monitor and regulate communicative and other cognitive enterprises. I begin by proposing a broader interpretation of communication concepts, one that emphasizes their fundamental commonalities with other cognitive processes. The concept of metacognition is then introduced and elaborated. After these stage-setting preliminaries, the model is presented, first in outline and then in detail. The chapter concludes with an examination of some possible implications for education.

A Broader Interpretation of Communication Concepts

What is not "communication"? Without making arbitrary and artificial restrictions on reference, what cognitive roles, goals, and processes can be excluded from communication concepts like "audience" and "message"? Very few, in my opinion (Flavell, 1976a). Consider the concept of an audi-

35

ence. If its essential meaning can be taken to be an individual or group that receives information, then it is clear that there are many kinds of audiences. Audiences may do all sorts of things to all sorts of information for all sorts of reasons. One type of audience is of course the "listener" of referential communication fame. But we are no less genuinely "audiences" when we listen to nonlinguistic sounds, when we perceive with other senses, and when we attend to our own inner thoughts and feelings. We are audiences to information when we listen, but we are also audiences to information when we feel, think, speak, gesture, write, read, and perceive. And what an audience perceives can be nonlinguistic as well as linguistic in form, social as well as nonsocial in content.

Audience goals and processes are equally diverse. We are audiences when we attend to information unintentionally or without special purpose, that is, when our audience-role behavior is accidental or idle. We are also audiences when we deliberately process information to achieve specific subgoals and goals. The subgoals prominently include comprehending and remembering the information. The main goals can also consist of comprehending and remembering, of course, as is the case when students study for exams. However, the main goals can also include numerous objectives in the areas of social and nonsocial thinking and problem solving.

Thus, the concept of "audience" becomes very broad unless we make what seem to me to be artificial distinctions among the many settings in which information is received. The same is true of "message," and true by the same line of reasoning. The essential meaning of the term seems to be something like "information." Thus, a clue word in the Password game is very clearly a "message." But so are the other noises we hear, the sights and smells around us, and the thoughts and feelings inside us. Likewise, what is said, gestured, or written is a message for both sender and receiver, since both are "audiences" to it. The tasks and problems that the child encounters in and out of psychological laboratories are all messages to be attended to, comprehended, remembered, solved, or otherwise dealt with. And again, these tasks and problems can be social as well as nonsocial.

There is not, therefore, a distinctive area of cognitive processing called "communication" that stands well apart from other areas called "perception," "attention," "comprehension," "memory," "thinking," "problem solving," "social cognition," and so on. From this it follows that the nature and development of communication monitoring may not be adequately understood if examined in isolation from cognitive monitoring in these "other areas."

Consider the following example. It is possible that young children's shortcomings in communication situations may partly stem from their tendency not to treat messages as analyzable cognitive objects (Flavell, 1976a, 1977). According to this hypothesis, they tend not to critically evaluate messages for what they assert and do not assert, imply and do not imply, *etc.* They do not scrutinize them completely and carefully for possible unclarities, ambiguities, and contradictions. We might say that young children are at one end of a continuum in the way they process messages—a continuum whose other end is occupied by biblical scholars, lawyers, diplomats, and other extremely analytical scrutinizers of messages.

However, very similar types of metacognitive or monitoring shortcomings may beset young children when they play the audience role with respect to other messages. They may not decenter on conservation and other Piagetian tasks, that is, allocate attention evenly to all important information in the task display in order to arrive at a judicious and balanced judgment of what is going on. They do not look at it like a lawyer looks at a ruling. They may also have difficulty in seeing how the same objects could be classified in different ways, how the same facts could be explained in different ways, or how the same physical or social situations could appear different from different perspectives.

The functional equivalent of adequate "comparison activity" (Asher, 1978) or "sensitivity to the referent–nonreferent array" (Glucksberg, Krauss, & Higgins, 1975) may be evident in a wide variety of cognitive enterprises. An older child may notice that the purely perceptual information available in a liquid quantity conservation task would allow or "afford" (Gibson, 1966) both the conclusion that this glass has more than the other because its liquid column is higher and the conclusion that it has less because its column is thinner. She may also see that a group of objects affords a classification by both form and color. She may further recognize that *water* is an inadequate clue word for *ocean* versus *river* in the Password game because it equally affords both *ocean* and *river* as associates (Asher, 1978). In all three cases, the information is held out at arm's length, so to speak, and carefully analyzed for the interpretations it does and does not afford. The information does not just trigger this reaction or that, while itself never becoming visible to the mind's eye.

Thus it is that a paper with a title as general as "Cognitive Monitoring" can make sense at a conference on a topic as specific-sounding as children's oral communication skills. As a friend of mine once put it: it is the same head, after all.

Metacognition

"Metacognition" is a somewhat fuzzy concept that has been used to refer to a variety of epistemic processes (Brown, 1978; Flavell, 1978a). It is probably best defined loosely and broadly, namely, as knowledge or cognition that takes as its object or regulates any aspect of any cognitive endeavor. Its name derives from this "cognition about cognition" quality. People have argued that metacognition plays an important role in oral communication of information (Flavell, 1976a), oral persuasion (Howie-Day, 1979), oral comprehension (Markman, 1977, 1979), reading comprehension

(Brown, in press; Brown & Smiley, 1978; Meichenbaum & Asarnow, 1979), writing (Nold, in press), language acquisition (Clark, 1977), attention (Miller & Bigi, 1979), memory (Brown, 1975; Flavell & Wellman, 1977), problem solving (Brown, 1978; Flavell, 1976b, 1978a; Hayes, 1976), social cognition (Flavell, 1978a, 1978b, in press), and diverse forms of self-control and self-instruction (Meichenbaum & Asarnow, 1979; Mischel & Mischel, 1977). Metacognition or similar concepts appear to be gaining currency in the fields of social learning theory, behavior modification, personality development, and education, as well as in the field of cognition and its development (Flavell, 1978b). As will be shown in what follows, metacognition can be differentiated into metacognitive knowledge and metacognitive experience, and one can distinguish between metacognitive and cognitive strategies.

The variety of possible forms of metacognition can best be introduced by considering memory development, the area in which there has been the most thinking and research concerning this sort of cognition. Flavell and Wellman (1977) have tried to classify the major categories and subcategories of memory metacognition ("metamemory") that a developing individual could conceivably acquire. The following from Flavell (1976a) summarizes the resulting taxonomy:

One major type of metamemory we have labeled *sensitivity*. The child presumably develops a sensitivity or sense for when the situation he is in calls for voluntary, intentional remembering efforts on his part. Adults and older children have learned that it is appropriate and adaptive in certain situations, but not in others, to deliberately initiate certain specialized cognitive activities which we call memory strategies. Some of these activities or strategies are designed to get information into memory (storage strategies); others are designed to get information out of memory (retrieval strategies). There is reason to think that this kind of sensitivity needs acquiring; that is, children may have to learn what it means to make an active, persistent, goal-instigated and goal-directed effort either to recall something now or to memorize something for later recall. . . . Spontaneous, automatic, passive memory of various kinds occurs early in life, of course. What develops later are these more active, intentional efforts at remembering, together with the knowledge of when one does and when one does not need to engage in such efforts.

A second major type of metamemory is called *variables*. It refers to knowledge of what factors or variables act in what ways to affect an individual's performance on a memory problem. We have distinguished three categories of such variables, namely, *person, task,* and *strategy* variables. Each of these three categories is in turn further divided into two subcategories.

The *person* category encompasses all the things an individual could learn or become aware of concerning himself and others as mnemonic beings. One subcategory of person metamemory refers to knowledge of what the self and others are generally like as storers and retrievers of information, that is, their enduring abilities and limitations in this area of cognitive functioning. Examples would be the acquired belief that you are better at remembering faces than names, that your spouse has a better memory for most things than you do, and that everybody's memory is fallible. The other subcategory of person metamemory refers to the ability to monitor and interpret one's own immediate mnemonic experiences in specific memory situations. Examples would be the sensation that something you are trying to recall is right on the tip of your tongue, or the feeling that something you are trying to memorize still needs more study. The first subcategory of person variables thus has more to do with knowledge of general memory *traits,* the second more to do with the monitoring of specific, here-and-now memory *states.* The *task* category includes knowledge of the task variables that affect the difficulty level of a memory problem. There is a great deal for the growing child to learn about what makes some mnemonic enterprises harder than others. First (one subcategory), a memory task can be harder or easier as a function of the amount and kind of information that must be remembered. As examples, it is hard to remember large bodies of information and it is hard to remember bodies of information which are low in meaningfulness or organization. Second (the other subcategory), some memory task demands are more difficult to meet than others, even with the amount and type of memory material held constant. It is usually easier to recognize things than to recall them, for instance, and memory for the gist of a story is better than memory for its exact wording. It can be seen, then, that the first subcategory of task variables has to do with the nature of the memory input, while the second concerns the nature of the retrieval demands.

The *strategy* category includes the attainable knowledge of the various things one can voluntarily do to help one's memory system achieve one's memory goals. The two subcategories here refer to knowledge concerning storage strategies and knowledge concerning retrieval strategies. The little girl's description of how she would go about remembering a phone number [cited earlier in the paper] is a good example of verbalizable knowledge about a possible storage strategy. On the retrieval side, most of us are aware of various tricks we can use to improve on rote, "brute force" recall. An example is trying to remember someone's name by deliberately searching for possible retrieval cues to it, such as the person's appearance or the initial letter of his name. . . . We also assume that there is knowledge to be acquired about *interactions* among person, task, and strategy variables, as well as about each one taken alone. An example would be the belief that, for oneself but possibly not for everybody, a certain type of strategy works better for one kind of memory task than for another [pp. 2–3].

A revised version of this taxonomy will see service in the model of cognitive monitoring I shall now present.

A Model of Cognitive Monitoring

The model described in what follows is intended to capture the variety of things that can happen during a cognitive enterprise in which the subject does at least some monitoring of cognitive goals, experiences, and actions. The enterprise could be as brief as the reading of a road sign or as lengthy as the lifelong study of the Elizabethan theater. There could, of course, be subenterprises within larger enterprises, as this last example suggests. As implied in the first section of the chapter, the model is meant to apply to oral communication (especially listener activities) but also to much else—to "Communication" in the broad sense as well as "communication" in the narrow sense. In the course of presenting the model, I will make suggestions about possible developmental changes in cognitive monitoring, as well as show how monitoring might work in metacognitively sophisticated adults.

Figure 2.1 shows the four basic components of the model: *cognitive goals* (or tasks), *cognitive actions* (or strategies), *metacognitive knowledge,* and *metacognitive experiences.* The arrows indicate which components can exert influence on or provide input to which other components. Cognitive goals are the tacit or explicit objectives that instigate and maintain the cognitive enterprise. Goals naturally vary from one enterprise to another and can also change in the course of any given enterprise. Metacognitive knowledge consists of long-term memory representations of the types of knowledge described in the Flavell and Wellman (1977) taxonomy—including, of course, their numerous counterparts in other, nonmemory kinds of cognitive activities. It can be thought of as that part of your accumulated world knowledge that has to do with people as cognitive agents and with their cognitive tasks, goals, actions, and experiences. Like any other type of stored knowledge, relevant portions of it may be retrieved and used during a cognitive enterprise either automatically or deliberately, and either with or without entering consciousness. I will make no proposals about the nature or format of its storage in long-term memory. Metacognitive experiences are conscious experiences (ideas, thoughts, feelings, "sensations") related to any aspect of the enterprise. The Flavell and Wellman (1977) "here-and-now memory states" of the person category which were described in the previous section are clear examples of metacognitive experiences. Others would be the feeling that you do not quite understand what was just said and the sudden realization that what you were trying to say has finally gotten through to your listener. Metacognitive knowledge and metacognitive experiences are not presently assumed to be qualitatively different in their basic nature from nonmetacognitive ones, only in their content and function. Cognitive actions

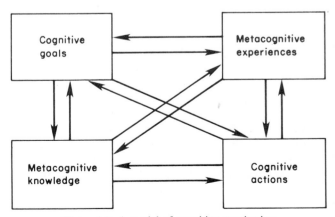

Figure 2.1. A model of cognitive monitoring.

are those undertaken to achieve the goals of the enterprise, for example, trying to understand the intended meaning of the speaker's utterance. They can also lead to metacognitive experiences and provide input to metacognitive knowledge.[1] No claim is made that there is nothing but wisdom, truth, and adaptiveness in the four components: Not all cognitive goals need suit the occasion; not all metacognitive knowledge need be veridical; not all metacognitive experiences need accurately reflect present reality; and not all cognitive actions need be good means to their intended goals. Let us now examine the four components and their relationships to one another.

Cognitive Goals

One of the most striking things about the goals of cognitive enterprises is their enormous variety and heterogeneity. Some enterprises seem to have virtually no goal, for example, daydreaming or idly observing people passing by. In other cases there is a cognitive goal, but it is not very well defined or clearly linked to future actions and outcomes. Reading a novel for pleasure could be such a case. In other enterprises the cognitive goal and associated practical outcomes are clearer. Examples include trying to figure out how to persuade someone to do something, trying to understand how to get to someone's house by listening to her directions, and trying to memorize the definition of classical conditioning for tomorrow's exam. Trying to find a new strategy or improve an old one in pursuit of a goal can itself also be a goal (or subgoal). Some enterprises have more than one goal. An instance would be simultaneously trying to comprehend what the used car salesman is claiming about his once-in-a-lifetime bargain and trying to evaluate the truth or importance of these claims. Some cognitive goals are self-selected, some are imposed by others or circumstances, and some are mixtures of the two. We might expect to find developmental trends in the ability to: be consciously aware of what cognitive goals, if any, are in play in which of one's enterprises; to clarify unclear goals whenever possible or desirable; to pursue several goals at once; to set explicit goals for oneself intentionally; and to adopt and deliberately pursue goals which are not self-selected.

Let us now examine the arrows emanating from the cognitive goals

---

[1] One can imagine adding other components to the model, such as *cognitive problem* and *problem setting* (I am indebted to Steve Yussen for calling my attention to this possibility). Knowledge about the problem setting or context might help the problem solver clarify the exact nature of the cognitive problem. Clarification of the problem might in turn help her specify the cognitive goal(s) she should try to achieve and the actions needed to achieve them. Metacognitive knowledge and metacognitive experiences might play useful roles at any and all points in this chain of events. The model contains only the above four components because they were the ones I used to generate my current ideas about how cognitive monitoring might work. A more complex model containing such additional components would undoubtedly provide a more complete representation of how it might work, but I prefer not to attempt such a model here.

component in Figure 2.1. The component of the model most obviously influenced by the cognitive goals component is that of cognitive actions. The depth (Craik & Lockhart, 1972; Baddeley, 1978) and type of processing done on the information available in any cognitive enterprise is likely to vary with one's cognitive goal. For example, Frederickson (1975) has shown that adults process a written passage very differently when their objective is to generate inferences from it in order to solve a problem than when their objective is just to remember the passage. The influence of cognitive goals on cognitive actions is especially apparent when subgoals vary within a single, extended cognitive enterprise. To illustrate, a reader may skim or skip the parts of a book that he does not need or care to know much about. On the other hand, he may process the important points quite deeply—the ones that seem important to the author, important to his teacher, or important to him, depending upon his objectives (cf. Anderson & Pichart, 1978). He may also make a special effort to understand and remember material relevant to any new goals that may emerge as he continues to read. One would expect to see similar goal-generated variations in cognitive actions within and between cognitive enterprises when the enterprises are of other types, such as telling, persuading, listening, looking, and social or nonsocial problem solving.

There also must be much for the growing child to learn about how to change his cognitive actions to accord with changes in his cognitive goals in a flexible and efficient manner. Indeed, the developmental literature on selectivity, adaptability, and control of attention (Brown & Smiley, 1978; Flavell, 1977, pp. 167–171) strongly indicates that this is the case.

The arrow from cognitive goals to metacognitive knowledge in Figure 2.1 is meant to indicate that the formation of a particular goal can serve to retrieve or activate those portions of one's stored metacognitive knowledge that are relevant to that goal. Consider again the goal of trying to understand how to get to someone's house by listening to her directions. Past experience with such problems may have built up a fund of metacognitive knowledge that the presence of this goal evokes. Examples might include the knowledge that you are particularly inept at generating spatial representations from verbal directions (person variables), that the number and nature of the steps in her directions will affect the difficulty of your comprehension and memory task (task variables), and that verifying your grasp of the instructions by repeating them back to her before driving off into the night might be a useful thing to do (strategy variables).

We would expect an increase with age in the tendency for cognitive goals to call up relevant segments of metacognitive knowledge. The most obvious reason is the undoubted increase with age in the sheer amount of such knowledge that has been acquired and stored. A more interesting possibility is that whatever knowledge is available in the younger child's memory has been less well learned, organized, generalized, *etc.,* and is therefore less accessible. The older child may have more and better retrieval routes from specific cognitive goals to appropriate metacognitive knowledge. A related possibility is that the older child may have learned to make a deliberate search of his metacognitive knowledge base when establishing and pursuing a cognitive goal.

The formation or inspection of a goal may trigger a metacognitive experience. For example, you may instantly recognize your current goal as one you have had great trouble achieving in the past and consequently feel unconfident and discouraged.

Metacognitive Knowledge

The Flavell and Wellman (1977) metamemory taxonomy presented earlier will serve as a convenient framework for illustrating various kinds of metacognitive knowledge (see also Flavell, 1976a, in press).

Sensitivity

As implied in the discussion of cognitive goals, there is a great deal of metacognitive knowledge that could be acquired concerning what depth and kind of cognitive processing is appropriate or adaptive in what life situation. Especially important is knowledge of what environmental events are implicit signals to pay close attention, listen intently, read carefully, store or retrieve information intentionally, try to solve a problem, and so forth. The child doubtless has to learn *how* to voluntarily carry out processing of different depths or kinds. However, it would seem that he must also learn *when* the situation calls for one versus another depth or kind of processing. It could be argued that such sensitivity is better construed as a subspecies of knowledge about task demands, and hence belongs in the task-variables category (Flavell, in press).

Person Variables

One subcategory of this category includes intuitions about intraindividual differences, interindividual differences, and universals. These intuitions help define our concepts of ourselves and others as cognitive processors (Flavell & Wellman, 1977, pp. 9–10). As to intraindividual differences, we may acquire beliefs that we are more skilled or interested in this type of cognitive processing than in that; we may also acquire similar beliefs about other people of concern to us. For instance, we might believe we are better at political than mathematical reasoning, and that the same is true of one of our parents. We may also acquire beliefs about interindividual differences, for example, that the parent in question cannot follow information presented through the ear as easily and accurately as we can.

Possible intuitions about universal properties of human beings as cognitive devices strike me as more interesting. They may also have greater functional utility in our cognitive lives. The following are a few generalizations of this type that anyone would do well to acquire: There are various degrees and kinds of understanding. Processing information through reading, listening, or observation is not synonymous with understanding it, nor does such processing guarantee that any desired level of understanding will occur. We can fail to understand something in two different ways: We cannot achieve any coherent representation of it or we can understand it incorrectly, that is, misunderstand it. Misunderstandings are especially pernicious because they usually produce the same satisfied feeling (or lack of feeling) that correct understandings do. The same distinction applies in such activities as communicating to others, perceiving, remembering, and problem solving. Moreover, it can sometimes be hard for us to find out whether or not we have understood something fully or correctly. (My favorite cases in point are Piagetian concepts like *reflective abstraction;* the comprehension monitoring attempts may take more time and effort than the actual comprehension attempts!) It can be especially hard to determine whether something has been processed adequately enough for the goal that motivated its processing in the first place (e.g., to recall it later or to explain it clearly to someone else). Although present feelings concerning the comprehensibility and memorability of information can certainly be very useful, they can also deceive us. Things that feel well understood and readily recallable now may not prove to be so easily recomprehended or remembered later. Conversely, the click of comprehension or memory that eludes us now may yet happen later, even with no additional conscious effort. Just because the meaning of the concept being explained is crystal clear to me, it need not be to everyone else in the audience, or to my listener (if I am doing the explaining). The egocentrism-based feeling that, if it feels *this* clear to me, it *must* be clear to others probably cannot be extinguished, but it should not be allowed to engender egocentric judgments and actions. More generally, we would do well to be on our guard against egocentrically attributing our current thoughts and feelings to others (or, indeed, attributing them to ourselves at times and states other than those of the present). For instance, we could *know* that we may not feel as depressed tomorrow as we do today, even though it presently *seems* inconceivable that we will ever feel happy again. Thus, there are conceptual, as well as perceptual, illusions and ambiguities, and intuitions about their existence can be valuable components of a person's metacognitive knowledge.

The other subcategory of Flavell and Wellman's (1977) person category referred to ideas and feelings that occur during an actual memory endeavor. In the present model, such ideas and feelings are assigned to the metacognitive experience component, and therefore will be discussed in detail later. Three things might be mentioned concerning them at this point, however.

First, both the occurrence of metacognitive experiences and the effects of their occurrence (what further experiences they engender, what inferences or other cognitive actions they lead to) can be strongly influenced by metacognitive knowledge. For example, if we suddenly feel vaguely puzzled when we encounter a certain sentence in a text, our metacognitive knowledge might automatically lead us to take that feeling seriously as a possible symptom of noncomprehension, to try to track down its cause, and to re-clarify our understanding of the text insofar as possible. Second, the metacognitive experience might actually contain an explicit idea or prescription drawn from our store of acquired metacognitive knowledge. An example would be the sudden conscious recollection, while adding up a column of figures, of our longstanding credo that we should always compute a sum twice to ensure accuracy. In fact, it is hard to imagine a metacognitive experience that has no metacognitive-knowledge content or scaffolding whatever. Third, the general belief that metacognitive experiences can be very useful in cognitive enterprise, and hence should be carefully attended to and even actively sought out, is surely an important part of metacognitive knowledge.

Task Variables

The first subcategory here has to do with the information involved in cognitive enterprises. It could be abundant or meager, familiar or unfamiliar, full of redundancies or densely packed, well or poorly organized, internally consistent and coherent or not, vivid and exciting or pallid and tame, interesting or dull, rapidly or slowly delivered, presented under distracting conditions or not—the possible variations seem endless. The metacognitive knowledge in this subcategory is knowledge of what such variations imply for how the cognitive task should best be navigated and how successful we are likely to be at it. Knowing what these variations portend is important in successfully communicating to others, comprehending others' communications to us, learning and remembering anything, solving problems, and other cognitive pursuits (cf. Flavell, 1976a).

The other subcategory includes metacognitive knowledge of task demands. Knowing the use to which processed information will have to be put has implications for how that information should be processed, and also for how it should be packaged and delivered as a message, if one is in the communicator role.

The achievement of knowledge of these implications is also an important developmental task for the child. For example, with such knowledge, we can understand that we need to process information differently depending upon whether we will subsequently have to just recognize it, repeat the gist of it, recall it verbatim, explain it clearly to others in speech or writing, solve problems with it, or use it to generate new ideas.

Strategy Variables

There is a great deal that the child needs to learn about what means (strategies) are likely to succeed in achieving what goals and subgoals in what cognitive undertakings. Discussion of possible strategies will be left to the section on cognitive actions, since many of these actions are in fact strategies of one sort or another. However, it should be clear that our stored knowledge about the nature and utility of cognitive strategies is definitely part of our metacognitive knowledge.

Interactions among Variables

One example (from Flavell, 1976a) should suffice to illustrate metacognitive knowledge about such interactions in an area other than memory: "Speaker A decides to communicate information X to listener B in one way rather than another, based upon a combined assessment of his own communicative abilities, B's receptive capacities, and the particular nature of information X [p. 6]." Most of the metacognitive knowledge that is accessed and used in cognitive enterprises is undoubtedly knowledge of how person, task, and strategy variables interact.

As to the arrows issuing from the metacognitive knowledge component in Figure 2.1, Table 2.1 gives concrete examples of how each type of knowledge can lead to or affect cognitive goals, cognitive actions, and metacognitive experiences. There is considerable redundancy in the table. This reflects both the interactions among the three types of variables and the fact that anything in the left and center columns would be reclassified as a metacognitive experience if it happened to be retrieved in the form of a conscious idea or feeling. (As indicated earlier, however, I assume that an item of metacognitive knowledge would *not* have to enter consciousness in order to affect the other three components.) This redundancy notwithstanding, the fact that all kinds of metacognitive knowledge can provide direct input to all three components seems to me to be a powerful argument for the importance of metacognitive knowledge in our cognitive lives. It also suggests how much there might be for a child to acquire in this general area.

Metacognitive Experiences

The rightmost column of Table 2.1 illustrates some of the types of metacognitive experiences we can have. As was just indicated, metacognitive knowledge in the other columns could also surface as conscious ideas or feelings. However, not all metacognitive experiences are items of metacognitive knowledge that have become conscious. For example, a feeling of surprise on encountering some unexpected information is not in itself such an

TABLE 2.1

Examples of the Effects of Various Kinds of Metacognitive Knowledge on Cognitive Goals, Cognitive Actions, and Metacognitive Experiences

Kind of metacognitive knowledge	Cognitive goals	Cognitive actions	Metacognitive experiences
Sensitivity	When the message is a set of directions rather than, say, some casual remarks, my goal as listener will be to attain a complete and explicit understanding of the message rather than just the general drift.	Repeated failure to solve a problem using this approach means I should try another approach.	I suddenly realize that I'll need to remember what she is talking about now, as contrasted with what she was talking about earlier.
Person	I have more aptitude for the social sciences than for the physical sciences, so I'd better try for a B.A. in some social science.	I feel I understand this. However, since I know such feelings can be deceptive and since a correct understanding is very important in this instance, I'd better go over it again.	While listening to a talk I am reminded of how hard it is for me to follow orally given information, compared to most of my professional acquaintances.
Task	I think I'll write my term paper on topic A rather than topic B because the concepts in A are more familiar and will be easier to write about.	Since I'll have to explain this to my friends as well as just learn how to do it myself, I'd better figure out how to express it in words and what points to cover first.	I have the sudden sinking feeling that I can't possibly learn all this in time for tomorrow's test.
Strategy	I'd better try to persuade my husband to do A rather than B, because I can make a better case and more convincing appeal for A than for B.	I know I am likely to forget things like these unless I write them down, and I simply must remember these things. So I'll write them all down.	It just dawned on me how to find out if A really likes me: I'll ask B, who knows and likes both of us.

item, although what you make of it and do about it would undoubtedly be guided by metacognitive knowledge. Similarly, some items of metacognitive knowledge may never become metacognitive experiences. Many metacognitive experiences concern persons (self, others, everyone), tasks, goals, or situations (the nature of the information, what the cognitive goals are or should be), strategies (what goal-directed actions are being or ought to be undertaken), and especially various interactions among these; a metacognitive experience could even concern some previous metacognitive experience. As further examples, we may currently experience the lack of some needed talent, puzzlement about some task-relevant information, an awareness of the difficulty of the task requirements, an inability to think of a means to the goal, or the opposites of these feelings.

Metacognitive experiences often have something to do with our progress toward the goal: We feel that we have just begun, or that the goal is still very remote. We feel we are almost there, that the sought-for memory, understanding, or problem solution is right on the tip of our tongue or frontal lobes. We feel we are in fact there—that the goal has definitely been achieved. Or we feel that the goal is possibly, probably, or definitely unattainable. We also have ideas and sensations about our rate of progress toward the goal: Progress is faster than anticipated (perhaps suspiciously so), is too slow, or has suddenly slowed down. We may be aware of differences or similarities between a current metacognitive experience and a previous one. For example, this concept feels better understood or easier to remember than it did a minute (day, year) ago. Such comparisons among experiences over time may in fact help generate our ideas about rate of progress. Indeed, comparison processes of all sorts must be a rich source of metacognitive experiences (e.g., when we compare our progress with the known or imagined progress of real or ideal others).

Finally, metacognitive experiences can be attitudinal or emotional in nature, and they can also have the psychological processes of others as their content. As to the former, we may feel critical, admiring, fond, moved, dubious, or disgusted regarding some body of information. As to the latter, most social cognition does seem intrinsically metacognitive in nature (Flavell, 1978a, 1978b); the listener's ideas about the communicative intent of the speaker and the speaker's ideas about the comprehension abilities of the listener are two examples pertinent to this volume. In fact, the monitoring of one's social cognition may be a promising new subject for developmental research (Flavell, in press).

It is important to underscore just how many varieties of metacognitive experiences there can be in any given type of cognitive enterprise. Consider the family of feelings that can occur in a comprehension enterprise. Most of us would probably first think of the feeling of noncomprehension. But this paradigmatic example could be differentiated and supplemented in numerous ways: I do not now, and could not ever, understand this. I do not now but conceivably/probably/definitely could understand this with more time and work. I may understand it, probably understand it, definitely understand it, and can prove it. I just failed to understand something because my mind wandered/because of that one puzzling sentence/because this part seems inconsistent with that part/because I do not understand the overall purpose or relevance of the information/and I have no idea why. The reader could no doubt add to this list.

When are metacognitive experiences most apt to occur (Flavell, in press)? Not surprisingly, they are probably most apt to occur whenever you do a lot of conscious cognition, thereby providing many cognitive events and contents about which to have metacognitive experiences. And when are you most apt to engage in a lot of conscious cognition (cf. Langer, 1978)? In some situations there is an explicit demand for it—your vocation or avocation expressly requires you to think up and evaluate alternative courses of action, solve complex problems of one sort or another, *etc.* In other situations the demand is more implicit but no less real. This is the case in situations where you have to think, speak, or otherwise behave in new and unaccustomed ways (e.g., when trying to communicate with someone from a very different culture). More conscious thought and attention are likely to be given to each step you take in such novel situations. Considerable conscious thought will also be explicitly or implicitly demanded in situations (including any of the foregoing) where the outcome of what you think and do is important to you. Making business, career, and marital decisions are examples. More generally, there is apt to be more ideation, and more monitoring of that ideation, when you are faced with risky decisions, especially if you believe you might reduce the risk by engaging in careful and sustained thought.

Metacognitive experiences are also likely to occur whenever your cognitions seem to have something wrong with them. As examples, you discover that your previous judgment about something was erroneous; you notice that your progress on some problem has slowed down or stopped; you are perplexed by something you just read; or there is ambiguity and uncertainty about whether you have reached your goal. Finally, at least the more complex and cerebral forms of metacognitive experiences (e.g., actively trying to figure out *why* you do not understand something versus merely noticing *that* you do not understand it) place heavy demands on attention and occupy considerable space in working memory (Markman, this volume). Consequently, you are more likely to have these kinds of experiences when attention and memory resources permit (e.g., when you have sufficient time to think about your cognitions, when you are not in a highly emotional state, and the like). The foregoing also suggest some of the conditions under which metacognitive experiences would not likely occur or, having occurred, would likely be terminated: when you can achieve your goals with little or no conscious thought, when your previous goals have been either achieved or abandoned, when you do not much care how the cognitive enterprise turns out, or when there is some kind of cognitive or affective overload.

Metacognitive experiences can have important effects on cognitive goals (see Figure 2.1). There may have been no goal active and a metacognitive experience activates one. For example, someone tells us something that puzzles us, and so we establish the goal of clearing up the mystery. Famous detective like Sherlock Holmes had a penchant for establishing their goals that way. Similarly, a metacognitive experience can lead us to abandon a previously active goal ("That's too hard for me.") or to switch goals ("I thought I needed to explain X to her, but I now see that it is information about Y that she really needs.").

The effect of metacognitive experiences on metacognitive knowledge is of a very different kind: They can add to, delete, or revise that knowledge, and can thus play an important role in its development. We can notice and store as metacognitive knowledge what cognitive actions and outcomes cooccur with what metacognitive experiences (cf. Flavell & Wellman, 1977). The feeling that we do not understand part of an instruction is, of course, often followed by an inability to follow it correctly, provided that we do not use that feeling to instigate further attempts at understanding. On the other hand, the outcome is liable to be more successful if the feeling elicits additional comprehension effort. The child could store and integrate such cooccurrences as part of her metacognitive knowledge. It would be interesting to find out what cooccurrences are most easily noticed, stored, integrated, and subsequently used in monitoring and regulating future cognitive enterprises.

Finally, metacognitive experiences can have obvious effects on cognitive actions. For instance, the realization that your communication (comprehension, memory, problem solving) effort is not faring well may lead immediately to actions designed to remedy that situation. There are other, less obvious effects, which will be described in the following section on cognitive actions.

As to possible developmental trends, there might be an increase with age in the tendency to notice and attend to metacognitive experiences, and to evaluate their meaning, importance, trustworthiness, and possible implications for cognitive action. We might gradually develop the belief, for example, that feelings of comprehension are liable to be less trustworthy than feelings of noncomprehension as predictors of the true state of our understanding. We may also learn to prefer and seek out direct, "criterion-referenced" evidence of cognitive progress by means that importantly involve metacognitive experience. The intended contrast here is between a student who decides he understands and will be able to retain the important information in his textbook simply because he read it, and one who makes the same decision only after testing himself or otherwise generating feelings and information about his actual state of mastery. In some cognitive tasks, at least, younger children may assume that they will achieve their goal merely by engaging in some arbitrary amount and kind of goal-directed activity. In contrast, older ones may realize that they need to check and make tests to determine what the activity has actually accomplished for them. Research showing age increases in the ability to know when one is ready for a recall test (Flavell, 1978a; Flavell & Wellman, 1977) might be examples of this hypothesized development.

Cognitive Actions

The best way to convey the various functions that cognitive actions may perform in the cognitive monitoring model is to examine their relationships to other phenomena right at the outset, rather than only at the end of the section. Figure 2.2 describes the possible combinations of antecedents, objectives, and outcomes that cognitive actions can have. "Other" means other-than-metacognitive experiences, as will be shown. Let us examine various left-to-right paths through Figure 2.2, beginning with the one at the bottom (Other → Other → Other).

The immediate antecedent of an action in this path could be a goal we have just established, together with some metacognitive knowledge that selected this particular action as an appropriate one for that goal. Or, the goal could already have been established, some relevant cognitive action could already have been selected and executed, and the action we are considering could simply be the one that would normally come next in progressing toward the goal; thus, its most immediate antecedent would consist of another action rather than a newly established goal. In either case—continuing to follow the bottom-most path in Figure 2.2—the sole objective of this action is to make progress towards the goal, and its sole outcome is a greater or lesser degree of progress (varying from none to more than expected). To illustrate this path, suppose we read a segment of text. It could be the initial segment, and was therefore immediately preceded by the goal of comprehending the text at some level, for some purpose. Or, it could be some later segment,

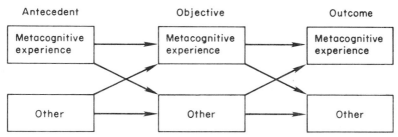

Figure 2.2. Possible combinations of antecedents, objectives, and outcomes of cognitive actions.

in which case it was immediately preceded by another reading-for-comprehension action. In both instances, the objective is solely to understand the segment and the only outcome is some cognitive representation of it. Actions showing this pattern of antecedent, objective, and outcome are of course both frequent and indispensable in all kinds of cognitive enterprises. They are the core goal-directed actions that get us to our goals. It is the other paths in Figure 2.2 that provide information about the roles of cognitive actions in cognitive monitoring, however.

Suppose we have the same action, with the same antecedent and the same objective, that is, a comprehension effort initiated by and for some type of comprehension goal. This time, however, a metacognitive experience unexpectedly accompanies whatever other, nonmetacognitive outcome may ensue. For example, we become aware that we did not understand this segment of text very well. Or, to take a memory example, we conclude that we have temporarily memorized that phone number, since we just carried out the cognitive action of rehearsing it correctly. This path illustrates an important fact, namely, that metacognitive experiences can be the unintended and unexpected fringe benefits of cognitive actions undertaken to achieve other, cognitive rather than metacognitive, objectives (cf. Markman, 1977, 1979).

The objective–outcome paths just described can also—or instead—have a metacognitive experience as their antecedent (see Figure 2.2). For instance, having just realized that our attention had wandered while listening to someone, we ask him to repeat what he has said. The objective instigated by this metacognitive experience is the nonmetacognitive one of simply comprehending the message. Again, the outcome of the cognitive actions we perform on our interlocutor's repetition of the message might only be some cognitive representation of what he meant (Other outcome only). Alternatively again, the outcome might be that cognitive representation plus some ideas or feelings about it (Other plus Metacognitive Experience outcomes).

Another significant possibility allowed for in Figure 2.2 is that cognitive actions can have as their specific objective the generation of metacognitive experience outcomes. The antecedent might be a metacognitive experience, some event in the Other category (e.g., the establishment of a goal), or both. Whatever the antecedent, it leads us to carry out a certain action. The express purpose of this action, however, is to provide us with ideas and feelings relevant to our cognitive progress or to other aspects of the cognitive enterprise. For instance, we suddenly get the vague sensation (metacognitive experience) that we may not fully understand what we have just read, so we review (cognitive action) the material and our interpretation of it in order to find out exactly what, if anything, is amiss (another metacognitive experience). Or we may decide to read something for some purpose (establish a goal) and start by skimming parts of it (cognitive action) in order to get some initial sense of how hard the going is likely to be (metacognitive experience). These actions will have secondary, nonmetacognitive (Other) outcomes as well, since they involve processing of the relevant information (cf. Flavell, Friedrichs, & Hoyt, 1970). In the two examples just given, both reviewing and skimming will lead to at least some change in our representation of the material reviewed or skimmed, as well as lead to the metacognitive experiences they were carried out to produce. These secondary outcomes are often beneficial in themselves. For example, the prior skimming may help the subsequent reading, and the reviewing may facilitate comprehension and memory.

We have seen that cognitive actions can either have both cognitive and metacognitive outcomes, or only cognitive ones. It is possible that some metacognitively sophisticated individuals may sense this fact, and sometimes carry out cognitive actions with both objectives in mind. For example, you might attempt to repeat my explanation back to me, but in your own words and with your own organization. Your conscious objectives in doing so might be to both (a) assess the correctness of your understanding of the explanation (metacognitive); and (b) increase your chances of being able to remember or explain it clearly to others (cognitive).

The foregoing discussion suggests some interesting distinctions in the domain of metacognition and cognitive monitoring: We develop cognitive actions or strategies for *making* cognitive progress, and we also develop cognitive actions or strategies for *monitoring* cognitive progress. The two might be thought of as cognitive strategies and metacognitive strategies, respectively. The former *can* yield metacognitive experiences as well as cognitive outcomes. The latter *will* yield cognitive outcomes as well as metacognitive experiences. Both are forms of metacognitive knowledge. That is, we know ways to make progress toward cognitive goals and we also know ways to monitor that progress. To say that we have metacognitive knowledge about metacognitive strategies and how to use them sounds peculiar. One "metacognitive" per sentence seems plenty (or even one too many, some might say). However, it is actually no less accurate than saying that we have metacognitive knowledge about metacognitive experiences and how to use them.

There are many cognitive actions that can be deliberately used to engender metacognitive experiences. Some can be initiated at or prior to the beginning of the cognitive enterprise. We can scout out, survey, sample, or skim the relevant information to get a feeling for what goals and associated means would be reasonable to select. The metacognitive experiences that result could thus serve the metacognitive functions that Brown (1978) refers to as *prediction* and *planning*. The same or other activities can be undertaken during the enterprise in order to evaluate one's progress. These might correspond to Brown's (1978) *checking* and *monitoring*. Finally, some actions come at the end of the enterprise. Brown (1978) speaks here of checking outcomes for *internal consistency* and against common-sense criteria (the latter is called *reality testing*).

The following are some of the more interesting actions that can intentionally or unintentionally generate metacognitive experiences about one's own comprehension. One is of course simply trying to comprehend. Furthermore, as Markman (1977, 1979) has aptly pointed out, the more actively and deeply we try to comprehend (inferential, constructive processing), the more likely we are to experience inconsistencies and other comprehension problems that more superficial processing could not bring to light. We may seek out metacognitive experiences by looking back or by looking forward: looking back to see if earlier information squares with present information; looking forward to see if upcoming information will be consistent with, or can be predicted by, present understanding (Markman, this volume). As in science, we are surer of our understanding if we have multiple converging evidence for it: if earlier information is consistent with present information; if subsequent information can be successfully predicted by our present understanding; and if all the information accords with the "previous literature and theory" housed in our knowledge base and cognitive schemata.

We may have a feeling of noncomprehension when a tacit or explicit expectation is not confirmed by information that we now encounter or when our comprehension effort is blocked for other reasons (unfamiliar concepts, ambiguous reference, hard-to-follow reasoning, *etc.*). Two events cooccur in these cases: (*a*) information processing slows down or stops; and (*b*) we have the metacognitive experience of not understanding (or possibly not understanding, *etc.*). Is the change in processing rate the cause of the experience, the consequence of it, or neither? Perhaps our processing rate and changes in that rate actually elicit metacognitive feelings and ideas: that this is easy, hard, or harder or easier than it was a moment ago, depending upon the rate and rate changes. And perhaps we have to learn to interpret rate information in these ways; that is, perhaps young children do not do it.

Finally, we may engender useful metacognitive experiences by "communication," loosely defined. We try to summarize, paraphrase, find examples of, make inferences from, expand on, ask questions about, or put into practice what we have tried to comprehend in order to find out how correctly and fully we have comprehended it. We may be the sole critical audience to these attempts, or we may invite others to join the audience—experts, who can answer our questions or otherwise verify our level of understanding, or novices, who can verify how clearly we understand and are able to formulate the main points. We may also use other external resources to help us monitor our understanding, such as natural and man-made objects and events, books and other written documents, and diverse audio-visual sources.

A metacognitive experience concerning comprehension can thus come about in a variety of ways. But what do we do once we have one? That is, what cognitive actions can ensue from such experiences? We may just keep on processing as before, for any of three reasons. First, our metacognitive experience is that comprehension is proceeding as well or better than expected, and that we should therefore just keep up the good work. Second, the experience is that something is amiss, but we do not do anything about it—because we do not want to, need to, or have the time to (mature "we"); or because we have not yet learned the implications of such feelings (immature "we"). Third, the experience is that something is amiss, but we decide to continue processing for a while to see if additional information will clear things up. If we do decide to act on the basis of the experience, we can try to verify, clarify, evaluate, or figure out the implications of the difficulty. Alternatively, we can use the same or different actions to try to clear up the problem. The ability to do either of these may require considerable learning and development.

Figure 2.1 shows arrows going from cognitive actions to the other three components. The one going to the metacognitive experiences component has already been abundantly illustrated. Cognitive actions probably affect cognitive goals most directly by achieving them, and thereby terminating them. Less successful outcomes of cognitive actions may lead to changes in goals, although perhaps mainly through the mediation of metacognitive knowledge and/or experiences. Information concerning cognitive actions can be stored as part of metacognitive knowledge. An especially important subset of this information is that which concerns their effectiveness as means to cognitive goals (i.e., as cognitive strategies) or to metacognitive goals (i.e., as metacognitive strategies for generating useful metacognitive experiences).

Finally, it should be emphasized that cognitive monitoring can appear to be an exceedingly complex affair, particularly if viewed over the course of an extended cognitive enterprise (cf. Flavell, 1978a). For instance, a cognitive action may lead to a metacognitive experience, which may instigate another action, which may produce another experience, and so on; cognitive goals and metacognitive knowledge will also play antecedent and outcome roles in such cycles. In other words, the ensemble of arrows in Figures 2.1 and 2.2 should be visualized as flashing on and off, simultaneously and in rapid alternation with one another.

Implications for Education

The cognitive-monitoring model has many potentially useful implications for the teaching of oral communication skills. If children could be gotten to monitor their speaking and listening efforts in the various ways specified by the model, I believe the quality of these efforts would generally be improved. Here are two possible examples, from the beginning and from the end of the previous section, respectively: First, we could consider teaching children to become aware of, and maintain in awareness, their communicative goals, at least in certain speaking and listening endeavors. Such heightened awareness could help them choose likely means to these goals, evaluate the effectiveness of these means, and generally monitor their progress in the communicative endeavor. Second, they might be taught ways to evaluate and clear up detected problems in understanding speakers and in getting listeners to understand them.

It would obviously be very space consuming to reexamine for its possible educational implications each point made in the preceding section. It would probably also be unnecessary, since any interested readers could no doubt do it themselves. What I would prefer to do instead is, first, to describe some general considerations that might guide the selection of educational objectives here and, second, to propose one such objective.

What would make a cognitive-monitoring process seem worth teaching in school? Several attributes seem particularly important (Borkowski & Cavanaugh, 1979; Brown, 1978; Brown & Campione, 1978). First, the process ought to be a highly useful one. This means that engaging in it should really help in those cognitive situations where it can be used, and also that the situations in which it can be used should be numerous. Thus, the ideal process should be both efficacious and broadly applicable.

A process would also be ideal to the extent that its learning by children would be easy to implement. This implies several things: The school system should regard it as educationally desirable. Teachers and teacher trainers should want it taught and know how to teach it. Parents should approve of it and perhaps also further its acquisition at home. It should be amenable to effective packaging into instructional materials. Last but hardly least, children should find it interesting and worthwhile to acquire because they can be shown that it helps them achieve cognitive goals and, in general, do better in school.

The process should also be of the sort that, once learned, is likely to be used whenever needed during any appropriate cognitive enterprise. This means that children should find it easy both to remember to use the process and to keep using it as long as needed. If it is hard to think of doing, it will often not be called into action when it should be; if, once initiated, it requires an undue amount of effort to keep doing, children will often not persist in doing it.

I think the fostering of metacognitive experiences and associated cognitive actions is an educational objective that may possess most of these attributes. Recall what metacognitive experiences have going for them. They can be deliberately sought out and evoked by metacognitive strategies. They can also occur as nondeliberate outcomes of cognitive strategies—and be no less useful for being unintended. Having occurred, they may instigate new goals, new cognitive strategies, and/or new metacognitive strategies; these in turn may yield new metacognitive experiences. Finally, concrete metacognitive experiences and associated actions can provide input to permanent metacognitive knowledge, which in turn will influence future experiences and actions.

How, then, might we set about fostering metacognitive experiences in the school? I obviously do not know but will prescribe as if I did: Try consciousness raising and training in introspection. Engage children in cognitive enterprises that should produce specifiable metacognitive ideas and feelings. Try to get them to attend to these ideas and feelings. Help them to understand their meanings and implications for subsequent cognitive action. Teach them how to generate metacognitive experiences, as well as respond appropriately to them. Since cognitive monitoring itself consumes attentional resources (Markman, this volume), we might select as training settings familiar cognitive enterprises that the child can already manage with relatively little attention.

In the specific case of oral communication monitoring, get speakers and listeners to keep exchanging roles. Do this to show children how easy and familiar information can feel when you are the knowledgeable speaker and how hard and unfamiliar it can feel when you are the unknowledgeable listener. Help them to understand the phenomenological chasm between the mind that already knows and the mind that does not yet know. Get speakers to probe the understanding of listeners and listeners the meaning of speakers. Get each to notice any feelings of surprise or puzzlement that this feedback about the other's mental contents may produce. (How could she have thought I meant *that*? Is *that* what he meant when he said _____?) Help them to analyze messages as cognitive objects, in order to understand the different cognitive experiences that different messages might stimulate in the heads of different speakers and different listeners. In short, try to stimulate conscious thoughts and feelings about speakers, messages, and listeners, using any methods that seem promising.

A recent educational experiment by Corno (1978) is of interest in this connection. Parents were provided with instructional materials for teaching an interesting set of oral communication skills to their third-grade children. The children were taught to understand and detect occurrences/nonoccurrences of the following teacher behaviors: reviewing information from a previous lesson; identifying the goals of a lesson; identifying its important points; providing summary information. These behaviors were introduced to the children as "tricks for making ideas orderly." They were also given instruction on the student behaviors of asking questions that are relevant to the lesson, of volunteering, and of giving relevant answers when called upon. The instructional procedure for reviewing will illustrate the way these concepts were taught. The meaning, purpose, and educational importance of lesson reviews were repeatedly explained and illustrated. The children were also given practice with feedback in distinguishing reviews from nonreviews in lesson material, in part by learning to spot key words or phrases that usually signal a review, for example, "In our last lesson we learned. . . ." Although the results of Corno's study were complex (there were several kinds of aptitude–treatment interactions, for example), they were generally positive. For example, the third graders who received the instruction outperformed their controls on vocabulary and reading comprehension tests, as well as on tests of the communication concepts taught. Corno's (1978) intervention is hardly the kind of training I am proposing, but it is a step in that direction.

Striving occasionally to practice what I preach, I have done some cognitive monitoring of this section of the chapter, and that monitoring has delivered me of the following metacognitive experience: All educational interventions have problems and flaws. The educational profit new interventions make in one place are likely to be offset by losses—often subtle ones—incurred elsewhere. Worse yet, even the profits may turn out to be only temporary, if not downright illusory. So will it surely be with the kind of intervention I have sketched here, my present optimism and enthusiasm for it notwithstanding. I do not know what the losses and temporary or illusory profits will be, but I do believe there will be some. The conclusion I draw from this rather somber metacognitive experience is that the above sort of intervention should be tried—but also monitored very, very carefully at every step.

Acknowledgements

The preparation of this chapter was supported by National Institute of Child Health and Human Development Grant HDMH 10429. A number of psychologists affiliated with the University of Illinois Center for the Study of Reading have recently begun what promises to be exciting theoretical and experimental explorations of metacognition. They have been trying to understand what role metacognition plays in skilled reading and how poor readers might be trained to use it to improve their reading comprehension and study strategies. The group has included Marilyn Adams, Richard Anderson, Thomas Anderson, Linda Baker, Ann Brown, Joseph Campione, Allan Collins, Ernest Goetz, Glenn Kleinman, Diane Schallert, and Rand Spiro. My thinking about cognitive monitoring has been much influenced by recent conversations with this group and by reading informal summaries of their research plans. For example, the idea that we sometimes wait to see if subsequent information will clear up a present comprehension problem (see the end of the section entitled "Cognitive Actions") is entirely theirs. I am very grateful to them. I wish to thank Ellen Markman for her patience in listening to my ideas in their various stages of malformation and for her predictably astute suggestions about how they might be improved. I may have also pirated some of her ideas as well as some of the Illinois group's, for which both she and they deserve my apologies as well as my thanks. I would like to express my deepest gratitude to my research collaborators James Speer, Frances Green, Rainer Kluwe, and Diane August for their many contributions to my thinking about matters metacognitive and monitoring. Finally, I am particularly grateful to Steve Yussen for his most helpful criticisms and suggestions for revision of the first draft of this paper.

References

Anderson, R. C., & Pichart, J. W. Recall of previously unrecallable information following a shift in perspective. *Journal of Verbal Learning and Verbal Behavior,* 1978, *17,* 1–12.

Asher, S. R. Referential communication. In G. J. Whitehurst & B. J. Zimmerman (Eds.), *The functions of language and cognition.* New York: Academic Press, 1978.

Baddeley, A. D. The trouble with levels: A reexamination of Craik and Lockhart's framework for memory research. *Psychological Review,* 1978, *85,* 139–152.

Borkowski, J. G., & Cavanaugh, J. C. Maintenance and generalization of skills and strategies by the retarded. In N. R. Ellis (Ed.), *Handbook of mental deficiency: Psychological theory and research* (2nd ed.). Hillsdale, N.J.: Lawrence Erlbaum Associates, 1979.

Brown, A. L. The development of memory: Knowing, knowing about knowing, and knowing how to know. In H. W. Reese (Ed.), *Advances in child development and behavior* (Vol. 10). New York: Academic Press, 1975.

Brown, A. L. Knowing when, where, and how to remember: A problem of metacognition. In R. Glaser (Ed.), *Advances in instructional psychology.* New York: Halsted Press, 1978.

Brown, A. L. Metacognitive development and reading. In R. J. Spiro, B. Bruce, & W. F. Brewer (Eds.), *Theoretical issues in reading comprehension.* Hillsdale, N.J.: Lawrence Erlbaum Associates, in press.

Brown, A. L., & Campione, J. C. Permissible inferences from the outcome of training studies in cognitive developmental research. In W. S. Hall & M. Cole (Eds.), *Quarterly Newsletter of the Institute for Comparative Human Development.* New York: Rockefeller University, 1978.

Brown, A. L., & Smiley, S. S. The development of strategies for studying texts. *Child Development,* 1978, *49,* 1076–1088.

Clark, E. V. *Awareness of language: Some evidence from what children say and do.* Paper presented at the Discussion Meeting on The Child's Conception of Language, Projektgrüppe für Psycholinguistik, Max-Planck-Gesellschaft, Berg en Dalsweg 79, Nijmegen, The Netherlands, May 1977.

Corno, L. *Effects of parent instruction on teacher structuring and student participation in the third grade: An aptitude–treatment interaction approach.* Unpublished doctoral dissertation, Stanford University, 1978.

Craik, F. I. M., & Lockhart, R. S. Levels of processing: A framework for memory research. *Journal of Verbal Learning and Verbal Behavior,* 1972, *11,* 671–684.

Flavell, J. H. *The development of metacommunication.* Paper presented at the Twenty-first International Congress of Psychology, Paris, July 1976. (a)

Flavell, J. H. Metacognitive aspects of problem solving. In L. B. Resnick (Ed.), *The nature of intelligence.* Hillsdale, N.J.: Lawrence Erlbaum Associates, 1976. (b)

Flavell, J. H. *Cognitive development.* Englewood Cliffs, N.J.: Prentice-Hall, 1977.

Flavell, J. H. Metacognitive development. In J. M. Scandura & C. J. Brainerd (Eds.), *Structural/process theories of complex human behavior.* Alphen a. d. Rijn, The Netherlands: Sijthoff and Noordhoff, 1978. (a)

Flavell, J. H. Metacognition. In E. Langer (Chair), *Current perspectives on awareness and cognitive processes.* Symposium presented at the meeting of the American Psychological Association, Toronto, 1978. (b)

Flavell, J. H. Monitoring social cognitive enterprises: Something else that may develop in the area of social cognition. In J. H. Flavell & L. Ross (Eds.), *Social cognitive development: Frontiers and possible futures.* New York: Cambridge University Press, in press.

Flavell, J. H., Friedrichs, A. G., & Hoyt, J. D. Developmental changes in memorization processes. *Cognitive Psychology,* 1970, *1,* 324–340.

Flavell, J. H., & Wellman, H. M. Metamemory. In R. V. Kail & J. W. Hagen (Eds.), *Perspectives on the development of memory and cognition.* Hillsdale, N.J.: Lawrence Erlbaum Associates, 1977.

Fredericksen, C. H. Effects of context-induced processing operations on semantic information acquired from discourse. *Cognitive Psychology*, 1975, *7*, 139–166.

Gibson, J. J. *The senses considered as perceptual systems*. Boston: Houghton Mifflin, 1966.

Glucksberg, S., Krauss, R. M., & Higgins, E. T. The development of referential communication skills. In F. D. Horowitz (Ed.), *Review of child development research* (Vol. 4). Chicago: University of Chicago Press, 1975.

Hayes, J. R. It's the thought that counts: New approaches to educational theory. In D. Klahr (Ed.), *Cognition and instruction*. Hillsdale, N.J.: Lawrence Erlbaum Associates, 1976.

Howie-Day, A. M. *Metapersuasion: The development of reasoning about persuasive strategies*. Paper read at the Society for Research in Child Development Meetings, San Francisco, March, 1979.

Langer, E. J. Rethinking the role of thought in social interaction. In J. H. Harvey, W. J. Ickes, & R. F. Kidd (Eds.), *New directions in attributional research* (Vol. 2). Hillsdale, N.J.: Lawrence Erlbaum Associates, 1978.

Markman, E. M. Realizing that you don't understand: A preliminary investigation. *Child Development*, 1977, *48*, 986–992.

Markman, E. M. Realizing that you don't understand: Elementary school children's awareness of inconsistencies. *Child Development*, 1979, *50*, 643–655.

Meichenbaum, D., & Asarnow, J. Cognitive-behavior modification and metacognitive development: Implications for the classroom. In P. Kendall & S. Hollon (Eds.), *Cognitive-behavioral interventions: Theory, research and procedures*. New York: Academic Press, 1979.

Miller, P. H., & Bigi, L. The development of children's understanding of attention. *Merrill-Palmer Quarterly*, 1979, *25*, 235–250.

Mischel, W., & Mischel, H. N. Self-control and the self. In T. Mischel (Ed.), *The self: Psychological and philosophical issues*. Totowa, N.J.: Rowman & Littlefield, 1977.

Nold, E. W. Revising. In C. Fredrickson (Ed.), *Writing: The nature, development and teaching of written communication*. Hillsdale, N.J.: Lawrence Erlbaum Associates, in press.

3

Comprehension Monitoring

ELLEN M. MARKMAN

Occasionally, while I am reading my mind begins to wander. As I become more engrossed in my daydream, I, of course, understand less and less of what I read. Yet, I keep on reading, sometimes for pages on end. I persist at such obviously profitless reading because at the time I am not aware that I do not understand. This is an extreme example of a failure to monitor one's own comprehension, but less extreme cases are probably fairly common in adults. I suspect that such problems are pervasive in children. As there is so little empirical work directly concerned with comprehension monitoring, I cannot document these beliefs with much evidence. However, there are several findings from the developmental literature that at least suggest that children often fail to notice when they do not understand. Here are some of the more striking examples. (For other relevant findings, see Crosgrove & Patterson, 1977, 1978; Dittman, 1972; Ironsmith & Whitehurst, 1978.) In one study, children were asked to serve as consultants to someone who was writing instructions for children on how to play a card game and perform a

61

magic trick (Markman, 1977). Although the instructions contained glaring omissions, young children claimed to understand them. For example, for the card game children were shown cards with letters of the alphabet on them. The children were told that an equal number of cards were dealt to each player. They then listened to the following instructions: "We each put our cards in a pile. We both turn over the top card in our pile. We look at the cards to see who has the special card. Then we turn over the next card in our pile to see who has the special card this time. In the end the person with the most cards wins the game." Although there was no mention of what the special card was, nor of how players accumulated cards, these young children were confident they understood how to play the game.

In another study, older elementary school children were enlisted as consultants to help evaluate essays (Markman, 1979). Children judged the essays to be comprehensible, even though they contained blatant inconsistencies. For example, children often claimed that an essay about fish made perfect sense and was easy to understand, even though it contained the following passage: "Fish must have light in order to see. There is absolutely no light at the bottom of the ocean. It is pitch black down there. When it is that dark the fish cannot see anything. They cannot even see colors. Some fish that live at the bottom of the ocean can see the color of their food."

In a referential communication task, children served as listeners and were told that they were permitted to ask questions (Patterson, Massad, & Cosgrove, 1978). Nevertheless, they almost never spontaneously questioned the speaker or requested more information, even when the messages were completely uninformative. In a similar setting, children sometimes informed speakers that they had understood what was said (Karabenick & Miller, 1977). Yet over half of these "confirmations" followed information that was ambiguous or incomplete.

The purpose of this chapter is to provide a preliminary conceptual framework in which such findings can be better understood. I begin to address questions such as: How do we decide whether or not we have understood something? What is the nature of the information upon which we base such decisions? How do we obtain this information about our own comprehension? What are the likely sources of developmental differences in comprehension monitoring? The central point of my argument will be to show how theories of comprehension can inform theories of comprehension monitoring. In the first section of this chapter, I describe two fundamental aspects of comprehension: (*a*) comprehension must involve a type of structure or organization of information; and (*b*) it often potentiates inferential processes or "going beyond the information given." In the second section of the chapter, I show how this view of comprehension provides insight into problems of comprehension monitoring and I extend the analysis to cover developmental change.

Comprehension

Requirements of Structured Information

It does not make much sense to say that I understand my phone number. I can learn, know, or remember a phone number, but not understand one. Why not? In recent discussions of understanding, Bransford and McCarrell (1974) and Moravcsik (1979) convincingly argue that only structured or organized information can count as meaningful or as a proper object of understanding. To the layman, at least, phone numbers do not have the relevant structure. We know of no rule or principle of organization that, for example, predicts the order of the numbers. As a consequence, it makes no sense to speak of understanding in this case.

We do speak of understanding words, sentences, stories, and events, among other things. In each of these cases, the domain under consideration must be described by some structural analysis. Since psychologists have begun studying the processing of meaningful material, they have begun to require structural descriptions. For example, theorists who believe that words have meaning argue that the words are analyzable or decomposable into primitives or that they can be placed in a system where they are defined by other words. Sentences are characterized by grammars, which, of course, are structural descriptions of how words interrelate. Stories have also been described by grammars, which give principles by which they are organized (Rumelhart, 1975). Events have been characterized by scripts, plans, and goals, which are conceptual structures explaining sequences of actions (Schank & Abelson, 1977).

In none of these domains is there yet an adequate structural description. For some domains this may not be possible. Yet progress has been made in the analysis of the structures and in finding empirical support for these analyses. An impressive variety of empirical consequences have been derived from structural descriptions. For example, what will be judged as well formed or not can be predicted from structural descriptions. Relative ease of comprehension, as measured, for example, by speed or accuracy, can be predicted from the relative complexity of structures (e.g., Fodor, Bever, & Garret, 1974). Predictions about which information is a story is most likely to be retained and which is most likely to be forgotten have also been based on structural descriptions (Mandler & Johnson, 1977; Thorndyke, 1977). Different structures can be imposed on stored information with predictable consequences as to what information is retrieved (Anderson & Pichert, 1978). Structural similarity can be the basis for predictions of facilitation or interference in memory (Bower & Black, Note 1).

There is no reason to believe that the principles of organization will be identical across a wide variety of domains of understanding. Even the few examples just mentioned involve principles that are very diverse: arbitrary, conventional rules, logical inference, causality, space, and time. The point is not that the structural principles must be similar, but that there exist such principles which organize the information and that they have empirical consequences for the way in which that information is understood. Any theory of understanding must fundamentally involve a theory of the organization of that domain. Later I will argue that these principles have implications for comprehension monitoring as well as for comprehension proper.

Inferential and Constructive Processing

Another reason why it does not make sense to say that I understand my phone number is that I cannot do much with it. I cannot paraphrase it, improve it, use it to predict other information, relate it to other knowledge, *etc.* About all one can do with a phone number is to rote memorize it, that is, reproduce it in a fixed form. Yet, understanding often involves transforming, extending, and relating information.

Some of the transformations and extensions of information that occur during normal comprehension are barely noticed, relatively automatic, and very mundane. These inferences are highly constrained by the context. For example, Bransford, Barclay, and Franks (1972) found that, after hearing a sentence such as "Three turtles rested on a floating log and a fish swam beneath them," people would often believe that they heard "Three turtles rested on a floating log and a fish swam beneath it." Because of knowledge about spatial relations, this inference is readily made. Another, more dramatic, example involved having people read a paragraph that began "The procedure is actually quite simple. First you arrange things into different groups. Of course one pile may be sufficient depending on how much there is to do. If you have to go somewhere else due to lack of facilities that is the next step [Bransford & McCarrell, 1974]." One group of people who read the passage had very poor recall of the information. Another group who read the identical passage had considerably better recall. The only difference between the two groups was that the latter was given the title: "Washing Clothes." Why should a title help so much? The answer to this is that, when one reads this vague material with the title in mind, one's stored knowledge of what happens when washing clothes provides a framework for interpreting the passage, for concretizing the vague information. This knowledge includes stereotyped knowledge of what objects are involved, how they are manipulated, the standard temporal sequence of actions that occur, and the standard sequence of spatial displacements that the objects undergo. This structured information guides the interpretation of the passage. That is, the context provides a structural representation onto which incoming information is mapped. Many minor details which are not explicitly mentioned in the passage are supplied by this representation.

Of course, not all inferences that people make are highly constrained. Some are brilliant insights reflecting a much fuller, more extensive understanding than is usual. Others are wild guesses which might reflect confusion rather than genuine understanding. What distinguishes these two types of inferences? This question is closely tied to questions of what makes a good explanation, or a good theory, of what counts as insight, *etc.* These are very complex questions in psychology and philosophy which I cannot begin to answer. However, I would like to argue that any account of these issues will necessitate discussions of the organization of knowledge. A brilliant insight or elegant theory often makes minimal extraneous assumptions to solve a specific problem yet also establishes many unforeseen interrelations and connections. By establishing these new relations, such an explanation enriches our understanding and becomes more enlightening. This contrasts with an explanation that is ad hoc, that is, that solves a given specific problem but does not further our understanding by completing or enriching our knowledge in other ways. A wild guess, like an ad hoc explanation, might "solve" a given problem, but its assumptions may be unwarranted and, again, no further insights gained. Inferences or insights can be exceptional by providing a reinterpretation of a phenomenon—a new way of looking at old facts. In other words they impose a new structure on old information. Good metaphors probably have this characteristic. A final example is when a higher order structure is created which can encompass others, resulting in the discovery of previously unrecognized commonalities. Recent excitement in physics over supergravity is due to this type of progress. According to Freeman and van Nieuwenhuizen (1978), supergravity may provide a single account of four forces in physics: strong, electromagnetic, weak, and gravitational. This would be considered a major theoretical advance because "a more satisfying understanding of nature could be achieved if the four forces could somehow be unified (p. 126)."

These examples reveal several points about the nature of comprehension:

1. Understanding is not all or none; it admits of degrees. In addition, it may be difficult to specify an end point of perfect understanding. Unlike rote recall, there may not be clear criteria for perfect understanding.
2. Understanding requires structured or organized information.
3. Understanding often involves inferential or constructive processes, operations that transform, elaborate, and extend incoming information.

These two aspects of understanding—structure and inference—are closely interrelated. Inferences range from the mundane to the exceptional. This range is at least partially determined by how much detail existing structures can supply. At one extreme, the structure dictates the nature of the inferential processes; at the other extreme, the inferential processes engender new structures.

Comprehension Monitoring

In this section, I will attempt to show how the characteristics of understanding described earlier are relevant to the study of comprehension monitoring and its development.

Variability and Vagueness of Criteria

Because understanding admits of degrees and kinds, and because there may not be a way of specifying complete understanding, it often may be difficult for people to judge their own comprehension. Whether or not someone is judged to understand something will depend upon the type of material. How we decide that we understand directions to someone's house will be different from how we decide that we understand a poem. Even when the material is identical (e.g., a specific novel), decisions about whether one understands it will vary with one's goal (e.g., reading for pleasure versus reading to write a literary critique). The point is that the lack of a straightforward criterion for judging comprehension makes these judgments complex, probabilistic, and open to error. Skilled judgments of one's own comprehension require adjusting one's desired level and kind of understanding to the material and goals.

Because the criteria for knowing when one has achieved comprehension are vague, children may have difficulty applying them. It is possible that there may be some confusion of comprehension with rote memorization. Appel, Cooper, McCarrell, Sims-Knight, Yussen, and Flavell (1972) have reported that initially children confuse memory with perception, but to my knowledge there is no analogous empirical work on the comprehension–memory distinction.

Children may have difficulty adjusting the standard to varying material and goals. To understand a story or an essay composed of sentences requires more than understanding individual sentences: Some higher order organization is necessary. Children may initially judge whether or not they understand prose by judging their comprehension of successive sentences rather than by attempting to integrate these sentences. If so, judgments of comprehension of individual sentences would lead to spuriously high judgments of comprehension of essays, *etc.* Thus, one possible developmental difference is that children attempt to judge comprehension of complex higher order structures on the basis of comprehension of the simpler structures that comprise them. As a consequence, they would tend to overestimate how well they understand.

A finding from Markman (1979) may be an example of this. Third- and sixth-grade children listened to essays that contained inconsistencies. They were asked to judge the essays for their comprehensibility. Half of the children were informed that there was a problem with each essay—something that did not make any sense—and that their job was to find it. The other half were asked to evaluate the essays but were not warned about the problem. A sizable proportion of children (mainly third graders) still failed to notice inconsistencies even after being set to search for a problem. However, these children did question the truth of individual claims more often than children in the other instructional group. To evaluate an essay for its consistency, one must relate the various portions of the text to each other. To evaluate single sentences for their truth, one need not make this the same type of interrelationship. Rather, each sentence can be tested individually for its correspondence to empirical fact. This finding suggests that children may tend to evaluate their comprehension of such prose in a piecemeal fashion, focusing on component sentences but not attempting to use a criterion that requires imposing a higher order organization on the material.

Requirements of Structure

Absence of Structure

Objects of understanding must be structured. If one finds it impossible to impose a structure on incoming information, that should serve as a signal that the information is not understood. We know quite readily that we do not understand *Now he or table in for type*. Doubly self-embedded sentences, for example, *The man, the boy, the girl knew, likes, sings,* though grammatical, are very difficult to understand. It is difficult to understand these sentences because it is difficult to parse them. Yet, for this same reason, being almost totally unable to discover a structure, we readily know that we do not understand. Analogous decisions can be made about stories or films, especially when people search for a plot structure. Stream of consciousness or flashback techniques often make such works difficult to comprehend because people are unable to fit the work to a standard plot structure, and not having other structural descriptions available, they are left puzzled. Again, the inability to determine an underlying structure makes the material difficult to understand, but it also makes it very simple to realize that one has not understood.

Within a given domain, the gross inability to discover an underlying structure should be a developmentally early sign that one has failed to comprehend the material. At the sentence level, even young children should be able to determine that they did not understand rapid or garbled speech, speech in a foreign language, completely ungrammatical speech, or extremely complex sentences. Minimal processing is required for such judgments. They can be made without having to formulate expectations, draw inferences, check implications against incoming information, etc. Similarly, a scrambled plot structure should be one of the first signs that children use to determine they have not understood a story. Note that, even at this crude level, sensitivity to the variety and appropriateness of organization is required. Children who judge the comprehensibility of a story based on their understanding of individual unrelated sentences would judge even an incoherent story as comprehensible. But, assuming that the appropriate structure is invoked, then extreme difficulty in imposing the structure on incoming material should be an early developing basis for intuitions about comprehension.

Multiple Structures

Information that can be given multiple structural descriptions can also signal a failure to comprehend. Examples of this type of message abound in the referential communication literature. Consider what it means when a referent is incompletely specified, as is the case in *John and Bill went to the store. He bought some bread.* The problem with this message is that, without any other information, *he* could refer to either John or Bill, and there is no nonarbitrary way of deciding between them. Recognizing ambiguity in referential descriptions could lead to the realization that one has not understood the speaker, or that the message requires clarification. (It is possible that the recognition of multiple interpretations leads to a particular type of phenomenological experience, one that is similar to indecision, analogous to reaching a choice point and not knowing which alternative to take.)

It would be misleading to suggest that whenever two or more interpretations are possible, one will judge that there is a comprehension problem. Multiple interpretations of a sentence are frequently possible; it is just that often the context constrains the interpretation so much that we do not notice the potential ambiguity (see Clark & Clark, 1977 for a discussion of this problem). The principle could be reformulated to state that, whenever two or more interpretations are *noticed,* one will judge that there is a comprehension problem. Again, I believe this would be an oversimplification. Many messages that we receive are incompletely specified and require some inferential processing to fully understand. Inferences that supply details that the speaker omitted, or bridge gaps that appear in written messages, are frequent and routine. The work of Bransford and his colleagues provides many demonstrations of this type of processing (Bransford & McCarrell, 1974). Clark and Haviland (1977) have formulated principles that characterize certain of these "repair" strategies that listeners use. Collins, Warnock, Aiello, and

Miller (1975) have characterized some common types of inferences people use when dealing with incomplete knowledge.

Given that people are continually operating on messages to bridge gaps and supply missing details, what implication does this have for their judgments of their own comprehension? It could be that for each of these inferences we momentarily suspect a problem but suspend concern as soon as an inference resolves it. This must happen, at least occasionally, although the automatic nature of many of these inferences could often preclude any awareness of a comprehension problem. In any case, certainly there are continua here in respect to whether or not we notice the ambiguity and, if noticed, whether we judge it severe enough to warrant concern about our comprehension. This lack of a clear boundary leaves room for individual differences, and for changing the criteria depending on one's interest, on how important complete understanding is, on what margin of error one can tolerate, *etc.*

In the clear cases, the context does not provide enough information to nonarbitrarily choose between alternatives. (Context here includes principles of communication; see Clark and Clark (Note 2) for an interesting analysis.) In such cases, to decide between alternatives, one would have to guess or make extraneous, unwarranted assumptions. Thus, one must implicitly judge how well the context constrains the interpretation, how legitimate the inferences are.

These kinds of judgments are subject to error. However, many of the errors can be spotted during the normal course of active comprehension. In some cases, when vagueness or ambiguity is noticed, we may immediately seek clarification by asking a question, reprocessing material, etc. Often, however, we may decide to wait to see if subsequent information will constrain the interpretation. Once alternative interpretations are noticed, we may tentatively decide on an interpretation and then revise that decision if subsequent information indicates it is wrong. All of these decisions require inferential processing and judgments about inferences. Some require that tentative decisions be remembered as tentative. If we forget that an interpretation was hypothetical, then we will have difficulty revising the decision once subsequent information conflicts with it. Thus, once an ambiguity has been detected, it may be necessary to make subtle judgments about what is a reasonable versus an arbitrary decision, and additional processing capacity can be consumed in assigning temporary decisions, in remembering that the decision is temporary and what the alternatives were, checking the decision against incoming information, and revising the decision when necessary.

When children have been presented with ambiguous messages in a referential communication task, they often have failed to ask for appropriate clarification (Cosgrove & Patterson, 1978; Ironsmith & Whitehurst, 1978; Patterson, Massad, & Cosgrove, 1978). In order for children to realize that more information is required in such cases, they must note the possibility of alternative interpretations and must realize that any decision they could make would be arbitrary. Both aspects of this requirement have developmental implications. It was hypothesized earlier that the first intuition that develops for realizing that one has not understood is the failure to come up with a single coherent interpretation. A child who is satisfied with obtaining one coherent structure may not notice, or be disturbed by, the alternative possibilities. Once a single consistent interpretation is found, the child would not seek alternative possibilities. There is some evidence for this in a referential communication study by Dickson (1979) reviewed by Asher (1978). In the study, the possible referents children could select from were lined up in an orderly array. If children settled on the first coherent interpretation of a message, then they would choose the first object they discovered that fit the description, and—assuming children scanned the array systematically—their referent selections would be predictable by the position of the objects in the array. This was, in fact, what Dickson (1979) found.

Whether or not a child is satisfied with this minimal criterion will most likely depend on the complexity of the task. For complex domains, children may be more likely to settle for the first structure obtained, whereas, for simple domains, they may carry through with the processing required to discover possible ambiguities or vagueness. The information-processing requirements certainly affect the quality of the messages children produce (see Asher, 1978 and Shatz, 1978, for reviews). Similar principles most likely will affect children's ability to evaluate the messages.

Once children notice an ambiguity, they must also realize that their own resolution would be arbitrary. This requires making judgments about how much the context constrains the inference, the plausibility of alternative interpretations, *etc.* I will defer discussion of this complex problem until the discussion of inferential and constructive processing.

Discovery of Inconsistencies

Another signal that there has been a failure to comprehend or that there is a problem in the material is provided when inconsistencies are discovered. In the multiple-structure cases just described, there are two or more alternative interpretations of information and insufficient context to decide between them. In the present case, some information already exists as a part of the structure, yet conflicting information is being presented. It is by attempting to incorporate two inconsistent types of information into a single structure that the incompatibility is noticed.

The studies reported in Markman (1979) where children evaluated essays that contained explicitly inconsistent material suggest that elementary school children may often fail to engage in the processing required to notice inconsistent information. For example, in an essay about ice cream, children heard the following information about Baked Alaska: "To make it they put the ice cream in a very hot oven. The ice cream in Baked Alaska melts when it gets that hot." They subsequently heard, "When they make Baked Alaska, the ice cream stays firm and it does not melt." Each essay was read twice before children were asked for their judgments. The children, who appeared cooperative and flattered to be asked for their opinions, were not in general reluctant to question or criticize the experimenter. Yet, despite the fact that the essays were read twice and that the children could later recall the relevant information, they often appeared oblivious to these problems. They seemed genuinely unaware that incompatible material had been presented. Unless children attempted to establish interrelationships among propositions, such inconsistencies could not be noticed. Each proposition could exist independent of the other and not in and of itself be seen as problematic.

Once a potential inconsistency is discovered, problems similar to those discussed in the multiple-structure case arise. One could search for an immediate clarification or solution, or could wait hoping that subsequent information would resolve the problem. One could tentatively offer a resolution, marking the resolution as tentative and leaving it open to further revision. Again, each of these alternatives could increase the complexity of the processing load.

Use of the Structure to Formulate Expectations

Probably the most important implication of a structural description of information is that it can be used to formulate expectations. Regardless of whether the principles of organization are linguistic, logical, causal, temporal, or of some other sort, they can provide a basis for predicting subsequent information. After hearing the first part of a sentence, one can often predict much about what the second half will be. When following a scientific discussion, at a colloquium for example, one can predict what the next study will be or what conclusions will be drawn from the data. An example of subjects' use of a structure to formulate expectations was provided by Greeno and Noreen (1974). Their subjects read paragraphs believing that they would later be asked questions about them. The time taken to read individual sentences of the paragraphs was recorded. It was found that sentences that were consistent with information presented earlier in the paragraphs were read more quickly than sentences that were unrelated. Sentences that were inconsistent with prior information took even more time to read. These findings suggest that subjects are formulating expectations based on the information that they read and that these expectations guide subsequent processing. Developmental work of this sort is needed.

In some cases, the predictions that one makes are wrong. Erroneous predictions result in a violation of one's expectations which in turn is an important source of information about one's own comprehension. This is a case in which there is an inverse relation between comprehension proper and knowledge about comprehension. A mismatch between one's expectations and the actual information is a sign of poor comprehension. Yet the discovery of such violations provides grounds for confident judgments about one's comprehension. These mismatches can be due to problems in the material, to misreadings of the material, or to inadequacies in one's initial representation. In other words, the source of the problem can be external or internal. I am assuming that knowledge of the actual locus of the problem is not critical for the initial detection of a violation. In both cases it is the use of a structure to formulate hypotheses which allows for disconfirmation. Subsequent review of the material may often be required to localize the reasons for the mismatch. Phenomenologically, violations of expectations might be similar to mild surprise. If the experience is similar to surprise, such violations could intrude into consciousness and provide a particularly salient signal of failure to comprehend.

Without expectations, one could not obtain this source of information about one's comprehension. There is a minor problem here in that incoming information may be distorted to conform to one's expectations. Though expectations are required to notice this sort of problem they could also prevent discovery of some problems. However, there is a self-correcting aspect to this system. Erroneous beliefs lead to incorrect expectations. Perhaps some initial information could be distorted, but repeated encounters with material would certainly increase the likelihood that violations would occur and eventually be noticed.

Violations of expectations might be especially salient information about one's own comprehension. In the absence of such violations, will people assume that they have understood? Certainly this is sometimes the case. The example of reading while distracted by a daydream may be an example of this. Had a surprising violation entered my awareness, I might have realized that I did not understand. In the absence of such an intrusion into consciousness, I continued reading. In active critical comprehension, however, there is another more positive source of information about one's own comprehension: the confirmation of one's expectations. People can be more confident that they have comprehended material when their expectations are repeatedly confirmed.

To my knowledge there are no developmental studies contrasting the use of violations versus confirmations as sources of information about one's own comprehension. It is possible that the use of violations as an index of how well one has understood may developmentally precede search for confirming evidence. Children may assume that they understand as long as there is no evidence to the contrary. If so, then, in cases where there is neither confirming nor disconfirming evidence about one's comprehension, children should be confident that they had understood, whereas adults should be hesitant to judge.

Inferential and Constructive Processing

Inferential and constructive processing is required in order to obtain information about one's own comprehension. Only by formulating an expectation can one discover that it has been confirmed or disconfirmed. Only by attempting to relate material can one discover that it is inconsistent. Each of these sources of information about how well one is comprehending requires transforming, extending, or relating material. Without attempts to operate on the material in such ways, important information about one's comprehension is lost.[1]

Although even quite young children operate upon material to draw inferences, make assumptions, etc., there are developmental differences in the extent to which children engage in such processing (Ackerman, 1978; Collins, Wellman, Keniston, & Westby, 1978; Paris & Lindauer, 1976; Paris, Lindauer, & Cox, 1977; Paris & Upton, 1976). Because children are more limited in the extent to which they engage in such processing, they will have less of this information about their own comprehension. As a consequence, they may often be left unaware of problems in their comprehension. An example of this was provided by Markman (1977) where children were asked to evaluate instructions which lacked crucial information about how to perform the tasks. These instructions specified temporal sequences of actions on objects. The incompleteness of the instructions meant that there was not enough information about transitions from one action or state to the next. By third grade, children very readily spotted the inadequacy of the instructions, but first-grade children often thought that the incomplete instructions were perfectly adequate. It was hypothesized that the reason children did not notice the problem was that they were failing to mentally execute the instructions. A child who mentally worked through the instructions, who attempted to represent the states and their transitions, could find the problem. A more passive processer—one who listened to and remembered the instructions but who did not attempt to mentally execute them—would fail to notice the problem. If children's failure was due to this insufficient processing, then, by

[1] In this discussion I have ignored a number of distinctions between various types of inferences. There are distinctions between invited and necessary inferences, presuppositions and implications, conditional and class logic, etc. Such distinctions may eventually prove relevant to discussions of comprehension monitoring. Differences in difficulty, or in the probability with which inferences are made, will predict how readily certain problems in comprehension will be uncovered. It is also possible that the violations of different inferences will have different implications for judgments about one's comprehension. For example, one may be less concerned about violations of invited inferences than of necessary inferences. It is also possible that the actions taken (e.g., the repair strategies that one uses) once a problem is noticed will vary depending on the type of inference involved. However, at present too little is known about these various inferences and their developmental history to infer much about their differential role in judgments of comprehension.

helping children accomplish some of the processing, it should be possible to improve their performance. Two findings from Markman (1977) support this conclusion. Children were more likely to notice the problem either when the instructions had been partially demonstrated for them or when they actually attempted to enact them. In both of these cases, the necessity for inferential and constructive processing is reduced. The transitions between one state and another should no longer have to be mentally inferred because the children actually see them. As a consequence, the inadequacy of the instructions should become more apparent and children should become more aware of the problems, as they in fact did.

The preceding example illustrates how insufficient processing precludes access to information needed for judging one's comprehension. An additional way in which inferential processes can provide information about our own comprehension occurs when we find ourselves unable to carry out such processing. An inability to paraphrase information, to draw implications,[2] to come up with a concrete example of a general principle, etc. can serve as an indicator that we have failed to understand. In cases where we find ourselves too rigidly bound to the precise form of the material, unable to rearrange, transform, or extend it, we have some information about the limitation of our comprehension. On the other hand, if we find that we are capable of such manipulations of the material, we may obtain evidence that we have comprehended. Of course, there must be some check on the validity of such manipulations, but presumably this would be analogous to the confirmation of expectations. The paraphrase, extensions, or concrete examples should lead to new predictions which can then be checked against additional information or knowledge.

Decisions about inferences are a final way in which inferential processing is relevant for comprehension monitoring. In much of the previous discussion, issues arose about the plausibility or appropriateness of inferences. These concerns are much broader than issues of whether an inference is valid or not, and the criteria for judgment are much vaguer than notions of logical validity. There are two broad types of ways in which decisions about appropriateness can be made.

The first is to see how useful an inference turns out to be in light of subsequent information. One might make an assumption to resolve a problem, hoping that subsequent information will either support or refute it. To use this strategy, one has to notice the problem, draw the inference, mark it as tentative, perhaps hold it in working store and recall what the alternatives

---

[2] One caveat is in order here (Ziff, 1972). There are bogus paraphrases and inferences that can be constructed with knowledge of English and logic but which would certainly not count as evidence of understanding. For example, after hearing an active sentence, one could paraphrase it into a passive form with only the most superficial understanding of the sentence. Similarly, knowing a little logic, one could always draw an inference from a poorly understood proposition "p," for example, "p or q."

were, check incoming information against the inference and revise it as necessary. Thus, as already noted, use of these procedures could be cognitively taxing and prone to a number of sources of error.

The second way in which decisions about inferences are made involves more direct judgments of the inferences. These will be judgments about, for example, whether or not the context sufficiently constrains the inference or whether assumptions are warranted or ad hoc. They are analogous to judgments of elegance and parsimony in evaluation of theories. It is the metacognitive evaluation of the inferences that is at issue, not the actual drawing of the inferences per se. As the prior discussion revealed, there are many cases in which, in order to appropriately judge one's own comprehension, these types of decisions about the evaluation of inference are required. Such evaluation of inferences must be fundamentally involved in comprehension monitoring. Yet, to my knowledge, there is virtually no empirical work on this important problem.

In summary, two essential characteristics of understanding—the systematization of knowledge and the use of inferential or constructive processing—were analyzed to determine how they could inform theories of comprehension monitoring. Note that it is not always necessary to have an explicit question "Do I understand?" in order to obtain information about one's own understanding. In the process of attempting to understand, one can obtain information about how well one does understand. Metacognitive knowledge and abilities probably play an important role in all aspects of comprehension. (For relevant discussions, see Brown, 1977; Brown & DeLoache, 1978; Flavell, this volume; Flavell & Wellman, 1977.) Active attempts to comprehend, judgments about material and task demands, judgments about potential explanations, etc. all require some metacognitive knowledge. Without minimizing the role that such metacognition plays, I would like to emphasize that much information about one's comprehension is a by-product of active attempts to understand and not just of attempts to monitor.

Developmental differences are expected when comprehension monitoring requires information that is difficult for children to obtain, a type of judgment that is difficult for them to make, a skill they may lack, or processing capacity beyond their limitations. I would like to consider a metaphor for developmental change that may help relate it to issues in comprehension and comprehension monitoring. The metaphor, borrowed from Brown & DeLoache (1978), is one of the novice versus the expert. In discussing developmental changes in metacognitive processes, Brown and DeLoache suggest that novices in general, not just children, lack knowledge about their own capabilities, about novel task requirements, and about strategies for achieving goals. "Children are universal novices, it takes experience before they build up the knowledge and confidence which would enable them to adopt routinely the self-interrogation mode of the expert (p. 14)." I would like to expand on their idea and suggest alternative ways in which changes in expertise could affect judgments about one's comprehension in particular.

Experts, by definition, know more than novices. They have accumulated more specific facts in a given domain than novices, who may have more vague, general, and perhaps erroneous beliefs. What also comes with expertise, I believe, is a greater systematization of knowledge. Experts detect more patterns, see more relations between discrete events, and know more principles that unite diverse facts than do novices. As one becomes more proficient in an area, knowledge becomes both more detailed and more systematized. There are three major types of benefits from this systematization of knowledge, each of which improves the ability to judge one's comprehension.

First, the systematization of knowledge unites separate facts into higher order structures. This process of "chunking" (Miller, 1956) should result in a savings of capacity. One example of this comes from Chase and Simon (1973), who found dramatic memory differences for legal chess positions between master and amateur chess players. Presumably, with greater expertise, the legitimate arrangements of pieces are recalled as larger and larger units, as opposed to the player having to recall the position of individual pieces. Chi (1978) has data on memory for the position of chess pieces that suggest that the standard memory differences between adults and children can be reversed if the children are more expert than the adults.

Another example comes from Smith, Adams, and Schorr (1978). They replicated the findings of Anderson and Bower (1973) that the more facts one has associated with a topic, the more they interfere with one another, and, thus, the more difficult it is to retrieve information about the topic. Yet, Smith *et al.* point out that this finding is paradoxical: It conflicts with our belief that with expertise one should become more (not less) proficient at answering questions. They suggest that when isolated facts can be integrated into a single coherent unit, this "fanning" effect should disappear (see Hayes-Roth, 1977, for a related argument). By providing subjects with a unifying theme, Smith *et al.* were able to eliminate the fanning effect. When material was effectively unitized, there was little cost for the increase in facts.

The additional capacity gained by such integration could be used in several ways, any of which could contribute to better awareness of one's own comprehension. One way in which the extra capacity could be used is for executive or control processes. Shatz (1978) has made a related suggestion. With capacity freed, the expert should be better able to monitor ongoing activity, to self-interrogate, to modulate processes, for example by adjusting the rate of processing to the nature of the material. In addition, the extra capacity could be used to perform the relevant inferential processes—to formulate expectations, to check of possible explanations for their plausibility, *etc*. If capacity is too limited to carry these processes, then valuable sources of information about one's comprehension will be lost.

The second way in which the systemization of knowledge can improve comprehension monitoring is that more detailed, more tightly organized structures will generate more expectations. The more expectations one has, the greater the opportunity to have them confirmed or disconfirmed. Consider, for example, differences in musical expertise. A relative novice might be able to categorize music into general types, for example, classical, rock, jazz. Suppose that when listening to a musical work a novice judges it to be classical. This will lead to expectations about the type of instruments involved, the tempo, *etc*. If a classical piece suddenly changed into a country and western song, the novice would notice the discrepancy. Yet, if the first movement of a Brahms piano concerto were followed by the second movement of a Mozart piano concerto, that would go unnoticed. Someone with greater musical expertise, having more specific expectations about what should follow, would be surprised or confused if the piece were suddenly transformed in this way. With still greater expertise, knowledge of who is conducting can lead to additional predictions about the character of the music. Expertise elaborates and refines predictions. As a consequence, it generates more information about how well one understands information.

The third possible benefit of expertise is that one can gain more explicit knowledge about the structures, about the organizational principles involved. The more explicit the knowledge of these principles, the more they can be used to guide hypothesis testing to detect alternative structures, to judge the appropriateness and worth of new inferences, *etc*. There is developmental work suggesting that, with age, tacit knowledge becomes more explicit. I will give examples from three domains: language, logical thinking, and prose comprehension.

With age or expertise, people become better able to analyze and examine aspects of language that they have previously mastered in a less self-conscious way. There is evidence in the domains of meaning, phonology, and syntax that children who have acquired certain principles of language may not necessarily be able to analyze these principles.

One linguistic example concerns the relationship between words and the objects that they signify (Markman, 1976). For the most part, this relationship is an arbitrary one. Except for onomatopoeia, there is no similarity or isomorphism between words and their referents. Yet, children do not appreciate the arbitrariness of this relation and instead judge that properties of objects are determined by their labels (Markman, 1976; Osherson & Markman, 1975; Piaget, 1929; Vygotsky, 1962). For example, Osherson and Markman (1975) found that children would allow that one could change the labels for objects, for example, that dogs could be called "cats." However, these same children, even while looking at a picture of a dog, now called "cat," claimed that it would meow. Obviously, children have no problem learning arbitrary or conventional relations between words and objects. Yet, they have difficulty examining aspects of this referential relationship that they have mastered. Objective examination of the word–referent relationship is one metalinguistic ability that develops considerably later than the linguistic ability upon which it is based.

All normal children differentiate words based on phonological properties. Even infants can discriminate between speech sounds (Eimas, Siqueland, Jusczyk, & Vigorito, 1971). Yet Gleitman and Rozin (1973) argue that certain reading problems are due to a failure of children to attend to and analyze the sounds of their language. Gleitman and Rozin (1973) review evidence that a more self-conscious, explicit analysis—a metalinguistic ability—is required to successfully learn an alphabetic writing system. Children who have no auditory deficit, who unquestionably have the linguistic ability to understand speech, can still have difficulty functioning in this more judgmental, analytic way.

The final example from language concerns metalinguistic awareness of syntax. There is evidence from a number of fields that children who presumably can speak grammatically might not perform well on tasks which require explicit analysis and self-conscious awareness of the structure of language (Shultz & Horibe, 1974; Shultz & Pilon, 1973; Yalisove, 1978; Hirsch-Pasek, Gleitman, & Gleitman, Note 4). Judgments of grammaticality, judgments of ambiguity, appreciation of humor and riddles all require metalinguistic analysis. In each case, marked developmental trends are found. Humor, for example, often depends on perceptions of ambiguity. Many jokes rely on people forming a particular interpretation of a sentence and then confronting an incongruity. The incongruity can be resolved by noticing the ambiguity of the original sentence. Developmental work suggests that children, who understand and speak the language, do not appreciate jokes or riddles that rely on syntactic ambiguity (see, e.g., Yalisove, 1978).

As in logical thinking, several different levels of structural awareness can exist. One could draw conclusions in accordance with the rules of logic without having explicit knowledge of the rules. With greater awareness of the rules, one could then appreciate the logical necessity of the conclusions that are drawn. At an end point of this continuum would be the logician, who can explicitly discuss, characterize, and formalize the rules. One domain in which there is evidence for this type of developmental trend is the part–whole comparisons of the Piagetian class inclusion problem (Markman, 1978). For finite classes, if one class is a proper subclass of another, then it follows that the whole or superordinate class has more members than the part or subordinate class. In the Piagetian class inclusion problem, children are asked to compare a superordinate class with the larger of its two subordinate classes (Inhelder & Piaget, 1964). For example, a child might be shown five roses and three daisies and be asked, "Are there more roses or flowers?'' At about 8 years of age, children finally become capable of correctly answering this question. They judge that there are more flowers than roses and explain their answer by mentioning that roses are flowers or that there are eight flowers and only five roses, *etc.* But these correct answers do not guarantee that the children have explicit awareness of the logical principle involved. Children can reason correctly without understanding that the conclusion is a logical consequence (rather than an empirical fact) of the inclusion relation. If they understand the logic of the relation, they would realize, for example, that as long as an inclusion relation is maintained, no addition or subtraction of flowers could result in there being more roses than flowers. Yet children who are fully capable of correctly answering the class inclusion question do not at first appreciate the logical necessity of their answers (Markman, 1978).

There is also developmental evidence that suggests that children with tacit knowledge of prose structure cannot readily make explicit judgments of the structure. Children and college students attempted to judge the relative importance of sentences contained in prose passages (Brown & Smiley, 1977). This was done by successively crossing out sentences according to their importance to the passage. This task requires some degree of structural analysis. The most important sentences would express the main idea of the passage, the least important would express more peripheral ideas. But main ideas and peripheral ideas must be defined with respect to structure. The main idea will be one that is tightly connected to the rest of the material. If the main idea were modified, it would require modification of many other portions of the passage as well. Peripheral ideas are ones whose modification would have little impact on the remainder of the passage. They are peripheral because they do not participate in many interrelations with other ideas. To return to Brown and Smiley's study, they found that college students and fifth graders could quite systematically judge relative importance of these units. Third graders could not make these explicit judgments about relative structural importance. However, at all grades tested, recall of the passage was predicted by its structure. Even third graders recall more of the main ideas and fewer of the peripheral ideas. Though their processing is guided implicitly by the prose structure, the younger children could not explicitly analyze it.

Nold (in press) reviewed a study by the National Assessment of Educational Progress (1977) where 9- and 13-year-olds were given a fixed amount of time in which to revise their own essays. The most marked developmental change occurred in the frequency of organizational revisions—rearrangements of clauses and paragraphs to improve the organization or addition of elements to facilitate transitions. Only 6.6% of the 9-year-olds made such organizational changes, compared to 17.7% of the older children.

In addition to judgments of structural importance, skilled readers probably have explicit knowledge of structural devices used in prose that they can use to guide comprehension monitoring activities. The words *thus, therefore, hence* announce that an argument has just been made and could serve as a reminder to check whether or not you have seen how the conclusion follows from the previous material. *Because* and *as a result of* mark causal connections. *Similarly* and *analogously* indicate that a comparison is being made. *However, but, in contrast* mark a contrast. Each of these conjunctions and adverbs marks relations and in addition provides clues as to the nature of the relation. These markers could well serve to warn skilled readers of appropriate places to check their comprehension. It would be useful to have empirical work in this area, especially developmental work or comparisons of skilled and unskilled readers and listeners. I assume, however, that these structural devices of prose are almost certainly used as important signals to check one's comprehension. Sophisticated readers would probably be disturbed by material that contained a spurious *thus* or by incorrect substitution of *but* for *and*. In these cases they would expect an argument that was not forthcoming or be set to find a contrast that did not appear. Because they establish relations, these conjunctions can provide valuable information about how to check one's comprehension.

In short, comprehension monitoring can suffer due to lack of expertise. Novices may not know enough about their own abilities, task requirements, or effective strategies (Brown & DeLoache, 1978). They may have to devote too much attention to component skills that experts have routinized (Shatz, 1978). The relative lack of systematization of information forces the novice to operate under more severe processing constraints. Also because of the impoverished organization, novices can generate fewer expectations. Finally, novices have less explicit knowledge of the principles of organization. All of these differences in expertise result in less ability to monitor one's comprehension.

Educational Implications

To the extent that the present analysis of comprehension and its relation to comprehension monitoring is correct, it suggests several methods that might foster comprehension monitoring. One implication of the analysis is that children should be given ample opportunity to listen to or read material that is well organized or tightly structured. Simple logical, temporal, and causal relations can be understood by quite young children (see Gelman, 1978). Yet, when glancing through textbooks written for young children, I noticed that highly structured, clearly organized material was infrequent. More often, paragraphs consisted of simple descriptive sentences which could be randomly rearranged with little loss in the comprehensibility of the passage. In other words, they contained very little structure. Perhaps children's reading material is deliberately written this way under the assumption that children could not understand the structural relations. Whatever the reason, we may be doing children a disservice by such oversimplification.

A second implication of the analysis is that practice at formulating expectations should be beneficial. Children could be asked to predict what word will come next in a sentence, to infer the consequence of a causal sequence, to guess a cause given an effect. This type of practice can involve a wide variety of inferences and hypotheses which can be calibrated to the appropriate level.

A third consequence of the analysis is that children should be given practice at making judgments about, and evaluations of, inferences and explanations. They could be asked to select which of two inferences is better, or more reasonable. They could be asked to explain why an inference follows, to explain why some solutions are clever and others far-fetched.

Finally, direct practice at finding problems should promote comprehension monitoring. Children could be challenged to find what is wrong with a passage, to find what does not make any sense. This could help promote the needed type of analysis, interrelation of material and inferential processing.

Empirical work is needed to be able to assess the value of these and other techniques. This would seem to be an important area for future research because of its clear educational implications. The ability to monitor one's comprehension is necessary for academic excellence. In order to study effectively, one must be able to differentiate what is understood from what still requires clarification. One must be sensitive to the level of one's comprehension to know what to re-read, when to ask questions, what additional information is needed, *etc.* Without such knowledge about comprehension, comprehension itself will suffer.

Acknowledgments

This chapter benefited from the many conversations I had with John Flavell. I thank John H. Flavell, Sam Glucksberg, and Edward E. Smith for their helpful comments.

Reference Notes

1. Bower, G. H., & Black, J. B. *Action schemata in story comprehension and memory.* Paper presented at Convention of APA, San Francisco, August 1977.
2. Clark, E. V., & Clark, H. H. *When nouns surface as verbs.* Unpublished manuscript, Stanford University, 1978.
3. Hirsh-Pasek, K., Gleitman, L. R., & Gleitman, H. *What did the brain say to the mind? A study of the detection and report of ambiguity by young children.* Unpublished manuscript, University of Pennsylvania, 1978.

References

Ackerman, B. P. Children's understanding of speech acts in unconventional directive frames. *Child Development, 1978, 49,* 311–318.

Anderson, J. R., & Bower, G. H. *Human associative memory.* Washington, D.C.: Winston, 1973.

Anderson, R. C., & Pichert, J. W. Recall of previously unrecallable information following a shift in perspective. *Journal of Verbal Learning and Verbal Behavior, 1978, 17,* 1–12.

Appel, L. F., Cooper, R. G., McCarrell, N., Sims-Knight, J., Yussen, S. R., & Flavell, J. H. The development of the distinction between perceiving and memorizing. *Child Development, 1972, 43,* 1365–1381.

Asher, S. R. Referential communication. In C. J. Whitehurst & B. J. Zimmerman (Eds.), *The functions of language and cognition.* New York: Academic Press, 1978.

Bransford, J. D., Barclay, J. R., & Franks, J. J. Sentence memory: A constructive versus interpretive approach. *Cognitive Psychology, 1972, 3,* 193–209.

Bransford, J. D., & McCarrell, N. S. A sketch of a cognitive approach to comprehension: Some thoughts about understanding what it means to comprehend. In W. B. Weimer & D. S. Palermo (Eds.), *Cognition and the symbolic process.* Hillsdale, N.J.: Lawrence Erlbaum Associates, 1974.

Brown, A. L. Knowing when, where, and how to remember: A problem of metacognition. In R. Glaser (Ed.), *Advances in instructional psychology.* Hillsdale, N.J.: Lawrence Erlbaum Associates, 1977.

Brown, A. L., & DeLoache, J. S. Skills, plans, and self-regulation. In R. Siegler (Ed.), *Children's thinking: What develops.* Hillsdale, N.J.: Lawrence Erlbaum Associates, 1978.

Brown, A. L., & Smiley, S. S. Rating the importance of structural units of prose passages: A problem of metacognitive development. *Child Development, 1977, 48,* 1–8.

Chase, W. G., & Simon, H. A. The mind's eye in chess. In W. G. Chase (Ed.), *Visual information processing.* New York: Academic Press, 1973.

Clark, H. H., & Clark, E. V. *Psychology and language: An introduction to psycholinguistics.* New York: Harcourt Brace Jovanovich, 1977.

Clark, H. H., & Haviland, S. E. Comprehension and the given–new contract. In R. O. Freedle (Ed.), *Discourse production and comprehension.* New Jersey: Ablex, 1977.

Chi, M. T. H. Knowledge structures and memory development. In R. Siegler (Ed.), *Children's thinking: What develops?* Hillsdale, New Jersey: Lawrence Erlbaum Associates, 1978.

Collins, A., Warnock, E. H., Aiello, N., & Miller, M. L. Reasoning from incomplete knowledge. In D. Bobrow & A. Collins (Eds.), *Representation and understanding: Studies in cognitive science,* New York: Academic Press, 1975.

Collins, W. A., Wellman, H., Keniston, A. H., & Westby, S. D. Age-related aspects of comprehension and inference from a televised dramatic narrative. *Child Development, 1978, 49,* 389–399.

Cosgrove, J. M., & Patterson, C. J. Plans and development of listener skills. *Developmental Psychology, 1977, 13,* 557–564.

Cosgrove, J. M., & Patterson, C. J. Generalization of training for children's listener skills. *Child Development, 1978, 49,* 513–516.

Dickson, W. P. Referential communication performance from age four to eight: Effects of referent type, target position, and context. *Developmental Psychology, 1979, 15,* 470–471.

Dittman, A. T. Developmental factors in conversational behavior. The *Journal of Communication, 1972, 22,* 404–423.

Eimas, P. D., Siqueland, E. R., Jusczyk, P., & Vigorito, J. Speech perception in infants. *Science, 1971, 171,* 303–306.

Flavell, J. H., & Wellman, H. M. Metamemory. In R. V. Kail Jr., & J. W. Hagen (Eds.), *Perspectives on the development of memory and cognition.* Hillsdale, N.J.: Lawrence Erlbaum Associates, 1977.

Fodor, J. A., Bever, T. G., & Garrett, M. F. *The psychology of language: An introduction to psycholinguistics and generative grammar.* New York: McGraw Hill, 1974.

Freedman, D., & Van Nieuwenhuizen, P. Supergravity and the unification of the laws of physics. *Scientific American,* 1978, *238,* 126–143.

Gelman, R. Cognitive development. *Annual Review of Psychology, 29,* 1978.

Gleitman, L. R., & Rozin, P. Teaching reading by use of a syllabary. *Reading Research Quarterly,* 1973, *8,* 447–483.

Greeno, J. G., & Noreen, D. L. Time to read semantically related sentences. *Memory & Cognition,* 1974, *2,* 117–120.

Hayes-Roth, B. Evolution of cognitive structure and process. *Psychological Review,* 1977, *84,* 260–278.

Inhelder, B., & Piaget, J. *The early growth of logic in the child.* New York: Norton, 1964.

Ironsmith, M., & Whitehurst, G. J. The development of listener abilities in communication: How children deal with ambiguous information. *Child Development,* 1978, *49,* 348–352.

Karabenick, J. D., & Miller, S. A. The effects of age, sex and listener feedback on grade school children's referential communication. *Child Development,* 1977, *48,* 678–684.

Mandler, J. M., & Johnson, N. S. Remembrance of things passed: Story structure and recall. *Cognitive Psychology,* 1977, *9,* 111–151.

Markman, E. M. Children's difficulty with word–referent differentiation. *Child Development,* 1976, *47,* 742–749.

Markman, E. M. Realizing that you don't understand: A preliminary investigation. *Child Development,* 1977, *48,* 986–992.

Markman, E. M. Empirical versus logical solutions to part–whole comparison problems concerning classes and collections. *Child Development,* 1978, *49,* 168–177.

Markman, E. M. Realizing that you don't understand: Elementary school children's awareness of inconsistencies. *Child Development,* 1979, *50,* 643–655.

Miller, G. A. The magical number seven, plus or minus two: Some limits on our capacity for processing information. *Psychological Review,* 1956, *63,* 81–97.

Moravcsik, J. *Understanding Dialectica,* 1979, *33,* 201–216.

National Assessment of Educational Progress. *Write/rewrite: An assessment of writing skills.* Denver, Colorado: U.S. Government Printing Office, 1977. (Writing report # 05-W-04)

Nold, E. W. Revising. In C. Frederickson (Ed.), *Writing: The nature, development and teaching of written communication.* Hillsdale, N.J.: Lawrence Erlbaum Associates, in press.

Osherson, D., & Markman, E. Language and the ability to evaluate contradictions and tautologies. *Cognition,* 1975, *3,* 213–226.

Paris, S. G., & Lindauer, B. K. The role of inference in children's comprehension and memory for sentences. *Cognitive Psychology,* 1976, *8,* 217–227.

Paris, S. G., Lindauer, B. K., & Cox, G. L. The development of inferential comprehension. *Child Development,* 1977, *48,* 1728–1733.

Paris, S. G., & Upton, L. R. Children's memory for inferential relationships in prose. *Child Development,* 1976, *47,* 660–668.

Patterson, C. J., Massad, C. M., & Cosgrove, J. M. Children's referential communication: Components of plans for effective listening. *Developmental Psychology,* 1978, *14,* 401–406.

Piaget, J. *The child's conception of the world.* London: Routledge and Kegan Paul, 1929.

Rumelhart, D. E. Notes on a schema for stories. In D. B. Bobrow & A. M. Collins (Eds.), *Representation and understanding: Studies in cognitive science.* New York: Academic Press, 1975.

Schank, R. C., & Abelson, R. P. *Scripts, plans, goals, and understanding.* Hillside, N.J.: Lawrence Erlbaum Associates, 1977.

Shatz, M. The relationship between cognitive processes and the development of communication skills. In B. Keasey (Ed.), *Nebraska Symposium on Motivation, 1977*. Lincoln: University of Nebraska Press, 1978.

Shultz, T. R., & Horibe, F. Development of the appreciation of verbal jokes. *Developmental Psychology, 1974, 10,* 13–20.

Shultz, T. R., & Pilon, R. Development of the ability to detect linguistic ambiguity. *Child Development, 1973, 44,* 728–733.

Smith, E. E., Adams, N. & Schorr, D. Fact retrieval and paradox of interference. *Cognitive Psychology, 1978, 10,* 438–464.

Terman, L. M., & Merrill, M. A. *Measuring intelligence: A guide to the administration of the new revised Stanford–Binet tests of intelligence*. Boston: Houghton Mifflin, 1937.

Thorndyke, P. W. Cognitive structures in comprehension and memory of narrative discourse. *Cognitive Psychology, 1977, 9,* 77–110.

Vygotsky, L. S. *Thought and language*. Cambridge, Mass.: M.I.T. Press, 1962.

Yalisove, D. The effect of riddle structure on children's comprehension of riddles. *Developmental Psychology, 1978, 14,* 173–180.

Ziff, P. *Understanding understanding*. Ithaca: Cornell University Press, 1972.

4

The Role of Role-Taking in Children's Referential Communication

CAROLYN UHLINGER SHANTZ

Children's understanding of their social world has become an increasingly important topic of theorizing and empirical study (Shantz, 1975b). The "social world" has been divided and subdivided into many aspects: the child's understanding of the psychological characteristics of individuals (such as their thoughts, feelings, intentions); the social relations between individuals (friendship, dominance, authority); and the social rules of groups within which they operate (social conventions and moral principles). Studies of these three levels of social representation—the individual, the dyad, and the group—along with studies of causal social inference constitute the bulk research on social-cognitive development.

The ways in which children learn about and "create" social information is still a matter of speculation, but on the face of it, there are probably a number of ways: observing others, imitating others, abstracting regularities in social behavior, taking the role of the other, and being told about the inner psychological experiences of others and existing rules, *etc.*—all of these events being assimilated to the child's existing level of conceptual functioning.

85

One of these means of gaining and creating social information has been of primary concern to many cognitive-developmental researchers: taking the role of the "other." This mechanism, at its base, is most often defined as the child's recognition that her/his own interpretation or viewpoint is only one of several possible interpretations or viewpoints. If the child assumes identity or high similarity between his/her viewpoints and the other's, the child is deemed "egocentric." The work of John Flavell (1968) served as a major impetus to American developmentalists in focusing on the developmental changes in the ability to take the role of the other, now a well-documented phenomenon. In addition, that work sought to relate the child's role-taking skills to a highly important social act: communication with others.

The relation between communication and role-taking has been viewed in terms of the facilitating effects role-taking has in increasing the likely effectiveness of a message. That is, as a speaker, one is more likely to emit an adequate message if one recognizes potential differences between the self and the other (the listener). But, as Flavell noted originally, the recognition of potential differences is not the "whole story" in being a good speaker or good listener: In a microgenetic sequence of specific communications, the speaker must recognize that such role-taking activity is needed, make reasonably accurate inferences about the other, use those inferences to "edit" the message, and continually monitor the ongoing message and feedback from the listener.

From this analysis, one would predict a substantial relation between role-taking ability and effectiveness in communicating. Is there empirical support for such a relation? This question was originally examined by Glucksberg, Krauss, and Higgins (1975) in a chapter summarizing research on the development of referential communication. They concluded that "the empirical support for this assumption is sparse [p. 320]." The support was sparse in several senses: There were relatively few studies that investigated the relation between role-taking and communication; of those that did, there were few that were not methodologically flawed, and fewer yet that found a significant positive relation between the two variables. In this chapter, additional empirical evidence, from both correlational studies and communication training studies, will be examined and an analysis made of the issues embedded in this area of research.

Correlational Studies

To establish a functional relation between role-taking and communication requires more than a demonstration that they are related across wide age spans. Both abilities increase with increasing age during childhood, but that does not answer the question of whether, at any and each age period, they are functionally related. Second, there are a number of studies in which both variables are measured from the same data: the message given. Because egocentric messages tend to be low in information, there is a strong potential for finding a relation between role-taking and poor communication when they are measured from the same data base.

In order to evaluate the empirical relation between role-taking and communication and to avoid the kinds of problems just noted, I selected studies from the literature in which (*a*) role-taking and communication were assessed independently; (*b*) the tasks differ substantially in content and the type of response required; and (*c*) chronological age is held constant either by examining the relation *within* each age group or by partialling out CA. A brief elaboration on the second point is in order. Role-taking and communication could be independently assessed, but by methods that are so highly verbal that any correlation between them might be due more to shared method variance (high verbal demands) than to the two conceptual abilities being assessed. One role-taking task that is relatively low in receptive verbal requirements and makes no demands for expressive verbal skills is spatial role-taking. In this task, a child selects a picture that represents the relation between another's spatial location and another's spatial perspective. The nonverbal response required and the spatial content make this task particularly suited to maximizing the differences with communication tasks. All the studies noted here used the Glucksberg and Krauss (1967) "stack-the-blocks" task or Cowan's checkerboard (1967) task to assess referential communication ability. Sometimes performance on such tasks is a dyadic measure in that the final product, the number of correct choices by the listener, is a function of both speaker adequacy and listener adequacy. More often such tasks are scored for speaker adequacy only by the number of criterial attributes given in each message. The nine studies that met the three criteria are listed in Table 4.1 (Shantz, 1975a).

Three studies showed consistent, significant positive relations between communication performance and role-taking (Berner, 1971; Cowan, 1967; Rubin, 1973) in various samples ranging from preschool to 11 years of age. Mixed results were found in three other studies, the relations between the variables sometimes being positive and sometimes nonexistent (Ceresnie, 1974; Coie & Dorval, 1973; Kingsley, 1971). For example, Kingsley found significant positive relations for third graders, but not for kindergarteners. And, finally, three studies showed quite consistent nonsignificant relations between role-taking and communication performance (Looft, 1972; Shantz & Steinlauf, 1976; Steinlauf, 1974). A mixed scoreboard, indeed!

To provide a close-up view of such studies, the study by Shantz and Steinlauf (1976) will be briefly presented. Eighty children from lower- and middle-income groups were randomly selected from grades 1–4 and individually administered a battery of tests. Referential communication was measured by a variant of Cowan's task (1967) in which the speaker selected from a set of six toy animals one animal which he/she placed on one of six squares

TABLE 4.1

Studies of the Relation between Referential Communication and Role-Taking Tasks

Author	Communication task	DV	Role-taking task	Subjects' CA	Results
Berner, 1971	Glucksberg & Krauss with familiar pictures	Dyad	DeVries' penny-guessing game	3–5	Significant + relation between communication and RT task
Ceresnie, 1974	Glucksberg & Krauss	Dyad	Spatial perspectives	$M = 8\frac{1}{2}$	Low-RT dyads significantly poorer communication than high-RT and mixed dyads
Coie & Dorval, 1973	Checkerboard	Speaker	Spatial perspectives	8–10	With age partialled, C/RT $r = .58$ for boys and .19 for girls
Cowan, 1967	Checkerboard	Speaker and Dyad	Spatial perspectives	8–10	Low-RT dyads poorest communication, mixed dyads middling, high-RT best on speaker DV; few differences on dyad DV; no statistical tests
Kingsley, 1971	Glucksberg & Krauss with familiar pictures and designs	Speaker	Spatial perspectives & spatial pictures task	5 & 8	No relation for 5-year-olds; for 8-year-olds, spatial and communication (a) adequacy $r = .63$ and (b) information $r = .45$
Looft, 1972	Checkerboard	Speaker and Dyad	Spatial perspectives	Young adults; elderly	No relation between communication and spatial scores for either age group
Rubin, 1973	Glucksberg & Krauss	Speaker	Spatial perspectives	$5\frac{1}{2}, 7\frac{1}{2}, 9\frac{1}{2}, 11\frac{1}{2}$	Space and communication significantly related with CA or MA partialled (.35); Factor I spatial loading .88 & communication loading .73–.84
Shantz & Steinlauf, 1976	Checkerboard	Speaker	Spatial perspectives	6–9	No relation with CA partialled for total sample, $r = .17$; no relation for 6- and 8-year-olds, but significant relations for 7- and 9-year-olds: .68 and .47
Steinlauf, 1974	Checkerboard	Speaker	Spatial perspectives	$5\frac{1}{2}–7$	No significant relation between space and communication scores

in a checkerboard. The speaker was to tell a listener who had identical materials which animal was selected and where it was placed. Speaker communication adequacy was assessed by the sum of the criterial attributes for distinguishing the animal and the location on the first four trials. The spatial task was a modification of Piaget's three-mountain task. For these Detroit children, a gas station array was used in which the child attempted to locate the correct picture of the relations among the station, pumps, and Esso sign from another's location. A weighted scoring system was used in which the children received no points when they attributed their own viewpoint to the other (egocentric response); one point for a picture in which the perspective was different from their own but would have been "impossible" from any location (the objects had been rearranged and photographed); two points for perspectives in which interobject relations were correct but the perspective wrong; and three points for a correct choice. A second role-taking task was employed which had more verbal demands: Flavell's privileged information (1968) task. A child constructed a story for a set of pictures in which a boy climbs a tree to escape a menacing dog. The dog pictures were then deleted and the child asked to construct a story that would be told by a person who had only seen the shorter set. Egocentrism was measured by the degree to which the child attributes knowledge of the fear-of-dog motive to the other person. Two decentration tasks were also administered, and will be described later.

The correlation between spatial role-taking and communication performance for the total sample ($N = 80$) was $+.14$; partialled for age, $+.17$. The correlation between communication ability and Flavell's role-taking task—one that requires expressive verbal skills—was significant, but modest ($r = +.32$, and partialled for age, $r = +.29$). These data were further analyzed and those results will be presented later. In summary, role-taking ability accounted for little of the variance in communication performance in the Shantz and Steinlauf study (except at particular age levels), and in the other studies cited seldom accounted for more than 25% of the variance.

How should such findings be interpreted? First, it is important to note some factors that might account, in part, for low correlations between role-taking and communication performance. A restricted range of scores in samples of children limits the magnitude of the correlations, as does low reliability of the tasks. In the latter instance, the reliabilities of many communication and role-taking tasks are seldom reported. In the Shantz and Steinlauf study, test–retest reliabilities assessed at a minimum of 2 weeks indicated .72 for spatial role-taking and .81 for communication performance, probably considered acceptable but not robust temporal reliabilities. Second, some nonstatistical aspects should be noted in interpreting the findings of the nine studies. Spatial role-taking should not be considered as "the" test of role-taking. Although it has the virtue of maximizing differences with communication tasks, it is not highly correlated with other measures of role-taking in most studies (Shantz, 1975b). In the Shantz and Steinlauf study, for example, spatial role-taking and Flavell's privileged information role-taking task correlated $+.36$, partialled for age, $r = +.38$, a rather typical finding when intercorrelating various role-taking tasks. Finally, in all studies examining the communication–role-taking relation, the role-taking performance has been measured as an ability, conceptualized as a continuous dimension in which the task assesses the *degree* of intrusion of self's knowledge or experience in relation to another. There is another tradition within this area of research in which the self–other relation is assessed on a qualitative, rather than quantitative, basis, specifying particular types of self–other relations (e.g., Selman, 1971). It appears that no study has examined levels of role-taking in relation to communication abilities.

Let us now return to the findings in the nine studies cited earlier, given this context of possible artifacts and limitations of this set of studies. For some, the very modest relationships found in the majority of studies of role-taking and communication might be surprising. This would be the case if one attributes a highly determining role to role-taking skills in referential communication, the most extreme form of which is to posit that role-taking is sufficient for adequate communication. At times in the research literature, it seems that such a position is attributed to Piaget, among others, because of his emphasis that egocentrism does play a role. However, the "sufficiency" position seems quite untenable given the evidence in the nine studies cited and other studies, not to mention common sense. Referential communication skill depends on multiple factors, the most obvious and documented ones being such factors as the perceptual abilities to distinguish attributes of the referents and nonreferents, comparison activity of the similarities and differences between the referent and nonreferents, linguistic abilities to encode the criterial differences, *etc.* (see e.g., Asher & Oden, 1976; Kingsley, 1971; Whitehurst & Merkur, 1977).

In short, not all poor communications are egocentric. One may well be able to take the role of the listener but unable to make the necessary discriminations or encode adequately, and, as a result, give messages that omit criterial information or are redundant. Some findings relevant to this discussion come from the Shantz and Steinlauf (1976) study cited earlier. A factor analysis (varimax rotation) of the data on spatial role-taking, Flavell's privileged information role-taking task, and the referential communication task revealed an interesting three-factor pattern in the data. The first factor appeared to be interpretable as primarily role-taking performance with Flavell's task performance loading .78, the spatial task .46, and with communication loading at the lower level of .31. The second factor was defined by mental age and the Flavell task, the loadings being .69 and .59, respectively. The third factor was composed of two "decentration" tasks (loadings of .47 and .67), and the communication task (.37). The last factor requires a bit of explanation. The ability to deploy attention over a wide field of experience, or decentration, is posited by Piaget as an underlying necessary factor in being able to take the role of another. Since decentration is a widely used construct in social-cognition, but has never been assessed independently of role-taking, this study was a first attempt at such an independent measurement. Two tasks were used which, traditionally, have been measures of divergent thinking: alternate uses for common objects and the number of similarities one can find among a group of objects. The notion here is that the child must go beyond the habitual uses of objects or the obvious attributes of objects, deploying attention to less salient properties and conceptualizing less common uses. Why would communication performance load with performance on such decentration tasks (Factor 3)? I would speculate that all three tasks require a common skill: analysis of different object properties—whether to inform a listener (communication task), to establish similarities among objects (decentration/similarities task), or to find different uses for objects (decentration/alternate uses task). These data, then, are but one more indication that skills other than the ability to take the role of the other are involved in adequate communication. At the same time, to find that these and other skills are involved does not mean that role-taking ability is irrelevant to communication. Indeed, the loading of communication performance with other role-taking tasks (Factor 1), albeit a low loading, is consistent with most other studies that find some relationship to role-taking ability.

Just as not all poor communications are egocentric, so, too, not all good communications are nonegocentric. We may, for example, code some information very privately, for ourselves and very idiosyncratically, and merely emit our private codings. If our listener, however, happens to share our "universe" relevant to the information, the private coding may be quite adequate for that particular listener. It appears that some referential communication tasks make quite modest demands for role-taking, given the similarity between speaker and listener and the knowledge (given by the experimenter) that they share the same universe of things to be communicated about. If the differences between speaker and listener are relatively minor, then it is difficult to determine whether a good message is the outcome of good private coding or good role-taking.

If, in fact, clear and substantial differences are not engineered between speaker and listener in many referential communication situations, then it is not surprising that communication performance only relates modestly to role-taking skills in a number of studies. In the spatial task, for example, a clear difference is made between the child and the other: They have very different (often opposite) perspectives of an array; the child, presumably, must inhibit attributing her/his perspective to the other, and infer exactly what the other's perspective is. Likewise, Flavell's task gives the child information that he/she must not attribute to the other, having instead to infer what the other would think given the other's experience. In contrast, the referential communication task would seem to minimize the differences between self and other. Hypothetically, the child might well describe his/her own actions as they are performed ("I'm picking up the green gorilla and I'm going to put it in the corner"), which, if said out loud (as the child is instructed to do), might well serve as a fairly adequate message. In short, the child only needs to *share* his/her experience, not inhibit it as in the role-taking tasks.

Is there any evidence that role-taking is related to communication performance when the speaker and listener do not share or do not know they share the same set of things about which to communicate? There is only one study, apparently, that has examined this. Cowan (1967) tested boys on the spatial egocentrism task, and, on the basis of their performance, paired them in three ways: Low–Low role-takers, High–High role-takers, and Mixed (High–Low). These dyads then participated in a referential communication task. The children were seated back-to-back with 16-square checkerboards and 16 objects apiece, and no one was designated speaker. They were told to take their objects, one at a time and place them, one in each square, so that the boards would wind up with the same objects in the same places. One measure was "metacommunication": talking about their task before starting to give messages or to place objects. For example, the children might ask "Do you have a red and yellow board?" or "Do you have a red star?" All High–High role-takers invariably checked that they were in "the same stimulus universe" first, whereas most Low–Low dyads (66%) did not, and, of High–Low dyads, 33% did not. This indicates a very high relation between role-taking and metacommunication. Also, the types of statements were ranked for the degree to which they took into account the listener's viewpoint: For example, a score of 3 = "If the yellow squares are on the top of your board, put the blue circle in the top right yellow corner"; 2 = "Put it in the first square on your left"; 1 = "Put it there." Low–Lows showed significantly more egocentric messages than High–High dyads, and mixed dyads showed an intermediate level. These results for metacommunication and for degree of egocentric message as a function of role-taking ability were found at each of three age levels, 8-, 9-, and 10-year-olds. The high role-takers, then, did not assume identity between their situation (the materials) and the other's situation, nor were they informed by the experimenter. They recognized the need to determine the degree of shared situations. Whether referential communication in situations that do not build in substantial speaker–listener similarities will also show variation with role-taking skills awaits future study.

To conclude this part of the discussion, it is worth noting that the fact that a speaker communicates with a listener as if the listener shares the speaker's perspective does not imply necessarily that the speaker is egocentric. Egocentrism refers to the basic *assumption* of identity (or of a high degree of similarity) between, in this case, the speaker and listener. But, a speaker may also communicate in what on the surface appears to be an egocentric way but does so because he/she has *inferred* identity (or high similarity), rather than assumed it. For example, in this chapter I did not give a description of the Glucksberg and Krauss referential communication task. Why? If I were egocentric in this instance, I omitted that information because *I* knew it and automatically attributed it to you (assumed similarity). If I were not egocentric, I analyzed my potential audience with interests in referential communication and inferred their familiarity with the task, and hence the lack of need to describe it. Thus, the same behavior, omission of a task description, may be the result of egocentrism or it may not; one can not tell by the outcome (message) alone. Inferred similarity, indeed, is probably an important means by which we make others' behavior comprehensible and predictable, and by which we avoid boring our listeners. The similarity is not the issue; whether it is assumed or inferred is.

Training Studies

The relation between role-taking and referential communication is addressed by a group of studies in which training communication has been attempted. Researchers who held the view that some important communication deficiencies in children are due to their egocentric functioning designed training programs focused on decreasing self-orientation by increasing children's awareness of the importance of the *relation* between self and other in achieving communicative effectiveness. Two particular methods of training derived from the premise of the importance of egocentrism as an obstacle to communication. The first was the reversal of roles between speaker and listener; the second was the confronting of the speaker with the inadequacies of the message for the listener.

Role reversal as a method of training is based on the notion that as the children experience the "perspective" from the role of the listener and from the role of the speaker, they will become sensitized to the demands of each role, become better able to infer what the "other" needs in the dyadic interchange in order to perform a task successfully, and, as speakers, better able to edit messages so that the task may be accomplished and, as listeners, better able to infer what the speaker means by what he/she says. The "confrontation" method is based on the notation that, as Piaget once put it, children as speakers believe they have made themselves perfectly clear, and children as listeners believe they have perfectly understood. To correct this often ill-founded optimism, the speaker needs to be confronted with information that indicates the message for the listener is not adequate and, likewise, the listener needs to be confronted with the inadequacies of the message for him/her to perform a given task.

Prior to examining the effects of training studies that have involved these methods, it is, perhaps, worthwhile to analyze further some aspects of the methods. Every child who enters training studies (typically in the age range of 4–9 years) has had years of role reversal, speaking and listening, with hundreds of thousands of "trials" per day, and extensive feedback about the adequacy of messages and adequacy of listening. Every child has developed some important communicative skills upon which intensive and short-termed training is superimposed to determine what experiences might be *sufficient* to elicit certain new skills or accelerate developing skills. (Training studies do not illuminate the *necessary* experiences for communicative competence.)

Is it likely that one of these two methods might be more effective in eliciting or accelerating communicative skills? Piaget has tended in his writings to emphasize the confrontation aspect, particularly between people of equal power, as the important means by which one's egocentrism declines, although, at least in one instance of spatial perspective-taking (Piaget & Inhelder, 1956), he has posited that occupying another's location is necessary. The emphasis on confrontation is consistent with his equilibration model of cognitive change in which either intrapsychic conflict or interpersonal conflict force decentration. Decentration, then, is seen as the important underlying factor in lessening egocentrism (Piaget, 1970). Whether or not decentration is the critical factor will have to await future research.

There are, however, aspects of the two methods that suggest that the confrontation method might be more effective in training communication skills than is role-reversal. One important aspect of communication is that children learn to make their messages and responses to messages contingent upon the others' characteristics and needs, whether they be task-related needs or person-related (see Higgins *et al.,* this volume). In short, a communicatively competent child (or adult) recognizes communication as a dyadic enterprise, a *relation* between two individuals around a task. How well various training procedures emphasize or make salient the social relation would largely determine, then, their efficacy in facilitating communicative abilities.

In this context, role reversal would not seem as effective because it does not make salient the relational aspect. Role reversal is basically a *sequential* experience, in which one is a speaker, then a listener, then, again, a speaker, ad infinitum. Children may well experience these roles as "false absolutes" rather than as dyadic relations. Absolutism, as originally proposed by Piaget, is a descriptive concept of the young child's tendency to accept and understand each perception or experience as a separate and independent entity, which evolves in ontogenetic development into a relativism, or the tendency to relate events and experiences to one another. There is evidence that the young child, in fact, often treats basic relational concepts and experiences as absolutes, such that "brother" is understood as an attribute of a person rather than a relation between persons ("brother to . . ."), an object as having the characteristic of being right or left rather than "to the right of . . .", or different visual appearances of an object from different locations as being separate, unrelated perceptions. In short, despite extensive experience in being a speaker and a listener, one might well understand them, not as related roles, but rather as separate roles (experiences), each having certain demands.

There are two ways in which the relation between speaker and listener roles might be made more salient, presumably by making experiences less sequential (or more simultaneous): by confronting the speaker while still in the role of speaker with the effects of his/her message on the listener, and by having the child observe the relation between another speaker's message and the listener's response (in this case, the child as the third-party observer of the relation). The confrontation method seems particularly likely to be effective because it has the potential for informing the speaker, for example, of two important things: (a) there is a difference between the speaker's needs (knowledge, situation, etc.) and the listener's; and (b) there is a relation between the speaker's message and what the listener can or does do (i.e., a causal relation). Feedback is the usual term in training studies for what is being discussed here as "confrontation." The types of feedback actually employed in different training studies will be described later.

The second method of highlighting the relation between speaker and listener, the child-as-third-party-observer method, is based on the idea that the children can more easily focus on the relation between speaker–message/listener–response when not themselves enmeshed in one of these roles. It is possible that the third-party experience is effective either because of the unique aspect of being a third party or by "vicarious" role reversal.

Because, as we shall see in a moment, no communication study has directly contrasted the efficacy of these various training procedures, it is instructive to briefly examine one study outside the communication area that has contrasted the two primary methods of role reversal and confrontation. A study by Cox (1977) posed the question of how one could most effectively train spatial perspective-taking. There is an apparent *formal* similarity between such a task and that of communication: How does one best induce the notion that there is a relation between what one sees in looking at an array of objects (what one knows about an array of designs) and what another person sees (knows or needs) when they do not share the same location (knowledge or needs)? In the spatial area, one method is to move around an array of objects and occupy another's position to see how objects look to another. A second method is confrontation in which the child does not move in space, but rather continues to experience his/her own perspective, while being shown or told by the other what the other's visual experience (perspective) is. Cox found that the confrontation training (whether visual or verbal) was much more successful in inducing spatial perspective-taking than "occupying" the place of another and experiencing the other's perspective. These results are best viewed as indirect evidence that confrontation may be more effective than role-reversal in children's learning the self–other relation. Certainly, this is not to imply that the occupation of another's role is irrelevant to learning about roles, but only to suggest the relative efficacy of the two experiences.

Let us turn now to communication studies. The earliest training studies of which I am aware (Fry, 1966, 1969; Shantz & Wilson, 1972) used both role-reversal and confrontation (feedback) to determine *whether* communicative skills could be improved, and if so, to what degree. Fry (1966, 1969) used a rather omnibus training program in which some children served only as speakers, others only as listeners, and others as both speakers and listeners. Messages were given for a rather typical referential communication task (describing a design for the listener to select from an array of designs) and a less typical task (in which a full description was needed so that a listener could draw the design). At the end of each message, the group analyzed the adequacy of the message (providing feedback for the speakers), and the procedure was repeated. The results of such training were largely negative. The latter study (Fry, 1969) used, in addition, role-reversal procedures and feedback, which also had little positive training effect. Flavell (1968) speculated that the failure of training may have been inadequate control over the actual feedback to the subjects (since the children, who largely controlled the message analysis phase, seemed to often find the messages much more adequate than the experimenter did!).

The study by Shantz and Wilson (1972) was designed to increase the amount and specificity of feedback to speakers about their messages, to duplicate Fry's procedure of having children reverse roles of speaker and listener, and, in addition, to have children be observers of speakers and listeners. This last aspect was designed, as previously described, to help children understand the relation between speaking and listening while not encumbered themselves by the demands of either role. The results of this study were a little more encouraging than Fry's in that the trained children were significantly better on the posttest communication tasks than a control group (who received only pretests and posttests). There were some, but not consistent, indications of generalization to other communication tasks (Krauss and Glucksberg's low-codable designs task, and a modified version of Cowan's checkerboard task), but no generalization to a persuasion task (indeed, the control group, inexplicably, showed superior persuasive abilities). In summary, this training procedure indicated it was possible to improve communication performance of second graders with six 30-minute sessions. The design of the study does not allow one to specify what aspect(s) of the training produced the effects. The results are consistent with the notion that role reversal and feedback improve performance, but are not definitive, as other factors could have been sufficient to elicit improvement (practice in communicating, experience in analyzing design attributes, *etc.*).

A somewhat similar and more recent study of training communication skills, in this case, of emotionally disturbed children (ages 9–14), has been reported by Chandler, Greenspan, and Barenboim (1974). The children, who evidenced very poor communication and role-taking skills, were divided into three groups: controls, training in role taking, and training in communication. Role-taking training consisted of children developing skits, enacting them, and then analyzing the video-taped skits. The referential communication training, patterned after Botkin (1966) and Shantz and Wilson (1972), involved role reversal and a good deal of feedback about the adequacy of communications in a walkie-talkie treasure hunt game, describing a baseball game, *etc*. Both types of training resulted in significant improvement, but the role-taking training resulted only in improved role-taking skills, whereas communication training improved both role-taking and communication performance. It may be that the communication training actually trained both skills, that is, taking the role of the other (listener or speaker) and translating that activity into better communications.

In summary, the training studies of Shantz and Wilson (1972) and Chandler *et al.* (1974) indicate that reversal of roles of speaker and listener combined with feedback results in significant increases in the adequacy of speaker skills. Is role reversal a necessary aspect of effective training of speaker skills? It is not possible to determine from these studies because, in both cases, role reversal experience always occurred with a good deal of feedback to speakers. The positive effects of training might be due to role reversal, or feedback, or both (or even other aspects of training, as noted previously). However, there is indication from a careful set of studies by Whitehurst and Sonnenschein, reported in this volume, of significant increases in informative messages by young children after training sessions with *no* role reversal, but with a specific kind of feedback.

We turn, then, to a discussion of feedback, previously presented as the "confronting" of the speaker with the adequacy or inadequacy of the message given. Feedback is defined operationally from various training studies as (*a*) success or failure of the listener operating from the message (see Whitehurst, and Sonnenschein, Experiment 6); (*b*) a reminder of a rule to contrast differences of referent and nonreferents (see Whitehurst and Sonnenschein, Experiment 2); (*c*) the specific problem of the listener (see Robinson, this volume); (*d*) a reminder of the goal of informing the listener (see Whitehurst and Sonnenschein, Experiment 3); or (*e*) some combination of these and general questions to lead the speaker to correct incomplete or redundant messages (Shantz & Wilson, 1972; Chandler *et al.*, 1974). Two sets of studies, those by Whitehurst and Sonnenschein and by Robinson, have examined the specific role of feedback in improving communication skills. As both sets of research are reported in this volume, they will not be described in detail here.

In a series of referential communication training studies, Whitehurst and Sonnenschein (this volume) found that the lack of feedback to the speaker consistently results in the lowest percentage of informative messages children give. But their research goes a good deal further in specifying the conditions for improved performance:

> Preliminary communication instructions that tell the child to describe things so that the listener will know which one he is talking about, coupled with corrective feedback that tells the child that he has or has not described how the referent is different results in large and significant training effects that generalize to other speaking tasks and that endure for at least a week.

These conclusions are based on experiments in which combinations of two types of instructions to the child prior to speaking and two types of feedback were used. The wording of each was as follows:

> Communication instruction: "Tell me about the triangle with the star above it so that I will know which triangle you are talking about," shortened after the fifth trial to "Tell me about it."
>
> Perceptual instruction: "The way to do a good job of playing the game is to tell how the triangle is different," shortened after the fifth trial to "How is it different?"
>
> Communication feedback: "That's good [or, "that's wrong," depending on which is true]. You told (didn't tell) about the triangle with the star above it so that I knew (didn't know) which one you were talking about."
>
> Perceptual feedback: "That's good (wrong). You told me (didn't tell) how the triangle with the star above it was different from the other."

The specific combination of instructions and feedback that consistently led to the highest percentage of informative messages was communication instruction plus perceptual feedback. Why is this particular combination the most effective? I would hazard the guess that it specifies, as no other combination does, the *goal* of communication and a *means* to achieve it. That is, the communication instructions focus on the listener's needs to know and thereby emphasizes the person (listener) aspect. It clearly makes the task a social one, whereas perceptual instructions focus only on the means, the rule to find differences. With the communication instructions setting the social goal, the particular effective feedback is the specification of how to reach that goal [You told (didn't tell) me how it was different]. But the feedback also includes success or failure of the message for the speaker. Perhaps *that* aspect of feedback is all that is really operative. Whitehurst and Sonnenschein, in Experiment 6, tested this possibility by providing "simple feedback"—"That's right" or "That's wrong"—and nothing further, that is, no rule reminder. This simple feedback was not significantly better than no feedback at all (62% and 53% informative messages, respectively); and both no feedback and simple feedback were significantly inferior to perceptual feedback (81% informative messages).

Some of Robinson's work (this volume) is consistent with Whitehurst and Sonnenschein's findings. She found that the most effective feedback to children who err in giving too general messages is to say, "I've got n [4, 2, or however many] like that. I'm not sure which one you mean. Can you help me?" This feedback tells the child the message is inadequate, specifies the inadequacy and the listener's reaction (uncertainty), and includes a request for help. Like Whitehurst and Sonnenschein's feedback, it tells the speaker about the success or failure of the message; unlike their feedback, it specifies the listener's problem but not the specific means to solve the problem (tell differences). The feedback quoted here was found to be much more effective than two other types of feedback: the listener guessing what the speaker was referring to or merely asking "Which one?" in a puzzled tone of voice. Although the exact instructions used are not reported (Experiment V), the instructions are essentially for the child to describe the clothes he se- lected for his doll so the experimenter could select the matching one for her doll, the stated aim being to have the dolls identically dressed. Apparently, there was no role reversal in this study, and the child served as speaker on all trials.

What, then, can be concluded from these various communication train- ing studies? First, studies that have employed some type of role reversal have (with the exception of Fry, 1966, 1969) resulted in some success in improving communication performance. But because these studies have also included various types of feedback, it is not clear, as was previously noted, to what extent improvement is the result of role reversal, feedback, or both. There appear to be no studies that have examined the effects of role reversal training with and without feedback. However, Whitehurst's studies involved no role reversal, and significant training effects resulted from a specific com- bination of instructions and feedback. Thus, role reversal does not appear to be an important aspect of a successful training program of speaking skills.

Overall, the evidence examined in this chapter indicates that role-taking skills, as variously assessed or used in training procedures, facilitate ade- quate communication skills, but that they certainly are not sufficient, as many other skills are also involved. Likewise, despite the fact that no study has examined the necessity of role-taking skills, one would hazard the guess that they are not necessary for, at least, some adequate communication (as has been suggested by Chandler *et al.,* 1974). That is, very able listeners and an informative context can make up for many omissions of role-taking by the speaker.

It seems that the research task before us should not be conceptualized as *whether* or *to what degree* role-taking is involved in communication ade- quacy. Rather, a much more productive venture would be to determine how such abilities function in the interpersonal act of communicating. For exam- ple, the dependent variables in communication tasks have been largely lim- ited to the number of criterial attributes of objects given by the speaker or the dyadic "success" of a communication (the listener selecting the correct referent). Redundant messages are often classed as "poor messages." Yet, in everyday life, a good speaker may be redundant precisely because the speaker knows that it is difficult for a listener to get the criterial information with only one oral presentation. Not only might we reconceptualize often-used dependent measures in light of the task of the listener, but we might also consider other dependent variables, which may well be more sensitive to the absence or presence of role-taking by the speaker: metacommunication about the items to be described, the organization of a message for a listener, the speaker's monitoring of the listener's comprehension of a message, and the types of messages (Cowan, 1967; Pratt, Scribner, & Cole, 1977; Spilton & Lee, 1977).

Likewise, the paradigm in such studies has been quite limited to highly structured, experimenter-requested communications. Certainly, studies of spontaneous communications of children in natural settings (e.g., Garvey & Hogan, 1973; Wellman & Lempers, 1977) will provide a needed expansion in the assessment and function of referential communication.

But these points do not directly address the issue of how role-taking abilities influence the communication enterprise. In fact, it will take a good deal of creative theory-building and research to determine the processes involved in "taking the role of the listener" in situation X given task Y. How does a speaker recognize a potential difference between himself/herself and the listener? What kinds of processes are involved in conceptualizing the listener's needs? What does one do, then, to one's initial message given such recognitions and inferences? To be able to answer such questions in the future will not only help us understand both communication and social cognition, but will also provide avenues for training such skills.

At the same time, it is important to note that role-taking is but one process by which the child has access to or creates social information relevant to communication with another. At the beginning of this chapter, it was suggested that there are many ways in which a child can acquire and create social knowledge. Clearly, not all social knowledge is the result of role-taking. But relatively little research has been devoted to how children conceptualize the subjective experiences of themselves and other individuals, of dyadic relations between individuals, and of social rules as these relate to communication. Some of the contributions in this volume are beginning this inquiry (for example, the study of development of metacognition, by Flavell; nonverbal aspects of communication, by Allen; intentions and expectations between communicative partners, by Higgins, Fondacaro, and McCann and by Olson and Hildyard). What we need to know is how social conceptualizations influence communicative performance, whether or not constructs of egocentrism and role-taking are invoked. On the other hand, if role-taking is defined in more structural terms as a particular kind of relation between self and other that changes with age, as Selman (1971) proposes, then one is always in some role-relation with others and it is necessary to specify the relation between communicative behavior and the kind of role relation as behaviorally expressed or represented by the child. Either way, the point is that communication is a social act of a self relating to another. Hopefully, future research will be focused on illuminating how social conceptualizations of self and other, and the dyadic relation, influences communication development.

References

Asher, S., & Oden, S. Children's failure to communicate: An assessment of comparison and egocentrism explanations. *Developmental Psychology*, 1976, *12*, 132–139.

Berner, E. S. *Private speech and role-taking abilities in preschool children*. Paper presented at the meeting of the Society for Research in Child Development, Minneapolis, 1971.

Botkin, P. T. *Improving communication skills in sixth-grade students through training in role-taking*. Unpublished doctoral dissertation, University of Rochester, 1966.

Ceresnie, S. J. *Communication and cooperation in dyads of children of varying levels of egocentrism*. Unpublished master's thesis, Wayne State University, 1974.

Chandler, M. J., Greenspan, S., & Barenboim, C. Assessment and training of role-taking and referential communication skills in institutionalized emotionally disturbed children. *Developmental Psychology*, 1974, *10*, 546–553.

Coie, J. D., & Dorval, B. Sex differences in the intellectual structure of social interaction skills. *Developmental Psychology*, 1973, *8*, 261–267.

Cowan, P. A. *The link between cognitive structure and social structure in two-child verbal interaction*. Paper presented at the meeting of the Society for Research in Child Development, Santa Monica, 1967.

Cox, M. V. Perspective ability: The conditions of change. *Child Development*, 1977, *48*, 1724–1727.

Flavell, J. H. *The development of role-taking and communication skills in children*. New York: Wiley, 1968.

Fry, C. L. Training children to communicate to listeners. *Child Development*, 1966, *37*, 675–685.

Fry, C. L. Training children to communicate to listeners who have varying listener requirements. *Journal of Genetic Psychology*, 1969, *114*, 153–166.

Garvey, C., & Hogan, R. Social speech and social interaction: Egocentrism revisited. *Child Development*, 1973, *44*, 562–568.

Glucksberg, S., & Krauss, R. M. What do people say after they have learned how to talk? *Merrill-Palmer Quarterly*, 1967, *13*, 309–316.

Glucksberg, S., Krauss, R., & Higgins, T. The development of communication skills in children. In F. Horowitz (Ed.), *Review of child development research* (Vol. 4). Chicago: University of Chicago Press, 1975.

Kingsley, P. *Relationship between egocentrism and children's communication*. Paper presented at the meeting of the Society for Research in Child Development, Minneapolis, 1971.

Looft, W. R. Egocentrism and social interaction across the life span. *Psychological Bulletin*, 1972, *78*, 73–92.

Piaget, J. Piaget's theory. In P. H. Mussen (Ed.), *Carmichael's manual of child psychology*. New York: Wiley, 1970.

Piaget, J., & Inhelder, B. *The child's conception of space*. London: Routledge & Kegan Paul, 1956.

Pratt, M. W., Scribner, S., & Cole, M. Children as teachers: Developmental studies of instructional communication. *Child Development,* 1977, *48,* 1475–1481.

Rubin, K. H. Egocentrism in childhood: A unitary construct? *Child Development,* 1973, *44,* 102–110.

Selman, R. Taking another's perspective: Role-taking development in early childhood. *Child Development,* 1971, *42,* 1721–1734.

Shantz, C. U. *Communication skills and social-cognitive development.* Paper presented at the meeting of the Society for Research in Child Development, Denver, 1975. (a)

Shantz, C. U. The development of social cognition. In E. M. Hetherington (Ed.), *Review of child development research* (Vol. 5). Chicago: University of Chicago Press, 1975. (b)

Shantz, C. U., & Steinlauf, B. *Perspective-taking and decentration abilities in children.* Unpublished manuscript, Wayne State University, 1976.

Shantz, C., & Wilson, K. E. Training communication skills in young children. *Child Development,* 1972, *43,* 693–698.

Spilton, D., & Lee, L. C. Some determinants of effective communication in four-year-olds. *Child Development,* 1977, *48,* 968–977.

Steinlauf, B. *Role-taking abilities of young children and maternal discipline strategies.* Unpublished master's thesis, Wayne State University, 1974.

Wellman, H. M., & Lempers, J. D. The naturalistic communicative abilities of two-year-olds. *Child Development,* 1977, *48,* 1052–1057.

Whitehurst, G. J., & Merkur, A. E. The development of communications: Modeling and contrast failure. *Child Development,* 1977, *48,* 993–1001.

//
Referential Communication Studies

5

Training Referential Communication Skills

STEVEN R. ASHER AND ALLAN WIGFIELD

In this chapter we examine research on the training of referential communication skills. To provide a context for this review, we first summarize the two major theoretical approaches to the study of children's referential communication ability. One approach, the egocentrism perspective, attributes communication failure to young children's inability to take the role of the listener. The other approach, a task-analytic perspective, emphasizes children's difficulty in coping with the specific demands of various communication tasks. After examining these approaches, we review research on the training of communication skills, most of which is derived from the role-taking perspective. Following discussion of these studies, we present a series of training experiments that we conducted from a task-analytic perspective. The chapter concludes with a discussion of ways to integrate the role-taking and task-analytic research traditions.

Children's Oral Communication Skills

Theoretical Accounts

The Egocentrism Explanation

Although it is well known that children's referential communication performance improves with increasing age (Glucksberg, Krauss, & Higgins, 1975), the developmental changes that underlie improvement are just beginning to be understood. Various skill acquisitions have been hypothesized to contribute to the development of children's competence. One widely held view is that the growth of communication accuracy is a function of the decline of childhood egocentricity. According to this view, as children grow older, they become more aware of the need to take the listener's role and the necessity of providing messages that meet the listener's informational needs.

This view stems from Piaget's work (Piaget, 1926), and has been elaborated by Flavell and his associates (Flavell, Botkin, Fry, Wright, & Jarvis, 1968). Piaget contended that communication develops from the egocentric speech of childhood to the socialized speech of adulthood. Childhood speech is not intended to meet listener needs, and is thus not adapted with the listener's perspective in mind. Adults, on the other hand, communicate with the intention to inform and recognize that the listener lacks information known to the speaker. Flavell and his colleagues (1968) term this ability to accomodate to the listener's informational needs as role-taking skill. In the view of Piaget and Flavell et al., development of the ability to take the other's perspective is a main component in the development of good communication skills.

In early studies of referential communication accuracy (e.g., Alvy, 1968; Glucksberg, Krauss, & Weisberg, 1966; Sullivan & Hunt, 1967), the egocentrism explanation was adopted to explain young children's communication failure. More recent research indicates, however, that this approach inadequately explains communication skill development (Asher, 1979). First, there is considerable evidence that even very young children alter their message content depending upon the particular listener they are addressing. Preschool children give different kinds of messages to adults than to young children (Shatz & Gelman, 1973), to a blindfolded listener than to a sighted listener (Maratsos, 1973; Meissner & Apthorp, 1976), and to a listener who is knowledgeable about a game than to a naïve listener (Menig-Peterson, 1975). This suggests that even children in Piaget's preoperational stage are capable of taking the listener's perspective.

Second, it appears that even when children fail to communicate adequately, their poor performance cannot be readily explained in terms of children's egocentrism. For example, the egocentrism formulation leads to the prediction that children's messages may have private meaning even though their messages lack public meaning. Asher and Oden (1976) tested this prediction by examining whether children's messages would have meaning for themselves when the messages were not meaningful to others. Results indicated that children whose messages provided little information to an adult listener also were unable to effectively use their own messages to select referents. This finding implies that children lack skills other than the ability to analyze listener characteristics.

Third, a large number of studies have examined the correlation between role-taking skill, as directly measured by various tests, and communication accuracy. Although children improve over age on both the role-taking and communication tasks, the correlation between these two kinds of tasks is usually modest or low (e.g., Cole & Dorval, 1973; Johnson, 1977; Kingsley, 1971; Piché, Michlin, Rubin, & Johnson, 1975; Rubin, 1973; Shantz, 1975). This implies that role-taking and communication tasks are assessing different skills.

Thus, a variety of sources of evidence indicate that the role-taking approach provides an inadequate account of the development of communication accuracy. We believe that there are two basic problems with this approach. One is the global nature of the role-taking construct. Most research on egocentrism and communication has proceeded without a clear conceptualization of the component skills that constitute role-taking ability. Often, role-taking ability is equated with simply being aware that listeners have different perspectives from one's own. As will be discussed later, there are other important elements of role-taking skill. The second problem is that there are other skills relevant to accurate communication that are ignored in the role-taking approach. A task-analytic model, considered next, gives attention to different sorts of skills.

The Task-Analytic View

The task-analytic view emphasizes the child's ability to cope with the specific features inherent in various communication tasks. Communication tasks vary in the demands they make upon speaker skills. For example, the task of giving someone directions to a location requires somewhat different skills than the task of teaching someone the rules of a board game. Nonetheless, most tasks have certain features in common. Rosenberg and Cohen (1966) have proposed a two-stage model of communication which attempts to specify the processes that are required in many communication tasks. Rosenberg and Cohen contend that, given the task of communicating a referent, the speaker first samples a response from a hierarchy of word associations to the referent. The probability of sampling a response is said to be proportional to its occurrence as a word associate. Next, the speaker is said to compare the sampled response to both the referent and potential nonreferents. If the associative value to the referent is greater, the message is likely to be emitted; if the value is smaller, the message probably will be rejected and another cycle of sampling–comparison activity begun.

This model suggests the relevance of certain cognitive processes to the development of communication effectiveness. First, improved performance over age could be due to the acquisition of a more elaborate vocabulary or knowledge base from which to sample a response. As children's knowledge of the world increases, they would be better prepared to communicate increasingly subtle distinctions. Second, children's improved communication performance over age could be due to increased awareness of the need to engage in comparison activity. Young children may be more likely to treat the communication task as though it simply requires an adequate association to the referent. Older children may be more likely to consider nonreferents as well as the referent when formulating a message.

There has been little research on the contribution of vocabulary development or world knowledge to the development of communication effectiveness. However, a growing number of studies have examined whether children engage in comparison activity on referential tasks (e.g., Asher, 1976; Asher & Parke, 1975; Bearison & Levey, 1977; Whitehurst, 1976). Asher and Parke (1975) had second-, fourth-, and sixth-grade children communicate messages for word pairs in which the referent was dissimilar to the nonreferent (e.g., *run*–bake) and for word pairs in which the referent and nonreferent were similar (e.g., *ocean*–river). On the latter type of word pair, comparison activity is required to ensure that the message generated is more highly associated to the referent than the nonreferent. On the dissimilar word pairs no comparison activity is needed. Asher and Parke found that children at each grade level gave adequate messages on nearly all of the dissimilar word pairs. However, on the similar word pairs, older children were significantly more accurate than the younger children. These findings suggest that younger children were failing to meet the demand for comparison activity posed by the similar word pair task.

Evidence that younger children fail to engage in comparison activity also can be found in recent studies of children's message appraisal ability. Asher (1976) asked second-, fourth-, and sixth-grade children to evaluate a standard set of 12 messages. Six of the messages were effective in that, although they were only moderately associated to the referent, they were completely unassociated to the nonreferent. The other 6 messages were not effective in that they were highly associated to both the referent and the nonreferent. In contrast to the communication task, this appraisal task requires no message production; children simply have to recognize which messages are effective and which are not. Results indicated that younger children did significantly worse than older children on the good clue and poor clue appraisal tasks.

Further evidence that children do not adequately engage in comparison activity comes from the Robinsons' work on message appraisal (Robinson & Robinson, 1976a, 1976b; Robinson, this volume). On their task, children evaluated whether the speaker or listener was to blame when a message is not understood. The task was actually structured so that the speaker was to blame in all cases, in that the speaker's message referred to both the referent and the nonreferent. Results indicated that 5-year-olds tended to blame the listener for the failure, whereas children 7 years and older correctly blamed the speaker. The Robinsons concluded that one reason why younger children do not adequately assess messages is that they do not compare the information in the message to each potential referent.

Whitehurst and his colleagues (e.g., Whitehurst, 1976; Whitehurst & Sonnenschein, 1978) have also investigated the extent to which children engage in comparison activity. Whitehurst has used a triangle description task in which the number of critical features distinguishing one triangle from another can be controlled. Three types of messages can be identified with this task: those that are incomplete because they fail to mention the critical attribute; those that are redundant in that they include both essential and nonessential information, and those that are truly contrastive in that only the critical attributes are mentioned. Whitehurst (1976) showed that children were more likely to produce contrastive messages when there were only two items in the display, the referent and the nonreferent. With two nonreferents, production of contrastive messages declined. In addition, Whitehurst found that older children, even though they produced discriminative messages, did not attempt to give the most efficient messages (contrastive ones), but instead gave more redundant messages. Similar results occurred in a second experiment in the same report. Children who heard a model produce contrastive messages showed a stronger increase in redundant than in contrastive messages. Apparently, children learned that their messages must distinguish the referent from nonreferents, but they followed the path of "least effort" in that they produced redundant rather than contrastive messages.

The task-analytic perspective has also been used to study the correlates of communication accuracy. One would expect communication performance on referential tasks in which the referent and nonreferent are similar to correlate with performance on other tasks that require comparison activity. We have begun to examine the correlation of communication accuracy with two other tasks. One is the Matching Familiar Figures (MFF) task developed by Kagan and his colleagues (Kagan, Rosman, Day, Albert, & Phillips, 1964) to study children's tendency to respond impulsively versus reflectively. The child is shown a picture and is asked to find the identical picture in a set of six highly similar alternatives. This task requires that the child carefully scan the alternatives in order to select the identical match rather than one of the similar "distractors." In a pilot study, children's accuracy on the word pair task correlated significantly with MFF accuracy; it seems that children who engage in comparison activity on one task are more likely to engage in a scanning process on the other.

Another task that presumably requires comparison activity is the multiple-choice reading achievement test. Here the child reads a paragraph and is presented with a test question and four alternative answers. One alternative is the correct answer and one or more is often quite similar and could easily be mistaken for the correct answer. The problem for the child is to avoid selecting the first answer that seems attractive and to compare among the alternatives. Wigfield and Asher (1978) correlated multiple-choice test reading achievement scores with communication accuracy on the word pair task. The correlation approached significance in third grade, r (18) = .43, p < .10, and was significant in fifth grade, r (14) = .57, p < .05.

These data suggest that similar processes may contribute to performance on multiple-choice achievement tests and referential communication tasks. Further research is needed to determine the extent to which comparison processing, in particular, is an important contributor to performance on multiple-choice achievement tests as well as referential communication tasks. If younger children's achievement test performance is affected by deficiencies in comparison processing, then their performance should be particularly affected by the placement of the correct alternative within the multiple-choice array. Dickson (1979) has recently reported that the placement of the referent in a stimulus display affects the probability that young listeners will correctly select the referent. It seems plausible that a similar finding would be obtained on multiple-choice test performance.

To summarize, research from a task-analytic perspective suggests that comparison activity is an important component of communication accuracy and that children increasingly engage in comparison activity as they grow older. Various studies have demonstrated the conditions that influence whether children engage in comparison processing. Finally, there is evidence that the task-analytic perspective leads to successful predictions regarding the correlates of referential communication accuracy.

Training Children's Communication Skills

The research reviewed thus far has employed a developmental-descriptive methodology. In this type of study, children of different ages communicate messages on one or more tasks or under one or more conditions. Investigators then make inferences about the types of skills that contribute to developmental changes in communication accuracy. An alternative research strategy for identifying skills that contribute to children's communication development is the training methodology. Hypotheses about the skill deficits that underlie communication failure can be experimentally tested by teaching a specific skill and observing the effects on subsequent communication performance. If children's communication performance improves following training, then it can be inferred that the trained skill is relevant to accurate communication and that children were initially lacking in that skill.

The utility of a training research strategy rests upon the careful specification of the skills to be trained. It does little good, from a theoretical perspective, to improve communication performance if little is learned about the specific skill deficits that were remediated. Confident interpretation of training studies also depends upon the utilization of teaching procedures with known effectiveness. Without the use of such procedures, failure to produce improved communication performance could be interpreted as being due to poor teaching procedures rather than inappropriate selection of skills.

The Role-Taking Approach to Communication Training

Referential communication training studies have primarily emphasized the importance of role-taking skill (Chandler, Greenspan, & Barenboim, 1974; Fry, 1966, 1969; Shantz & Wilson, 1972). These training studies have had limited success in producing changes in communication performance. More important, even when improvement in performance is obtained, it is not clear what particular skill deficits were remediated. In order to understand why the studies have produced unclear results, each will be considered in detail.

The first training studies were conducted by Fry (1966, 1969). As the two studies were similar, only the latter (Fry, 1969) will be described here. Fry based his study on Piaget's contention that it is the disconfirmation of one's own perspective, mainly by peers, that fosters role-taking skill. Fifth-grade children were given a pretest and posttest on various speaker communication tasks that involved distinguishing referents from various non-referents. Half of the children received training between the pretest and posttest. They met in groups of six and seven for 1 hour a week over a 6-week period. During each hour, children alternated in the speaker and listener roles. Following each child's performance as a speaker, a tape recording of the child's message was played back and listeners criticized the message and indicated other possible messages that might have been sent. As in Fry's (1966) earlier study, the results indicated few positive effects of training.

A number of factors may explain the weak training effect. First, the age group chosen (11-year-olds) may have had relatively well developed skills prior to training. A training study is more likely to be effective with children who have neither undeveloped nor well developed skills. A second difficulty lies with the use of peers as a source of feedback. No control over the quality of peer feedback was provided nor was any assessment made of the quality of feedback given by peers. The most basic problem with the study, however, was the lack of prior articulation of relevant skills. Even if the training had resulted in improved performance, it would have been impossible to determine what communication skills had improved, given the nature of the training procedure.

Shantz and Wilson (1972) also investigated whether communication skills can be improved through training children to be more aware of listener needs. However, in contrast to Fry, their interest was less in the role of peer feedback than it was in the development of a controlled "curriculum." Shantz and Wilson worked with 7-year-olds, because research by Piaget and Flavell indicated this to be an age of rapid transition in communication skills.

The research design was as follows. Children were randomly assigned to either the training or control conditions and were pretested. Children in the training condition then received six 30-minute sessions; in each session, the children served as speaker, listener, and listener–observer. The experimenter actively questioned listeners and observers about message adequacy and encouraged constructive peer criticism. As part of the training procedure, the children communicated the same referent on two tasks, a description and a discrimination task. On the description task, the child had to describe a referent so that a listener could draw it. On the discrimination task, this same referent appeared in the context of nonreferents that differed on a number of dimensions (size, color, position, and shape). The child's task was to provide a message that discriminated the referent from the non-referents.

Following training, children received the posttests which, in addition to the training tasks, included generalization tasks: a checkerboard task in which the speaker tried to communicate so that a listener could place six objects in certain positions on a checkerboard; the novel forms task of Glucksberg et al. (1966), and a persuasion task used by Flavell et al. (1968) in which the child was asked to try to sell a tie to a prospective buyer. Results on the training tasks showed that both the training and control children improved significantly on description and discrimination tasks, with the training group improving significantly more than the control group. Results from the generalization tasks were mixed. On the checkerboard task, the two groups did not differ in the amount of information judged useful; however, the training group was significantly superior on listener accuracy. On the novel forms task, the two groups did not differ on total errors but showed significant differences on the last trial in favor of training subjects. Finally, on the persuasion task, children in the control group actually gave more arguments and more types of arguments than children in the training group.

From these results, Shantz and Wilson concluded that training produced improved performance on description and discrimination tasks, generalization to tasks similar to those used in training (the checkerboard and novel forms tasks), but no generalization to a highly dissimilar task (the persuasion task). There are difficulties with this conclusion. The ambiguity of findings on both "near-generalization" tasks (checkerboard and novel forms) and the reversal from expectation on the "far-generalization" persuasion task is not convincing evidence for generalization. Also, it is not clear whether the significant effects that did occur were due to training or simply to practice alone. The improvement of the control group on the description task suggests that "descriptive ability may improve substantially with minimal repetition and no feedback [Shantz & Wilson, 1972, p. 697]." This result suggests the necessity of including comparable practice opportunities in the control condition, which Shantz and Wilson did not do.

Assuming, however, that training was responsible for the training group's relative improvement, it is not clear what skills were learned. Shantz and Wilson suggest that the procedure of including the same standard card for discrimination and description tasks may have alerted children to the importance of attending to listener needs. However, providing multiple attributes (i.e., size, color, position, shape) may have shown children that communication requires discriminative messages. Further, the training may have alerted children to certain dimensions such as size and color for making discriminations. Because the training procedure was complex, it is impossible to choose among these various possibilities.

The Shantz and Wilson study suggests that practice, or practice and feedback, can be effective in improving children's referential communication ability. A study by Chandler et al. (1974) points in a similar direction. Emotionally disturbed, institutionalized children aged 9–14 years were divided into three conditions: a role-taking training group, a referential training group, and a nontreatment control group. The role-taking training consisted of working in a group with other children to produce videotaped dramas. The rationale for this procedure was that the production of dramas would provide children with practice in stepping outside their own role and in assuming different roles or perspectives. The referential communication training group practiced and received feedback on a variety of communication tasks. This training did not include any formal or didactic communication skill training. Instead, it was intended that the children find and correct their own errors. The control group received neither role-taking nor referential communication training.

Results indicated that the group receiving referential communication practice and feedback made sizable gains on the posttest communication measure, and these gains were significantly greater than those of the role-taking and control groups. Role-taking training produced gains on the communication measure that were no different from the gains in the control condition. This suggests that a better conceptualization is needed of the role-taking skills to be trained and of the links between role-taking training procedures and the objective of improved communication accuracy. Without a more adequate conceptualization, it is unlikely that future role-taking training will greatly improve communication accuracy.

In summary, studies in which the goal was to train role-taking skill have not been very successful in improving children's communication skills. These results demonstrate in another way that the role-taking explanation provides an inadequate account of the development of children's communication skills. When success has occurred, it was due primarily to practice on various communication tasks, followed by unstructured feedback from either the experimenter or same-age peers. The problem with this approach is that it is difficult to specify exactly what children have learned, and thus any improvement in their communication performance is open to a number of alternative explanations.

The Task-Analytic Approach to Communication Training

The task-analytic approach has only recently been used as a framework for the design of training studies. As discussed earlier, the developmental-descriptive studies conducted from this perspective suggest that young children's poorer communication performance results in part from failure to engage in comparison activity. Elementary-aged children should be able to make such comparisons; however, they may not be aware that it is important to do so on referential tasks. Thus, teaching children to be aware of the importance of comparing messages to both the referent and the nonreferent should improve their communication performance.

We will describe three training studies we conducted, each concerned with the effects of comparison training on children's communication accuracy. All three experiments examined the immediate effects of training on the task used during training. The first study also assessed whether training effects were maintained over time and whether the effects generalized to another referential task. In the second study, the major issue assessed was whether children's communication performance is constrained by difficulties in thinking of particular messages even when children understand the importance of comparison activity. In the third experiment, the main issue was again whether training effects generalized to another referential task. We will also briefly describe a fourth training study in which we further attempted to examine generalization effects. Because the procedures used in this study differ from the other three, the study will receive separate attention in the section on generalization effects of training.

The Comparison Training Procedure

As discussed earlier, the success of a training program depends not only on the program content (i.e., the skills to be trained), but also on the teaching methods employed. The training procedure used in our research was derived from the modeling plus self-guidance statement procedure used by Meichenbaum and Goodman (1971). This method consists of three components: (*a*) the child sees a model who overtly verbalizes the correct problem-solving strategy; (*b*) the child has an opportunity to practice the strategy; and (*c*) the child then receives feedback. Meichenbaum and Goodman used this procedure to successfully train impulsive children to more carefully scan arrays on the Matching Familiar Figures task. The success of their training procedure and the seeming similarity of scanning to comparison activity made the modeling plus self-guidance statement procedure attractive for our purposes.

The procedure for the training conditions in the studies was generally as follows: Children were first pretested on a set of word pairs, each consisting of a referent and nonreferent that had similar meanings. Children communicated their messages for an imaginary listener, a procedure that has been used frequently in previous studies (e.g., Asher & Parke, 1975; Kingsley, 1971; Shantz & Wilson, 1972), and which poses no conceptual difficulty for elementary-school children. After the pretesting, children received training, which consisted of watching a videotaped model communicate clues for 10 word pairs, practicing giving clues for 10 word pairs, and receiving structured feedback from the experimenter about message adequacy. The word pairs used in training were different from both the pretest and posttest word pairs.

The experimenter began the training with the following instructions: "I'm here to help the kids in your class learn how to do well on games like this. But before we practice I want to show you a person doing the word pairs. I want you to pay close attention so that you will learn the best way to play the game, okay?" The child then saw a modeling film depicting either an adult male (for boys) or adult female (for girls) generating clues for word pairs. The model's script for the first pair (child-*baby*) was as follows: "Let's see, there's 'child' and 'baby' and 'baby' has a line under it. How about 'play' as a clue? A baby plays. No, that's no good, because a child plays too, and the person won't know which word has the line under it. How about 'mother,' because a baby has a mother. No, a child has a mother too. Oh, I've got one. 'Rattle.' Because a baby plays with a rattle and a child doesn't. 'Rattle.' "

After the model selected a clue for the first pair, the child was asked to give a clue for the first practice pair. The following instructions were given: "Okay, now you try one. Think out loud just like the person on TV. I'll help you if you need help." When the child gave a poor clue, the experimenter said: "No, that might not be a good clue because. . . . Try again." After two unsuccessful tries by the child, the experimenter said: "No, that's not a good clue because. . . . Let's go on to the next pair." When the child gave a good clue the experimenter said: "Yes, that's a good clue because. . . . Let's go on to the next pair."

The modeling, practice, and feedback continued in a similar fashion for six word pairs for both the model and the child. For the next four word pairs the model was seen thinking to himself or herself and then emitting a good clue. For example, on the seventh word pair, the model said: "There's 'crayon' and 'chalk' and 'crayon' has a line under it. A good clue is 'wax.' 'Wax.' " Before the child gave a clue for the seventh practice pair, the experimenter said: "Now do it like the person on TV. Think to yourself and come up with a good clue." After the child gave a clue, the experimenter gave feedback as above. This procedure continued until the model and child had each given 3 more clues, for a total of 10 clues each.

Design of the Training Studies

The first experiment using this comparison training procedure was conducted with third- and fourth-grade children, and the other two experiments were conducted with fourth-grade children. In each of the studies children were divided into two groups; a training group that received the modeling plus self-guidance procedure and a practice–control group. Children in the practice–control group practiced on the same word pairs used in the training condition but received no comparison training. In this way the effects of modeling and feedback could be separated from other effects such as practice or familiarity with the experimental situation. In all three experiments, children were first pretested with one set of word pairs, Set A. (See Table 5.1 for each set of word pairs.) As a posttest measure, children produced clues for 10 word pairs unrelated to those used in the training and practice–control conditions. In Experiments 1, and 2, Set B was used as a posttest measure; in Experiment 3, Set C was used. In all three experiments, children's clues were scored by having three adult judges evaluate the adequacy of each clue.

TABLE 5.1
The Pretest and Posttest Word-Pair Sets[a]

Set A	Set B	Set C
cook–*bake*	*plant*–flower	*steak*–hamburger
say–*tell*	*ship*–boat	*piano*–violin
wash–clean	dish–*plate*	*wrestling*–boxing
music–song	*mad*–angry	pond–*lake*
city–town	hot–*warm*	*yellow*–blue
sleep–*rest*	river–*ocean*	*soap*–detergent
road–street	wheel–*tire*	motorcycle–*bicycle*
write–*print*	mitten–*glove*	*tree*–bush
short–small	*rubbers*–boots	*slippers*–shoes
sound–*noise*	*world*–earth	butter–*cheese*

[a] The referent word in each pair is in italics. Word pairs in each set are displayed in the randomly selected order in which they were presented to children.

(See Asher, 1976; Asher & Oden, 1976 for the rationale for this type of scoring procedure.)

Experimental Findings

Immediate Effects of Training

To assess immediate posttest performance in each study, an analysis of covariance was performed using the Set A pretest scores as the covariate. Table 5.2 presents the adjusted posttest scores. In each study, children in the training condition performed significantly more accurately than children in the practice–control condition. These results support the hypothesis that teaching children to engage in comparison activity on the word pair task improves their communication accuracy.

Maintenance of Training Effects

One month after training, children in Experiment 1 were tested again on two additional 10-item word pair sets. One was Set A, the word pairs that had served as the original pretest, and the other was Set C, an entirely new group of items that had not been seen by the children before. Children in the training condition again communicated significantly more effectively than children in the practice–control condition (3.56 versus 2.59 for Set A, and 5.13 versus 3.52 for Set C).

Alternative Explanations of Low Communication Accuracy

The results presented thus far demonstrate that comparison training is more effective than practice alone and that the effects of training are maintained over time. The results provide support for the task-analytic approach in that teaching children a task-specific strategy facilitated their perfor-

TABLE 5.2
Average Posttest Communication Accuracy in the Three Experiments (Adjusted Scores)

	Condition	
Experiment	Practice control	Comparison training
Experiment 1 (Set B)	2.50	3.51
Experiment 2 (Set B)	2.09	3.54
Experiment 3 (Set C)	2.34	6.79

mance. However, children's performance was still low relative to the total possible score on each set of items. Even on the easiest set of items, Set C, children who received training averaged only 5.13 out of a possible 10 correct in Experiment 1, and 6.79 in Experiment 3. Thus, the comparison training did not lead to high scores. One possibility is that children simply failed to engage in comparison activity on some items. Another possibility is that children consistently engaged in comparison actively but still had difficulty generating appropriate messages, due to other factors such as their knowledge of the items used in the word pairs.

These alternatives were evaluated in Experiment 2 by testing children on a message appraisal task as well as on the message production task. The appraisal task consists of 12 word pairs and potential clues (see Asher, 1976, p. 22). Six of the clues are good in that they are more highly associated to the referent than the nonreferent and six of the clues are poor in that they are highly associated to both the referent and the nonreferent. For each item, the child's task was to say whether the clue would help a listener who did not know which word was underlined to pick the correct word. The appraisal task provides a more sensitive test of a child's understanding of the comparison concept than does a message production task. It makes fewer demands on children's knowledge because the clues were chosen to reflect the world knowledge of middle-elementary-school children. Good performance on this task in combination with relatively low performance on the word pair task would suggest that children did learn the comparison concept but were constrained by other production factors. Relatively low performance on both tasks would suggest that children did not learn to engage in comparison activity.

Results indicated that children in the comparison training group did significantly better than children in the practice–control group on both good clue appraisal accuracy (5.57 versus 4.71) and poor clue appraisal accuracy (4.92 versus 2.99). Note that children's scores in the training group were relatively close to the highest possible score of six on each subset of items. These data suggest that children learned the importance of engaging in comparison activity.

To provide perspective on children's performance, we collected data on adults' communication and appraisal ability. College students received no training, but simply gave clues for each word pair set and appraised the good and poor clues. Adults' scores on the good clue ($\bar{X} = 5.55$) and poor clue ($\bar{X} = 5.86$) appraisal sets are similar to trained children's scores. On the communication production task, the average score for adults was 5.13 on Set A, 5.06 on Set B, and 8.06 on Set C. These data indicate that many of the items were difficult even for competent speakers and that children's performance following training approached the level of adult performance.

Why might children have learned the comparison concept yet still have achieved relatively low scores on the message production task? Perhaps children lacked specific strategies for generating clues. A second session in Experiment 2 was designed to investigate this issue. Children who had received comparison training in the first session were matched based on posttest scores and randomly assigned either to a "comparison reminder" condition or to a "comparison reminder plus strategy training" condition. In the latter condition, children were taught two specific strategies for generating messages—first, to think of a word that goes with the referent in a sentence; and second, to think of an example of the referent. These two strategies were selected based on an examination of the types of effective clues speakers gave in our earlier research. If children's communication performance was constrained by their lack of strategies for generating messages, comparison plus strategy training should improve performance beyond the level of comparison training alone. The results provided partial support; girls' communication performance improved significantly as a result of this strategy training, but boys' performance did not. One possibility is that girls had a more adequate vocabulary repertoire and were better able to utilize the strategies that were taught. This hypothesis could be assessed in future research by testing children's knowledge of the particular lexical items used in the word pairs. It could then be examined whether children with the most knowledge benefit most from comparison and strategy training.

To summarize, the appraisal data show clearly that the comparison training procedure was quite effective in teaching children to appreciate the need to attend to nonreferents as well as referents in formulating a message. Children in the comparison training condition were quite adept at evaluating the quality of both good and poor messages. What accounts, then, for trained children's relatively low performance on the communication task? Tentatively, it appears that some children lack specific strategies for thinking of clues, and others may be limited by their knowledge about the various word pair items. Thus, the present findings qualify to some extent our earlier conclusions that emphasized the importance of inadequate comparison processing as the reason for young children's communication ineffectiveness (e.g., Asher, 1976; Asher & Parke, 1975). The discrepancy between children's communication accuracy and appraisal accuracy scores, along with the "example" and "sentence" rules training data, suggest that other message production factors also play an important role.

Generalization of Training

As discussed earlier, previous attempts to achieve generalization of training in the communication literature have met with limited success (e.g., Fry, 1966, 1969; Shantz & Wilson, 1972). One problem in assessing generalization effects of training is the selection of appropriate transfer tasks (Brown, 1978). From a task-analytic perspective, not all communication tasks could serve as tests of generalization of training. Our criteria for selecting generalization tasks were twofold. First, the task should require that children engage in comparison activity; that is, the referents to be communicated should appear in the context of highly similar nonreferents. Second, features of the generalization task, although different from the training task, should not place demands on the speaker that override the speaker's ability to manifest his or her comparison ability.

The issue of generalization of training was initially examined in Experiment 1. At immediate posttest, children were given a snowflake description task adapted from one used by Rosenberg and Markham (1971). The speaker was shown a series of 10 pairs of snowflake photographs, one pair at a time. The snowflakes in each pair were highly similar in appearance and one of the two snowflakes was designated as the referent. The speaker's task was to provide a message of any length that would enable a listener to select the referent in each pair. Like the word pair task, the snowflake description task requires speakers to engage in comparison activity; speakers must ensure that their messages are more highly related to the referent than to the similar nonreferent. The results for this task indicated no significant difference between children in the comparison training versus practice–control conditions. Thus, the training procedure that was successful in producing 1-month maintenance on the trained task did not generalize to a different task administered immediately after training.

The issue of generalization was examined again in Experiment 3. Here the generalization task was Baldwin, McFarlane, and Garvey's (1971) picture-description task. In this 10-item task, the referent in each item is a picture of an animal or person and the nonreferents are six highly similar versions of the same object. The speaker was asked to describe the referent so that a listener could pick it from the alternatives. The message could be of any length. In contrast to the snowflake task, there is a maximum of four critical features distinguishing the referent and nonreferents in each picture set, and the number of critical features varies systematically across picture items. The results for this task were quite similar to the results of the first experiment; there was a nonsignificant difference between the trained condition and the practice–control condition. Thus, once again, comparison training did not generalize to a task other than the one used in training.

One possibility is that generalization did not occur because children received comparison training on just one task. To examine this issue we conducted a fourth training study, in collaboration with Peter Renshaw, the purpose of which was to determine if comparison training on more than one task would produce more generalization than comparison training on the word pair task alone. Third- and fourth-grade children were randomly assigned to different training conditions. One group received word pair comparison training that was identical to that of our other studies. The other children received training on two tasks, the word pair task and a triangle description task. The training on the triangle task was similar to the word pair training in that the model emphasized the importance of comparing the message to both referents and nonreferents. The posttests consisted of 10 word pairs and a modified version of the Baldwin *et al.* (1971) picture-description task.

An examination of children's pretest and posttest data indicated that once again comparison training led to improved performance on the word pair task. Children showed an average gain of approximately 2.5 from pretest to posttest. However, the scores on the picture description task varied only slightly across conditions. Thus, the results indicated that although comparison training was once again successful in terms of word pair performance, training effects did not generalize to picture description.

What, then, have we learned about generalization effects of communication training? Our first and third experiments showed that comparison training on the word pair task did not transfer to performance on other referential tasks. Our fourth experiment indicated that generalization is not obtained simply by providing comparison training on more than one task. This failure to obtain generalization in our research is similar to results from training studies conducted in other topic areas in which generalization has been a concern (Brown, 1978; Brown & Campione, 1977; Kuhn, 1974). Why is generalization of communication training so difficult to obtain? One possibility is that third- and fourth-grade children may not adequately analyze the demands of different communication tasks. That is, they may communicate without first considering the features of the task that require attention. Analyzing task demands can be viewed as a type of metacommunicative activity (Flavell, 1976; this volume). Perhaps teaching children, not only to engage in certain processes, but also to recognize that a new task requires these processes would facilitate generalization. This training could be done using the "modeling plus self-guidance statement" procedure. Children could be shown a model examining a series of referential tasks. Before communicating on each task, the model could think out loud about the particular dimensions or features of the task items that require attention. Modeling this type of task-analytic activity might facilitate generalization of comparison training.

Other Task-Analytic Training Studies

When we began our comparison training research program, there were no task-analytic communication training studies reported in the literature. This situation has changed; other chapters in this volume report task-analytic work on teaching speaker skills (Whitehurst and Sonnenschein) and listener skills (Patterson and Kister). These studies, like those reported here, support the view that attending to component skills will lead to improvement in children's communication performance.

In their chapter, Whitehurst and Sonnenschein discuss the important distinction between "novel skills" and "accustomed skills." In the first case, children lack the necessary component routines to do the task; whereas, in the latter case, children have the routines at their disposal but have not organized them or do not appreciate when to apply them. Whitehurst and Sonnenschein conducted a series of referential communication training experiments from which they concluded that children have comparison processing routines at their disposal but fail to use them because they do not recognize their necessity. This conclusion is consistent with earlier evidence that children seem unaware of the need to engage in comparison processing (Asher, 1976; Asher & Oden, 1976; Asher & Parke, 1975). It is also consistent with the findings of the studies we report here.

Whitehurst and Sonnenschein argue that the most important component of their training package is telling the child that he or she should describe how the referent is different from the nonreferent. A question that might be asked is whether the instruction to tell how they are different is as or more effective than the modeling plus self-guidance procedure used in the present research. Whitehurst and Sonnenschein present evidence of maintenance which suggests that children were internalizing the concept of describing differences rather than simply responding to an external command. On the other hand, the training did not generalize to a listener task in which children had to indicate when a message was not discriminative. These findings suggest that children were "telling how it's different" when in the speaker role without fully comprehending that it is the speaker's responsibility to provide discriminative messages. In our training studies reported here, trained children did quite well on the message appraisal task. This suggests that children may have more fully understood the comparison concept, at least on the task used in training. Further research is necessary to clarify the conditions under which the direct instruction to tell how it is different will be as effective as the more complicated training procedure used here.

Integrating the Role-Taking and Task-Analytic Approaches

Finally, we would like to suggest that the role-taking and task-analytic training perspectives described earlier in this chapter can become better integrated. Training studies that have emphasized role-taking training have not been successful in improving children's communication performance, largely because the role-taking construct as used in these studies has been too global. A better understanding of the components of role-taking ability and their relationship to communication accuracy should lead to training studies that improve both role-taking and communication skills.

Flavell (1974) has proposed a model that provides a more detailed conceptualization of the various component skills in role taking. This model goes beyond the view that role taking can be equated with simply being aware that others have different perspectives from one's own. Flavell suggests that the child initially becomes aware that people have perspectives and other psychological attributes (e.g., feelings or abilities). Second, the child begins to appreciate that an analysis of the other's perspective is important in different situations. Third, the child develops the inferential skills to make appropriate attributions about the other person's perspective. Finally, the child becomes able to translate the inferences about the other's perspective into effective behavioral applications. These four components are referred to by Flavell as Existence, Need, Inference, and Application.

This model makes explicit the fact that, in communication situations, communication failure can occur as a result of problems in inferences or application even if speakers are aware of the existence of other perspectives and of the need to consider those perspectives. Several studies mentioned earlier (e.g., Maratsos, 1973; Menig-Peterson, 1975; Shatz & Gelman, 1973) demonstrate that preschool children are aware of the existence of different perspectives and do appreciate the need to take the listener's perspective into account. These results imply that children's failures in communicating are not due to limited awareness that others have different perspectives, or to a lack of appreciation that these perspectives must be taken into account. Instead, children's failures may be attributable to problems in making accurate inferences or applications. Flavell's model of the components of role-taking could be used as a basis for developing training programs to facilitate both role taking and communication skill. Different kinds of training could be provided depending on the particular components that children are having difficulty with.

Another way to integrate the role-taking and task-analytic traditions would be to adapt task-analytic training procedures for the purpose of teaching role-taking skill. Role-taking training studies have often employed relatively indirect or unstructured training procedures that have not greatly improved children's communication performance. In contrast, task-analytic studies have used a rather direct instruction method of training; children are either shown or told the type of process they should engage in. As demonstrated in this chapter, these procedures have been successful in improving children's communication performance. This direct approach to instruction could be readily adapted to teaching role-taking skills. For example, children could be shown models who consider the kinds of listener characteristics that are important and take into account how those characteristics should influence their messages. This type of training procedure should be more effective than the less direct methods of instruction associated with the majority of previous role-taking training studies.

Summary

This chapter described two theoretical accounts of the development of children's referential communication ability. The first approach, the role-taking perspective, explains improvement in communication accuracy in terms of the development of children's ability to take another person's perspective. This explanation appears to offer an inadequate account due in large part to the global nature of the role-taking construct and the neglect of other relevant skills. The second theoretical account, the task-analytic approach, explains the development of communication accuracy in terms of children's increasing ability to meet the specific cognitive demands of various communication tasks. A number of studies utilizing this approach indicate that engaging in comparison activity is a particularly important component of communication effectiveness.

The major portion of the chapter was devoted to a discussion of studies that have attempted to train children's communication skills. Studies that have attempted to improve children's communication performance by training role-taking skills have not been very successful. Again, this is primarily because the relationship between role taking and communication accuracy has not been clearly specified. The studies reported in this chapter utilized the task-analytic approach. Specifically, an attempt was made to improve children's communication accuracy by teaching them to engage in comparison activity on a referential task. Three main issues were assessed: whether the training improved children's communication accuracy; whether the training effects were maintained; and whether the training effects generalized to other referential tasks.

Results indicated that comparison training was quite effective in improving children's performance and in maintaining these changes over time. However, the training effects did not generalize to other tasks. One plausible explanation is that children did not adequately analyze the demands of different tasks, and thus did not apply the comparison concept to those tasks. Future research might employ the modeling plus self-guidance statement procedure to teach children how to better analyze the demands of different communication tasks. The chapter concludes with a discussion of ways to integrate the task-analytic and role-taking perspectives.

References

Alvy, K. T. Relation of age to children's egocentric and cooperative communication. *Journal of Genetic Psychology*, 1968, *112*, 275–286.

Asher, S. R. Children's ability to appraise their own and another person's communication performance. *Developmental Psychology*, 1976, *12*, 24–32.

Asher, S. R. Referential communication. In G. J. Whitehurst & B. J. Zimmerman (Eds.), *The functions of language and cognition*. New York: Academic Press, 1979.

Asher, S. R., & Oden, S. L. Children's failure to communicate: An assessment of comparison and egocentrism explanations. *Developmental Psychology,* 1976, *12,* 132–140.

Asher, S. R., & Parke, R. D. Influence of sampling and comparison processes on the development of communication effectiveness. *Journal of Educational Psychology,* 1975, *67,* 64–75.

Baldwin, T. L., & Garvey, C. J. Components of accurate problem-solving communication. *American Educational Research Journal,* 1973, *10,* 39–48.

Baldwin, T. L., McFarlane, P. T., & Garvey, C. J. Children's communication accuracy related to race and socioeconomic status. *Child Development,* 1971, *42,* 345–357.

Bearison, D. J., & Levey, L. M. Children's comprehension of referential communication: Decoding ambiguous messages. *Child Development,* 1977, *48,* 716–721.

Brown, A. L. Knowing when, where and how to remember: A problem of metacognition. In R. Glaser (Ed.), *Advances in instructional psychology.* New York: Halstead Press, 1978.

Brown, A. L., & Campione, J. C. *Memory strategies in learning: Training children to study strategically* (Tech. Rep. No. 22). Urbana: Center for the Study of Reading, University of Illinois, 1977.

Chandler, M. J., Greenspan, S., & Barenboim, C. Assessment and training of role-taking and referential communication skills in institutionalized emotionally disturbed children. *Developmental Psychology,* 1974, *10,* 546–557.

Cole, J. B., & Dorval, B. Sex differences in the intellectual structure of social interaction skills. *Developmental Psychology,* 1973, *8,* 261–267.

Dickson, W. P. Referential communication performance from age 4 to 8: Effects of referent type, target context position. *Developmental Psychology,* 1979, *15,* 470–471.

Flavell, J. H. The development of inferences about others. In T. Mischel (Ed.), *Understanding other persons.* Totowa, N.J.: Rowan and Littlefield, 1974.

Flavell, J. H. *The development of meta communication.* Paper presented at the Symposium on Language and Cognition, International Congress of Psychology, Paris, July 1976.

Flavell, J. H., Botkin, P. T., Fry, C. L., Wright, J. C., & Jarvis, P. E. *The development of role taking and communication skills in children.* New York: John Wiley, 1968.

Fry, C. L. Training children to communicate to listeners. *Child Development,* 1966, *37,* 674–685.

Fry, C. L. Training children to communicate to listeners who have varying listener requirements. *Journal of Genetic Psychology,* 1969, *114,* 153–166.

Glucksberg, S., Krauss, R. M., & Higgins, E. T. The development of referential communication skills. In F. D. Horowitz (Ed.), *Review of child development research* (Vol. 4). Chicago: University of Chicago Press, 1975.

Glucksberg, S., Krauss, R. M., & Weisberg, R. Referential communication in nursery school children: Method and some preliminary findings. *Journal of Experimental Child Psychology,* 1966, *3,* 333–342.

Johnson, F. L. Role-taking and referential communication abilities in first- and third-grade children. *Human Communications Research,* 1977, *3,* 135–145.

Kagan, J., Rosman, B. L., Day, D., Albert, J., & Phillips, W. Information processing in the child: Significance of analytic and reflective attitudes. *Psychological Monographs,* 1964, *78,* (1, Whole No. 578).

Kingsley, P. *Relationship between egocentrism and children's communication.* Paper presented at the biennial meeting of the Society for Research in Child Development, Minneapolis, 1971.

Kuhn, D. Inducing development experimentally: Comments on a research paradigm. *Developmental Psychology,* 1974, *10,* 590–600.

Maratsos, M. P. Nonegocentric communication abilities in preschool children. *Child Development,* 1973, *44,* 697–701.

Meichenbaum, D. H., & Goodman, J. Training impulsive children to talk to themselves: A means of developing self-control. *Journal of Abnormal Psychology,* 1971, *77,* 115–126.

Meissner, J. A., & Apthorp, H. Nonegocentrism and communication mode switching in black preschool children. *Developmental Psychology*, 1976, *12*, 245–249.

Menig-Peterson, C. L. The modification of communicative behavior in preschool-aged children as a function of the listener's perspective. *Child Development*, 1975, *46*, 1015–1018.

Piaget, J. *The language and thought of the child.* New York: Harcourt and Brace, 1926.

Piché, G. L., Michlin, M. L., Rubin, D. L., & Johnson, F. L. Relationships between fourth graders' performances on selected role-taking tasks and referential communication tasks. *Child Development*, 1975, *46*, 965–969.

Robinson, E. J., & Robinson, W. P. Developmental changes in the child's explanation of communication failure. *Australian Journal of Psychology*, 1976, *28*, 155–165. (a)

Robinson, E. J., & Robinson, W. P. The young child's understanding of communication. *Developmental Psychology*, 1976, *12*, 328–333. (b)

Rosenberg, S., & Cohen, B. D. Referential processes of speakers and listeners. *Psychological Review*, 1966, *73*, 208–231.

Rosenberg, S., & Markham, B. Choice behavior in a referentially ambiguous task. *Journal of Personality and Social Psychology*, 1971, *17*, 99–106.

Rubin, K. H. Egocentrism in childhood: A unitary construct? *Child Development*, 1973, *44*, 102–110.

Shantz, C. U. *The generality and correlates of egocentrism in childhood: An interim report.* Paper presented at the biennial meeting of the Society for Research in Child Development, Denver, 1975.

Shantz, C. U., & Wilson, K. Training communication skills in young children. *Child Development*, 1972, *43*, 693–698.

Shatz, M., & Gelman, R. The development of communication skills: Modifications in the speech of young children as a function of listener. *Monographs of the Society for Research in Child Development*, 1973, *38*, (5, Serial No. 152).

Sullivan, E. V., & Hunt, D. E. Interpersonal and objective decentering as a function of age and social class. *Journal of Genetic Psychology*, 1967, *110*, 199–210.

Whitehurst, G. J. The development of communication: Changes with age and modeling. *Child Development*, 1976, *47*, 473–482.

Whitehurst, G. J., & Sonnenschein, S. Referential communication: Attribute variation leads to contrast failure. *Journal of Experimental Child Psychology*, 1978, *25*, 490–504.

Wigfield, A., & Asher, S. R. *Age differences in children's referential communication performance: An investigation of task effects* (Tech. Rep. No. 96). Urbana: Center for the Study of Reading, University of Illinois, 1978.

6

The Development of Informative Messages in Referential Communication: Knowing When versus Knowing How

GROVER J. WHITEHURST AND SUSAN SONNENSCHEIN

A Theoretical Distinction in Skill Acquisition

The distinction between knowing how to do something and knowing when to do it is subtle but important. The whole do-it-yourself marketing approach is based on recognition that many if not most of us know how to do carpentry, plumbing, auto repairs, *etc.* It's just a matter of convincing us that we are capable and telling us *when* to produce the simple tool-using routines that are the components of these seemingly complex tasks.

One could argue for two categories of skill, or more appropriately skill deficit. The first consists of those things that we do not do because we lack the necessary component routines to do them. To acquire these skills requires laborious practice and feedback over some considerable period. One will not find booklets for sale at the supermarket check-out counter entitled "Composing for the symphony orchestra in five easy steps" or "The beginner's guide to piloting a Boeing 747." The second category of skill deficit consists of those things that we do not do because we have not tried to do them or do not know when to do them or do not know how to organize them.

127

These skills may be acquired with comparative ease through observational learning, simple verbal instructions, or, in some cases, through a few instances of trial-and-error feedback. One *will* find booklets for sale at the supermarket entitled "How to grow tomatoes" or "Fixing a leaking toilet."

We need a way of talking about this distinction that has some generality. Although the examples so far have had a dichotomous character, a simple typology is not likely to prove useful. The problem is that acquisition of many skills involves both learning how and learning when. For instance, certain previously acquired subroutines may be called forth in learning to ride a bicycle through modeling or instruction (e.g., "pump the pedals," "lean away from the way you're falling," "sit up straight"). But the child still will not know how to ride the bicycle until a relatively large number of routines are learned directly. What is needed, then, is a vocabulary for apportioning a new skill into that part that can be constructed from subskills the learner already possesses and that part that requires the acquisition of new elements. We will call the former, *accustomed* elements, and the latter, *novel* elements.

A procedure for dividing a to-be-learned skill into accustomed and novel parts might go something like this. First, a task analysis would be conducted to identify the major components of the skill. Given some specification of the elements of the skill, the procedural test for accustomedness would be to determine which of those elements the child can already perform in the context of other tasks or as a result of simple instructions or modeling. The elements that the child cannot produce on such tests would need to be generated.

One reason this accustomed–novel analysis may be important is that it will tell us much about the difficulty of a particular skill for children of given ages or stages. If a task to be given to 5-year-olds is determined to consist of a large number of novel elements and few accustomed elements, we should not be sanguine about teaching it quickly or easily. When we find a skill that most children at a particular point in development do not have, and yet that is composed of elements most of which are accustomed for these children, relatively straightforward instruction is likely to be successful. As we conduct analyses of this type for varieties of tasks and varieties of children we learn more and more about the developmental process.

The distinction between accustomed and novel skills is superficially similar to Flavell's (1976; this volume) concept of *metacommunication,* which distinguishes between the act of communicating and cognitions about communication. A related distinction has been made by Ammon (this volume), who discusses *knowing how* (practical knowledge of a skill) versus *knowing about* (more theoretical knowledge). Knowing how, according to Ammon, can only be acquired through actual practice, whereas knowing about can be acquired through explanations. The accustomed–novel distinction is hierarchically subordinate to knowing about or metacognition. Novel skills and accustomed skills both refer to activities that the child needs to produce, but has not yet produced, in a communicative setting. When the child is successful in producing a novel or accustomed skill in the correct context, we might say that he *knows how,* in Ammon's term. Later, he might *know about.* Thus the logical sequence of development is from novel skill to accustomed skill to knowing how to knowing about (metacommunication).

Referential Communication Skills

The distinction between accustomed and novel components of skills is well fitted to current approaches to referential communication. Evaluative reviews of the communication literature that have appeared since 1975 (Asher, 1979; Glucksberg, Krauss, & Higgins, 1975; Shatz, 1978) have conceptualized communicative competence as consisting of a number of components or subskills rather than a single underlying factor such as role-taking ability. Glucksberg *et al.* (1975), for instance, suggest that production of informative messages includes at least a comparison component in which the speaker analyzes a set of stimuli to determine which attributes of a referent distinguish it from nonreferents, a listener component in which the speaker takes characteristics of the listener into account, and an evaluative component in which the speaker rejects incipient messages that would be uninformative and formulates alternatives.

A child may fail at communication if he lacks any of these component skills. Much recent research has been directed at determining the particular subskills at which the young child is deficient. Clearly, children often do take listener characteristics into account when producing messages (Maratsos, 1973; Meissner & Apthorp, 1976; Menig-Peterson, 1975; Shatz & Gelman, 1973). Of the two remaining critical subskills, stimulus comparison and message evaluation, the comparison component seems logically primary. That is, if a child is unable to identify a differentiating attribute of a referent, he will not be able to evaluate the quality of a message, because presumably evaluation occurs by comparing stimuli to determine if the message actually describes a differentiating attribute.

The child's comparison skills loom very large, then, when one considers the development of referential communication. The standard questions are: Does the child compare at all in the process of formulating messages? If so, how well does he compare? The purpose of this chapter is to apply the accustomed–novel distinction to a consideration of comparison skills. When the child fails to compare referents with nonreferents in formulating messages, does he have the requisite comparison skills but not know how to deploy them, that is, are these to-be-learned skills largely accustomed? Or, do comparison failures result from not knowing how to compare, that is, are these to-be-learned skills largely novel?

The Extent of Comparison Failure

Data on the extent of comparison failure in referential communication have been reviewed elsewhere (Asher, 1979; Asher & Wigfield, this volume), so the present coverage will be brief. The major evidence comes from manipulations of the difficulty of the comparisons that are required for an informative message. Asher and Parke (1975), for instance, using a Password type game, found that 7-year-olds were very poor at giving an effective clue for a word when it was paired with a highly similar word (e.g., *ocean*–river), but were virtually perfect when the referent word was paired with a dissimilar nonreferent (e.g., *ocean*–tree). Similar results indicating that poor communicators do not compare referent and nonreferents have also been found by Asher (1976) and Asher and Oden (1976).

The results from studies utilizing the similar–dissimilar word pairs are ambiguous, however, because children might in fact be comparing *ocean* with *river* but lack the precise vocabulary to produce a contrastive message. The vocabulary demands obviously would be greater in the similar word pair condition than in the dissimilar one. Unfortunately, it is not possible to compare the clues produced by children in the similar and dissimilar conditions because Asher and Parke (1975) used different referents for the two conditions.

Whitehurst and Sonnenschein (1978) investigated comparison failure in a task requiring 5-year-olds to describe for a listener and designated member of a pair of multidimensional triangles. Pretests showed that all children had the requisite vocabulary. The procedure involved varying the amount and type of dimensional variation in the triangle pairs across trials. In the simplest condition, the only variation was in the value of the relevant dimension of the referent. For instance, either a red triangle or a black triangle was the referent on each trial. In the most complex condition, both relevant and irrelevant dimensions varied across trials. The differentiating attribute was sometimes color, sometimes size, and sometimes pattern. Intermediate conditions of complexity had either fixed irrelevant dimensions with varying relevant dimensions or vice versa.

The results from this study were clear. Children produced a high level of informative messages in the simplest condition, basing their performance on a comparison of the referent with the nonreferent. However, the introduction of any between-trial variation, whether in the relevant dimensions, the irrelevant dimensions, or both, resulted in a complete breakdown of comparison.

A study using pictorial stimuli (Tenney & Apthorp, 1978) throws some light on the process underlying the poor performance of children in complex visual tasks. Children, ranging in age from 4 to 11 years, had to communicate to a listener about one of two dolls. The two dolls were located in separate houses and differed solely in one article of clothing. The dependent variable was whether the child looked in the nonreferent doll's house; and, if not, how many prompts were required to get the child to look. The results indicated that the children did not look at both the target and nontarget stimuli until age 11. These data, along with related research (Alvy, 1968; Ford & Olson, 1975; Garmiza & Anisfeld, 1976; Price & Shilkret, 1975; Whitehurst, 1976; Whitehurst & Merkur, 1977) suggest that young children's communicative deficiencies are due primarily to an inability to locate the differentiating characteristics of a referent when it is paired with similar nonreferents. If the child cannot detect distinctive features in related arrays of stimuli, then none of the other communication subskills can function either. That is, the child can hardly respond to listener characteristics by selecting the most listener-appropriate distinctive characteristics of a referent if he cannot detect the difference between distinctive and nondistinctive features. Similarly, the child cannot evaluate an incipient message and reject it if he is unable to perform the analysis required for such an evaluation.

It is this sort of conclusion—that children cannot do something because they do not do it—that demonstrates the need for the accustomed–novel distinction. Do young children fail at comparison activity in referential communication because they do not have comparison skills, or do they fail because they do not understand the relevance of deploying their comparison skills? Is stimulus comparison an accustomed skill which fails to generalize to referential communication, or is it a novel skill which will need to be freshly assembled? The data we have reviewed indicate that children do not compare stimuli before communicating; however, the data do not address the issue of whether they can compare.

The research presented in what follows begins with an attempt to determine whether comparison activity is a novel skill or whether it is an accustomed skill that the child fails to mobilize in a communication setting. An answer to this question leads to a series of studies in which children are trained to communicate based on the assumption that comparison is an accustomed skill. Finally, we will use the accustomed–novel distinction to integrate a variety of data on referential communication.

Comparison Skills: Accustomed or Novel?

The purpose of the first experiment was to ascertain whether young children know how to compare stimuli in order to isolate distinctive features for labeling or whether they lack this skill. In other words, is comparison an accustomed skill, one which young children do not know *when* to use, or is it a novel skill, one which they do not know *how* to use?

The subjects were 40 5-year-old kindergartners, evenly divided as to sex. These children received a sequence of 30 pairs of triangles; one triangle in each pair, the referent, was marked with a star above it. The triangles were constructed by combining the three two-valued dimensions of color, size, and pattern. Each pair of triangles differed on only one attribute while sharing the values of the other two attributes. (For a detailed description, see the complex-constant condition of Experiment 2 in Whitehurst & Sonnenschein, 1978). One third of the trials required a size discrimination, one third a pattern of discrimination, and one third a color discrimination.

Children were seen individually for one 20-minute session, which began with either communication or perceptual instructions. All children were told that they would be playing a game with the adult experimenter involving talking about triangles. Subjects in the communication group were told preceding each of the first five trials, "Tell me about the triangle with the star above it so that I will know which triangle you are talking about." Beginning with Trial 6, this instruction was shortened to "Tell me about it." The parallel instruction for the perceptual group was "Tell me how the triangle with the star above it looks different from the other triangle," which was shortened on Trial 6 to "How is it different?"

The results were analyzed via a two-way ANOVA. The first factor, a between subjects factor, was the type of instructions the child heard. The second factor, a within subjects factor, was the type of informative message given—contrastive or redundant. A contrastive message contains the minimal necessary to be informative (e.g., "The red one"), whereas a redundant message contains more than is minimally necessary to be informative (e.g., "The big red one"). The dependent variable was the number of informative messages that the child gave.

The children in the perceptual instructions group produced significantly more informative messages than the children in the communication group (73% versus 50%, $p < .01$). Children in the perceptual condition produced significantly more contrastives than children in the communication condition (70% versus 34%, $p < .001$). The reverse effect occurred for redundants, with more in the communication condition than in the perceptual condition (16% versus 3%, $p < .001$). In addition, there was a significant main effect for type of message, with more contrastive messages occurring than redundant messages (52% versus 19%, $p < .001$).

These results are dramatic in the context of the many previous studies suggesting that children of this age are unable to compare and contrast stimuli in a referential communication task of any complexity (Alvy, 1968; Asher & Parke, 1975; Ford & Olson, 1975; Price & Shilkret, 1975; Whitehurst, 1976; Whitehurst & Merkur, 1977; Whitehurst & Sonnenschein, 1978). The increase in contrastive messages under the instruction to "Tell how it is different" is very large. Our conclusion is that comparison activity is largely an accustomed rather than novel skill for 5-year-olds. Children of this age know how to compare, at least they know better than anyone expected, but they do not know when to compare. Specifically, they do not know that in a communication task (i.e., when you are describing something to someone), you describe how that thing is different from other things with which it might be confused. *The young child does not know that comparison is relevant to communication.*

Developing a Training Technique

In view of our conclusion that comparison is an accustomed skill, the next step was to attempt to teach children to compare stimuli when communicating. Experiment 2 was directed toward that goal. The study was also designed to assess the role of feedback and the nature of transfer to related communication tasks.

Sixty-four 5-year-old kindergartners were used as subjects. Three tasks were employed in this experiment. The first, or training task, was the same triangle description task employed in Experiment 1, but shortened from 30 to 20 trials. The second, or speaking transfer task, was a more complex 20-trial form of the training task, involving between-trial variation in irrelevant as well as relevant attributes (see the description for the complex-diverse task in Whitehurst & Sonnenschein, 1978). The third, or listening transfer task, was adopted from Ironsmith & Whitehurst (1978). In this task the child served as listener rather than speaker. The adult experimenter gave the child a series of 20 messages about four-item arrays of cartoon-like figures. Half of the messages were ambiguous, composed of a two-adjective description that referred to two of the four items in the array. The remaining messages were informative, composed of a two-adjective description of just one of the four items in the array. The child's task was to point to a button when a message described "more than one" and pick an object when the message described "just one."

Children were seen individually for one 30-minute session, which began with either communication instructions, as in Experiment 1, or communication plus perceptual instructions that went as follows: "Tell me about the triangle with the star above it so that I will know which triangle you are talking about. The way to do a good job of playing the game is to tell how the triangle is different." The stock phrase "Tell me about it" was then used to introduce subsequent trials for all subjects. A feedback variable was crossed with the instructional variable in a 2 × 2 design. Perceptual-feedback subjects received praise or reproof that emphasized the importance of describing distinctive features of the referent: "That's good; you told me how the triangle with the star above it was different from the other." Or, "That's wrong; you did not tell me how the triangle with the star above it was different from the other." The children were not given the opportunity after feedback to reformulate their messages. Children in the noncontingent social feedback group received a noncommital nod or "okay" following each trial.

Following these training trials, the subjects were introduced to the speaking transfer test with the instruction to play this new game in the same way they played the other one. No feedback occurred for any subjects in the speaking transfer test. The listening transfer test followed. Subjects were told that the object of the game was to tell when the experimenter had done a good or bad job of telling about the pictures; a good message described just one picture and a bad message described more than one. Children were to point to a button for bad messages and to the referent for good messages. There was no feedback for any subjects on the listening transfer task.

Performance on each of the three tasks was analyzed separately. There was a significant feedback effect on Task 1, with the perceptual feedback subjects doing better than the noncontingent social feedback subjects (79% versus 68% informative; $p < .025$). The perceptual groups produced more contrastive messages than the communication groups (45% versus 30%); this pattern was reversed for redundant messages (30% versus 42%). No significant differences among the groups were found in the speaking or listening transfer tasks, however.

The level of informative responding (83%) achieved by the communication instruction–perceptual feedback group was remarkably high—by far the highest level of informative message production shown by children in this age range on tasks of comparable difficulty (Whitehurst & Sonnenschein, 1978). Furthermore, the effect is unexpected in that communication instructions alone produced the lowest level of informative responding in previous research, but these same instructions combined with feedback stressing the importance of perceptual differences produced the highest level of informative responding here.

A third study was carried out to clarify the earlier results. The first purpose of Experiment 3 was to examine perceptual and communication instructions in combination with perceptual, communication, and noncontingent social feedback. A second issue addressed was the lack of transfer in Experiment 2. In Experiment 3, we used different sets of materials for the speaking transfer task and the training task. Hypothesizing that the lack of transfer to the listening task might be due to the reluctance of 5-year-olds to point out the mistakes of an adult speaker, we varied the age of the speaker factorially.

Sixty 5-year-old kindergartners were used as subjects, evenly divided as to sex. Three tasks were employed in this study. The training task was identical to that used in Experiment 2. The speaking transfer task consisted of pictures of everyday objects, two per trial, which differed on color, size, or pattern; there were 20 trials in all. The listening transfer task was the same as in Experiment 2, except that the messages were on tape. The speaker for half the children was another child; the remaining children heard an adult speaker. The children saw a picture of either a female child or a female adult.

The design was a 2 (instructions) × 3 (feedback) ANOVA. Children received either perceptual or communication instructions, as in Experiment 2. Children in the social and perceptual feedback groups received instructions as in Experiment 2, whereas children in the communication feedback group were told: "That's good; you told about the triangle with the star above it so that I knew which one you were talking about" on correct trials and "That's wrong; you did not . . ." on incorrect trials. The instructions for the speaking and listening transfer tasks were identical to those for Experiment 2 except for an additional explanation of the taped messages for the listening task in this experiment.

In general, the results replicate and clarify the findings from Experiment 2 (see Table 6.1). The most effective condition on the training task was the combination of communication instructions and perceptual feedback (83% informative messages). A priori contrasts revealed that this group performed significantly better than the other groups combined ($p < .05$). The group also performed significantly better than the communication–noncontingent social feedback group ($p < .05$) and the perceptual–noncontingent social feedback group ($p < .05$), and tended to perform better than the communication–communication feedback groups ($p < .10$). These results generalized to the novel speaking task with the communication instructions with perceptual feedback group again being superior in performance. In general, no meaningful positive transfer between the speaking training and the listening task was observed.

TABLE 6.1
Percentage of Informative Responding on Speaker Tasks for Experiment 3 [a]

| | Instructional Group | | | | | |
| | Communication | | | Perceptual | | |
Feedback	Contrastive	Redundant	Total	Contrastive	Redundant	Total
			Training task			
Social	36	31	67	38	26	64
Communication	36	33	69	59	15	74
Perceptual	47	36	83	46	29	75
			Transfer task			
Social	42	15	57	52	10	62
Communication	58	16	74	68	9	77
Perceptual	67	26	93	69	16	85

[a] The instructional and feedback groups refer to which type of training the child received on the training task.

These results demonstrate that there is something critical about the particular content of instructions and feedback given to the child. Over several tasks, communication instructions telling the child that he must describe something so that the other person can tell which thing he is talking about, coupled with perceptual feedback that tells the child he has or has not described a difference between stimuli, has emerged as the most potent instructional technique. The results over all three experiments suggest that the most important factor is telling the child that he should describe perceptual differences.

Our fourth study examined the precise role of the content of the feedback. All of the comparisons had been between noncontingent social feedback and a detailed feedback statement stressing either perceptual or communication rules. This experiment compared simple corrective statements with the more elaborated perceptual feedback in order to ascertain whether the content of the feedback statement was in fact important.

Thirty 5-year-old kindergartners were used as subjects. The standard training task from the previous experiments was employed. All subjects received communication instructions as described in previous experiments. Ten subjects received perceptual feedback as previously described; 10 subjects received noncontingent social feedback as previously described; and 10 subjects got simple corrective feedback: "That's good" on correct trials, and "That's wrong" on incorrect trials. The children were not allowed to reformulate their messages after feedback.

The feedback effect was significant ($p < 0.25$). The perceptual feedback group (81%) did significantly better than the simple feedback (62%) or noncontingent social feedback (53%) groups, which did not differ between themselves. There was also no difference between the simple feedback group and the communication feedback group (69%) from Experiment 3.

Clearly the content of the feedback is critical in teaching children to describe distinctive differences. Perceptual feedback is more effective than noncontingent social, simple, or communication feedback, which do not differ in their effects. Apparently, if we want children to describe differences between stimuli, we must give them feedback telling them when they have or have not described differences.

Transfer of Training

We have developed a technique for teaching referential communication skills to young children; however, it is important to show that its effectiveness is not limited to the particular materials on which the training occurred or to a particular age group. Our fifth experiment was concerned with these two questions. Twenty 5-year-old kindergartners and 20 4-year-olds enrolled in summer camp were used as subjects. The training task using triangles and the speaking transfer task using pictures of common objects were employed in the same form as described in Experiment 3. Training occurred using two conditions, the communication instructions–perceptual feedback procedure and the communication instructions–noncontingent social feedback procedure. Subjects were exposed to one of these procedures on the 20 trials of the training task in Experiment 3. One week later, the children were brought back and tested on the speaking transfer task. Each child was told that the game would be like the one played before and that the child should do what he or she was doing before.

The communication instructions–perceptual feedback group performed significantly better than the communication instructions–noncontingent social feedback group for both the 5-year-olds (84% versus 51%) and the 4-year-olds (55% versus 36%). These differences tended to remain significant when the children were tested 1 week later, for both the 5-year-olds (83% versus 60%) and the 4-year-olds (54% versus 25%). These results show that the training procedures work with 4- and 5-year-old children, that they transfer to a different task, and that the effects endure at least 1 week. Interestingly, the communication–perceptual feedback condition appears to have resulted in more contrastive messages and fewer redundant messages in the 5-year-old group (66% versus 17%) and the reverse pattern in the 4-year-old group (7% versus 47%). The predominance of redundant messages with the 4-year-old group is consistent with previous research (Whitehurst, 1976; Whitehurst & Merkur, 1977), if we assume that the task was more difficult for the younger group.

When to Compare: A Novel Skill

Our purpose when we started this series of experiments was to determine whether comparison skills are accustomed or novel for 5-year-olds. The data indicate that young children can compare but often fail to do so and consequently are ineffective communicators. Hence, knowing how to compare is an accustomed skill for young children. By using a training program that stressed mentioning differentiating features, we successfully trained children to become more effective speakers. However, knowing what to do as a speaker did not generalize to adequate performance as listener.

Experiments 2 and 3 had sought evidence of transfer of training from a speaking task to a listening task, but little consistent evidence of transfer was found. The purpose of this experiment was to use a more direct method of measuring speaking-to-listening transfer in order to assess the degree to which knowing when to compare is a novel skill. The listening transfer task in Experiments 2 and 3 was quite different from the speaking training task.

In order to test whether the lack of transfer was due to the listening task differing considerably from the speaking task, a sixth experiment involved training on the triangle speaking task followed immediately by a listening transfer test on that same task. Twenty 5-year-old kindergartners were used as subjects. The training task was identical to that used in Experiments 2–5. The listening task involved 20 trials using the same stimuli as the training task, with half informative and half ambiguous messages. Training occurred with communication instructions–perceptual feedback and communication instructions–noncontingent social feedback procedures. The listening transfer task followed immediately, with no feedback.

The training effects replicated: The perceptual feedback group was more informative than the social feedback group (81% versus 53% of the trials). The feedback variable did not produce a significant effect on the listening task, but there was a significant feedback condition times message type interaction, caused by the fact that the subjects who had received the perceptual feedback training were much worse at identifying ambiguous messages than the social feedback subjects (20% versus 71%, $p < .005$).

These findings are curious. Something about the effective perceptual feedback training on the speaking task inhibits the children's ability to detect ambiguous messages on the listening task. One would think that a child who has learned that a good message describes a difference would recognize a bad message as one that does not. Apparently the limits of knowing when to compare are narrow. That a child has learned to utilize comparison skills when producing messages does not necessarily mean the child will utilize these skills correctly when responding to messages. In fact, several of the children who had received training commented on their ability to detect differences: They always managed to find differences between the stimuli. Unfortunately, 50% of the time the detected differences were imaginary! In other words, the children were responding as if they believed that if a good message mentions differences between stimuli, then one can make a message good by finding differences between the stimuli.

Final Discussion

This chapter began with a consideration of two types of skill deficit. A not-yet-learned skill that can be assembled from components that have been exercised elsewhere in the subject's behavioral repertoire was termed an *accustomed* skill. A skill that consists of components that the child has not mastered in any context was termed a *novel* skill. Skills consisting of many components might be represented for a given child or group of children by a ratio of accustomed to novel elements.

Referential communication deficits for young children have been thought to be due largely to failures in the process of comparing referents with nonreferents to extract distinctive differences. Research varying the complexity of perceptual arrays (e.g., Whitehurst & Sonnenschein, 1978) had suggested that complex perceptual comparison might be a novel skill for preschoolers, setting limits on the informativeness of their communication.

The present series of studies shows this conclusion to be in error: Children in the 4–5 age range are capable of high levels of comparison activity on relatively complex tasks. Instructions to describe differences result in very high levels of informative messages.

This is an important theoretical point. One way to approach the process of referential communication theoretically is to specify the essence of the communication skill. Much recent debate, as for example between egocentrism and componential theories (cf. Glucksberg *et al.*, 1975), has revolved around this issue of what the child is doing when he communicates effectively and what he does not know when he fails at communication. The present research offers an answer to this question, which, if it is not the only answer, is at least an important answer: *The young child does not know that to communicate referentially is to describe differences.* He may sometimes describe differences, particularly if the differences are perceptually salient (Whitehurst & Sonnenschein, 1978), he knows how to describe differences, but he does not deliberately describe differences. In other words, for referential communication tasks, comparison activity is an accustomed skill for the young child.

Comparison skills may account for deficits in children's listener skills as they do for speaking skills. A number of studies have shown that young listeners do not ask questions when given ambiguous messages (see Patterson & Kister, this volume). The fact that modeling and instructions have resulted in strong and immediate improvements in listeners' questions when confronted with ambiguous messages suggests that listeners know how to compare but fail to do so. As our procedural test for accustomed skills is that they can be acquired through modeling or instructions rather than laborious practice, the success of these methods suggests that listening failures are due to a deficiency in mobilizing existing comparison skills. Similarly, Robinson and Robinson (reviewed in Robinson, this volume) have shown that feedback training that focused on the importance of describing differences between stimuli resulted in a significant increase in the likelihood that children would blame speakers rather than listeners for the consequences of ambiguous messages. Evaluation skills, like listening skills and speaking skills, seem to develop as a result of learning that effective messages describe differences.

The conclusions from all this research are consistent in pointing toward a deficiency in the young child's knowledge of the relevance of stimulus comparison for referential communication and toward the possibility of ameliorating this deficit through straightforward modeling and instructional interventions. However, the confusing and counterintuitive pattern of transfer between speaking training and listening tests suggests that investigators need to exercise caution in interpreting the breadth of the learning that has been induced through training. Children who do not know the relevance of comparison for any communication task are unlikely to induce a general rule on the basis of training on a limited set of tasks. Those interested in practical training procedures will have to induce comparison activity on speaking tasks, listening tasks, and evaluation tasks of varying content and complexity.

Acknowledgements

Some of the research reported herein was supported by Special Project Grant # 974 NP from the Suffolk County Department of Labor to Early Intellective Development, Inc. The authors wish to thank Barbara Foorman and Scott Paris for their helpful comments on an earlier draft of this chapter. Portions of this chapter were presented at the meetings of the Society for Research in Child Development, San Francisco, March 1979.

References

Alvy, K. T. Relation of age to children's egocentric and cooperative communication. *Journal of Genetic Psychology,* 1968, *112,* 275–286.

Asher, S. R. Children's ability to appraise their own and another person's communication performance. *Developmental Psychology,* 1976, *12,* 24–32.

Asher, S. R. Referential communication. In G. J. Whitehurst & B. J. Zimmerman (Eds.), *The functions of language and cognition.* New York: Academic Press, 1979.

Asher, S. R., & Oden, S. L. Children's failure to communicate: An assessment of comparison and egocentrism explanations. *Developmental Psychology,* 1976, *12,* 132–139.

Asher, S. R., & Parke, R. D. Influence of sampling and comparison processes on the development of communication effectiveness. *Journal of Educational Psychology,* 1975, *67,* 69–75.

Flavell, J. *The development of meta-communication.* Paper presented at the Symposium on Language and Cognition, Twenty-first International Congress of Psychology, Paris, July 1976.

Ford, W., & Olson, D. The elaboration of the noun phrase in children's description of objects. *Journal of Experimental Child Psychology,* 1975, *19,* 371–382.

Garmiza, C., & Anisfeld, M. Factors reducing the efficiency of referent communication in children. *Merrill-Palmer Quarterly,* 1976, *22,* 125–136.

Glucksberg, S., Krauss, R. M., & Higgins, E. T. The development of referential communication skills. In F. D. Horowitz (Ed.), *Review of child development research* (Vol. 4). Chicago: University of Chicago Press, 1975.

Ironsmith, M., & Whitehurst, G. J. The development of listener abilities in communication: How children deal with ambiguous information. *Child Development,* 1978, *49,* 348–352.

Maratsos, M. P. Nonegocentric communication abilities in preschool children. *Child Development,* 1973, *44,* 697–701.

Meissner, J. A., & Apthorp, H. Nonegocentric and communication mode switching in black preschool children. *Developmental Psychology,* 1976, *12,* 245–249.

Menig-Peterson, C. L. The modification of communicative behavior in preschool-aged children as a function of the listener's perspective. *Child Development,* 1975, *46,* 1015–1018.

Price, S., & Shilkret, R. B. *An interactionist view of the development of communication efficiency: Referential communication as a function of the interaction of age and task variables.* Paper presented at Fifth Annual Symposium of the Jean Piaget Society, 1975.

Robinson, E. J., & Robinson, W. P. The roles of egocentrism and of weakness in comparing in children's explanations of communicative failure. *Journal of Experimental Child Psychology,* 1978, *26,* 147–160.

Shatz, M. The relationship between cognitive processes and the development of communication skills. In B. Keasey (Ed.), *Nebraska Symposium on Motivation, 1977* (Vol. 25). Lincoln: University of Nebraska Press, 1978.

Shatz, M., Gelman, R. The development of communication skills: Modifications in the speech of young children as a function of the listener. *Monographs of the Society for Research in Child Development,* 1973, *38,* (5, Serial No. 152).

Tenney, Y. J., & Apthorp, H. *The development of knowledge about distinctive features and referential messages in children.* Unpublished manuscript, Harvard University, 1978.

Whitehurst, G. J. The development of communication: Changes with age and modeling. *Child Development,* 1976, *47,* 473–482.

Whitehurst, G. J., & Merkur, A. The development of communication: Modeling and contrast failure. *Child Development,* 1977, *48,* 993–1001.

Whitehurst, G. J., & Sonnenschein, S. The development of communication: Attribute variation leads to contrast failure. *Journal of Experimental Child Psychology,* 1978, *25,* 454–490.

7

The Development of Listener Skills for Referential Communication

CHARLOTTE J. PATTERSON AND MARY C. KISTER

Development of the ability to communicate effectively by means of the spoken word is certainly one of the momentous achievements of childhood. A great deal of information about children's communication skills and their development has been generated using the referential communication paradigm developed by Glucksberg and Krauss (Glucksberg & Krauss, 1967; Glucksberg, Krauss & Higgins, 1975; Glucksberg, Krauss & Weisberg, 1966; Krauss & Glucksberg, 1969). In this paradigm, one person (the speaker) is asked to describe a referent object or picture so that another person (the listener) can select that target referent from a group of potential referents on the basis of the speaker's verbal message. The number of correct referent choices made by the listener provides a measure of the pair's communicative success or accuracy. Studies using this paradigm have consistently found that communication of information between preschool children is often quite ineffective, and that accuracy of communication improves gradually over the elementary school years (Glucksberg *et al.*, 1975; Krauss & Glucksberg, 1969).

In an effort to uncover the causes of young children's communication

143

Copyright © 1981 by Academic Press, Inc.
ISBN 0-12-215450-9

failures, investigators sought to evaluate the relative responsibility of the speaker versus the listener. Results of early studies (Glucksberg *et al.*, 1966; Krauss & Glucksberg, 1969) led to the view that, although listener skill might show some improvement during childhood, even young children are relatively effective in this role. Hence, the major sources of children's communication failures were thought to lie in the inadequacies of messages produced by young speakers (Glucksberg *et al.*, 1975, p. 331).

In this chapter, we present the view that a number of listener skills are relatively poorly developed in preschool children, and that these skills show considerable improvement over the elementary school years. We review the results of recent research that demonstrate development in the ability to assess message adequacy, in the knowledge that message quality affects communicative performances, and in the ability to respond appropriately to both informative and uninformative messages. Evidence is also reviewed to show that at least some of these skills are susceptible to training in school-aged children, and that such training of listeners facilitates children's communicative performances. In light of these data, a reassessment is made of the listener's role in children's referential communication: Listener behavior is viewed as influential in determining communicative success, particularly among young children. Overall, recent findings on the development of listener skills point to the importance of viewing referential communication as an interactive process.

Children as Listeners: Early Studies

The idea that inadequate speaker performances are the primary cause of the frequently observed failures of communication among young children arose in part from the results of a series of studies conducted by Glucksberg and Krauss. In the first of these studies (Glucksberg *et al.*, 1966), preschool children were asked to play the role of the listener. An adult confederate served as the speaker and produced messages that had been independently judged as sufficient to permit identification of the target referent on each trial. The children performed very well under these circumstances, choosing the correct referent on the great majority of trials. However, performance deteriorated when the adult was replaced by a same-aged peer who produced spontaneous messages.

In a second study (Krauss & Glucksberg, 1969), adult "listeners" (the messages were actually conveyed in writing) were given messages formulated by speakers of different ages, and were asked to identify the target referent from a group of potential referents on the basis of each message. Consistent with the earlier findings, these adult "listeners" made more correct choices in response to the messages of older (e.g., third- and fifth-grade) as compared to younger (e.g., kindergarten and first-grade) subjects.

In a further unpublished study (described in Glucksberg *et al.*, 1975 and in Krauss & Glucksberg, 1969), the ages of both speaker and listener were systematically varied, and communication accuracy in the resulting pairs was assessed. Both speakers' and listeners' ages were related to the success of communication, but the age of the speaker was a much better predictor than the age of the listener. These findings led the authors to conclude that although both the ages of the speaker and the listener are "likely to be associated with overall dyad performance, the proportion of variance attributable to the speaker role [is] by far the greater of the two [Glucksberg *et al.*, 1975, p. 318]."

The image of the listener emerging from these studies, then, was that of a passive recipient whose main task was to make use of the information contained in the speaker's message. Although the ability to do this appeared in these and other studies to exhibit developmental trends (Glucksberg *et al.*, 1966, 1975; Maccoby, 1967, 1969; Maccoby & Konrad, 1966), even preschool and kindergarten children were relatively successful at the task in the referential communication setting. As listener ability appeared to be fairly well developed early in childhood, the major causes of children's communication failures were thought to be children's deficiencies in the speaker role.

Children as Listeners: A Reassessment

The Glucksberg and Krauss studies explored the role of one major kind of listener skill—the ability to make effective use of information in the speaker's message—and the picture of listener competence that resulted was largely limited to the exercise of that skill. More recently, however, other kinds of listener skills have been investigated, and a number of developmental trends have been noted with respect to these skills. When these data are considered, a broader conception of listener competence and of the importance of the listener role in children's referential communication emerges.

In their review of the literature on children's referential communication, Glucksberg and his colleagues remarked that there were at least three things that listeners could do that might improve communication performances:

> First, they can judge or estimate their confidence or certainty of understanding. That is, they can recognize ambiguous or noninformative messages as such. Second, if they recognize that a message or communication is inadequate, they can make this known to the speaker. Finally, they can specify the additional information that is needed in order to clarify the message [Glucksberg *et al.*, 1975, p. 331].

Although they were able to find little evidence at the time concerning children's abilities to perform these activities, subsequent research has explored these suggestions in some detail. The evidence will be considered under four major headings: assessment of message quality, knowledge that message quality affects communicative success, responses to adequate messages, and responses to inadequate messages.

Assessment of Message Quality

One factor that may influence children's listener performances is their ability to recognize when a message is ambiguous or uninformative.[1] This ability involves what Asher (1976) has called "comparison processes." In order to decide whether or not a message is adequate to allow identification of the target referent, the listener must compare the information in the message with the characteristics of the set of potential referents. The evidence suggests that younger children are generally less successful at this task than older ones.

Flavell, Botkin, Fry, Wright, and Jarvis (1968) reported one of the first studies of this ability. Third-, seventh-, and eleventh-graders were asked to report inadequacies in a set of directions for getting from one location to another on a map. Third-graders were notably unsuccessful in this regard, reporting on the average only one in four of the ambiguities in the directions. Performance improved markedly over the age range studied, with seventh- and eleventh-graders detecting more than twice as many errors as third-graders. The difficulty of the task is suggested by the fact that even the eleventh-graders reported fewer than 75% of the inadequacies in the directions.

In another study (Asher, 1976), second-, fourth-, and sixth-grade children were asked to judge the adequacy of a number of messages in a Password game. Younger children were less successful than older children in identifying adequate and inadequate messages, regardless of whether they themselves had generated the messages or whether another child had done so. At every age, appraisal of poor messages was significantly less accurate than appraisal of good messages. At the second-grade level, children recognized an average of four out of six adequate messages, but only one or two of the six inadequate ones. By sixth grade, while almost all children recognized adequate messages as such, they still appraised roughly a third of the ambiguous messages incorrectly.

[1] In this chapter, we use the terms "adequate message" and "informative message" interchangeably, and as opposites of the term "ambiguous message." In the referential contexts we consider here, an informative message has only one referent, whereas an ambiguous message has more than one. Moreover, in these contexts, an informative message is almost always understood as such by the listener—i.e., it is adequate to allow successful communication. We recognize that in other referential contexts, "informative" messages can at times be misunderstood as a result of difficulties in what are called lexical, syntactic, or pragmatic aspects of comprehension; however, these are not our main interest here.

Bearison and Levey (1977) also found younger children less able than older ones to distinguish adequate from ambiguous messages. An experimenter read sentences to kindergarten, second-, and fourth-graders, and asked the children to respond to questions about the sentences. The questions contained pronouns that were either clear or ambiguous in their reference to the sentences. The children were asked to indicate whether the questions were "good" or "bad." All of the children recognized adequate or "good" questions with relatively little difficulty. However, consistent with Asher's (1976) findings, younger children were much less successful in identifying ambiguous questions than older children. Whereas kindergartners correctly identified only one or two of the six ambiguous questions, fourth-graders were nearly perfect in their recognition of question ambiguity.

These studies, using a variety of experimental tasks, support three generalizations about the research on children's message appraisal skills. First, across a range of ages, materials, and procedures, age trends are consistently reported. Second, and perhaps more striking, the level of performance reported for any given age group varies markedly over studies by different investigators. Third, inadequate messages appear consistently more difficult to recognize than adequate ones, across all of the ages studied. These generalizations are remarkably well supported by other studies (Markman, 1977 and this volume; Meissner, 1978; Patterson, O'Brien, Kister, Carter, & Kotsonis, 1980; Robinson & Robinson, 1976a, 1976b, 1977a, 1977b).[2]

Part of the explanation for variations across studies in performance at any particular age level is almost certainly to be found in the variations in materials and procedures employed by different investigators. A number of such factors, including degree of message inadequacy, salience of the outcome of a communicative episode, size and clarity of the array of potential referents, instructional set, and response mode, appear to influence the success with which children respond to message inadequacy. We will consider the evidence regarding each of these factors in turn.

Although it seems clear that children correctly appraise adequate messages earlier than inadequate ones, it has been more difficult to establish exactly how the degree of message inadequacy affects these judgments. Robinson and Robinson (1977a), in their initial study of this issue, asked children to play a referential communication game with an adult; when communication failed, the children were asked to ascribe blame to either the speaker or the listener. Using this "whose fault" technique with 5-, 6-, and 7-year-old children, the Robinsons found no relationship between degree of

---

[2] The one apparent exception to the first generalization is a study by Meissner (1978), in which kindergartners were significantly better than second-graders at identifying poor messages that they themselves had produced as speakers in a standard referential communication setting. However, this study employed no control for message quality across ages; hence, it seems likely that kindergartners were more accurate in their judgements because their messages were more obviously inadequate than those of the older children.

message inadequacy (messages referred to one, two, or four of the potential referents) and tendency to blame the speaker; most of these children blamed the listener, regardless of the degree of message inadequacy. They interpreted these findings to mean that "very young children do not have a rudimentary idea of the role of the message in communication failure [Robinson & Robinson, 1977a, p. 161]."

In a subsequent study using the "whose-fault" technique, however, these investigators (Robinson & Robinson, 1977b) presented 6-year-olds with messages which were either informative, ambiguous (referring to two potential referents), or inappropriate (referring uniquely to a card other than the target referent). Children who blamed the listener for communication failures when the message was ambiguous nevertheless blamed the speaker when the message was inappropriate. Thus, 6-year olds evidenced some ability to detect poor messages, but only under conditions of extreme inadequacy.

Patterson, O'Brien, Kister, Carter, and Kotsonis (1980) also studied message appraisal skills in kindergarten, second-, and fourth-grade children. Children played the role of the listener in a standard referential communication situation. The speaker gave messages that referred to one, two, or four potential referents, and the child was asked if he or she knew the identity of the target referent or needed another clue in order to choose correctly. The likelihood of judging a message as inadequate increased markedly with increasing message ambiguity; correct appraisal of ambiguous messages was easier when the messages were highly inadequate.

The degree to which the outcome of a communicative episode is salient to the child also appears to affect message appraisals at the point when children are beginning to understand the role of the message. Robinson and Robinson (1977a) asked children between the ages of 6½ and 8 to judge the adequacy of a number of messages, and found that, at the younger end of this age range, many children's judgments about message adequacy–inadequacy were based on the outcome of the episode. Thus, an ambiguous message that nevertheless led to communication success (e.g., by chance) was more likely to be judged adequate than the same message when it resulted in failure. Older children, of course, blamed the speaker for inadequate messages, even when the listener chose the correct card. This result was confirmed in a later study (Robinson & Robinson, 1977b). These findings are reminiscent of young children's outcome-centered judgments in other domains (Miscione, Marvin, O'Brien, & Greenberg, 1978; Piaget, 1932/1965), and indicate that communicative outcomes may often provide cues that mislead these children in their efforts to appraise message quality.

Another factor that almost certainly affects children's message appraisal performances is the size and clarity of the array of potential referents. How many nonreferents must the target referent be distinguished from? How obvious is it to the child exactly what the array of nonreferents consists of?

Studies that have yielded relatively low age norms for the development of message appraisal skills (e.g., Bearison & Levey, 1977; Patterson, O'Brien, Kister, Carter, & Kotsonis, 1980) have generally employed quite simple, clear arrays of potential referents. For example, in the Bearison and Levey study, there were only two potential referents and their identity was established by the experimenter. Patterson and her colleagues varied the size of the array and found that children performed more effectively with small arrays of potential referents than with large ones. On the other hand, studies yielding higher age norms for the emergence of these skills (e.g., Flavell *et al.*, 1968; Markman, 1977) employed far more complex paradigms, in terms of both the number of potential referents and the clarity with which the array of potential referents was specified for the child. The actual size of the nonreferent array would seem to be potentially separable from whether or not the array of potential referents has been clearly set out by the experimenter or whether subjects must construct it for themselves. Both factors seem likely to affect message appraisal performance.

Markman (1977) has shown that the instructions a child receives can also affect message appraisal performance. She presented first- and third-graders with directions for performing a task. The directions were inadequate in that they omitted information that was crucial to successful task performance. She then queried the children concerning the adequacy of the directions and their ability to perform the task based on the directions they had heard. Whereas third-graders generally recognized message inadequacy after hearing the directions, first-graders had to be instructed to enact the directions or to watch a demonstration before they gave any indication of recognizing message inadequacy. Markman (1977) argued that young children's insensitivity to message inadequacy is due to their relative lack of constructive processing of the message. She argued that because the enactment or demonstration of the task reduce the demand for such processing, the young child is better able to recognize difficulties in the message under these conditions.

An additional factor that affects assessments of children's message appraisal skills is the response mode chosen for study. In particular, whereas most investigators have studied only verbal responses to variations in message quality, a few have also included nonverbal measures. One such study, reported by Bearison and Levey (1977), has already been described in part. Although only the oldest children in that study gave appropriate verbal responses to message ambiguity on a consistent basis, even the youngest subjects (kindergartners) showed significantly longer reaction times on the ambiguous, as compared to the unambiguous, trials. Thus, although these kindergartners rarely gave verbal responses that would indicate discrimination of message types, their nonverbal behavior varied quite consistently with message adequacy.

Patterson, Cosgrove, and O'Brien (1980) also studied nonverbal responses to message ambiguity. In this study, 4-, 6-, 8-, and 10-year-olds served as listeners in a standard referential communication task. An adult speaker produced messages that were informative or ambiguous. Although the 4-year-olds' verbal responses did not vary across message types, analyses of videotape records revealed that children at each of the four ages exhibited markedly different nonverbal behavior on informative as compared to ambiguous message trials. Children at all ages showed more hand movement over the page of potential referents and longer reaction times when messages were uninformative. Preschoolers made more eye contact with the speaker when the message was uninformative, but their amount of body movement was unaffected; the reverse was true for older children.

The fact that young children who did not show different verbal responses as a function of message type responded discriminatively in their nonverbal behavior indicates that at some level they must have identified these messages as differing in some respect. Exactly what degree of awareness concerning their own level of comprehension these children possess, however, remains uncertain. In general, the findings suggest that nonverbal measures may provide particularly sensitive indicators of the early emergence of message appraisal skills. However, further research will be required in order to understand how these nonverbal responses are transformed over the course of childhood into the complex verbal monitoring skills discussed elsewhere in this chapter.

Thus, several points emerge from the literature on children's appraisals of message adequacy. Appraisal of adequate messages seems to be more accurate across a range of ages than appraisal of inadequate messages. Older children are clearly more effective than younger ones in assessing message quality in a variety of situations; however, different studies suggest different age norms for the development of these skills. A number of factors, including degree of message inadequacy, salience of the outcome of a communicative episode, size and clarity of the array of potential referents, instructional set, and response mode all appear to affect children's assessments of message adequacy. It seems likely that variations in factors such as these may be responsible for the variations in age norms suggested by different studies in the literature.

Knowledge That Message Quality Affects Communicative Success

Another factor that may affect listener performance is a listener's recognition (or lack of recognition) that the quality of a speaker's message can affect communicative accuracy. Listeners' knowledge about the role of the message in communication might affect their communicative performances in a number of ways. For example, having judged a message as inadequate, children might still be unlikely to request additional information or to blame the speaker unless they understand that poor messages can lead to communication failure. Indeed, children who are unaware of the role of the message might, whether through inability or disinclination, fail to complete the relevant comparisons to ascertain that a message is inadequate.

Consistent with the idea that children who blame the listener for communication failure may be unaware of the influence of the message on communicative success, Robinson and Robinson (1978b) reasoned that these "listener blamers" should be unable as speakers to produce good and bad messages upon request. Failing to understand the role of the message, these children should also find problematic the concept of modifying the difficulty of a communication task by altering the message, and consequently should perform poorly on a message alteration task. Confirming these expectations, the Robinsons' results showed that children who blamed the speaker for communication failures in the "whose-fault" situation were significantly more successful than listener blamers in producing good and bad messages at will. Results of the early Robinson and Robinson (1976a, 1976b, 1977a) studies may also be interpreted as consistent with the idea that children only gradually acquire an understanding of the role of the message in communication.

In another study, the Robinsons (1977b) showed that young children who blamed the listener for communication failures when messages were ambiguous blamed the speaker when messages were inappropriate. The fact that the children performed more effectively with the inappropriate messages (which are presumably easier to appraise as inadequate) might suggest that children's difficulty in the ambiguous message condition was indeed with completion of the comparison activities necessary for accurate message appraisal, rather than with understanding the role of the message. On the other hand, the young child's concept of message adequacy might be limited to an understanding that the message must refer to the referent but might not yet include the idea that the message should refer *exclusively* to the referent. If this were the case, the ambiguous message would have been viewed as adequate, because it would meet the child's criterion for adequacy, whereas the inappropriate message would have been viewed as inadequate, because it would not (Robinson & Robinson, 1977b).

Results of another series of studies by the Robinsons (1978a) also suggest the importance of the child's knowledge about the role of the message. In these studies, a number of younger children were able to note and describe ambiguities in a speaker's message yet still blamed the listener for communication failures. Although these children were aware of message ambiguity, they did not suggest alterations in the message as a method of improving communication, and could not think of any justification for the suggestion that the speaker might deserve blame for communication failures. In further studies, it was established that these children possessed the relevant comparison skills, yet did not apply them in making judgments about the causes of communication failure (Robinson & Robinson, 1978a, 1978c).

Robinson and Robinson (1978a) also proposed that in order to recognize that an inadequate message may be a cause of communication failure, the child must appreciate the concept of distal causation. In the context of referential communication failure, the listener's response is the closest in time and space to the outcome; it is the proximal cause. The speaker's message, on the other hand, is more removed or distant; it is the distal cause. If the child fails to understand distal causation in general, then he or she might also fail to recognize that the speaker's message could be a cause of communication problems. To test this notion, the Robinsons (1978a) compared children's ascriptions of cause (proximal versus distal) in communication- and noncommunication-related contexts. As predicted, children who blamed the listener in the communication failure situation were also more likely to ascribe blame to proximal causes in noncommunication situations.

It appears, then, that completing relevant comparison activities for message appraisal and understanding that message quality affects communication accuracy are distinct abilities. Understanding the role of messages in communication may, in turn, involve the ability to appreciate distal causation. In some children, acquisition of comparison abilities appears to precede knowledge about the role of the message; in others, this order may be reversed (Robinson & Robinson, 1978a). In any case, recognition of the role of the message is clearly an important listener ability that undergoes considerable change during childhood.

Verbal Responses to Adequate Messages

Given that a child can distinguish an adequate from an inadequate message, and that he or she understands the role of the message, it still remains for the child to provide an adequate response. Although most referential communication paradigms do not require that the listener give a verbal response to an adequate message, explicit verification of message adequacy can indicate to the speaker that further elaboration is unnecessary. This might serve to minimize redundancy and to maximize the efficiency with which accurate communication takes place. Thus, although a nonverbal response to an adequate message is generally acceptable, verbal confirmation might often facilitate communication efficiency. In examining the naturally occurring conversations of different age groups, Dittman (1972) found clear age trends in the tendency to give such verbal confirmations. Although confirmations were rare in the conversations of elementary-school children, their frequency increased gradually with the age of the subjects.

Karabenick and Miller (1977) observed the occurrence of confirmations during referential communication among pairs of 5-, 6-, and 7-year-olds.

Confirmations were relatively infrequent overall, and no age effects were reported within this narrow age range. As one might expect from the results of research reviewed in the preceding sections, over half of the confirmations occurred following an ambiguous message from the speaker. Thus, the meager evidence suggests that young children rarely employ explicit verbal confirmations of adequate messages, and that they are likely to employ them inappropriately. A more adequate understanding of the developmental trends in the use of confirmations and their functions in the communication setting must await further research.

Verbal Responses to Inadequate Messages

Although verbal responses to adequate messages are not necessary in order to achieve accurate communication, a verbal response may be essential to the success of communication when the speaker's messages are ambiguous. Having determined that a message is inadequate, the listener should indicate this fact to the speaker and, if possible, specify the missing information. Certainly, studies of adult subjects in the listener role (Krauss & Weinheimer, 1966) show that they typically provide both such types of feedback in response to ambiguous messages.

In the Glucksberg–Krauss studies, however, "children . . . said very little as listeners [Glucksberg et al., 1975, p. 331]." Alvy (1968) studied communication between 6-, 8-, and 11-year-olds in same-age pairs, and found that 6-year-olds made fewer requests for clarification of speakers' messages than did older children. Dickson (1974) also reported that older children asked more questions in the listener role than younger children. In contrast, Karabenick and Miller (1977) found no clear age trends in number of listener requests for more information.

Some difficulty is experienced in the interpretation of these findings. In each case, children were asked to respond either to fully adequate messages formulated by an adult speaker (as in Glucksberg et al., 1966) or to spontaneous messages of varying informational adequacy produced by same-aged speakers (Alvy, 1968; Dickson, 1974; Karabenick & Miller, 1977). In the former situation, children may say very little because they have already been provided with all of the information that they need. In the latter situation, any differences in the listeners' behavior as a function of age would be difficult to interpret, as they would be responding to speakers the adequacy of whose messages is known to vary with age (Krauss & Glucksberg, 1969).

An adequate assessment of the development of children's skills in responding to ambiguous messages would require that listeners of different ages respond to standardized messages that vary in informational adequacy. Cosgrove and Patterson (1977) created such a situation by using an adult speaker who produced equal numbers of fully informative (adequate), partially informative (referring to two of four potential referents), and uninformative (referring to all four potential referents) messages in the context of a referential communication task. Children at each of four age levels (preschool, kindergarten, second, and fourth grades) played the role of the listener. Any questions asked by the listener during the communication task were answered in a straightforward manner. Dependent measures assessed both the number of requests for more information and the number of correct referent choices by each listener. In accord with earlier findings (cf. Glucksberg *et al.*, 1975), even the youngest listeners were quite successful in using the information contained in the speaker's initial message. Developmental trends emerged, however, when the speaker's initial message was ambiguous. Under these conditions, fourth-graders were significantly more likely than younger children to request clarification. As a result, they received more information and made more correct referent choices. Preschoolers, kindergartners, and second-graders asked relatively few questions, and made relatively few correct referent choices. There were no significant differences within these three younger age groups.

Similar findings were reported by Ironsmith and Whitehurst (1978a). In their study, an adult speaker's messages were either ambiguous or informative, and listener responses were coded as either appropriate or inappropriate. Making a choice among the referents was considered the appropriate response to informative messages, whereas requesting clarification was considered appropriate when the messages were ambiguous. The subjects were kindergarten, second-, fourth-, and sixth-grade children. As in earlier studies, there was little increase in appropriate responding with age when messages were informative, as all children did quite well in selecting the target referent on these trials (i.e., there was a ceiling effect). On the ambiguous message trials, however, fourth- and sixth-graders made many more appropriate responses (i.e., requests for additional information) than did younger children.

Summary

Early studies reported that listeners as young as 4 or 5 years of age are quite well able to make effective use of the information contained in speakers' messages. This finding led to the view that listener skill is relatively well developed early in childhood, and to an emphasis on the speaker's responsibility for communication failures. More recent studies have revealed, however, that when children are presented with inadequate messages, significant age differences are found in four areas of listener skill: assessment of message quality, knowledge that message quality influences communicative success, ability to respond effectively to adequate messages (e.g., confirmations), and ability to respond effectively to inadequate messages (e.g., questions). Consideration of these data indicates that, like speaker skills, listener skills undergo considerable development over the course of childhood and suggests that listeners may have a greater influence than previously suspected on the success of referential communication among children.

Training Children's Listener Skills

Relatively few researchers have attempted to train referential communication skills in children. In line with the general emphasis of the referential communication literature, almost all such efforts have focused on the training of speaker skills (Dickson, 1974; Fry, 1966, 1969; Shantz & Wilson, 1972; Whitehurst, 1976; Whitehurst & Merkur, 1977).

One study that attempted to facilitate children's performances in the listener role was reported by Cosgrove and Patterson (1977). As described in the previous section, children of different ages played the role of listener, and an adult speaker produced messages that varied in informational adequacy. Following the pretest (results of which have already been discussed), half of the children at each age level were given a plan for effective listening (instructions that emphasized the importance of asking for more information if the speaker's message was inadequate). On a posttest, children who received the plan asked more useful questions, got more information from the speaker, and hence made more correct referent choices than those in the no-plan control condition. These comparisons were significant for fourth-graders, second-graders, and kindergartners, but the instructions had no effect on the performance of preschool children.

One possible interpretation of the rapid improvements evidenced by older children in response to such brief intervention (cf. Asher, 1978) might be that initial failures resulted from a belief (despite instructions to the contrary) that question asking was inappropriate or impolite in this situation. As a check on this interpretation, seven additional second-graders were asked to play the role of the listener in the referential communication game. The procedure was just like that used for the "no-plan" condition of the Cosgrove and Patterson (1977) study, except that, after completion of the pretest trials, each child was asked whether it was all right to ask questions in the game. All seven children answered that questions were permissible. In spite of this, however, not one child asked even a single question on the subsequent posttest trials. Thus, it seems unlikely that children's failure to ask questions during the pretest trials resulted from any feeling that question asking was inappropriate behavior.

A second study (Cosgrove & Patterson, 1978) explored the possibilities of modeling of effective listener behavior as a technique for training young listeners, and also investigated the idea that instructions and modeling together might be more effective in facilitating listener performances than either method individually. The effects of these types of training on first-graders' listener performances were assessed in an immediate test, using both familiar and unfamiliar stimulus materials, and also in a delayed test, after an interval of 2–3 days. Results showed that children who had received either instruction or modeling gave better listener performances than those in a no-training control condition on the immediate test, with both types of referent items. Moreover, these effects were maintained on the delayed test. However, the two types of training together were no more effective than either type separately.

An important question raised by these results concerns the features of the modeling and instructional manipulations that were responsible for their efficacy. One cause of children's initial failures might have been a "comparison deficit"—a failure to compare each of the potential referents to the information contained in the speaker's message. By suggesting that listeners look carefully at the referents and formulate discriminating questions, the Cosgrove–Patterson instructional techniques may have encouraged comparison activities of this kind. On the other hand, even if they had completed the relevant comparison activities, children still may not have known what to do when a message was inadequate. This would be an "action deficit"—the children would know that a message was inadequate, but would not know what to do to reduce uncertainty. Of course, the Cosgrove and Patterson (1977) instructions suggested the nature of actions to be taken in these circumstances.

To test these two possible interpretations, Patterson, Massad, and Cosgrove (1978) systematically varied the presence and absence of instructions about a plan to engage in comparison activities ("comparison plan") and instructions about a plan to request more information if the speaker's message was ambiguous ("action plan"). Elementary school children were asked to play the role of the listener in the communication task. As before, the speaker was an adult confederate who produced messages of varying informational adequacy. Results showed that on an immediate test, children who received the action plan asked more questions when messages were ambiguous and made more correct referent choices than other subjects. These effects persisted on a delayed test administered 2 weeks later, and were observed for both easily nameable and more abstract items. No significant effect of the comparison plan was observed.

These findings fail to support a comparison deficit interpretation of children's difficulties as listeners, but are clearly consistent with an action deficit hypothesis. One possible explanation of the comparison plan's failure to affect performance might be that the comparison plan instructions were insufficient to elicit appropriate comparison activities. This seems unlikely, however, in view of the success of the action plan alone. It seems more likely that the comparison plan had no effect because children spontaneously completed comparison activities in this setting. Considered as a whole, the results suggest that knowing when and how to request additional information from a speaker is an important listener skill that can be facilitated using brief procedures. The results of a recent study by Ironsmith and Whitehurst (1978b) are also consistent with this conclusion.

To summarize, studies attempting to facilitate children's listener performances have focused on children's responses to inadequate messages. Results of these studies have shown that both modeling and the introduction of a plan emphasizing the importance of asking questions when messages are unclear can be effective techniques for facilitating elementary school children's listener performances, and that the effects of such interventions persist over periods of days and weeks. However, failure of training to affect preschoolers' listener performances suggests that other, more rudimentary skills (e.g., failure to understand the role of the message or failure to complete comparison activities) may be necessary, but not sufficient, for training to be effective. Future attempts to train listener skills might well focus on these types of activities as well as on the ability to provide appropriate verbal responses to speakers' messages.

Influence of the Listener on Children's Communication

A number of listener skills show development during childhood, and at least one of these is subject to facilitation with brief training. What implications do these facts have for conclusions about the listener's influence over the success of communication among children? If listeners request clarification of ambiguous messages, are young speakers likely to respond by offering more informative messages? If so, then the role of the listener in determining communication accuracy among children may be highly significant.

Speaker Responses to Listener Feedback

How sensitive are young speakers to feedback from the listener? It is well to note at the outset that "feedback" from the listener is not a unitary phenomenon. Listener feedback to ambiguous messages may be verbal (e.g., questions) or it may be nonverbal (e.g., expressions of puzzlement). Verbal feedback can be of a general nature, indicating only that more information is needed, or it can be highly specific, indicating exactly what kind or kinds of information the listener needs. Variations in factors such as these might be expected to affect the degree to which listener feedback influences the speaker's behavior.

In an early study, Alvy (1968) found that 6-year-olds were more likely than older children to persist in producing the same ambiguous descriptions of target referents over trials, even after visual feedback that these descriptions sometimes led the listener to make incorrect choices. However, interpretation of these data is complicated by the fact that considerable time apparently elapsed between trials in this study. Hence, the failure of young speakers to modify their descriptions might have resulted from memory deficiencies as to which messages had been successful.

Karabenick and Miller (1977) asked children between the ages of 5 and 7 to play a referential communication game in same-aged pairs. Speakers attempted to answer 91% of the relatively few questions listeners asked, but succeeded in providing additional useful information only 41% of the time. This result suggests that, although young speakers may be sensitive to a listener's indication that more information is needed, they may have difficulty modifying their messages to meet this demand. However, the finding might also be attributable to ambiguities or inadequacies in the listener's questions; no information about the nature of these questions was reported. In general, studies of referential communication between naïve, same-aged pairs (e.g., Alvy, 1968; Karabenick & Miller, 1977) are unlikely to provide conclusive evidence with regard to age differences or the effects of other factors (e.g., quality of feedback) on speakers' reactions to feedback, as listener responses remain uncontrolled in these studies and may vary with age.

Another approach to the study of speakers' responses to feedback has been to give young speakers standardized feedback from an adult confederate serving in the listener role. In the first study of this type, Glucksberg and Krauss (1967) provided kindergarten, first-, third-, fifth-grade, and adult speakers with general feedback on specified trials, indicating that the listener did not know the identity of the target referent. Verbal responses to this kind of feedback were offered by almost all speakers, suggesting that even the youngest speakers were aware that a response to this type of listener feedback would be desirable. However, kindergartners were more likely to repeat their previous description than to offer new information. The reverse was true for older children and adults. The tendency to give more information after listener feedback increased with age.

Similar results were reported by Jarvis (in Flavell et al., 1968). Second-, sixth-, and ninth-grade speakers were asked to describe complex geometric forms so that an adult could reproduce them from the subject's description. After general feedback indicating that the speaker's first description was inadequate, he or she was given an opportunity to reformulate the message. Second-graders' messages showed less improvement as a result of this feedback than did older children's.

Peterson, Danner, and Flavell (1972) also studied young speaker's responses to listener feedback. In their study, 4- and 7-year-olds served as speakers in a referential communication task. On specified trials, the adult listener provided one of three types of feedback indicating that the child's message was ambiguous. When the listener gave "facial" feedback, consisting of a puzzled look, few of the children at either age reformulated their messages. When the listener provided general verbal feedback with an implicit request for more information (e.g., "I don't understand; I don't think I can guess that."), most of the older children offered further clarification, although only a few of the younger ones did. When the listener's request for information was more explicit, however, (e.g., "Look at it again. What else does it look like?"), all of the children at both ages provided at least one reformulated message.

Similarly, Cosgrove and Patterson (1979) found that 5-year-old speakers gave more informative messages when an adult listener provided general feedback (indicating that he did not know the identity of the target referent, and asking for more information) than when no feedback was provided. Virtually all speakers produced perfect messages when the listener provided specific feedback indicating the exact nature of the information that was needed.

Visual feedback indicating that the listener picked the wrong item has also been effective in influencing the messages of even very young speakers (Copple, Coon, & Lipscomb, 1977; Fishbein & Osborne, 1971). In the Copple et al. study, for example, kindergarten speakers gave more informative messages after visual feedback regarding the listener's incorrect choices. In the absence of this visual feedback, only quite specific verbal feedback (e.g., "There were several red ones and I picked the wrong one. I picked a red circle. . . .") influenced children's performances.

Although the age at which speakers respond effectively to different kinds of feedback will depend on the exact nature of the task involved, several general conclusions seem justified by the research. First, older children are generally more likely than younger ones to respond effectively to listener feedback (Flavell et al., 1968; Glucksberg & Krauss, 1967; Peterson et al., 1972). Specific feedback is more effective than general feedback in eliciting message reformulations, and general feedback is more effective than none at all (Copple et al., 1977; Cosgrove & Patterson, 1979; Peterson et al., 1972). Although they may not provide more information, even speakers as young as 5 attempt to respond when the listener requests more information (Cosgrove & Patterson, 1979; Glucksberg & Krauss, 1967; Karabenick & Miller, 1977). Finally, even 4- and 5-year-olds, at least under some conditions, are able to improve their messages in response to feedback (Copple et al., 1977; Cosgrove & Patterson, 1979; Peterson et al., 1972).

Influence of the Listener

In general, then, the data suggest that systematic variations in listener behavior affect the adequacy of young speakers' messages, and hence influence communicative success. Positive effects of listener feedback seem most likely to occur when listener questions are explicit in indicating what information is needed. As these are exactly the kinds of questions that the "trained" listeners in the Cosgrove and Patterson (1977, 1978) studies were most likely to ask, the data suggest that training listeners in this way might be an effective means of facilitating successful communication among young speaker–listener pairs.

Although some of the data (e.g., Karabenick & Miller, 1977) suggest that listener questions may affect communicative success among children, only one attempt has been made to facilitate referential communication among children using systematic manipulation of listener behavior. In this study (Patterson & Massad, 1980), pairs of first- and third-grade children participated in a referential communication game, with the younger child serving as the speaker and the older one as listener. Half of the listeners were taught to ask questions, much as in earlier studies (Cosgrove & Patterson, 1977). Results showed that, as expected, trained listeners asked more questions than those in the no-plan condition. Because speakers provided useful message reformulations in response to 92% of the listener questions, listeners in the plan condition received more information and made more correct referent choices than did other subjects.

There are at least two ways in which listener questions might have had an impact on speakers' performances in this setting. Questions might have served on a trial-by-trial basis to indicate the listener's informational needs; this will be termed the *trial-by-trial effect* hypothesis. In addition, questions might have had a cumulative effect on the speaker's performance, such that the speaker would have gradually learned over trials what kinds of information should be included in his or her messages. We will call this the *cumulative effect* hypothesis.

To investigate these hypotheses, Patterson and Massad (1980) analyzed speakers' messages into "initial" messages (everything the speaker said before the listener asked a question) and "final" messages (everything the speaker said before the listener made a choice among the potential referents, including any answers to questions). If the trial-by-trial hypothesis is correct, then final messages should have shown improvement with listener feedback. If the cumulative effect hypothesis is correct, then initial messages should have shown improvement over trials as a result of listener feedback. To examine the possibility of a cumulative effect, Patterson and Massad divided the 16 trials of their communication task into 4 trial blocks of 4 trials each, and compared the number of distinguishing attributes mentioned in the speakers' initial messages for the first trial block to those for succeeding trial blocks.

The results showed that listener feedback facilitated communication on a trial-by-trial basis, and also showed a cumulative effect. Although the number of distinguishing attributes mentioned in initial messages did not differ as a function of condition for Trials 1–4, speakers who interacted with a trained listener named more distinguishing attributes in their initial messages for later trial blocks than those who interacted with an untrained listener. Over trials, then, listener feedback served to teach speakers how to produce more adequate initial messages.

These findings point to the significance of the listener role in determining the success of referential communication among children. Young listeners who received the instructional plan not only were able to obtain additional necessary information from the speakers on a trial-by-trial basis, but also managed to transform naïve first-graders into more effective speakers over the course of only 16 trials. The data, then, clearly show that listener behavior can have an important impact on both speaker performance and communicative success among children.

Summary and Conclusions

Early studies of the role of the listener in referential communication among children investigated children's skill in using the information contained in a speaker's initial message. Because this ability appeared to be relatively well developed even in 4- and 5-year-old children, the listener's role was thought to contribute comparatively little to variations in the success of communication among children. As a result, major responsibility for failures of communication among children was thought to lie with the speaker.

However, more recent work has employed a broader conception of the listener's role. This research has shown that young children are relatively deficient in a number of skills relevant to performance in the listener role, including ability to appraise message quality, knowledge that message quality affects communicative success, and ability to respond effectively to adequate and inadequate messages. When children's performances of some of these listener activities have been facilitated through training, more effective communication among children has been the result. Therefore, deficiencies in young children's performances in the listener role also appear to be a major cause of communication failure among children.

The recent findings serve to emphasize the importance of viewing referential communication as an interactive process. Although studies of speakers' "encoding" behavior in isolation from listeners and studies of listeners' "decoding" behavior in isolation from speakers can provide useful information about some communication skills, they can never produce a complete understanding of the causes of success and failure in ongoing communication. We have already considered the ways in which the use of a static encoder–decoder approach led to an underestimation of the listener's role in early research (e.g., Glucksberg *et al.,* 1966; Krauss & Glucksberg, 1969).

More recent uses of this model (e.g., Quay, Mathews, & Schwarzmueller, 1977) continue to obscure important sources of variance in the communicative process. For example, the listener questions that facilitated successful communication among children in the Patterson and Massad (1980) study would be unlikely to occur outside the context of actual interaction with a speaker. Similarly, young speakers' reformulations of ambiguous messages are undoubtedly useful in achieving accurate communication, but they are unlikely to occur without clear evidence of the listener's need for more information. Therefore, recognition of the listener's potential influence over communication success among children should serve not to minimize the significance of the speaker's contribution, but to underline the importance of interactions between speaker and listener.

Educational Implications of Research on Listener Skills

It is perhaps surprising that relatively little attention has been devoted to the educational implications of research on the development of listener skills, especially in view of the importance of these skills for children's cognitive development (Dickson, Hess, Miyake, & Azuma, 1979) and school achievement (Atkin, Bray, Davison, Herzberger, Humphreys, & Selzer, 1977). Using a longitudinal design, Dickson and his colleagues (1979) found that, in both the United States and Japan, referential accuracy of mother–child pairs when the child was 4 was significantly correlated with the child's school readiness score a year later, even when the effects of potentially related variables (e.g., socioeconomic status) had been partialled out. Also using a longitudinal design, Atkin et al. (1977) found that measures of listener skill provided the single best predictor of academic achievement in their sample.

As one of us (Patterson, 1978) has argued elsewhere, the potential educational significance of research on the development of listener skills is impressive. A great deal of children's time during school hours is spent in referential communication tasks—that is, in listening to their teachers' oral presentations of a variety of curricular materials. The child's likelihood of deriving benefit from such classroom instruction certainly depends in part on his or her ability to listen effectively. Naturally, most teachers strive to present lessons in a clear and informative manner. Even with the clearest and most informative presentation, however, some children will not understand. Research by Markman (e.g., 1977) and others suggest that children often do not even detect these comprehension failures. If children do notice comprehension problems, research by Cosgrove and Patterson (e.g., 1977) and others suggest that they may not think of asking questions as a possible strategy for solving these problems.

The educational image that these arguments suggest is one of a classroom of students listening passively to a teacher presenting material that they often do not understand. Overdrawn as such an image may appear at first glance, a substantial body of educational research exists to support it. One of the more striking and consistent findings of observational research in school classrooms is that, although teachers often ask many questions of their students, the students themselves initiate very few questions. For example, in a study of several first-grade classrooms, Susskind (1969) found that, whereas teachers asked an average of over 80 questions per hour of instruction, the children averaged only 2 or 3 per hour. Similar findings have been reported not only for elementary, but also for junior and senior high school, classrooms (cf. Cowen, 1977; Gall, 1971). These data might be less compelling if teachers were adept at identifying nonverbal signs of comprehension failure in their students, but research on this point (Allen, this volume; Jecker, Maccoby, Breitrose, & Rose, 1964) suggests that they are not.

There are, of course, many possible explanations for children's failure to ask questions in class. Not least of these, however, is one that focuses on teacher responses. Ross and Balzer (1975) reported a study relevant to this issue. They showed a number of pictures of unfamiliar places and people to first-, third-, and fifth-graders, and solicited children's questions about the pictures. Results showed that, regardless of the children's age, those whose questions were answered in a consistent and informative manner learned more and subsequently asked more questions than those whose questions sometimes went unanswered. When this finding is considered together with those of Susskind (1969) and others, one possible implication is that children may ask few questions in class because teachers—wittingly or unwittingly—discourage them from doing so. Thus, whereas effective listening may often require students to ask questions, teachers may inadvertently foster the belief that good listening requires the listener to remain silent.

Laboratory studies of children's listener behavior, however, suggest that their performances may be subject to considerable facilitation, using relatively brief instructional procedures or modeling techniques (e.g., Cosgrove & Patterson, 1977, 1978). Such interventions have been shown to remain stable, at least over periods of days or weeks (Patterson, Massad, & Cosgrove, 1978), and to facilitate accuracy of communication in both adult–child (Cosgrove & Patterson, 1977) and child–child (Patterson & Massad, 1980) pairs. Thus, although children may not normally think to ask questions in class when something is not clear to them, results of the laboratory studies suggest that a number of procedures might facilitate their tendency to do so. If children could be led to ask questions in this way when they are confused or do not understand something presented in class, perhaps they would also learn more than they do by remaining silent.

Another possible application of the laboratory findings on children as listeners might be to the growing practice of peer tutoring. The literature shows that, although peer tutoring may often have beneficial effects on the tutors, evidence for a positive impact on tutees' mastery of curricular material is limited (Feldman, Devin-Sheehan, & Allen, 1976). On the basis of the research on children as speakers (Glucksberg *et al.*, 1975), it seems reasonable to assume that young tutors may simply give inadequate presentations of the material. If so, then the findings of the Patterson and Massad (1980) study may be useful in this context. In that study, trained listeners were able to elicit considerable improvement in message adequacy from naïve first-grade speakers in a matter of only 16 trials on a referential communication task; this resulted in more effective communication. The possibility that brief listener training for tutees might enhance the effectiveness of peer tutoring is an intriguing one.

In short, there are a number of ways in which the laboratory findings on children's referential communication skills might be brought to bear on problems of communication in educational settings. As yet, however, there has been almost no research designed to do this. Nowhere in our review of the literature have we found the need for further research to be more acute.

References

Alvy, K. T. Relation of age to children's egocentric and cooperative communication. *The Journal of Genetic Psychology*, 1968, *112*, 275–286.

Asher, S. R. Children's ability to appraise their own and another person's communication performance. *Developmental Psychology*, 1976, *12*, 24–32.

Asher, S. R. Referential communication. In G. J. Whitehurst and B. J. Zimmerman (Eds.), *The functions of language and cognition*. New York: Academic Press, 1978.

Atkin, R., Bray, R., Davison, M., Herzberger, S., Humphreys, L., & Selzer, U. Cross-lagged panel analysis of sixteen cognitive measures at four grade levels. *Child Development*, 1977, *48*, 944–952.

Bearison, D. J., & Levey, L. M. Children's comprehension of referential communication: Decoding ambiguous messages. *Child Development*, 1977, *48*, 716–720.

Copple, C. E., Coon, R. C., & Lipscomb, T. J. *Effects of listener feedback on the messages of kindergarten children in a referential communication task*. Paper presented at the Annual Meeting of the Eastern Psychological Association, Boston, 1977.

Cosgrove, J. M., & Patterson, C. J. Plans and the development of listener skills. *Developmental Psychology*, 1977, *13*, 557–564.

Cosgrove, J. M., & Patterson, C. J. Generalization of training for children's listener skills. *Child Development*, 1978, *49*, 513–516.

Cosgrove, J. M., & Patterson, C. J. Adequacy of young speakers' encoding in response to listener feedback. *Psychological Reports*, 1979, *45*, 15–18.

Cowen, E. L. Baby-steps toward primary prevention. *American Journal of Community Psychology*, 1977, *5*, 1–22.

Dickson, W. P. The development of interpersonal referential communication skills in young children using an interactional game device (Doctoral dissertation, Stanford University, 1974). *Dissertation Abstracts International*, 1974, *35*, 3511-A. (University Microfilms No. 74-27,008).

Dickson, W. P., Hess, R. D., Miyake, N., & Azuma, H. Referential communication accuracy between mother and child as a predictor of cognitive development in the United States and Japan. *Child Development*, 1979, *50*, 53–59.

Dittman, A. T. Developmental factors in conversational behavior. *The Journal of Communication*, 1972, *22*, 404–423.

Feldman, R. S., Devin-Sheehan, L., & Allen, V. L. Children tutoring children: A critical review of the research. In V. L. Allen (Ed.), *Children as teachers: Theory and research on tutoring*. New York: Academic Press, 1976.

Fishbein, H. D., & Osborne, M. The effects of feedback variations on referential communication of children. *Merrill-Palmer Quarterly*, 1971, *17*, 243–250.

Flavell, J. H., Botkin, P. T., Fry, C. L., Wright, J. C., & Jarvis, P. E. *The development of role-taking and communication skills in children*. New York: Wiley, 1968.

Fry, C. L. Training children to communicate to listeners. *Child Development*, 1966, *37*, 675–685.

Fry, C. L. Training children to communicate with listeners who have varying listener requirements. *The Journal of Genetic Psychology*, 1969, *114*, 153–166.

Gall, M. The use of questions in teaching. *Review of Educational Research*, 1971, *40*, 707–721.

Glucksberg, S., & Krauss, R. M. What do people say after they have learned to talk? Studies of the development of referential communication. *Merrill-Palmer Quarterly*, 1967, *13*, 309–316.

Glucksberg, S., Krauss, R. M., & Higgins, E. T. The development of referential communication skills. In F. D. Horowitz (Ed.), *Review of Child Development Research* (Vol. 4). Chicago: University of Chicago Press, 1975.

Glucksberg, S., Krauss, R. M., & Weisberg, R. Referential communication in nursery school children: Method and some preliminary findings. *Journal of Experimental Child Psychology*, 1966, *3*, 333–342.

Ironsmith, M., & Whitehurst, G. J. The development of listener abilities in communication: How children deal with ambiguous information. *Child Development*, 1978, *49*, 348–352 (a)

Ironsmith, M., & Whitehurst, G. J. How children learn to listen: The effects of modeling feedback styles on children's performance in referential communication. *Developmental Psychology*, 1978, *14*, 546–554. (b)

Jecker, J., Maccoby, N., Breitrose, H. S., & Rose, E. D. Teacher accuracy in assessing cognitive visual feedback from students. *Journal of Applied Psychology*, 1964, *48*, 393–397.

Karabenick, J. D., & Miller, S. A. The effects of age, sex, and listener feedback on grade school children's referential communication. *Child Development*, 1977, *48*, 678–683.

Krauss, R. M., & Glucksberg, S. The development of communication: Competence as a function of age. *Child Development*, 1969, *40*, 255–266.

Krauss, R. M., & Weinheimer, S. Concurrent feedback, confirmation and the encoding of referents in verbal communication. *Journal of Personality and Social Psychology*, 1966, *4*, 343–346.

Maccoby, E. E. Selective auditory attention in children. In L. Lipsitt, & C. Spiker (Eds.), *Advances in child development and behavior* (Vol. 3). New York: Academic Press, 1967.

Maccoby, E. E. The development of stimulus selection. In J. P. Hill (Ed.), *Minnesota Symposia on Child Psychology* (Vol. 3). Minneapolis: University of Minnesota Press, 1969.

Maccoby, E. E., & Konrad, K. W. Age trends in selective listening. *Journal of Experimental Child Psychology*, 1966, *3*, 113–122.

Markman, E. M. Realizing that you don't understand: A preliminary investigation. *Child Development*, 1977, *48*, 986–992.

Meissner, J. A. Judgment of clue adequacy by kindergarten and second-grade children. *Developmental Psychology*, 1978, *14*, 18–23.

Miscione, J. L., Marvin, R. S., O'Brien, R. G., & Greenberg, M. T. Children's understanding of the words "know" and "guess." *Child Development*, 1978, *49*, 1107–1113.

Patterson, C. J. Teaching children to listen. *Today's Education*, 1978, *67*, 52–53.

Patterson, C. J., Cosgrove, J. M., & O'Brien, R. G. Nonverbal indicants of comprehension and noncomprehension in children. *Developmental Psychology*, 1980, *16*, 38–48.

Patterson, C. J., & Massad, C. M. Facilitating referential communication among children: The listener as teacher. *Journal of Experimental Child Psychology*, 1980, *29*, 357–370.

Patterson, C. J., Massad, C. M., & Cosgrove, J. M. Children's referential communication: Components of plans for effective listening. *Developmental Psychology*, 1978, *14*, 401–406.

Patterson, C. J., O'Brien, C., Kister, M. C., Carter, D. B., & Kotsonis, M. E. *Stimulus complexity, message ambiguity, and the development of comprehension monitoring*. Unpublished manuscript, University of Virginia, 1980.

Peterson, C. L., Danner, F. W., & Flavell, J. H. Developmental changes in children's response to three indications of communicative failure. *Child Development*, 1972, *43*, 1463–1468.

Piaget, J. *The moral judgment of the child*. New York: Free Press, 1965. (Originally published, 1932).

Quay, L. C., Mathews, M., & Schwartzmueller, B. Communication encoding and decoding in children from different socioeconomic and racial groups. *Developmental Psychology*, 1977, *13*, 415–416.

Robinson, E. J., & Robinson, W. P. Developmental changes in the child's explanations of communication failures. *Australian Journal of Psychology*, 1976, *3*, 155–165. (a)

Robinson, E. J., & Robinson, W. P. The young child's understanding of communication. *Developmental Psychology*, 1976, *12*, 328–333. (b)

Robinson, E. J., & Robinson, W. P. Children's explanations of communication failure and the inadequacy of the misunderstood message. *Developmental Psychology*, 1977, *13*, 156–161. (a)

Robinson, E. J., & Robinson, W. P. Development in the understanding of causes of success and failure in verbal communication. *Cognition*, 1977, *5*, 363–378. (b)

Robinson, E. J., & Robinson, W. P. The young child's explanations of communication failure: A re-interpretation of results. *Perceptual and Motor Skills*, 1977, *44*, 363–366. (c)

Robinson, E. J., & Robinson, W. P. *Development of understanding about communication: Message inadequacy and its role in causing communication failure*. Unpublished manuscript, Macquarie University, 1978. (a)

Robinson, E. J., & Robinson, W. P. The relationship between children's explanations of communication failure and their ability deliberately to give bad messages. *British Journal of Social and Clinical Psychology*, 1978, *17*, 219–225. (b)

Robinson, E. J., & Robinson, W. P. The roles of egocentrism and of weakness in comparing in children's explanations of communication failure. *Journal of Experimental Child Psychology*, 1978, *26*, 147–160. (c)

Ross, H., & Balzer, R. Determinants and consequences of children's questions. *Child Development*, 1975, *46*, 536–539.

Shantz, C. U., & Wilson, I. E. Training communication skills in young children. *Child Development*, 1972, *43*, 693–698.

Susskind, E. C. The role of question-asking in the elementary school classroom. In F. Kaplan, & S. B. Sarason (Eds.), *The psycho-educational clinic: Papers and research studies*. Massachusetts Dept. of Mental Health, 1969.

Whitehurst, G. J. The development of communication: Changes with age and modeling. *Child Development*, 1976, *47*, 473–482.

Whitehurst, G. J., & Merkur, A. E. The development of communication: Modeling and contrast failure. *Child Development*, 1977, *48*, 993–1001.

8

The Child's Understanding of Inadequate Messages and Communication Failure: A Problem of Ignorance or Egocentrism?

E. J. ROBINSON

A fashionable trend in work on the capacities of children is to emphasize the intellectual strengths of the very young, and to question the usefulness of certain Piagetian notions of development. This is particularly noticeable in work on communication; focus on the behavioral skills of the very young child has led to the conclusion that Piaget's (1926/1959) description of the preschool child as egocentric is at best too global and at worst misleading and inaccurate. Asher and Oden (1976) have asserted that "the egocentricity explanation of poor communication performance is called into question [p. 139]," citing memory factors and absence of comparison activity as alternative explanations for behavior observed. Bearison and Levey (1977) likewise cite absence of appropriate comparison activity and claim no influence of "egocentrism" to explain kindergarten children's weakness in decoding ambiguous questions. Maratsos (1973) and Shatz and Gelman (1973) have shown that preschool children differentiate between listeners in terms of the way they speak to them, although these authors do not explicitly argue for an absence of egocentrism in the speech of their children.

However, in none of this work has there been any attempt to analyze

167

whether or not the child understands what he is doing. Piaget's egocentric child does not *understand* that for communication to be successful, the message must meet the listener's information requirements; evidence that the child frequently does meet these requirements does not decrease the potential validity of this aspect of the concept of egocentrism. In *The Language and Thought of the Child,* Piaget (1959) states

> In the first place, neither the child's social ego-centrism nor the ego-centrism of his knowledge of the physical world is a quality which can be observed within his self-consciousness or by watching his external behaviour. Social ego-centrism, as much as purely intellectual ego-centrism, is an epistemic attitude: it is a way of understanding others just as ego-centrism in general is a way of looking at things [pp. 272–273].

The capacity of 2-year-olds to respond sensibly to a *What?* request for clarification has been used to "hypothesize that very young children have a basic understanding of communication failure [Valian, Caplan, & de Sciora, 1977]." In a series of experiments carried out jointly with W. P. Robinson, we have been more wary of making inferences about understanding based solely on performance. We have asked children to account for the success or failure of communications and have examined relationships between their accounts and their performance. Does the child say that messages can be inadequate and that they can be responsible for communication failure? In this way we avoid the need to make inferences about understanding from performance characteristics alone.

In this introductory section, I shall first describe the game we play with the child to test his understanding about communication, and then summarize some of the ways we have used the game to begin to find out what is involved in this understanding. In the next two sections, I shall present some new results which make clearer just what the young child's capabilities and problems are, and show how these latter can be and are perpetuated by the adults who interact with him. In the last section I shall discuss some of the implications of these results. In the studies reported here the experimenter was always female (myself), whereas only half of the child subjects were female, so I shall eliminate ambiguity of reference by reserving the pronoun *she* for the experimenter and by using *he* for the child.

Each child is tested individually. Child and experimenter sit at opposite ends of a table with a screen across the middle. The players have identical sets of cards bearing drawings. The six cards in one of the sets have a man with a black pointed hat, a black top hat, a red flower, a blue flower, a red flag up high, and a red flag down. The initially stated object of the game is for one player, the speaker, to choose a card and describe it so that the other player, the listener, can choose the matching card from his set. The listener's role is a passive one in that he is not invited to ask for more information, nor is the child listener given any should he spontaneously make such a request.

The experimenter introduces the game to the child by showing him the two sets of cards and telling him they are identical. The experimenter explains and then demonstrates the game, giving a good message which identifies her chosen card uniquely. The child picks the correct card, then he has a turn as speaker. The players continue to take turns. On some of her turns as speaker, the experimenter introduces communication failure by giving messages that refer to two cards, such as "I've got the one I want you to pick, it's a man with a flower," with an array from which the child could choose a man with a red flower or one with a blue flower. Whichever card the child chooses, the experimenter shows that she was talking about the other one. Normally, genuine communication failures arise when the child is speaker: Most children spontaneously give one or more inadequate messages that are followed by the experimenter's choosing wrongly.

Most often, our immediate interest has not been in the child's messages, but in his explanations of communication failure when the message was inadequate: Why did the listener pick the wrong card? We have developed a standard sequence of questions, the "whose fault" sequence:

> We've got different cards, we went wrong that time. Whose fault was that, mine, yours? Why? Did I/you tell you/me properly which one to pick? [If the child says no: "What should I/you have said?"] Whose fault was it we went wrong? Why?

The child is asked this sequence of questions following at least two communication failures (usually three or four), and usually both when he is listener and when he is speaker. From each child we find out: first, the role blamed for communication failure, listener or speaker, and the reasons for this allocation of blame (we found empirically that children blamed roles not persons); and, second, whether or not he thinks the speaker told properly (or said enough), and if not, what he thinks was missing from the message.

On occasions when from the adult point of view it was the speaker and his message that were responsible for failure, we have taken the role blamed and the reason given as an indicator of whether or not the child understands that an inadequate message can cause communication failure: When a child says, "It was the speaker's fault because he didn't say what color the flower was," then we conclude that he understands that the inadequate message caused the failure. If, on the other hand, he says, "It was the listener's fault because she picked the wrong card," we have as yet no grounds for concluding such understanding.

We consider the reasons given by the child to be more important indicators of understanding than the locus of blame alone. This form of questioning was developed because it proved to be a useful way of drawing from the child comments about message inadequacy and the role of the speaker in causing communication failure; it was not that we were particularly interested in locus of blame as such. Should a child refuse to ascribe blame, if he nevertheless made a clear statement that the speaker gave insufficient information for the listener to make a confident correct choice, we would categorize him with those who blamed the speaker and gave appropriate reasons. In the age range of 5–8 years, which we have commonly used, no children blamed the listener on the grounds that he should have asked for more information, although this reasoning has occurred very rarely among older children. We would not have categorized a child who reasoned in this way with our listener blamers.

We have taken the child's judgments about whether or not the speaker told properly, and what he should have said, as an indicator of his understanding about message inadequacy. If the child says, "The speaker didn't tell properly, he should have said red," and can pick out different missing attributes from other messages (see Robinson & Robinson, 1978a), we infer that he understands that the message was inadequate because it did not uniquely identify the speaker's card. If, on the other hand, the child says that the speaker did tell properly when in fact the message referred to more than one card, we do not infer that he understands about the inadequacy of the message.

In what follows, a *listener blamer* is a child who blames only the listener for the failures and always says the speaker did tell properly when the message in fact referred to more than one card. A *speaker blamer* is a child who, when it is appropriate from the adult point of view, always blames the speaker for failures on the grounds that the message was inadequate, says the speaker did not tell properly, and identifies at least one attribute missing from each inadequate message. Normally in data analysis we use two or more *intermediate* categories, into which are put children who blame the speaker on at least one but not all appropriate occasions, and children who on one or more appropriate occasions judge the message to be inadequate despite blaming only the listener. For investigating some problems, it has proved to be important to separate these last two groups of children, for example, when distinguishing knowledge about message inadequacy from knowledge about inadequacy as a cause of failure (Robinson & Robinson, 1978a).

We have found strong age-related differences in children's ascriptions of blame for communication failure. Younger children, of around 5 years, commonly fall into the listener-blaming category. Speaker blamers become common by around 7 years, and all the 11-year-olds we have tested blamed the speaker when appropriate (Robinson & Robinson, 1976a, 1976b).

The same age-related differences were obtained using the Krauss and Glucksberg (1969) abstract shapes (Robinson & Robinson, 1976b) and using inkblots (Robinson & Robinson, 1976a), instead of drawings of men. We have also used picture stories involving communication failures (Robinson & Robinson, 1977a). For example, one of these is about a boy who asks his mother for a drink. She gives him an orange drink but he really wanted a green drink. Whose fault was it the boy did not get the drink he wanted? With these more life-like communication failures, it seemed to be a little easier for the child to recognize the significance of the role of the speaker and his message in communication failure, although the age-related trend from listener to speaker blaming remained the same. Having the child observe a communication game between dolls, rather than the child himself playing the roles of listener and speaker, yielded substantially similar results (Robinson & Robinson, 1977c).

Asking the child to ascribe blame is not the only way of eliciting such information; an alternative is to ask the child, "How would we make sure we got it right next time?" Children who blamed the speaker for failure with our normal procedure said that the message would have to be improved, whereas children who blamed only the listener with our normal procedure, did not mention the message. They said "We'll have to think harder" or "Guess it right" (Robinson & Robinson, 1978a). Countersuggestion used in the Piagetian manner—asking the child to justify an allocation of blame different from the one he has just given—had virtually no effect. Hardly any child produced reasoning different from that given spontaneously (Robinson & Robinson, 1978a).

Messages can be inadequate for different reasons. In the examples we have given so far, the inadequacy has lain in the fact that message is too general: Both speaker and listener would agree that it refers to the card the speaker had in mind but also to at least one other card. We have also looked at messages that are idiosyncratic in that they have a different reference for listener and speaker (Robinson & Robinson, 1978a), and at messages that are inappropriate in that they do not refer to the card the speaker has in mind (Robinson & Robinson, 1977c). Idiosyncratic and too-general messages appear to be equally difficult for the child to identify, but understanding about inappropriate messages seems to develop somewhat earlier. That is, some children classified as listener blamers on the basis of their judgments about too-general messages, judge inappropriate messages to be inadequate and blame the speaker of inappropriate messages for communication failure.

A finding that can be related to this is that, in a game in which inadequate messages were too general, listener blamers were less likely than speaker blamers to engage in comparison activity when producing messages (Robinson & Robinson, 1978a), even though many listener blamers could perform the necessary comparisons in a description completion task. In this task the child completed a description of which of a pair of cards was turned face down (Robinson & Robinson, 1978c). The results with both inappropriate messages and comparison activity are consistent with the suggestion that the listener blamer decides about the inadequacy of messages on the basis of the answer to the question "Does the message fit the speaker's card?" If the answer is yes, the message is judged to be adequate and the blame for communication failure is ascribed to the listener only. If the answer is no, the message is judged inadequate and the blame is ascribed to the speaker. At a later stage of development, adequacy is defined by the answer to the question "Does the message fit *only* the speaker's card?" As with the first question, if the answer is yes, the message is judged to be adequate and the listener is blamed, and, if the answer is no, the blame is located with the speaker and his message (Robinson & Robinson, 1977b).

A working conclusion from the results summarized so far could be that the listener blamer does not know that a message should refer uniquely to whatever the speaker has in mind. For him it is sufficient that the message refers to this item, regardless of whether or not it refers to other things as well.

However, one hint that this account was not entirely satisfactory came from a result that, when accounting for the success of a communication, not only did some listener blamers mention the message, but some of them did this only when the message was in fact adequate and not when it was too general (Robinson & Robinson, 1977b). That is, some listener blamers appeared to recognize the contribution of a good message to successful communication, even though they did not recognize that a bad message could cause communication failure.

It becomes important therefore to look more deeply into the listener blamer's conception of the communication situation. What are the stages of development of understanding about the causes of communicative success or failure? In the next section, I shall present some attempts to find out to what extent the listener blamer knows that a message should refer uniquely to whatever the speaker has in mind.

Reformulation: The Child's Response to His Listener's Nonunderstanding

If our listener blamers do not understand the role of inadequate messages in causing communication failure, we would not expect them to think of improving their messages when the listener fails to understand. Peterson, Danner, and Flavell (1972) found that, whereas all of the 7- and 4-year-olds in their study could supplement their messages when explicitly asked to do so, only a few of the 4-year-olds produced further speech in response to the experimenter commenting that she did not understand. These authors suggest that the 4-year-olds did not know what sort of help was needed; their results are also consistent with the view that these young children did not realize that inadequate messages could be the cause of communication failure. Foorman (1977) likewise found that "I still don't know which one it is. Is there anything else you can tell me about it?" was by itself insufficient to evoke significant improvements in the number of discriminating attributes mentioned. In experiments by Cosgrove and Patterson, young children of about 4–8 years faced with ambiguous messages did not spontaneously ask disambiguating questions. When they were explicitly advised to do so by the experimenter, all but the 4-year-olds did so and continued to employ this tactic across materials and occasions (Cosgrove & Patterson, 1977, 1978; Patterson, Massad, & Cosgrove, 1978).

We have conducted three experiments to try to find out the relationship between children's ascriptions of blame for communication failure and their responses to their listener's nonunderstanding. In particular, we were interested in the performance of listener blamers: Do they say more when their listener says she does not understand? Results are said to be significant if $p < .05$.

In our first investigation, Experiment 1, we found that nearly all the children in the sample (28 children aged between 5:11 and 7:7), whether they were listener blamers or speaker blamers, rephrased their messages in our communication game when the experimenter said, "I'm not sure which one you mean. Can you help me?"

This led us to wonder if reformulation was an indicator of understanding. Perhaps the children had learned a simple rule "If the listener doesn't respond appropriately, say something else"; some of them might not know why this rule worked or what sort of help was appropriate. In this first experiment, the children were sending messages about one of a set of nine inkblots (Robinson & Robinson, 1976a); the materials were such that we could not objectively code message quality, we could only tell whether or not a message reformulation was adequate for that particular listener playing the game. In Experiments 2 and 3, we used a set of six drawings such that messages could be coded according to the number of cards they referred to: All cards had a man with a blue flag, and four binary features varied for the men (each attribute being represented three times): flower (red versus blue), hat (tall versus short), footwear (boots versus shoes), and mouth (smile versus sad).

As all the men had blue flags, the child would not help his listener to choose the correct card by mentioning that attribute. Similarly, as all the men with red flowers also wore boots, and all those with blue flowers also wore shoes, mentioning both color of flower and footwear would not reduce the number of potential referents from the listener's point of view. On the other hand, having told the listener that the chosen man held a red flower, it would reduce the number of potential referents to tell her whether he had a tall or a short hat. In general, then, we could code each item of information given by the child in terms of how much it reduced the number of cards to which the total message referred.

In Experiment 2, our subjects were 58 children aged between 5:7 and 6:2. During the course of the game with these cards, the experimenter asked the child the whose-fault sequence of questions following four communication failures (two when the child was speaker and two when the experimenter was speaker). On two further occasions when the child gave an inadequate message, the experimenter said, as in Experiment 1, "I'm not sure which one you mean, can you help me?"

As in Experiment 1, if we simply examined whether the child said something *new* in response to the listener's request for help, there were no significant differences between children in the different blame categories. Neither were there any significant differences between them in length or quality of messages given prior to the listener's requests for help.

However, there were marked differences between children in the different blame categories in the quality of the help given once the listener had said "I'm not sure which one you mean, can you help me?" Across the four categories—from listener blamers, through two intermediate categories, to speaker blamers—there was a significant increase in percentage of responses to requests for help that reduced the number of choices available to the listener. There was also a significant increase over the four blame categories in the proportion of children whose messages referred to only one card following the request for help, given that the message had referred to two cards prior to that request. The more advanced the child's answers to the whose-fault sequence of questions, the more likely he was to give helpful information following the listener's request for help.

These results are consistent with the view that the child with less advanced understanding about inadequate messages and their role in communication failure may have merely learned to say more in the face of perceived listener nonunderstanding; in contrast, those with greater understanding about the causes of communication failure know what sort of help to offer, and they give it.

In Experiment 3, we gave the children more information about what sort of help was needed, to see whether our listener blamers could perform better when given more explicit instructions. This time, following the child's inadequate messages, the experimenter said, "I've got four/two [or however many cards the message referred to] like that. I'm not sure which one you mean. Can you help me?" That is, the child was told how many cards his message referred to. This pinpointing of the problem helped our listener blamers dramatically, bringing their performance up to the level of the speaker blamers; in this third experiment there were finally no discernable differences between children in the different blame categories, even though there was still room for improvement among the children in each category. It appears that our listener blamers were capable of producing a message that referred uniquely to their chosen card, but that they needed to be prompted into doing so. Even though a child may not be aware of the relationship between a too-general message and communication failure, if his listener points out in what way the message is too general, the child knows what to do to help.

One possible interpretation of these results is that the child finds it easier to identify a too-general message when his listener has refused to choose (as she does when she asks for help), than when she makes a wrong choice (as she does prior to asking the whose-fault sequence of questions in our standard game). We tested this by asking each of a fourth sample of children the whose-fault sequence of questions both when the listener had chosen wrongly and when she said she could not choose. There were, however, no differences in the children's answers under these two conditions.

We are left, then, with the interpretation offered earlier, that at least some of our listener blamers know what a good message should be like, but that they need to be prompted into producing a message that identifies their chosen card uniquely.

Could it be that with even more prompting the child would begin to indulge spontaneously in appropriate comparison activity when producing messages? As was mentioned, we have found that listener blamers are less likely than speaker blamers to do this even if they can perform the necessary comparisons in a description completion task. Our first attempt at improving the communicative performance of listener blamers is presented in the next section, in which we relate our method of "prompting" to modes of adult–child interaction in everyday life.

The Effect of Adults' Responses to Children's Inadequate Messages

What information about communication is offered to the child in his everyday life? How do adults and other children deal with the child's inadequate messages or with their own? What might the child learn from observing successful or unsuccessful communication between others? If we knew what experiences the child has, we could attempt to work out how these experiences might be interpreted by the child to produce the developmental sequences we have observed in our experiments.

In an attempt to find out what the child's experiences are, we are in the process of analyzing some data collected in Australia by other researchers for other purposes. Data collected by Clough (1971) in Melbourne consists of transcripts of verbal exchanges between teacher and child in preschools. The children were aged between 3:4 and 5:3 and were mainly of low socioeconomic status. The teacher wore a microphone for the collection of two samples from each of six preschools. Each sample included 20 minutes of "normal indoor activity" and 20 minutes of "small group activity" if such was normally included; the teachers followed their usual programs. We have also analyzed part of the data collected by Cambourne (1971) in Queensland; these consist of transcripts of verbal exchanges in the home (mainly between mother and child) and in the classroom (between teacher and children). Each child in the sample wore a radio microphone transmitter for about 1 hour in the morning while having breakfast and getting ready for school, and again in the classroom. The children were aged between 5 : 2 and 6 : 7.

We have coded these data to find out how frequent misunderstandings or inadequate messages are in adult–child interaction, and how they are dealt with. As an indication that an utterance was inadequate, we have taken either the listener's subsequent utterance, or the speaker's next utterance following the listener's response or lack of response. In each of the three sets of data—preschool, school, and home—messages that were obviously inadequate for the listener were surprisingly rare: Of the exchanges in the preschool, only about 2% of adults' utterances and about 9% of children's utterances appeared to be inadequate; in the school, the corresponding figures were 1% and 8%.

By far the most common way for listeners to deal with an apparently inadequate message was to use a conventional means of requesting a repetition: "What was that?" "Pardon?" (Those requests were in fact followed by repetitions.) The next most common response to an inadequate message was to request more information, usually by employing a *Wh*-question: "What sort of something?" "Where?" "You point to it." "Trevor who?" "Round the side where?" Other ways of dealing with an inadequate message were to verbalize a guess "In a car?" "The microphone?"); to verbalize alternative meanings ("Does she live in the country or the city?"); to repeat or expand the original message; or to ignore it. The frequency of occurrence of each of these modes of dealing with inadequate messages is shown in Table 8.1.

TABLE 8.1
Frequency of Occurrence of Different Modes of Dealing with Inadequate Messages

Speaker inadequate message given by	Number of inadequate messages	Conventional request for repetition by listener (%)	Request for more information by listener (%)	Guess verbalized by listener (%)	Alternative meanings verbalized by listener (%)	Repetition/ expansion by speaker (%)	Inadequate message ignored (%)
Preschool							
Child	94	60	17	13	4	6	—
Adult	15	33	20	—	—	20	27
Home							
Child	258	57	24	10	—	7	4
Adult	159	48	25	7	—	18	1
School							
Child	60	35	23	8	—	7	—
Adult	14	—	—	14	—	71	—

It was only in the preschools that ignoring a child's nonunderstanding of an adult's message was at all common, but it was also in the preschools that the most explicit information that occurred about message inadequacy was given: verbalizing alternative meanings of the child's message (and only 4% of inadequate messages were dealt with in this way, as shown in the table). Preschool teachers occasionally gave explicit instructions about appropriate forms of requests (e.g., "What do you say? 'Please, Mrs. C., would you put the veil on?' That's what you say.") and about appropriate noise levels of messages, but they gave no information about essential content of messages, such as "You should tell me whether you mean the blue one or the red one."

In the schools, the number of exchanges (as opposed to monologue by the teacher) was so small that it was difficult to identify inadequate messages from the transcripts; it was only in these schools, however, that explicit references to nonunderstandings or misunderstandings occurred ($N = 5$): "Oh, I thought you meant that one," "No, you misunderstood me."

From these data, it is clear that the children in these samples, presumably not unrepresentative of their age group, were given very little information about communication effectiveness. The focus of attention of the adults appeared to be upon maintaining pleasant social relationships or the communication content, rather than the communication process. Asking the child a *Wh*-question may successfully extract from him the information necessary for his listener's understanding, but it may not inform him about the nature of the communicative problem.

Yet communicative problems rarely occurred. The children managed quite well even though, we assume, many of them would have answered as listener blamers in our communication game. If the children communicate effectively without understanding about the causes of communicative success and failure, what advantages does the achievement of such understanding give him?

One might hold the view that, in general, knowledge is better than ignorance; it is surely preferable that an attentive child understand the reasons for his own failures to respond appropriately to instructions from adults, rather than always accept the blame for failure. We have identified experimentally some improvements in communicative performance associated with the change from listener blaming to speaker blaming (Robinson & Robinson, 1978a, 1978b), but improvements in the short term will not be dramatic, because performance is already proficient. Presumably, it is only if the child's performance is already good that he can come to see why failures occur. Unless success is the rule, why should he seek to explain failure? When the child comes to understand about the role of the message, his approach to a problem in communication will change: It will become analytic and deductive, rather than experimental and intuitive. The child should be able to reflect upon his speech with its successes and failures in a way that the child without understanding cannot. If this is so, the child who understands about communication has a potential for intellectual growth that is qualitatively superior to that of his listener-blaming peer.

If, then, it is an advantage to children to understand about communication instead of just using rules of thumb, it may be worthwhile to teach children the reasons for successful and unsuccessful communication. As it appears that children are usually not told explicitly when and why their messages are not understood, we wondered if the child might be able to learn about communication if he was informed directly about problems that arose. We decided to find out how children interpreted the various possible adult responses to an inadequate message. If the child says, for example, "Mum, do you know where my cardigan is?" does he interpret the response "Which one?" as an indication that his message was inadequate, or does he treat the question like, for example, "Why do you want it?" which is not an indicator of message inadequacy? We thought it possible that the child might find it easier to recognize the inadequacies of his messages if adults told him explicitly when and why they did not understand instead of simply asking a question.

In Experiment 4, we constructed six snatches of dialogue between imaginary children and their mothers. We chose mother rather than a stranger so as to mimic as closely as possible our child subjects' everyday circumstances. In each case, the child depicted had lost an article of clothing and asked his mother for help. Each child was represented by a cardboard cutout doll, and the lost object by a picture which was attached in a "thought bubble" near the doll's head as the dialogue was presented. The task was introduced in this way: "I've got some pictures of boys and girls here. They've all lost something and they ask their Mum for help. Here's _____; he's [or she's for the pictures of girls] lost his _____. This is the _____ he wants. This is the one he's thinking about [as the article was attached near the doll's head]."

Each of the dolls said, "Mum, have you seen my _____ please?" and each of the doll's mothers gave a different reply: One of the mothers did know where the article was, another one said she did not know where it was, and the others gave more or less explicit indicators of not understanding what was wanted: "Which gloves?" "Do you want your red hat?" (the doll did); "Do you want your green jacket?" (the doll wanted his purple one); and "I dont know which cardigan you want. You've got two cardigans. You should tell me which one". There was also a seventh item, in which the child subject was given no response from the doll's mother, or so it was not possible to tell whether or not the mother had understood. This item was always given first.

After the experimenter had recited each snatch of dialogue to the child, she asked two questions: "_____'s Mum knows _____ wants a _____. Does she know *this* is the one he wants?" (While asking, the experimenter pointed to the article in the thought bubble.) If the child said no, he was asked why not: "Did _____ say enough about what he wanted? He said 'Mum, have you seen my _____ please?' Did he say enough about what he wanted?" If the child again said no, he was then asked "What should he have said?"

Each child was individually tested and presented with all the items in one of four orders. In addition, each child was tested for his understanding about inadequate messages and their role in causing communication failure using one of the "life-like" communication failure stories described in Robinson and Robinson (1977a): Steven asks his mother for a drink; he is given an orange drink, but really wanted a green drink. Whose fault was it Steven didn't get the drink he wanted? On the basis of his answers to the whose-fault sequence of questions, the child was categorized into one of four blame categories: listener blamers, two intermediate categories, and speaker blamers. In this experiment we tested 63 children aged between 5:2 and 6:6.

There was a clear difference between listener and speaker blamers in their judgments about the first item, the item in which there was no response from the mother. Most of the listener blamers said that the mother did know just what was wanted; in contrast, two-thirds of the speaker blamers thought that the mother did not know, or were not sure whether she did or not. The first assumption of the listener blamers, apparently, was that the message would be understood; this was less often true of the children with more advanced understanding about message inadequacy and communication failure.

Many of the listener blamers held to their assumption even when the mother's indicator of nonunderstanding was given. Of the 19 listener blamers, only 4 recognized the inadequacy of *any* of the messages given by the dolls, whereas 22 of the 28 speaker blamers judged at least some of them to be inadequate.

In this experiment, we wanted to see whether certain forms of mother's response made it easier for the child to identify listener's nonunderstanding and message inadequacy. We were therefore mainly interested in the children who gave different judgments in the different items.

Preliminary analyses of the data suggest that it was easier for the child to recognize the mother's nonunderstanding or the message inadequacy, or both, if the mother either made the problem explicit, instead of just asking for the missing information; made a wrong guess, instead of just asking for the missing information; or verbalized a wrong rather than correct guess. Many children thought that the mother who said she did not know where the lost article was did not understand what the doll wanted. There was an apparent confusion between a listener's ignorance and his nonunderstanding.

These results suggest that the young child may have difficulty in recognizing on the basis of the listener's response that a message has not been understood, but that this difficulty may be less pronounced if the listener makes explicit what the problem is, or verbalizes an incorrect guess about the meaning of the message. Even if the child realizes that the listener does not understand, he may not locate the problem with the message. He was less likely to spot the inadequacy of a message if the listener guessed correctly rather than incorrectly, even though both guesses took the form of a question, which to an adult might indicate uncertainty in the listener.

One implication of these results is that the common adult response to a child's inadequate message is unlikely to be the most suitable one for teaching him about communication. If the adult simply asks "Which one?" the child may not realize that his original message was incomplete. The apparent confusion between nonunderstanding and ignorance could presumably also be helped by giving more explicit responses: "I know what you want but I don't know where it is," rather than simply "I don't know." It could also be the case that the better the adult listener is at understanding the child, and hence the better he is at guessing correctly what is wanted (despite uncertainty), the less that child is informed about the requirements of effective communication.

If giving the child explicit information about nonunderstanding and message inadequacy helps him to comprehend the immediate situation, it might also help him to do better and understand better in the future. The experiment summarized in what follows was designed to see whether this is the case.

In Experiment 5, each child played individually with the experimenter a game that involved choosing clothes for dolls to wear. Fifty-two children between the ages of 5:2 and 6:5 were tested. Child and experimenter sat on either side of a screen, and had identical dolls with sets of clothes. There were six different types of garment (sweaters, trousers, shirts, etc.), and eight of each type. The types of garment were displayed on different rows of a stand, so on any one trial the child dealt with eight items. The eight examples of a type of garment differed along three dimensions, each of which had two values. For example, the sweaters had wide or narrow stripes, long or no sleeves, and round or V necks. As the child selected which of each type of garment his doll was to wear, he described it so that the experimenter could select the matching one for her doll. The stated aim was that both dolls would be wearing the same clothes.

Whenever the child gave an inadequate description of a particular item, that is, one that did not identify it uniquely, the experimenter took one of three courses of action:

1. For one third of the children, she simply made a guess.
2. For another third of the children, she asked "Which one" in a puzzled tone of voice, waited for the child's response, and then chose as best she could.
3. For the remaining children she made explicit what was missing, for example, "Well, there are four like that, I don't know whether it's

got long sleeves or short sleeves, and I don't know whether it's got stripes or squares [checks]." The experimenter made her choice when the child had supplied the missing information.

In all cases, the child's and experimenter's selected clothes were compared to see if they were the same before the child went on to another type of garment.

The child was tested before and after this game for his understanding of inadequate messages and their role in causing communication failure. To test this, child and experimenter played with a second matching set of dolls and clothes. This time, child and experimenter took turns at choosing clothes, and, whenever an inadequate message sent by either resulted in the listener's choosing wrongly, the experimenter asked the whose-fault sequence of questions. On the basis of his answers to the whose-fault sequence of questions given at the beginning and at the end of the game, each child was placed twice into one of four categories (listener blamers, two intermediate categories, and speaker blamers)—once on the basis of his performance at the beginning of the game, and once on the basis of his performance at the end of the game.

Each of the child's initial descriptions of the chosen articles of clothing (i.e., before the experimenter had given any of the three forms of feedback on that trial) referred to one, two, four, or eight garments, and on this basis was given an ambiguity score of 1, 2, 3, or 4. Each child gave six such initial descriptions. The total ambiguity score for these six was our measure of the adequacy of the child's initial descriptions.

We found that, of the children categorized as listener blamers at the beginning of the game, those who were given explicit information about the inadequacies of their message gave less ambiguous messages than those in the other two feedback conditions (guessing or being asked which one). And it was apparently not the case that the listener blamers who were given explicit feedback were merely learning to say more: The listener blamers in the three feedback conditions did not differ in the number of irrelevant attributes mentioned.

Finally, we looked at the answers to the whose-fault sequence at the end of the game; not all the children were given this test. Of those tested with the whose-fault sequence both at the beginning and the end, only two of the nine in the explicit feedback condition who were listener blamers at the beginning of the game, were still listener blamers at the end; the others had moved into more advanced blame categories. In contrast, only two out of nine in the guessing condition had moved out of the listener blamer category by the end of the experiment, as had only three out of six in the "which one?" condition.

It appears, then, that those who at the start of the experiment showed no sign of understanding about the role of inadequate messages in causing communication failure, benefited in two ways from being given explicit information about the inadequacies of their messages. First, they gave better messages spontaneously (before being given any information about that particular message) than did those in the other two feedback conditions. Second, they were more likely than those in the other two feedback conditions to have improved in their understanding about communicating by the end of the experiment.

Among children who at the start of the experiment fell into the more advanced blame categories (lower and higher intermediates and speaker blamers), there was no difference in quality of messages between the three feedback conditions. There were but few advances in blame category by the end of the experiment among the intermediates, and no differences in this respect between the feedback conditions. Although the speaker blamers (in all three conditions combined) gave better messages than the listener blamers in the explicit feedback condition, they still had room for improvement. Presumably, these speaker blamers were not helped by the explicit feedback because they already knew what the problem was—they were already trying to identify uniquely their chosen article of clothing, and perhaps they simply had difficulty in making the necessary comparisons and producing a suitable message.

The results of this experiment appear to demonstrate that adults could productively utilize opportunities for helping children to learn about communication effectiveness. The common adult responses to children's inadequate messages—guessing or asking a *Wh-* question, seem to be much less effective than giving explicit information as a means of improving a child's communicative performance and his understanding about communication.

Ignorance or Egocentrism?

When we first discovered and identified listener blamers, they appeared not to know that a message should refer uniquely to whatever the speaker had in mind. Even if in a description completion task they could perform the comparisons necessary for judging the inadequacy of too-general messages, we could not enable them to make such judgments in the communication game. Countersuggestion was ineffective, as were analytic descriptions of the events, in which we offered comments such as "But you didn't know which one, did you? I just said 'A flower' and you picked a flower. I didn't tell you it was the red flower." These comments had absolutely no effect on message evaluation or on future performance. The experimenter in the role of observer and commentator could not persuade these children to give an inadequacy judgment when confronted with a too-general message, whether the message was his own, the experimenter's, or a doll's.

However, from the evidence presented in the second and third sections of this chapter, it now seems that if the experimenter in the role of listener makes explicit what her problems are in interpreting a too-general message, the listener blamer can improve his message. Moreover, experience of doing this apparently enables the child to improve his understanding of message inadequacy and also the quality of his subsequent messages.

Might we then suggest that the child really understood about message inadequacy all the time? This could be misleading. However, it would also be unnecessarily complex on this evidence alone to describe the child as egocentric, if use of that term implies an incapacity to conceive of the problems of dealing with another's information requirements. The simpler description would be that the child was ignorant about the problems of perspective in verbal communication. Once given the information he needs, he is able to restructure his thinking and his behavior immediately.

In *The Language and Thought of the Child,* Piaget (1959) gives an example which may be extended to clarify this distinction:

> A simple ignorant man who has lived since his birth in a small corner at the foot of mountains of which he has a good view but which he has never explored. From the point of view of physical knowledge, this observer will obviously fall prey to all sorts of illusions. . . . He will see the world as a system of which he occupies the centre and all the mountains and valleys grouped in relation to the place in which he lives. Similar illusions will colour his knowledge of other people . . . the intellectual, enjoying a holiday, will be looked upon as a lazy rentier . . . [pp. 268–269].

This man is ignorant: Presumably, if the intellectual were to break his holiday by presenting the man with the "three mountains" problem, the man would demonstrate the capacity to handle the spatial relations involved. If he were persuaded to travel around the countryside surrounding his home, he would restructure his view of it without difficulty. The case of this imaginary man can be contrasted with that of his imaginary 2-year-old son: Taken on the same travels, he would not use the information available to him to restructure his view of the world. He could usefully be described as egocentric rather than simply ignorant.

If the child at the stage we have been investigating (5-year-olds in our sample) is merely ignorant about certain aspects of the communicative process, why is he ignorant?

If the infant is to attempt to communicate with others (verbally or nonverbally), he will presumably first of all behave in a way consistent with having a tacit assumption that his messages will be effective. Without necessarily having any awareness of understanding or nonunderstanding, we would expect the child to make modifications to his messages when his listeners do not respond appropriately. This would be the case with any attempt to achieve a certain goal: If a child is trying to open a box and fails with his first mode of attack, he is likely to try a different way. Without introducing the concept of "understanding about" communication at all, one could expect the child to

- Learn by trial and error (repeat his utterance when he fails to achieve the desired result, and modify it in a limited way such as shouting more loudly)
- Build up a store of general effective modifications which are not listener-specific (speaking more slowly may be more effective than speaking more loudly)
- Accumulate knowledge of particular techniques suitable for particular listeners (such as infants or animals) and generalize to new listeners having similar characteristics
- Learn to apply directly taught rules for effective communication (such as making requests in a polite way; saying *please* and *thank you*)

Relying upon these techniques alone, the young child may manage to communicate successfully much of the time; he need not necessarily understand the reasons for the success or failure of communications. He may operate quite well while remaining ignorant about the requirements of effective communication.

We have seen that when he is between the ages of 3 and 6, the child's adult listeners apparently do very little to remove him or help him remove himself from his state of ignorance. They give very little information about the inadequacy of messages and about the reasons for communication failure. They simply act to generate and extract the information missing from the child's inadequate messages without informing him that they were inadequate, and they may reformulate their own inadequate messages without telling the child why.

This focusing of attention on the communication alone, rather than upon the process, would appear to be appropriate when the infant is first learning to speak. Performance limitations would prevent the infant from taking his listener's needs into account in any but the very simplest way (e.g., talking more loudly to somebody further away). In any case, there will normally be little need to do so as his first referential comments are often about objects visible or audible to the listener, and he will commonly be communicating with somebody who knows how he spends his day and who knows what he is likely to be commenting on. Given that at this stage of development (perhaps up to about 2 years) the infant is often incapable of producing messages that could be understood by a listener who did not know the context or the range of likely utterances, one might predict that the greater the range of shared experience between the infant and his listener, the more successful communication between them will be and the more quickly the infant will master language. It might even be the case that, if language learning is to be successful, the infant must be allowed to remain in ignorance about discrepancies in information requirements between the speaker and his listeners.

At this early stage in the mastery of language, even if the infant were given information about the inadequacy of messages and the reasons for the success or failure of communication, he would presumably be unable to understand, let alone use, the information. The child must be able to perform the simplest comparisons if he is to conceive of the inadequacy of a too-general message. He must be able to handle distal causes if he is to conceive of the speaker's message as being responsible for communication failure (Robinson & Robinson, 1978a). He must have the capacity to keep a number of components in mind at the same time if he is to conceive of a listener's information requirements as being different from his own. That is, quite apart from problems in production of messages, one might expect that the 1- to 2-year-old would be unable to understand that a message should refer uniquely to whatever the speaker has in mind. If so, then in this respect he could be described as egocentric rather than simply ignorant.

By the time the child is 2 or 3, not only will his mastery of language be much greater, but he might also have acquired at least some of the skills that have been listed, and, if so, he will be in a position to benefit from information about the process of communication. There are at least four reasons why this information might rarely be given. First, as with the infant, many pre-school children may be communicating mainly with adults who know what they are likely to say. There may in fact be few communication failures. However, once the child reaches school age, he is likely to try to relate to his mother or his teacher events of which they are ignorant. One might therefore expect to observe more frequent attempts by adults to inform the child about the requirements of effective communication; yet, the children in Clough's and Cambourne's samples did already attend preschool or school, and such attempts were still rare. Second, adults may not be aware that the child is ignorant about the process of communicating. They may fail to realize that saying *Which one?* is not seen by the child as an indicator of message inadequacy. They may fail to realize that the child finds it difficult to identify nonunderstanding in his listener, and that, even if he does identify it, he may not locate the problem with his message. Third, perhaps the focus of attention of the adult when he is interacting with a child is on maintaining smooth discourse flow. Even in adult conversation, it can be considered rude to tell a speaker that you have not understood what has been said. The same rule of politeness may apply to adult–child conversation. Adults have perhaps learned to pretend to understand, and may have acquired responses that allow conversation to continue despite incomplete understanding of what has been said. Fourth, at other times, such as in the classroom, the focus of attention of the adult may be upon relaying information or making the child emit some particular response. In order to achieve this, there may be no need to talk about communication, and to do so may even distract the child from the task at hand.

The situation may be, then, that the infant first behaves as if his communications will be effective. In fact, they often are in the early stages of the mastery of language because the child and his listener have shared the experience upon which he is commenting; and, subsequently, because the child has acquired various useful rules of thumb. On occasions when his communications are not effective, he may be unaware of nonunderstanding in his listener because his listener fails to inform him or even misleads him; on occasions when he does not understand an adult's message, again he may be unaware of his own nonunderstanding.

If this is an accurate description, giving information to the child about communication does appear to help both his communicative performance and his understanding. This would be expected on a learning theory view of development, but at first sight it might appear to be inconsistent with a Piagetian view. Piaget (1926/1959), after making the point that adults take the child into account so efficiently that they allow his egocentrism to continue, goes on to argue that it is peer interaction that is responsible for the breaking down of egocentrism. His view is that development occurs as a result of conflict between equals rather than by means of learning from a relationship based on inequality, such as the parent–child relationship. This is quite consistent with his general mechanism of development by equilibration, as applied, for example, to the acquisition of conservation of quantity (see Peill, 1975). In this case, the conflict leading to development is between judgments arising from two aspects of appearance.

Even if this general model of cognitive development (conflict between equals rather than imposition from a higher level) is valid, one could argue that, in the case of learning about communication, information from adults *would* be helpful to the child. Informing the child "I don't know which one you mean because there are two like that" is merely letting him know the effects of his action (in this case a message), and is not equivalent to telling him adult criteria for judging changes in quantity. It is perhaps equivalent to allowing him to observe the effects on appearance of his manipulations of clay. That is, consistent with the Piagetian view that increasing the child's experience of relevant physical transformations may help him to acquire concepts of quantity conservation, one could argue that giving the child more information about the quality of messages and the success or failure of communications may accelerate the development of his understanding about communication. That is, it would be quite consistent with a Piagetian view of development, as with a learning theory view, to argue that, if adults behaved differently, children could develop more quickly.

The problem for the child in coming to understand about communication may not be that adults take his needs into account too efficiently; rather, it may be that adults are quite unaware of the child's need to be informed explicitly about the success or failure of communications. Is it the adult or the child who is egocentric?

Acknowledgements

Most of the research reported here was financially supported by the Education Research and Development Committee of the Australian Commonwealth; the Social Science Research

Council (U.K.) is currently financing extensions of the work. Grateful acknowledgement is made to both these bodies. I would like to thank W. P. Robinson for his help with this chapter. Patrick Dickson, Margery Heber, Angela Hildyard and Gary Price all made comments on earlier drafts which were very helpful in producing this final version.

References

Asher, S. R., & Oden, S. L. Children's failure to communicate: An assessment of comparison and egocentrism explanations. *Developmental Psychology*, 1976, *12*, 132–139.

Bearison, D. J., & Levey, L. M. Children's comprehension of referential communication: Decoding ambiguous messages. *Child Development*, 1977, *48*, 716–720.

Cambourne, B. L. *A naturalistic study of language performance in grade I rural and urban school children.* Unpublished doctoral dissertation, James Cook University, Queensland, 1971.

Clough, J. R. *An experimental investigation of the effects of a cognitive training programme on educationally disadvantaged children of pre-school age.* Unpublished doctoral dissertation, Monash University, Victoria, 1971.

Cosgrove, J. M., & Patterson, C. J. Plans and the development of listener skills. *Developmental Psychology*, 1977, *13*, 557–564.

Cosgrove, J. M., & Patterson, C. J. Generalization of training for children's listener skills. *Child Development*, 1978, *49*, 513–516.

Foorman, B. R. *A neo-Piagetian analysis of communication performance in young children.* Unpublished manuscript, 1977. (Available from author at University of California, Davis, Department of Applied Behavioral Sciences, Davis, California 95616).

Krauss, R. M., & Glucksberg, S. The development of communication: Competence as a function of age. *Child Development*, 1969, *40*, 255–266.

Maratsos, M. P. Non-egocentric communication abilities in preschool children. *Child Development*, 1973, *44*, 697–700.

Patterson, C. J., Massad, C. M., & Cosgrove, J. M. Children's referential communication: Components of plans for effective listening. *Developmental Psychology*, 1978, *14*, 401–406.

Peill, E. J. *Invention and discovery of reality.* London: Wiley, 1975.

Peterson, C. L., Danner, F. W., & Flavell, J. H. Developmental changes in children's responses to three indications of communicative failure. *Child Development*, 1972, *43*, 1464–1468.

Piaget, J. *The language and thought of the child* (3rd ed.). London: Routledge and Kegan Paul, 1959. (Originally published, 1926.)

Robinson, E. J., & Robinson, W. P. Developmental changes in the child's explanation of communication failure. *Australian Journal of Psychology*, 1976, *28*, 155–165. (a)

Robinson, E. J., & Robinson, W. P. The young child's understanding of communication. *Developmental Psychology*, 1976, *12*, 328–333. (b)

Robinson, E. J., & Robinson, W. P. The child's understanding of life-like communication failures. *Australian Journal of Psychology*, 1977, *29*, 101–109. (a)

Robinson, E. J., & Robinson, W. P. Development in the understanding of causes of success and failure in verbal communication. *Cognition*, 1977, 363–378. (b)

Robinson, E. J., & Robinson, W. P. The young child's explanations of communication failure: A re-interpretation of results. *Perceptual Motor Skills*, 1977, *44*, 363–366. (c)

Robinson, E. J., & Robinson, W. P. Development of understanding about communication: Message inadequacy and its role in causing communication failure. *Genetic Psychology Monographs*, 1978. (a)

Robinson, E. J., & Robinson, W. P. The relationship between children's explanations of communication failure and their ability deliberately to give bad messages. *British Journal of Social and Clinical Psychology*, 1978, *17*, 219–225. (b)

Robinson, E. J., & Robinson, W. P. The roles of egocentrism and of weakness in comparing in children's explanations of communication failure. *Journal of Experimental Child Psychology,* 1978, *26,* 147–160. (c)

Shatz, M., & Gelman, R. The development of communication skills: Modification in the speech of young children as a function of listener. *Monographs of the Society for Research in Child Development,* 1973, (Serial No. 152).

Valian, V., Caplan, J. S., & de Sciora, A. M. *Children's use of syntactic knowledge in a failure of communication.* Unpublished manuscript, 1977. (Obtainable from V. Valian, Department of Psychology, Columbia University, New York.)

9

Referential Communication Activities in Research and in the Curriculum: A Metaanalysis

W. PATRICK DICKSON

This chapter has three goals: (*a*) to summarize findings from a metaanalysis of the referential communication research literature; (*b*) to discuss some uses of referential activities in elementary school classrooms; and (*c*) to make some methodological suggestions for future work on referential communication.

Metaanalysis of Referential Communication Research

Other chapters in this volume have reviewed the substantive findings concerning children's referential communication skills (Asher & Wigfield; Whitehurst & Sonnenschein; Patterson & Kister; and Robinson). The additions to our understanding of children's communication skills contained in those chapters speak well of the referential communication paradigm and bear testimony to the fact that experimental research in laboratory settings

189

Children's Oral Communication Skills

can make important contributions to our understanding of children's communication. On the basis of this research, we now have good reason to believe that a number of fundamental communication skills can be taught and we know techniques that are successful in teaching them. Specifically, children can be taught to make comparisons among various referents in a display and use those comparisons to encode better messages (Asher & Wigfield); children can be taught that to communicate in referential situations means to describe differences (Whitehurst & Sonnenschein); children can be taught to ask increasingly specific questions when faced with uncertainty, the effect of which is to lead to more accurate communication between children (Patterson & Kister); and children can be taught that communication failure can result from failures on the part of the speaker rather than always being due to the listener (Robinson).

Much of the research on which these conclusions are based is included in a review of the referential communication research literature (Dickson & Moskoff, 1980). In this search we attempted to locate every study that used referential communication tasks. We first located every published study cited in the Glucksberg, Krauss, and Higgins (1975) review. Next, we searched every issue of major journals from 1972 through early 1979. Finally, we searched the citations of all sources we had located in the search. In the end, a total of 66 referential communication publications were located. These publications reported 80 separate experiments, in which a total of 114 referential tasks were administered; a total of about 6200 subjects participated in the studies. It seems safe to say that our search included most studies of referential communication that have attracted the attention of researchers in the field. (The additional studies reported in the present volume are not included in the review.) The 66 publications located are listed in Appendix A.

Each study was coded on a number of dimensions, such as the number of subjects, age of the youngest and oldest subjects, type of referential task, number of trials, type of experimental design used, and so on. In addition to the characteristics of the studies, we also coded whether significant effects were found for a number of commonly examined factors, including age, sex, socioeconomic status, and egocentrism or roletaking. These data were then entered into a computer file and an SPSS system file (Nie, Hull, Jenkins, Steinbrenner, & Bent, 1975) to facilitate our "metaanalysis." Metaanalysis, a term made popular by Glass (1976), refers to techniques for summarizing the results of a number of studies.

A number of substantive findings emerged from our analysis of factors related to communication performance. In almost every study where age was a variable, performance was strongly related to age, even when the age range was only 1 year. With respect to sex-related differences, it was interesting to discover that, in every study where subjects were paired with each other, same-sex pairs were used. Furthermore, although a few differences were reported between male–male pairs and female–female pairs, most were higher order interactions and the total number of results showing sex-related differences occurring in the studies appears to be considerably less than would have occurred by chance with a probability level of .05. In the absence of more compelling logic than has motivated most analyses of sex differences, it would appear that no further research on this variable is needed and that unreplicated, unhypothesized higher order interactions ought not to be reported. Research comparing same-sex with mixed-sex pairing might be of interest, however, given the total absence of any research on this factor.

Verbal ability (or IQ) does not appear to be strongly related to referential communication skill, although significant correlations were observed in a few studies. Differences related to socioeconomic status of the participants were found in 8 of the 10 studies that included this factor, but the confounding of other factors with socioeconomic status renders these results uninterpretable. Seventeen studies included some test of the egocentrism or role-taking hypothesis, but the pattern of results gave little support to the view that referential communication performance is influenced to any great extent by egocentrism or role-taking (a conclusion also reached in Shantz's chapter in this volume).

What can be said about the characteristics of the research leading to these substantive findings? The typical study was published in *Child Development* or *Developmental Psychology* and reported a single experiment in which approximately 60 white, English-speaking, middle-class children of about 5 or 6 years of age communicated on a single referential task. In most of the studies, the children spoke or listened to an experimenter, not to other children, and, in the studies where children did communicate with other children, the children were often not allowed to see each other, talk back and forth, or ask questions. The typical task involved about nine trials in which one of a set of about four pictures was described or chosen; the most commonly used referents were abstract line drawings or pictures that differed on fixed attributes such as color and size.

The concentration of referential research on younger children can be seen in Figure 9.1, where the ages of the youngest and oldest subjects in the 80 experiments are displayed. We know little about the communication skills of children from age 11 until they reappear in our research as undergraduates. The communication skills of individual subjects were rarely studied in depth. Over 75% of all the tasks involved trials with less than 20 items. Similarly, only a few of the studies measured children's performance on multiple referential communication tasks, and of those that did, only a few report the correlations across the measures.

Each of the 114 referential tasks was coded according to who sent to whom (i.e., who was the speaker and who was the listener) in the task. Four basic categories were used: subject-to-subject, subject-to-tester, tester-to-

Youngest subjects			Oldest subjects		
N	Age	Histogram	N	Age	Histogram
0	1	*	0	1	
2	2	**	0	2	
4	3	****	0	3	
10	4	*********	2	4	**
16	5	****************	6	5	******
9	6	********	1	6	*
11	7	***********	7	7	*******
5	8	*****	4	8	***
2	9	**	8	9	********
3	10	***	5	10	*****
0	11		10	11	**********
1	12	*	2	12	**
0	13		0	13	
1	14	*	0	14	*
0	15		2	15	**
0	16		0	16	
0	17		0	17	
16	18	***************	1	18	*
	35		2	35	**

Figure 9.1. Distribution of experiments by age of youngest and oldest subjects. (College students are coded as 18-years-old; other adults as 35-years-old. Thirty studies in which only one age group was studied do not appear in the "Oldest" distribution.)

subject, and subjects-through-tester. (Parent-child studies are a special case of the subject-to-subject category.) In the first category, pairs of subjects interact with each other; in the next two, the tester serves as listener or speaker; the last category contains studies in which the tester recorded messages produced by subjects and then presented them to subjects who now acted as listeners. Clearly, the subject-to-subject design is the only one that permits natural interaction between the subjects. Figure 9.2 shows the changes over time in the frequency with which these four types of designs have been used. Over the 20 years spanned by this review, there has been a trend away from the more natural subject-to-subject design toward those designs in which the tester serves as the listener, or more recently, as the speaker.

Each task was also categorized according to the type of referential activity used. The tasks were grouped into four broad categories. In the first, *words* serve as referents; this category includes word pairs as well as tasks in which the subjects have to judge the adequacy of fixed messages. In the second category, subjects are required to describe one of a set of pictures having *fixed attributes;* this category includes tasks in which pieces with fixed attributes are selected and placed in an array. In the third type of task, subjects describe one of a set of pictures having *"fuzzy" attributes,* such as

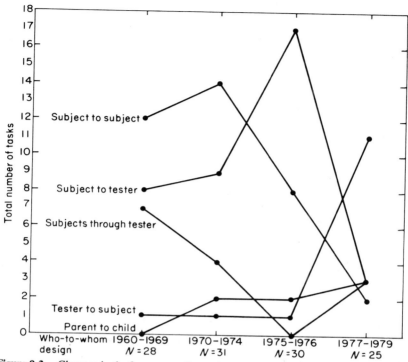

Figure 9.2. Changes in the frequency of use of experimental designs over time: Who sends to whom in the study.

abstract figures or color chips, for which language does not have ready labels. The fourth type of task involves *telling how* to do something, where the listener must carry out a sequence of steps. Included here are model-building tasks, map directions, game rules, telling how to draw symbols or trace a route on a map, or recounting game rules or events in a story. Changes over time in the types of tasks used are shown in Figure 9.3. The tasks involving referents with fixed attributes have greatly increased in popularity and those using word pairs have returned to popularity, whereas both the tasks involving "fuzzy" attributes and those in which subjects tell how to do something complex have declined sharply.

The pattern of changes over time in these two aspects of the research designs raises concerns about the ecological validity of this work. The subject-to-subject design and the telling-how task appear to most closely resemble the kinds of referential communication that might be encountered in natural settings. Children do engage in discussions about construction of a fort, for example, and the ability to give directions on a map or tell how to assemble parts in a kit is called for in a number of contexts. Yet it is precisely this type of task that has come to receive decreasing attention in referential research.

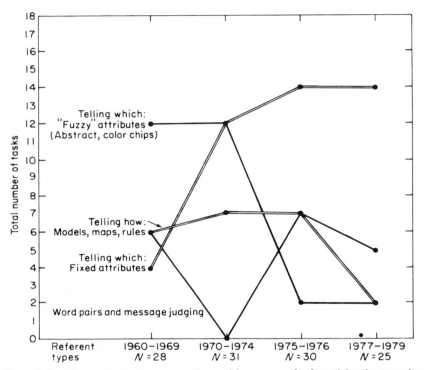

Figure 9.3. Changes in the frequency of use of four types of referential tasks over time.

It is quite possible that the shift away from the more natural and complex communication settings was a necessary step in the evolution of our discipline. Certainly, the accomplishments summarized at the beginning of this chapter support that view. Nevertheless, perhaps referential communication researchers should attempt to take the findings from tightly controlled situations into more complex, natural referential settings.

Referential Communication Activities in the Classroom

Now is an opportune time for research and development on the use of referential communication activities in classrooms. The U.S. Office of Education recently added speaking and listening skills to the list of "Basic Skills" under Title II (Lieb-Brilhart, 1979). This action has focused considerable attention on the need to develop curricular activities for teaching oral communication skills, as well as techniques for assessing these skills.

Feeling that referential activities have a number of features that make them potentially useful in the classroom, Patterson and I began a search for existing curriculum materials that call upon referential communication skills. Our search made us aware of a terminological difference between developmental psychology and speech communication, where referential skills are referred to as "informing" skills. (See Allen and Brown, 1977, p. 251, and Larson, Backlund, Redmond, and Barbour, 1978, pp. 1–3, for definitions commonly used in the field of speech communication.) In addition, we found that oral communication in the curriculum encompasses a broad range of meanings, including rhetoric, drama, poetry, reading, as well as referential ("informing") communication. Nonetheless, our search turned up a number of commercially available communication activities similar in form to referential tasks used in research (Dickson & Patterson, 1979).

Several of these activities will be described briefly. One example is the game "Talk and Take," originally developed by Olds (1968; 1973) as a part of his dissertation. This game is played by two children on a checkerboard and requires the players to follow instructions written on cards. The instructions combine referential and logical meanings; for example, "If you have a big blue circle on an orange space, you may move it two spaces." The use of conditional logic in this game resembles the research task used by Pozner and Saltz (1974), whereas the referential aspect of the game resembles the array construction task used by Shantz and Wilson (1972). Another referential game, developed in a curriculum project in England, is called the "Symbol Drawing Game" (Wright, Norris, & Worsley, 1974). In this game, two children are separated by a barrier. The speaker has a booklet filled with drawings of geometric shapes and abstract figures. His task is to tell the listener how to draw the figure, and when they feel the drawing is complete, they compare it with the original. This task strongly resembles the research task used by Brilhart (1965) and the description task used by Fry (1966). Other activities included a map directions task and worksheet activities in which children had to follow oral directions and write letters on particular pictures described by the speaker (Harnishfeger, 1977).

After pilot testing these materials, we concluded that some research tasks were potentially more interesting and challenging to children than were many of the commercially available materials, in particular, tasks calling for model building (Baldwin & Garvey, 1973; Piché, Michlin, Rubin, & Johnson, 1975; Dickson, Miyake, & Muto, 1979), map directions (Baldwin & Garvey, 1973; Ratner & Rice, 1963), placing in an array (Karabenick & Miller, 1977), and picture choosing (including the widely used abstract figures, color chips, and pictures with fixed attributes). Criteria for judging the suitability of referential communication activities in the classroom are discussed in our review of these curriculum materials (Dickson & Patterson, 1979).

In addition, it was disappointing to note that not one of the curriculum activities was supported by any evaluation of its effectiveness. What children were expected to learn from these activities was rarely specified, nor were suggestions made as to how teachers might assess individual children's performance in these activities. Nevertheless, our pilot tests confirmed that these activities do appeal to teachers and children. In my summary of trends in referential research, I called for increased research using complex referential tasks in which children interact freely with other children. We have found teachers eager to have their students participate in activities of this type. Research and evaluation of the use of referential communication activities in classrooms would seem to open up the kind of involvement of participants in research called for by Shuy and Griffin in their chapter in this volume.

Future Directions for Research on Referential Communication

Several questions that have occupied much attention in the past decade seem to me to be worth declaring null and void. The first of these is the age at which children are "able to communicate." The referential communication tradition found that even school age children are quite incompetent in communication, whereas the sociolinguistic tradition found that even infants are quite skillful in communication. The one tradition set out with the presupposition that children were "egocentric" and showed them to be so; the other set out to show the natural competence of children and succeeded in doing so. The apparently contradictory results can largely be reconciled by observing that task demands and criteria for "competence" determine the results of the study. Research aimed at establishing *the* age at which children achieve communicative competence will be less illuminating than research dealing with the more difficult questions of how task demands, cognitive development, and experience interact to produce a level of performance for an individual.

Another uninteresting question would seem to be that of the relationship between role-taking skill and communication skill. Whatever the relationship, it is clear that the percentage of variance in communication performance attributable to role taking is very small. In many ways, research on communication skill got off on the wrong foot. Rather than being an object of interest in its own right, communication has often been only a domain in which to look for manifestations of egocentrism. The original training studies often were poor training studies indeed. Only recently, in studies such as those presented in this book, has intensive research on training communication skills themselves been carried out.

Perhaps the most pressing problem for researchers and educators is the need for techniques for measuring the speaking and listening skills of the *individual* by observing the individual's interaction with others in essentially natural communication tasks. The lack of attention to this problem is perhaps due to the methodological difficulties in making such measurements in view of the fact that communication accuracy scores are jointly produced by the two participants in the communication act. This dyadic score includes three sources of variance: that due to the speaker, that due to the listener, and that due to the interaction of the speaker and listener characteristics (statistical interaction rather than social interaction). The methodological difficulties posed by this complexity may be referred to as the "two-body" problem.

Two solutions to the two-body problem are possible. The first (and most common) takes the pair as the unit of analysis, carrying out analyses of variance or correlations on the *dyadic* scores. The second (which has rarely been used) employs experimental designs permitting the separate assessment of *individual* scores.

The Pair as Unit of Analysis

Dyadic scores of same-age pairs can be useful as long as the focus of the research is on general developmental trends in communication performance. Such studies shed light on mean levels of the performance of dyads but cannot tell us anything about the mean levels of performance of the individuals in the dyads.

Correlational analyses of dyadic performance are also possible. Taking the pair as the unit of analysis, one can analyze the generalizability (Cronbach, Gleser, Nanda, & Rajaratnam, 1972) of dyadic performance across task conditions and time without addressing the question of whether the speaker or listener skills of the members of the dyad would generalize when they were paired with other partners. Surprisingly few studies in the referential communication literature report reliability and generalizability analyses for the dyads.

The few reliability coefficients reported in the literature, however, suggest some degree of stability of dyadic performance in referential communication tasks. Baldwin and Garvey (1973) report correlations for dyadic scores across three referential tasks, ranging from a correlation of .53 between a picture-choosing task and a map task to a correlation of .40 between the picture-choosing task and a model-building task. Dyadic performance showed high internal consistency across all tasks, yielding a Cronbach's alpha of .72. In further analyses of the data described in Dickson (1979), I found partial correlations across four types of referents which ranged from .19 to .45, after controlling for age and verbal ability; the partial correlations across four trials ranged from 14 to .60. The internal consistency of performance of mother–child dyads on a 24-item picture-describing task had an alpha coefficient of .61 in the United States and .49 in Japan (Dickson, Hess, Miyake, & Azuma, 1979). Thus, dyadic performance at a given point in time appears moderately stable. No studies of the stability of dyadic communication accuracy scores across time (test–retest reliability) have been found in the literature.

Measuring the Communication Skills of Individuals

Although dyadic scores (especially those based upon long-term relationships, such as the mother–child pair) are appropriate for certain purposes, measures of individual performance in dyadic situations are essential if we are to gain insights into the underlying processes accounting for communication skill. Two types of experimental design can yield data on individuals' speaking and listening skills: The first involves *holding messages constant;* the second involves *repeated pairings* of speakers and listeners (Dickson, Miyake, & Muto, 1979).

The technique of holding messages constant has been widely used in research on referential communication. Listening skill is measured by presenting listeners with a standard set of referential messages and scoring the accuracy of the listeners' responses, thereby holding constant the variance due to speaker. Speaking skill is measured in a similar fashion: Speakers are asked to communicate certain information to an experimenter who functions as a "standard listener," asking either no questions or standard probe questions. The speakers' messages are recorded and scored, either by use of a coding manual in which the essential information is counted or by use of a "jury" of listeners who respond to the recorded messages. The major limitation of this technique is that speaker–listener interaction is eliminated or highly constrained; to the extent that communication skill includes a large component of such skills as questionning, answering, and monitoring the comprehension of one's partner, this technique will yield less valid measures of speaking and listening skills.

The repeated pairings technique is more difficult to employ in research, but has the advantage of permitting the speakers and listeners to engage in more natural interaction. In these designs, each speaker is paired with a number of listeners and each listener is paired with a number of speakers. Ideally, each person in the experimental design would be paired with every other person in both the speaking and listening role. Brilhart (1965) had college students describe geometric shapes to classmates who attempted to draw the shapes. The accuracy of the drawings was scored and students received speaking and listening scores. In Brilhart's design, however, each person served as speaker only once but served as listener 16 times, and, no speaker–listener questions were allowed. A more balanced repeated pairings which did permit speaker–listener interaction design was employed by Dickson, Miyake, and Muto (1979). Students alternated as speakers and listeners in a block assembly task. Each student was paired with every other student, and served 4 times as speaker and 4 times as listener. In contrast to Brilhart's study which found no correlation between speaking and listening scores, speaking and listening scores in the block assembly task correlated .45.

Assuming individual differences in communication skills can be reliably measured, the correlates of communication skills need to be investigated. These can be grouped into several categories which differ in their potential importance to the field. With respect to subject characteristics, it seems safe to say that no further research is needed to show that performance improves with age or that no differences exist between male–male and female–female dyads. Similarly, correlations of social class with global measures of communication accuracy will not contribute to our understanding of individual differences in communication skill, nor will demonstrations that performance will be worse when tasks are more difficult. What is needed is more specific hypotheses concerning the interaction between specific task characteristics and subject characteristics, especially where these hypotheses are examined in training studies aimed at experimentally manipulating the subject characteristics.

Finally, research in classroom applications of referential activities may increase the validity and generalizability of our research, especially if tasks and designs that allow more natural interaction between children are used. We have recently completed a study in which all the children in a classroom paired up and engaged in referential communication activities patterned after the picture-choosing tasks commonly used in research (Dickson, Patterson, & Tracy, 1980). For example, a class of 24 children was divided up into 12 pairs and seated at tables positioned around the edge of the room. One member of each pair was designated as the speaker, and on signal each pair began communication about sets of pictures in notebook (see Dickson, Hess, Miyake, & Azuma, 1979). After 3 minutes they stopped, and speaker–listener roles were reversed on a second 3-minute trial. Next, one member of each pair rotated to the next table and the process was repeated.

The teachers and children responded enthusiastically to these activities. This type of classroom activity engaged all of the children in the classroom in rich verbal interaction, characterized by much higher frequencies of speaking, listening, and questioning by the children than typically occurs in the classroom routine. I believe that a sociolinguist examining this potentially "natural" classroom activity would conclude that the social and verbal interaction had many educational aspects (see Cazden, 1972, Chapter 10; Moffett & Wagner, 1976). At the same time, the activity yields quantifiable measures of the efficiency with which dyads and individuals across partners communicate, making it useful for research and assessment.

Conclusion

Our metaanalysis of research in the referential communication tradition over the past two decades revealed a trend toward more tightly controlled experimental designs. These studies have suggested ways in which a number of communication skills can be taught but have offered little evidence that either the skills or the training generalizes to more natural settings. Recently, increased concern has been expressed about the ecological validity of much educational and psychological research (Bronfenbrenner, 1979), which accounts in part for the increased interest in the more qualitative, sociolinguistic approaches to research discussed in the introduction to this book. Coincidentally, actions by the U.S. Office of Education have placed priority upon the development of techniques for teaching and assessing oral communication skills in classrooms. These developments offer researchers an exceptional opportunity to extend the body of knowledge gained through research on referential communication skills in experimental settings to natural settings involving more complex and representative tasks. Although there presently exist curriculum materials that involve referential communication skills, little research has been done on these materials. One can be optimistic that increased attention by researchers to children's referential communication skills in more natural settings will benefit both theory and practice in the area of oral communication skills.

Acknowledgements

The preparation of this chapter was supported by a grant from the National Institute of Education to the Wisconsin Research and Development Center for Individualized Schooling.

Appendix: References for Metaanalysis of Referential Communication

Asher, S. R. Children's ability to appraise their own and another person's communication performance. *Developmental Psychology*, 1976, *12*, 24–32.

Asher, S. R., & Oden, S. L. Children's failure to communicate: An assessment of comparison and egocentrism explanations. *Developmental Psychology*, 1976, *12*, 132–139.

Asher, S. R., & Parke, R. D. Influence of sampling and comparison processes on the development of communication effectiveness. *Journal of Educational Psychology*, 1975, *67*, 64–75.

Baldwin, T. L., & Garvey, C. J. Components of accurate problem-solving communications. *American Educational Research Journal*, 1973, *10*, 39–48.

Baldwin, T. L., McFarlane, P. T., & Garvey, C. J. Children's communication accuracy related to race and socioeconomic status. *Child Development*, 1971, *42*, 345–357.

Bearison, D. J., & Cassel, T. Z. Cognitive decentration and social codes: Communicative effectiveness in young children from differing family contexts. *Developmental Psychology*, 1975, *11*, 29–36.

Bearison, D. J., & Levey, L. M. Children's comprehension of referential communication: Decoding ambiguous messages. *Child Development*, 1977, *48*, 716–720.

Brilhart, B. L. The relationship between some aspects of communicative speaking and communicative listening. *Journal of Communication*, 1965, *15*, 35–46.

Chandler, M. J., Greenspan, S., & Barenboim, C. Assessment and training of role-taking and referential communication skills in institutionalized emotionally disturbed children. *Developmental Psychology*, 1974, *10*, 546–553.

Chapanis, A., Ochsman, R. B., Parrish, R. N., & Weeks, G. D. Studies in interactive communication: I. The effects of four communication modes on the behavior of teams during cooperative problem-solving. *Human Factors*, 1972, *14*, 487–509.

Cohen, B. D., & Klein, J. F. Referent communication in school age children. *Child Development*, 1968, *39*, 597–609.

Cosgrove, J. M., & Patterson, C. J. Plans and the development of listener skills. *Developmental Psychology*, 1977, *13*, 557–564.

Cosgrove, J. M., & Patterson, C. J. Generalization of training for children's listener skills. *Child Development*, 1978, *19*, 513–516.

Danks, J. H. Encoding of novel figures for communication and memory. *Cognitive Psychology*, 1970, *1*, 179–191.

Dickson, W. P. The development of interpersonal referential communication skills in young children using an interactional game device (Doctoral dissertation, Stanford University, 1974). *Dissertation Abstracts International*, 1974, *35*, 3511-A. (University Microfilms No. 74-27, 008).

Dickson, W. P., Hess, R. D., Miyake, N., & Azuma, H. Referential communication accuracy between mother and child as a predictor of cognitive development in the United States and Japan. *Child Development*, 1979, *50*, 53–59.

Dickson, W. P., Miyake, N., & Muto, T. Referential relativity: Culture-boundedness of analytic and metaphoric communication. *Cognition*, 1977, *5*, 215–233.

Dickson, W. P., Miyake, N., & Muto, T. *Generalizability of encoding and decoding skills across two referential communication tasks* (Working Paper No. 261). Madison: Wisconsin Research and Development Center for Individualized Schooling, 1979.

Feffer, M., & Suchotliff, L. Decentering implications of social interactions. *Journal of Personality and Social Psychology*, 1966, *4*, 415–422.

Fishbein, H. D., & Osborne, M. The effects of feedback variations on referential communication of children. *Merrill-Palmer Quarterly*, 1971, *17*, 243–250.

Ford, W., & Olson, D. The elaboration of the noun phrase in children's description of objects. *Journal of Experimental Child Psychology*, 1975, *19*, 371–382.

Friedenberg, L., & Olson, G. M. Children's comprehension of simple descriptions of vertical arrays. *Child Development*, 1977, *48*, 265–269.

Fry, C. L. Training children to communicate to listeners. *Child Development*, 1966, *37*, 675–685.

Garmiza, C., & Anisfeld, M. Factors reducing the efficiency of referent communication in children. *Merrill-Palmer Quarterly*, 1976, *22*, 125–136.

Genesee, F., Tucker, G. R., & Lambert, W. E. Communication skills of bilingual children. *Child Development*, 1975, *46*, 1010–1014.

Glucksberg, S., Krauss, R. M., & Weisberg, R. Referential communication in nursery school children: Method and some preliminary findings. *Journal of Experimental Child Psychology*, 1966, *3*, 333–342.

Greenspan, S., & Barenboim, C. *A matrix test of referential communication.* Paper presented at the fifth annual symposium of the Jean Piaget Society, Philadelphia, June 1975.

Gruschow, R., & Gauthier, J. P. Effects of stimulus abstractness and familiarity on listener's performance in a communication task. *Child Development*, 1971, *42*, 956–958.

Heider, E. R. Style and accuracy of verbal communications within and between social classes. *Journal of Personality and Social Psychology*, 1971, *18*, 37–47.

Higgins, E. T. Communication development as related to channel, incentive, and social class. *Genetic Psychology Monographs*, 1977, *96*, 75–141.

Hoemann, H. W. The development of communication skills in deaf and hearing children. *Child Development*, 1972, *43*, 900–1003.

Hoy, E. A. Measurement of egocentrism in children's communication. *Developmental Psychology*, 1975, *11*, 392.

Ironsmith, M., & Whitehurst, G. J. The development of listener abilities in communication: How children deal with ambiguous information. *Child Development*, 1978, *49*, 348–352. (a)

Ironsmith, M., & Whitehurst, G. J. How children learn to listen: The effects of modeling feedback styles on children's performance in referential communication. *Developmental Psychology*, 1978, *14*, 546–554. (b)

Johnson, R. L., & Gross, H. S. Some factors in effective communication. *Language and Speech*, 1968, *11*, 259–263.

Johnston, R. P., & Singleton, C. H. Social class and communication style: The ability of middle and working class five year olds to encode and decode abstract stimuli. *British Journal of Psychology*, 1977, *68*, 237–244.

Karabenick, J. D., & Miller, S. A. The effects of age, sex, and listener feedback on grade school children's referential communication. *Child Development*, 1977, *48*, 678–683.

Krauss, R. M., & Glucksberg, S. The development of communication: Competence as a function of age. *Child Development*, 1969, *40*, 255–266.

Krauss, R. M., & Rotter, G. S. Communication abilities of children as a function of status and age. *Merrill-Palmer Quarterly*, 1968, *14*, 161–173.

Krauss, R. M., Vivekananthan, P. S., & Weinheimer, S. "Inner speech" and "external speech": Characteristics and communication effectiveness of socially and non-socially encoded messages. *Journal of Personality and Social Psychology*, 1968, *9*, 295–300.

Krauss, R. M., & Weinheimer, S. Concurrent feedback, confirmation, and the encoding of referents in verbal communication. *Journal of Personality and Social Psychology*, 1966, *4*, 343–346.

Krauss, R. M., & Weinheimer, S. Effect of referent similarity and communication mode on verbal encoding. *Journal of Verbal Learning and Verbal Behavior*, 1967, *6*, 359–363.

Longhurst, T. M., & Turnure, J. E. Perceptual inadequacy and communicative ineffectiveness in interpersonal communication. *Child Development*, 1971, *42*, 2084–2088.

Maratsos, M. P. Nonegocentric communication abilities in preschool children. *Child Development*, 1973, *44*, 697–700.

Meissner, J. A. Use of relational concepts by inner-city children. *Journal of Educational Psychology*, 1975, *67*, 22–29.

Meissner, J. A. Judgment of clue adequacy by kindergarten and second-grade children. *Developmental Psychology*, 1978, *14*, 18–23.

Meissner, J. A., & Apthorp, H. Nonegocentrism and communication mode switching in black preschool children. *Developmental Psychology*, 1976, *12*, 245–249.

Menig-Peterson, C. L. The modification of communicative behavior in preschool-aged children as a function of the listener's perspective. *Child Development*, 1975, *46*, 1015–1018.

Patterson, C. J., Massad, C. M., & Cosgrove, J. M. Children's referential communication: Components of plans for effective listening. *Developmental Psychology*, 1978, *14*, 401–406.

Peterson, C. L., Danner, F. W., & Flavell, J. H. Developmental changes in children's response to three indications of communicative failure. *Child Development*, 1972, *43*, 1463–1468.

Piché, G. L., Michlin, M. L., Rubin, D. L., & Johnson, F. L. Relationships between fourth graders' performances on selected role-taking tasks and referential communication accuracy tasks. *Child Development*, 1975, *46*, 965–969.

Pozner, J., & Saltz, E. Social class, conditional communication, and egocentric speech. *Developmental Psychology*, 1974, *10*, 764–771.

Ratner, S. C., & Rice, F. E. The effect of the listener on the speaking interaction. *The Psychological Record*, 1963, *13*, 265–268.

Robinson, E. J., & Robinson, W. P. The young child's understanding of communication. *Developmental Psychology*, 1976, *12*, 328–333.

Robinson, E. J., & Robinson, W. P. Children's explanations of communication failure and the inadequacy of the misunderstood message. *Developmental Psychology*, 1977, *13*, 156–161.

Rosenberg, S., & Cohen, B. D. Referential processes of speakers and listeners. *Psychological Review*, 1966, *73*, 208–231.

Rubin, K. H. Relationship between egocentric communication and popularity among peers. *Developmental Psychology*, 1972, *7*, 364.

Rubin, K. H. Egocentrism in childhood: A unitary construct? *Child Development*, 1973, *44*, 102–110.

Samuels, M., Reynolds, A. G., & Lambert, W. E. Communicational efficiency of children schooled in a foreign language. *Journal of Educational Psychology*, 1969, *60*, 389–393.

Schmidt, W. H. O., & Hore, T. Some nonverbal aspects of communication between mother and preschool child. *Child Development*, 1970, *41*, 889–896.

Shantz, C. U., & Wilson, K. E. Training communication skills in young children. *Child Development*, 1972, *43*, 693–698.

Susswein, B. J., & Smith, R. F. Perceptual discriminability and communication performance in preschool children. *Child Development*, 1975, *46*, 954–957.

Triandis, H. C. Cognitive similarity and communication in a dyad. *Human Relations*, 1960, *13*, 175–183.

Whitehurst, G. J. The development of communication: Changes with age and modeling. *Child Development*, 1976, *47*, 473–482.

Whitehurst, G. J., & Merkur, A. E. The development of communication: Modeling and contrast failure. *Child Development*, 1977, *48*, 993–1001.

Wood, D., & Middleton, D. A study of assisted problem-solving. *British Journal of Psychology*, 1975, *66*, 181–191.

References

Allen, R. R., & Brown, K. L. (Eds.). *Developing communication competence in children.* Skokie, Ill.: National Textbook Company, 1977.

Asher, S. R., & Wigfield, A. Training referential communication skills. In W. P. Dickson (Ed.), *Children's oral communication skills.* New York: Academic Press, 1981.

Baldwin, T. L., & Garvey, C. J. Components of accurate problem-solving communications. *American Educational Research Journal*, 1973, *10*, 39–48.

Brilhart, B. L. The relationship between some aspects of communicative speaking and communicative listening. *Journal of Communication*, 1965, *15*, 35–46.

Bronfenbrenner, U. *The ecology of human development: Experiments by nature and design.* Cambridge, Mass.: Harvard University Press, 1979.

Cazden, C. B. *Child language and education.* New York: Holt, Rinehart & Winston, 1972.

Cronbach, L. J., Gleser, G. C., Nanda, H., & Rajaratnam, N. *The dependability of behavioral measurements: Theory of generalizability for scores and profiles.* New York: Wiley, 1972.

Dickson, W. P. Referential communication performance from age 4 to 8: Effects of referent type, context, and target position. *Developmental Psychology*, 1979, *15*, 470–471.

Dickson, W. P., Hess, R. D., Miyake, N., & Azuma, H. Referential communication accuracy between mother and child as a predictor of cognitive development in the United States and Japan. *Child Development*, 1979, *50*, 53–59.

Dickson, W. P., Miyake, N., & Muto, T. Referential relativity. Culture-boundedness of analytic and metaphoric communication. *Cognition*, 1977, *5*, 215–233.

Dickson, W. P., Mikaye, N., & Muto, T. *Generalizability of encoding and decoding skills across two referential communication tasks.* (Working Paper No. 261.) Madison: Wisconsin Research and development Center for Individualized Schooling, 1979.

Dickson, W. P., & Mioskoff, M. *A computer readable literature review of studies of referential communication: A meta-analysis* (Technical Report). Madison: Wisconsin Research and Development Center for Individualized Schooling, 1980.

Dickson, W. P., & Patterson, J. H. *Criteria for evaluating curriculum materials which use referential communication activities to teach speaking and listening skills* (Working Paper No. 273). Madison: Wisconsin Research and Development Center for Individualized Schooling, 1979.

Dickson, W. P., Patterson, J. H., & Tracy, K. *A classroom communication game for teaching speaking and listening skills.* Unpublished manuscript, University of Wisconsin, Madison, 1980.

Fry, C. L. Training children to communicate to listeners. *Child Development,* 1966, *37,* 675–685.

Glass, G. V. Primary, secondary, and meta-analysis of research. *Educational Researcher,* 1976, *5,* 3–8.

Glucksberg, S., Krauss, R. M., & Higgins, E. T. The development of referential communication skills. In F. D. Horowitz (Ed.), *Review of child development research* (Vol. 4). Chicago: University of Chicago Press, 1975.

Harnishfeger, L. *Basic practice in listening: Games and activities.* Denver: Love Publishing Company, 1977.

Karabenick, J. D., & Miller, S. A. The effects of age, sex, and listener feedback on grade school children's referential communication. *Child Development,* 1977, *48,* 678–683.

Larson, C., Backlund, P., Redmond, M., & Barbour, A. *Assessing functional communication.* Urbana, Ill.: ERIC Clearinghouse on Reading and Communication Skills, and Falls Church, Va.: Speech Communication Association, 1978.

Lieb-Brilhart, B. Update on basic skills legislation. *Spectra: A Bimonthly Publication of the Speech Communication Association,* February 1979, pp. 11–12.

Moffett, J., & Wagner, B. J. *Student-centered language arts and reading, K-13* (2nd ed.). Boston: Houghton Mifflin Co., 1976.

Nie, N. H., Hull, C. H., Jenkins, J. G., Steinbrenner, K., & Bent, D. H. *SPSS: Statistical package for the social sciences.* New York: McGraw-Hill, 1975.

Olds, H. F., Jr. *An experimental study of syntactical factors influencing children's comprehension of certain complex relationships* (Report No. 4). Cambridge, Mass.: Harvard University, Center for Research and Development on Educational Differences, 1968. (Available as thesis from Widener Library, Harvard University).

Olds, H. F., Jr. *Talk and take.* Boston: Houghton Mifflin Co., 1973.

Piché, G. L., Michlin, M. L., Rubin, D. L., & Johnson, F. L. Relationships between fourth graders' performances on selected role-taking tasks and referential communication accuracy tasks. *Child Development,* 1975, *46,* 965–969.

Pozner, J., & Saltz, E. Social class, conditional communication, and egocentric speech. *Developmental Psychology,* 1974, *10,* 764–771.

Ratner, S. C., & Rice, F. E. The effect of the listener on the speaking interaction. *The Psychological Record,* 1963, *13,* 265–268.

Shantz, C. U., & Wilson, K. E. Training communication skills in young children. *Child Development,* 1972, *43,* 693–698.

Wright, J., Norris, R. A., & Worsley, F. J. *Concepts for communication.* Niles, Ill.: Developmental Learning Materials, 1974.

///
Sociolinguistic Studies

10

Communication in Small Instructional Groups: A Sociolinguistic Approach

LOUISE CHERRY WILKINSON, MARY CLEVENGER, AND CHRISTINE DOLLAGHAN

The purposes of this chapter are to discuss a sociolinguistic approach to communication in the classroom and to provide an example of the use of this approach in an investigation of interaction among students in first-grade reading groups.

A Sociolinguistic Approach to the Study of Communication in the Classroom

Sociolinguists make assumptions about language and the social world, including the concept of *communicative competence* and the importance of meaning in context. They study an area of content that includes models of the use or function of language in social contexts, as well as models of social roles and relationships as expressed in communicative behavior. Sociolinguists use a variety of research methods, employing both naturalistic observational techniques and experimental techniques.

Children's Oral Communication Skills

Assumptions:
Communicative Competence and Meaning in Context

The fundamental assumption that underlies the sociolinguistic approach to language is the concept of *communicative competence,* which consists of knowledge of the rules of language structure and function. Communicative competence includes

> [the] knowledge of sentences, not only as grammatical but also as appropriate. [The child] acquires the competence as to when to speak, when not, and as to what to talk about with whom, when, where and in what manner. In short, a child becomes able to accomplish a repertoire of speech acts, to take part in speech events, and to evaluate their accomplishment by others [Hymes, 1974, p. 277].

Communicative competence enables children to participate in society. The sociolinguistic approach emphasizes the importance of conversational experiences; that is, social contexts, such as the classroom, within which children develop communicative competence.

An important issue in the study of interaction is the context within which the data are collected. Specification of context is essential for interpreting findings, as human behavior varies according to the situation within which it occurs (Mischel, 1977). Labov (1972) has asserted that the goal of social science should be to specify the conditions under which a particular rule applies or a particular relationship holds; Labov has formulated this as "variable rules." This view stands in contrast to a positivist model of social science which holds that the scientists' quest is to discover general rules or specify relationships that hold across situations. As Labov and Fanshel have stated (1977), these goals are not mutually exclusive:

> Eventually we must construct discourse rules that are quite general and stand free of context; but with our present state of knowledge, the only way we can be sure that these rules are developing in a useful direction is to show that they apply over and over again in many different contexts. In any particular context, we will not know if a particular rule applies unless our knowledge of the contextual conditions is accurate [p. 73.].

Mishler (1978) has argued that the study of meaning in context within social science is paradoxical. One side of the paradox is that human action is context dependent and may only be understood within its context. The other side of the paradox is that this common sense understanding has been excluded from the main tradition of theory and research in the social sciences.

It is necessary to specify the context within which human behavior is observed, in both laboratory and naturalistic studies. For example, in naturalistic studies, data may be collected for different groups in comparable situations, such as the speech events of snack- or lunch-time in the preschool

(Cherry, 1975) and the lesson in the elementary school (Cherry, 1978; Mehan, Cazden, Coles, Fisher, & Maroules, 1976). Likewise, in laboratory studies, the specification of contexts is important; as Bronfenbrenner (1977) has argued, the experimental laboratory is a particular type of "ecological context" with its own specific effects. He argues that it cannot be assumed that the findings from experimental studies are necessarily any more context free, or universal, than findings from other studies. Similar positions have been argued by Abelson (1976) in cognitive psychology, Cazden (1970) in developmental and educational psychology, Goffman (1971) in sociology, McGuire (1973) in social psychology, and Mischel (1977) in personality psychology. Mischel (1977) has argued that a reasonable goal for the social sciences is an interactional theory, which would include the study of "person by situation interactions," that is, of "how the environment influences behavior and how behavior in people who generate it in turn shapes the environment in endless interaction [p. 251]."

Content: The Functions of Language in Social Contexts

The content area of sociolinguistic research includes at least two distinct foci: (a) the functions of language (i.e., pragmatics); and (b) the relationship between, on the one hand, social variables, such as roles and status, and, on the other, linguistic expression, in terms of both its form and its function.

One of the basic principles of the sociolinguistic analysis is that there are many alternative ways of expressing at least approximately the same meaning or accomplishing the same function. The choice of a particular form of expression is determined by the social and contextual factors, such as the topic being addressed or the communicative abilities attributed to the listener (Hymes, 1974). This principle is the *paradigmatic* relationship that holds among language elements, or the rules of alternation (Ervin-Tripp, 1973).

Another basic sociolinguistic principle is that there is an interdependence among the chosen forms of expression. The choice of the initial, particular form of the expression affects all succeeding choices within the language unit. This principle is the *syntagmatic* relationship that holds among language elements, or the rules of cooccurrence (Ervin-Tripp, 1973).

Rules of sequencing account for coherence in any sequence of utterances in a conversation. Labov (1972) has argued that coherence involves formulating rules of interpretation, which relate "what is said"—statements, interrogatives, imperatives—to "what is done"—actions such as refusals, assertions, denials. There is no simple match between utterances and actions. Analysis of the linguistic structure of the utterances will not reliably provide their meaning, even though the utterances are made possible by, and performed in accordance with, the rules of linguistic structure. Two utterances may accomplish different actions even though they have the same grammatical representation, as shown by the following utterances, both declaratives: *You are standing on my foot,* and *You are going to be audited next week.* The first utterance is a request for the listener to remove his or her foot, whereas the second utterance provides information to the listener. Two utterances may have different grammatical representations but accomplish the same action, as in the following utterances: *You are standing on my foot,* and *Get off my foot!* Both utterances are requests for the listener to remove his or her foot. The first utterance is declarative whereas the second is imperative. Rules of interpretation and production relate utterances to actions, and sequencing rules operate between actions performed with utterances themselves.

These principles of sociolinguistic analysis have implications for the kind of data that will be collected by the researcher. The principle of the paradigmatic relationship among language elements makes it mandatory that contexts be specified in sufficient detail that the elements of language use and social contexts may be defined. The principle of syntagmatic relationships and the rules of sequencing among language elements make it likely that complex systems of analysis, such as the hierarchical coding system, multidimensional coding system, and sequential-analysis coding system may be employed in data analysis (see, e.g., Cherry, 1978).

An example of a study of the functions of language, or pragmatics, is found in Read and Cherry (1978), which examined the development of one function of language: the request for action or object, that is, the directive. This research revealed a developmental progression in the complexity of the linguistic expression of the request for action or object with increasing age during the preschool years.

Previous research by Cherry (1978) provides an example of sociolinguistic analysis in studying the relationship between social variables and linguistic expression. In this research, the teacher expectation model (Brophy & Good, 1974) was tested. Cherry examined how the quantity and quality of certain aspects of teachers' language differed according to their expectations of students' communicative competence. The results of the study provided partial support for the "self-fulfilling prophecy" hypothesis. On some measures of teachers' requests for information, either one or both of the teachers provided different opportunities for the "above average" students than for the "below average" students. The two teachers differed from one another in the patterns of their attempts to request more information from the "above average" students. The teachers also differed from one another in their use of explicit positive feedback with the two groups of students, but these differences were not as strong as the differences in requests for information. This study provides an example of the use of sociolinguistic analysis for testing the adequacy of one social psychological model.

Methods: Data Collection and Analysis

Sociolinguists use a wide variety of research methods, including naturalistic observational techniques such as ethnographic description, and elicited or experimental techniques such as the Corpus Extension Instrument (Shuy & Griffin, this volume).

The technique of ethnographic description has been useful (Hymes, 1974) in describing context. Sociolinguists often use ethnographic techniques to specify the contexts within which speech events occur so that further analysis of behavior may be carried out. Conventional ethnographies include descriptions of culture as a set of established categories devised by society for organizing human behavior (Cahir, 1978). Mehan (1978) has criticized conventional ethnographies for (a) having an anecdotal quality; (b) not making explicit adequate criteria for categorizing behavior; and (c) using summaries of data and excluding detail necessary for interpretation of the results. Thus, conventional ethnographies are typically nongeneralizable, nonreplicable, and noninterpretable.

Recently, new ethnographic techniques have been developed to remedy these problems. The new ethnographies are characterized by a focus on the behavior of participants in social interaction—"what is going on" in the "here and now" (Goffman, 1974). The observation of behavior is attempted without an a priori schema for categorization. Both verbal and nonverbal behaviors are described at macro and micro levels. The aim of this research is complete and adequate description of human behavior in context. For example, Mehan (1978) has extended and modified the conventional ethnographic approach, yielding what he calls the "constitutive study," which describes the interactional processes in social behavior. The goal of this procedure is the same as that of the conventional ethnography, but the methods of analysis are specified in greater detail so that the data can be adequately understood in context. According to Mehan, an adequate description of language use in classroom contexts requires a thorough analysis of a representative sample of classroom interactional behavior. In sum, careful ethnographic research attempts to provide, through adequate and complete description, a means for segmenting behavior and revealing recurring patterns (Cahir, 1978).

Because a goal in sociolinguistic research is the collection of complete and accurate data so that fine-grained analysis can be carried out, audio and video recording of interactions with sufficient contextual information to allow subsequent analysis has emerged as the most desirable method of data collection. Dunkin and Biddle (1974), Jackson (1968), and Adams and Biddle (1970) have all observed that there are literally thousands of discriminable verbal and nonverbal behaviors enacted in classroom interactions such as the lesson or reading group activity. Techniques of data collection that preserve these phenomena are crucial if data analysis is to reflect the richness of interaction in context.

Many sociolinguists believe that audio and video recordings are the most effective means of data collection, in contrast to live observational techniques for at least two reasons. First of all, live observational techniques allow only unidimensional coding systems, since it is not possible for a human information processor to analyze sequences of discrete utterances at two levels simultaneously. For example, sequences of utterances cannot be reliably analyzed at both syntactic and functional levels by on-the-spot observers. Observers' attention to selected speech behavior is mandatory in classroom contexts, which are characterized by an overwhelming quantity of data. A second problem with live observational techniques is the extent to which methods of data collection alter the phenomenon under investigation. The problems include techniques for investigating speech behavior in classrooms; observers often edit some utterances, disregard others, and either overlook, correct, or neglect to record grammatical "errors" (Soskin & John, 1963). Clearly, the speech of teachers and students is likely to be altered in unspecified ways with live observational techniques of data collection.

A goal of sociolinguistic research is adequate description and analysis of the data collected, so that particular research questions may be addressed. Describing the speech situation and extracting the unit of sample from the ongoing stream of behavior are the primary problems facing the sociolinguistic researcher. Erickson and Schultz (1977) have developed a procedure for describing classroom interaction that is useful in this respect. Their analysis involves a process of viewing videotapes made during classroom interaction.

Ideally, sociolinguistic analyses and descriptions, like linguistic descriptions, identify categories of language and specify the relationship among these categories and social contexts. Thus, these descriptions are often hierarchical in nature. Ideally, these categories are mutually exclusive and jointly exhaustive, so that each instance of a category can be identified as belonging to only that category. Multilevel coding systems, such as hierarchical coding systems, have been employed in linguistic analyses. These systems allow both the separation of various levels of communicative behavior and the establishment of relationships among these levels. Again, the availability of accurate and complete raw behavioral data is crucial if interrelationships are to be described in the complexity that may be necessary to reflect the phenomena.

The Study

The authors recently conducted a study that applied some of the principles discussed in the preceding section and thus illustrated the use of the sociolinguistic approach. Two research issues are addressed in this section of the chapter. One issue involves a detailed examination of two functions of language—the request for action and the request for information—in the speech of first-grade children. The second issue concerns the relationship between one social variable and these language functions in a particular context. Specifically, we will examine whether speakers exhibit a preference for listeners of the same or opposite sex in making these requests of fellow students in first-grade, all-student reading groups. The two issues that we have chosen to focus on are representative of the content area of sociolinguistic research: the function of language and the relationship between a social variable and linguistic expression.

First-Grade Reading Groups

The three first-grade, all-student reading groups studied here were composed of four to six children, of approximately 6 years of age, and had at least two members of each sex. The all-student reading group, in which students work without the teacher's presence in the group, is very common in early elementary school classrooms.

The small size of the reading groups studied meant that some of the qualities of small groups, such as cohesiveness (Hartup, 1974) and active participation by individuals (Hare, 1976), would probably be observed. The age of the children, however, suggested that, despite the smallness of the groups, some splitting into subgroups might occur. Smith (1973) found that groups of 5- and 6-year-olds working on a common task split into subgroups to work toward the goal. Smith suggests that children of this age are not capable of dealing with group size and complexity (Smith, 1973, p. 545). Therefore, it was expected that dyadic interaction between children, which was the focus of the study, would occur.

Reading groups are unique in their task orientation and organization in that they can be classified as neither cooperative (shared goal, interdependent) nor competitive (individual goal, independent, one "winner" only). Instead, the groups are organized around individual tasks (each member usually having the same task) yet members are encouraged to cooperate in the completion of these tasks. Rewards are individually distributed yet attainment of a reward by one member does not preclude reward attainment by another (as it would in competition). Also, in addition to individual task rewards, the group may be reprimanded or rewarded as a whole for its behavior. One effect of such an organization may be an encouragement—or at least a lack of discouragement—of the dyadic interaction typical of this age group.

Membership of reading groups has been found to be fairly stable after the first month of school [Groff, 1962 (grades 2–4); Hawkins, 1966 (grades 1–6); Weinstein, 1976 (grade 1)]. As the present study examined groups near the end of the school year, it is likely that group members were familiar with each other and with the process of interacting in this context. Membership stability is likely to affect group functioning in that status hierarchies are already defined in groups that have had stable membership (Hare, 1976).

Previous research on small groups and reading groups, then, leads us to expect a good deal of peer interaction, primarily oriented to the tasks assigned to the group. Both dyadic and larger units of interaction can be expected to occur in this context.

Requests for Action and Information

The study dealt with the general request function of language, specifically, the request for action and the request for information. The request function of language was chosen as a primary focus for four reasons. First of all, requests are inherently social; in the course of a request, both speaker and listener say or do something. A second reason for the focus on requests is the fact that request forms can serve both informational and interpersonal functions. Third, a number of investigators have presented data that show that request forms of various types are prevalent in the classroom situation between teacher and student (Cherry, 1978; Mehan *et al.*, 1976; Sinclair & Coulthard, 1975) and between student and student (Cazden, 1977; Mishler, 1978). Finally, the study of request forms was chosen because there exist in the field of pragmatics some formal criteria for the identification and structural analysis of these linguistic forms (Garvey, 1975; Labov & Fanshel, 1977). A discussion of these two types of requests is appropriate.

Requests for Action

The request for action conveys a speaker's intention that a listener perform some action. Requests for action are also known as directives, and have the imperative (e.g., *Give me some*) as their underlying form. Labov and Fanshel (1977) formulated a general rule of requests for action which specifies the conditions under which a listener will understand a speaker's utterance as a request for action on the listener's part:

> If A addresses to B an imperative specifying an action X at time T_1, and B believes that A believes that

1a. X should be done (for a purpose Y) [need for action]
b. B would not do X in the absence of the request [need for request]
2. B has the *ability* to do X (with an instrument Z)
3. B has the *obligation* to do X or is willing to do it
4. A has the right to tell B to do X.

then A is heard as making a valid request for action [p. 78].

Labov and Fanshel (1977) also describe a rule for indirect requests, by which a request for action is issued without use of an imperative. Indirect requests are frequently accomplished by reference to the preconditions 1–4 in the general rule of requests (need for the action, need for the request, ability of the listener to comply, obligation or willingness of the listener to comply, and right of the speaker to make the request). For example, an indirect request could be made by referring to the precondition of ability: *Can you pick him up at the airport?* No imperative is issued, but the directive intention is nonetheless expressed. Similarly, by saying *I'm hungry,* a speaker can make reference to the first precondition, the need for the action, which in this case would be interpreted as a request that the listener do something to alleviate the speaker's hunger. Garvey (1975) found that preschool children frequently justified or explained their direct imperatives by producing *which*-adjuncts referring to the preconditions (or the sincerity conditions) of the requests. She also found that children constructed indirect requests by referring to the preconditions underlying the request for action, much the same as adults do.

Labov and Fanshel (1977) discuss the reasons that indirect requests are frequently used. They state that there is a continuum of mitigation and aggravation, mitigation being the "softening" of requests so as to "avoid creating offense [p. 84]." Mitigation can be accomplished by the use of expressions such as *please* or *if you don't mind,* or through the use of indirect requests for action. These appear to allow the listener more options in responding than direct imperatives, which do not appear to give the listener a choice as to whether to comply. It has been argued that the degree of mitigation or aggravation built into a request for action may reflect the relative statuses of the speaker and listener, with mitigation serving to soften requests to higher status listeners and aggravation indicating the speakers' relative dominance (Henley, 1977).

Some researchers have investigated requests for action produced by preschool children (Bates, 1975; Ervin-Tripp, 1976; Garvey, 1975; James, 1975; Read & Cherry, 1978). These studies have revealed that children are able to produce indirect requests at an early age, although development appears to progress from the use of direct imperatives to the use of indirect forms. Garvey (1975) found twice as many indirect requests in the speech of 5-year-old dyads than that of 4-year-old dyads. A study by Read and Cherry

(1978) defined four main surface forms used by preschool children to convey requests for action, including imperatives (*Give me a cookie*), embedded imperatives (*Can I have a cookie?*), expressions of want or need (*I want a cookie*), and declarative statements with directive intentions (*That cookie sure looks good*).

Requests for Information

The request for information is used by a speaker who wants to obtain information from a listener. As Labov and Fanshel (1977) point out, requests for information are closely related to requests for action; in the latter type, the speaker may say *Give me X*, whereas in the former, he may say *Give me information about X* (Labov & Fanshel, 1977, p. 88). Labov and Fanshel formulate the rule for requests for information as follows:

> If A addresses to B an imperative requesting information I, or an interrogative focusing on I, and B does *not* believe that A believes that
>
> a. A has I
> b. B does not have I
>
> then A is heard as making a valid request for information [p. 89].

Requests for information are frequently expressed through interrogative forms, although other syntactic structures may be used. Research by one of the authors (Cherry, 1980) examined the use of the request for *known* information, a request type frequently observed in instructional contexts where the teacher asks students for information already known to her.

Preferences of Speakers for Same-Sex or Opposite-Sex Listeners

The other major aspect of this study concerns the interaction between the social variable of sex role and the request functions of language in the context of the first-grade reading group. Specifically, we wanted to know whether children in these reading groups make requests to listeners of the same or opposite sex.

Sex of speaker and addressee have been found to affect the communicative choice of adults, and there is some indication that children's communicative behavior may be influenced by variables involving gender. Previous research indicates that children in first grade prefer same-sex peers in making playmate or affiliative choices (Campbell, 1964; Haskett, 1971; Maccoby & Jacklin, 1974; Moore & Updegroff, 1964; Moreno, 1953; Parten, 1933). These studies, however, have not dealt with preferences in small groups composed of members of both sexes. It may be that in free-forming groups children gravitate toward same-sex partners, but that in mixed-sex, task-oriented groups their communication patterns will not reveal a same-sex preference. Hartup (1974) points out that, even though same-sex preference is the norm, there is no evidence that this preference is based on a strong rejection of the opposite sex. In fact, in a study of first-grade pairs, Haskett (1971) found that cross-sex cooperative pairs showed a significant increase in partner preference although preinteraction choices tended to be same-sex. A similar increase in partner preference was not found for same-sex partners, which suggests that one reason for the infrequency of cross-sex choice may be lack of interaction.

In sum, although evidence to date supports the hypothesis that same-sex preferences exist in children's affiliative choices, the degree to which a similar pattern is present in the context of the mixed-sex reading group remains an open question.

Methods

Subjects

The subjects for this study were 15 first-grade students constituting three reading groups in three separate classrooms of one school. Each reading group was the most advanced in its classroom.

Assessment showed that the children performed at least as well as expected for their age group according to existing norms on the standardized tests (Loban, 1976; Miller, personal communication, 1978; Miller & Yoder, 1975). In addition, there were no significant differences on any of the language measures across groups or across gender.

The 15 students were all middle-class, Caucasian, native speakers of English, ranging in age from 6 to 8 years. Three other students normally in reading groups under investigation were excluded from the present study; one student lacked parental permission, and two students were absent on the days when the videotaping occurred. There were eight females and seven males in the three groups: Group A consisted of two females and two males; Group B consisted of two females and three males; Group C consisted of four females and two males. All of the reading groups had been in existence for several months.

Procedures

Identifying the Speech Situation

The first author visited the three classrooms, spending an entire day in each classroom to observe the activities of the reading groups and their relationship to the structure of the school day. The teachers designated 9:00 A.M. to 9:50 A.M. as reading-activity time. The first author returned for a second visit to each classroom to observe and take notes on the reading activity from 9:00 to 9:50 in each of the classrooms. The teacher announced the beginning of the reading activity. Students chose their seats at the table. Two of the teachers provided instructions for their reading groups while the students were in the whole-group formation; one of the teachers provided those instructions after the students had entered into their reading groups. The groups were ended by the teacher.

Data Collection

Audio- and video-taping was scheduled for early April of 1978; the days selected for each classroom were chosen randomly and were regarded as typical days for reading by the classroom teachers. Each reading group was video- and audio-taped on one day. Video- and audio-recording began before the students assembled at the reading group tables and continued for about 5 minutes after the end of the reading activity. One stationary camera and one portable video camera were used to record the activity of each group; cameras were visible to the group members and were positioned across from one another so that nearly full-face views of all group members would be on one or the other camera. Two microphones were placed in the middle of each group's table.

Prior to, during, and following the taping, two observers prepared ethnographies of the ongoing events in the group, including the behavior of the students, in order to supplement the recordings with relevant contextual information which might not have been taped. The two observers were in the same room and visible to the students, so that, including the two members of the research team operating the cameras, there were a total of four adults in addition to the teachers and staff. According to the school principal, the subjects in this study were accustomed to being videotaped and to the presence of several adults in the classroom in addition to the teacher.

Analysis of Data

The indexing of the videotapes was guided by the methods suggested by Erickson and Schultz (1977) and Griffin and Shuy (1978). The major events that occurred on the tapes were written down on index forms. The phases of the reading event were identified on the basis of both verbal and nonverbal behavior. Information in the ethnographies was used to identify these boundaries.

The videotapes made for each group were transcribed using the method described by Cherry (1974). The videotapes were transcribed from beginning to end; the transcriber used both the ethnographies and the tape indexes in this process. The tapes were viewed in their entirety several times by the transcriber before the actual process of transcription began. A relatively long segment of all-student interaction for each group was chosen for detailed analysis (36 minutes for Group A, and 21 minutes each for Groups B and C). During this segment, the teacher was not with the group; typically, she was in the classroom assisting other students. A transcription was made from one of the audio tracks first, and then the track from the second tape was transcribed and integrated into the first transcript. Transcripts were rechecked against both tapes a second time. Reliability on these data for word and utterance boundaries (Cherry, 1974) exceeded 80%. Following completion of the verbal transcription, the tapes were viewed for relevant nonverbal and spatial information which was included on the transcripts. In order to determine the efficacy of the videotaping and audiotaping procedure in producing both accurate and complete data, the number of completely intelligible, partially intelligible, and completely unintelligible utterances were marked and tallied for each group. Close to 90% of the utterances transcribed were completely intelligible.

The comparability of the three groups and the comparability of the all-student segments is discussed in this section. The general context of the reading lesson provided the basic commonality for the three groups; however, the degree of similarity across groups varied with respect to several dimensions, including:

1. *Physical environment.* All groups were seated at small tables of varying shapes in classrooms that also contained other groups of students as well as the teacher; therefore, background noise and general environmental characteristics appeared to be quite comparable among the groups.

2. *Materials.* All groups used similar materials in completing their tasks during the all-student phase, such as books, paper and pencils or crayons. However, Group B differed from Groups A and C in one respect: Students in this group were allowed to use puppets to "help" them as they worked. Because the teacher did not assign puppets to group members, possession of the puppets was a fairly frequent topic of conversation for this group.

3. *Activities during the all-student segment.* The three groups appeared to be quite similar in terms of the tasks and activities undertaken during all-student sections. The dominant activity was reading, either silently or aloud, but all three groups performed one or more activities directly related to the stories read and requiring a written (printed) response, such as completing worksheets (Groups A and C), drawing a picture of the events they had read about (Group B), or printing sentences from the story (Group B).

The samples of data selected for analysis were coded into the following categories:

1. *Request for information.* This category involved an attempt by a speaker to obtain information from a listener. The request for information

function is most frequently marked by the use of the interrogative form. Examples of requests for information include *What's the answer to the next one?* and *Two plus two is* ———?

2. *Request for action.* Requests for action can be expressed through a wide variety of forms, all based on an underlying imperative form. Requests for joint or mutual action (e.g., *Let's get our books*), requests for permission (e.g., *Can I sit here?*), and directives based on an appeal to obligation (e.g., *You're supposed to read this now*) are included within this general category. Other examples of the directive forms include the imperative form (*Sit down*); the embedded imperative form with the modal verb, as in *Could you sit down now;* use of the word *please* standing alone; the declarative statement (*You are standing up while everyone else is sitting down*); and expressions of want and need, as in *I need that pencil*. Reliabilities on these categories were computed as the number of agreements divided by the number of agreements plus disagreements; reliabilities exceeded .80.

After the requests had been classified, each was examined in order to determine whether or not it unambiguously signaled an intended listener. Unambiguous signals or markers indicating the intended listener were of two types, overt and nonovert. Overt signals included the use of the intended listener's name in the request, head orientation or eye gaze to the intended listener concomitant with the uttering of the request, and increased physical proximity to the intended listener. The presence of any one of these signals served to mark the intended listener of the request. In addition to the overt signals, nonovert, contextual information sometimes unambiguously identified the intended listener. If a request lacked one of the overt markers, the transcript was examined to determine (*a*) whether the listener had been signaled overtly in the previous utterance; and (*b*) whether any utterances from other group members had been directed to this listener in the interval between the prior signaling and the present speaker's request. If the first condition was met and the second was not, it was decided that the intended listener was identified. For example, in the transcript from Group C, the following exchange occurred:

Mitch: (pointing to Ann's worksheet): *That's supposed to be the red rabbit.*
Ann: *Yah, but what's this word?*

When Ann makes this request for information she is looking down at her paper and does not overtly signal the intended listener. The intended listener could be identified, however, on the basis of the previously established interaction between Ann and Mitch—that is, the gestural pointing to Ann's worksheet. An intended listener was also identified, despite the lack of an overt marker, if the speaker's request concerned an action or utterance performed by the listener immediately prior to the speaker's present request (i.e., prior to any intervening utterances from other group members). An example of this is found in the transcript of Group B:

Evan: *Amy married a dog.*
Joanie: *Where does it say married?*

Joanie's request for information does not name Evan as the intended listener, but it clearly concerns Evan's previous utterance.

In order to address the second research question—that of speaker preference for same-sex versus opposite-sex listeners—two measures were computed for each student: the number of requests directed to a member of one's own sex (same-sex score), and the number of requests directed to members of the opposite sex (cross-sex score). As the groups differed with regard to duration and sex composition, an effort was made to standardize them. The duration of Group A was 36 minutes, whereas Groups B and C both had durations of 21 minutes; thus, the raw scores of students in Group A were multiplied by 21/36 and rounded to raw scores that would be predicted if Group A's duration had been 21 minutes instead of 36.

Students' same-sex and cross-sex scores were adjusted for sex composition of their groups by dividing raw scores by the number of possible same-sex or cross-sex listeners in the group. For example, in Group B, which had three boys and two girls, each boy's cross-sex score was divided by 2 (because there were two cross-sex listeners), and his same-sex score by 2 (because there were two same-sex listeners). A girl in Group B would have her cross-sex score divided by 3, her same-sex score by 1. In this way, raw cross-sex and same-sex scores were converted into "number of cross-sex requests per cross-sex listener" and "number of same-sex requests per same-sex listener."

Results

By way of introduction to the results of the study, we would like to present an excerpt from Group B which provides an example of the kind of data we are analyzing.

Sally:	*Look at what page we get to do.*	(1)
Chuck:	*She didn't tell us to work in that book. She just*	(2)
	told us the white pieces. Hey, when can we get up?	(3)
Sally:	*Beats me. You can talk out loud if you want.*	(4)
Chuck:	*I know.*	(5)
Sally:	*We should do these two pages.*	(6)
Chuck:	*No, we can't.*	(7)
Sally:	*Yeah, she said 58 and 59.*	(8)
Chuck:	*No, she said—didn't. Did she say 58 and 59, Chip?*	(9)

Sally:	*Yes. We're supposed to do it.*	(10)
Chuck:	*Uh-uh.*	(11)
Terry:	*Not that.*	(12)
Sally:	*We're not supposed to do the test.*	(13)
Chuck:	*Not this. We did that already, didn't we? We did*	(14)
	that. Where is it? (looking through book)	(15)
Terry:	*We're supposed to do that.* (points to Sally's book)	(16)
Chuck:	*Oh-oh.* (book falls apart) *Not again.*	(17)
Sally:	*What is it? Oh-oh.*	(18)
Terry:	(laughs) *Oh, not again.*	(19)
Sally:	*Oh-oh.*	(20)
Chuck:	*Oh-oh.*	(21)
Sally:	*Now your book is really falling apart.*	(22)
Chuck:	*Three parts.*	(23)
Sally:	*Oh boy.*	(24)
Chuck:	*I know there were. . . . Hey, didja watch Flint-stones last night?*	(25)
Terry:	*Oh yeah.*	(26)
Sally:	*No. It's on every Friday night at every—*	(27)
Chuck:	*No.*	(28)
Terry:	*Every S-*	(29)
Sally:	*Thursday.*	(30)
Terry:	*Thursday.*	(31)
Chuck:	*How come she stapled this part?*	(32)
Terry:	(laughs) *That's to get it all in one place.*	(33)

There are several notable features in this segment. First, the participants seem to maintain their attention to the task, at least at some underlying level, even when the topics introduced have little or no connection with the reading assignment. Superimposed on this underlying attention to the task is a rich and well-managed social interaction among the children in which they use a variety of linguistic strategies and forms. The ease with which the interaction progresses demonstrates the degree to which the participants are aware of and cooperating with each others' communicative efforts. Even when the topic of conversation shifts abruptly, as it does several times, all of the participants make the transition skillfully and rapidly.

It should also be noted that the children occupy different roles with respect to the interaction—not all of them participate equally or have equal influence. Chip says nothing during this sequence, although one question is addressed to him. At the other extreme is Chuck, who dominates the interaction in terms of both quantity of verbalization and his ability to initiate and terminate various topics. We turn now to the two main research issues of the study.

Issue 1: Analysis of Requests for Action and Information

Requests for Action

The first issue with which we were concerned was the request function. Examination of the requests for action produced by the children in this study reveals that they had at their disposal a variety of alternate forms with which to accomplish requests for action. Requests for information accounted for 10% of all utterances, and requests for action accounted for 11% of all utterances. Requests for action were classified into five categories defined by Read and Cherry (1978) after Ervin-Tripp (1976). These categories are (*a*) *imperative*, a command that is not embedded (e.g., *Stop kicking me*); (*b*) *embedded imperative*, an interrogative containing a modal verb (e.g., *Can I use that?*); (*c*) *expressions of want or need*, an utterance in which *want, wish*, or *need* appears (e.g., *I want a puppet*); (*d*) *declarative*, a statement with a directive intention (e.g., *I'm supposed to sit by him*). The use of *let's* plus the desired action can also convey a request for action (e.g., *Let's go get our reading books now*). As can be seen in Table 10.1, direct imperatives accounted for the majority of requests for action, and this result corroborates similar results obtained by Garvey (1975) for preschool-age peers and by Ervin-Tripp (1976) for adult peers. A study by James (1975) suggests that preschool

TABLE 10.1
Frequencies of Forms Used to Request Information and Action or Object

Form	Group A	B	C	Total
Requests for information				
Wh-question	7	6	32	45
Yes–no question	5	2	6	13
Tag question	2	1	1	4
Intonational marker	0	1	2	3
Declarative	0	0	0	0
Imperative	0	0	0	0
Total	14	10	41	65
Requests for action or object				
Direct imperative	8	25	20	59
Embedded imperative	2	5	0	9
Expression of want or need	1	1	1	3
Declarative statement	2	12	3	17
Let's	1	3	0	4
Total	14	46	24	92

children are aware of these distinctions in constructing their requests for action in various contexts. In contrast, adults infrequently use the direct imperative (Labov & Fanshel, 1977).

The findings of the present study show that first-grade children know a variety of linguistic forms for making requests for action. They have some knowledge of the paradigmatic rules governing their initial choice of a form for a particular context, as shown by the fact that the direct imperative form is very appropriate in the context of communication among familiar peers. Similarly, the paucity of want or need statements corroborates findings by Ervin-Tripp (1976) for adults; she noted that statements of personal need or desires were primarily addressed to subordinates, and such forms would not be appropriate in the familiar peer context of the present study. The results also give evidence that first-grade children understand the syntagmatic rules whereby the initial paradigmatic choice constrains subsequent forms, for no glaring inconsistencies of form occur in the transcripts.

Mitigation and Aggravation

The five types of requests for action that have been discussed were modified by speakers in a number of ways to mitigate or aggravate their strength or force, just as has been found in studies of adults and preschool children (Ervin-Tripp, 1976; Garvey, 1975; Labov & Fanshel, 1977). Examples of mitigation found in the present study (mitigating portions in bold face italics) included explaining the need for the request: *Oops. Hey, can I borrow your eraser again? **I made a mistake;*** or using politeness markers such as *please* and *may:* ***May I borrow that, Terry?*** In addition, some speakers mitigated their requests for action by allowing their listeners to choose the time of implementation: *Jake, **after you get through,** could I have him?*

Aggravation of a request for action, on the other hand, strengthens its force, as in the following example where a request for action in the declarative form, which is normally fairly "weak," is aggravated both nonverbally and through repetition: *I'm supposed to sit by him. [**pushes Jake off chair**] I'm supposed to sit by Evan. Evan's supposed to sit by me.* Children are able to control and modify their requests for action, even though the majority of requests for action produced by children in this study were immediately successful (i.e., resulted in listener compliance). In the following example, Kim provides a justification which results in success (4), after she makes an unsuccessful request for action (she wants Evan to stop poking at her puppet):

(Evan pokes at Kim's puppet)	(1)
Kim: *Don't, Evan.*	(2)
(Evan pokes at her puppet again)	(3)
Kim: *You could poke somebody's eye out.*	(4)
(Evan desists)	(5)

Similarly, Jake makes two attempts to get Joanie to trade with him, mitigating his second request (3) by making it sound like a merely temporary arrangement. This strategy, however, fails (4):

Jake:	*Joanie, you want to trade puppets?*	(1)
Joanie:	(shakes her head no)	(2)
Jake:	*Just for a while.*	(3)
Joanie:	*Nope.*	(4)

Aggravations of unsuccessful requests were infrequent, perhaps due to the relatively equal status of the group members. It should also be noted in passing that children in this study often used intonational cues to signal mitigation or aggravation of their requests (i.e., the use of "wheedling" versus "threatening" intonational patterns).

As has been noted, most of the requests for action produced by the children in this study were successful in the sense that they resulted in listener compliance. It is interesting to examine more closely the cases in which listeners did not comply. Both Garvey (1975) in her study of preschool children and Labov and Fanshel (1977) in their study of adults found two types of refusals (or noncompliant acknowledgments): outright refusals, and responses in which the listener appears to postpone compliance. The latter type of refusal is called "temporizing" by Garvey (1975) and "putting off a request" by Labov and Fanshel (1977). In addition, Labov and Fanshel point out that "in ordinary, face-to-face interaction, the only way in which a request may be refused with reasonable politeness is to give an accounting: an unaccounted refusal can lead to a break in social relations . . . [pp. 87–88]." In other words, adults most frequently explain their refusals.

In contrast, we found that nearly half of the children's refusals were not accompanied by accountings in our study, as illustrated in the following examples:

| Al: | *Lookit this. Lookit this. Mitch, Mitch.* | (1) |
| Mitch: | *No! Just read.* | (2) |

| Mitch: | *Will you help her, Al?* | (1) |
| Al: | *No.* | (2) |

Jake:	*Joanie, you want to trade puppets?*	(1)
Joanie:	(shakes head)	(2)
Jake:	*Just for a while?*	(3)
Joanie:	*Nope.*	(4)

In one case, Kim initially refuses a request by Evan without giving an accounting (2), however, after he whispers something to her she justifies her refusal (4) on the basis of the absence of a precondition (her willingness as the listener):

Evan:	*Can I use that?*	(1)
Kim:	*No.*	(2)
Evan:	(whispers to her)	(3)
Kim:	*I don't wanna trade with you.*	(4)

In addition to outright, unaccounted refusals, there were several occasions on which requests for action were simply ignored by listeners, who acted as though they had not heard the requests. It is difficult to know whether this was actually the case (a possibility when there are several conversations going on simultaneously, along with background noise) or whether the listeners were deliberately ignoring the requests, which would be interpreted as being extremely impolite in adult interaction.

The examples of unaccounted refusals may show that this aspect of pragmatic competence is incompletely developed in children of this age, as such instances are apparently fairly rare in adult conversation. Of course, more data on both adults and children are needed before this conclusion can be verified.

Refusals and Accountings

Another important issue involves the kinds of accountings or explanations given by listeners in refusing speakers' requests. Labov and Fanshel (1977) state that "refusals based on needs and abilities are generally mitigating, while refusals based on rights and obligations are extremely aggravating [p. 87]." Garvey's (1975) preschool children used a variety of reasons to support their refusals, including reference to the lack of a need for the request or for the action, or to their inability, unwillingness, lack of obligation, or conflicting rights. Although there were only a few instances of accounted refusals in our data, we can see several of the strategies described by Garvey (1975) and Labov and Fanshel (1977).

The following two examples show the listener refusing by asserting that he is not the appropriate person to carry out the action requested, thus apparently referring to his lack of obligation or the absence of the speaker's right to make the request:

| Ann: | *I want some.* | (1) |
| Mitch: | *Ya gotta get your own crayons.* | (2) |

| Ann: | *Judi, what's in this?* | (1) |
| Judi: | *You gotta read the directions by yourself.* | (2) |

In another instance, Mary responded to a request for action issued by Ann by asserting that there is no need for the request:

Ann: *Mary, don't look.*   (1)
Mary: *I'm not.*   (2)

The same reason, the lack of a need for the request, is used by Kim in responding to Evan:

Evan: *I want a puppet.*   (1)
Kim: *You got one.*   (2)
Evan: *No I don't.*   (3)
Jake: *If you go back to ask Susie, she will trade.*   (4)

Evan responds to Kim's refusal (2) by reasserting the need for the request (3). Jake then responds with a refusal, but mitigates it by offering an alternative listener (4). Jake later uses the same strategy, offering a substitute while refusing, in response to another request from Evan:

Evan: *Can I have him?*   (1)
Jake: *I'll let ya read the book.*   (2)

Finally, we present two separate interactions between Chuck and Sally that demonstrate Chuck's use of highly developed strategies to avoid complying with Sally's commands without refusing outright. In the first sequence, some pages in Chuck's book have become loose, and he holds them up as if inquiring what should be done:

Sally: *Just pull 'em apart.*   (1)
Chuck: *She stapled 'em together.*   (2)
Sally: *Just go like this* (makes tearing motion).   (3)
Chuck: *Then the whole book will fall apart.*   (4)
Sally: *Goody, goody.*   (5)
Chuck: *The pages would be flying all over the room*
          (laughs) *into the wastebasket.*   (6)
Sally: *Yeah, and then they have to get a new book.* (7)

In (1), Sally directs Chuck to rip out the remaining pages, using an imperative form. Chuck refuses, but gives an accounting (2), pointing out that her suggestion would undo the teacher's repair job. Sally reiterates and increases the clarity of her request for action with a nonverbal explanation (3), and Chuck again points out the negative consequences of her request for action (4), which are apparently just what Sally had in mind (5). Chuck finally sees that Sally is seriously encouraging him to damage his book, and he disguises his final refusal by describing a humorous imaginary scene which would result if he complied with her request for action (6). Sally goes along with the flight of fantasy and drops her request for action entirely—at least for the moment (7).

A similar interchange occurs a few minutes later:

Chuck:	*I'm gonna tear this book apart. Tear, tear, tear.*	(1)
Sally:	*Do it.*	(2)
Chuck:	*Huh?*	(3)
Sally:	*Do it.*	(4)
Chuck:	*Tear this apart? Do "ch'ch'ch?"* (tearing noise)	(5)
	Unh-uh.	(6)
Sally:	*Why?*	(7)
Chuck:	*It already is broke.*	(8)
Sally:	*But that's why I want you to tear it apart.*	(9)
Chuck:	(to Terry): *Are you tearing yours apart?*	(10)
Terry:	(shakes her head "no")	(11)
Chuck:	*Darn, I just lost my page.*	(12)

Here Chuck jokingly introduces the idea of tearing his book (1) and Sally immediately and bluntly directs him to do it (2). Chuck first responds by making two requests for clarification, acting first as though he has not heard her (3), next as though he does not understand her (5), and finally refusing outright (6). Sally questions the reason for his refusal (7) and he explains it (8), but Sally uses his reason to support her request for action (9). Chuck then checks with another group member (10), and when he learns that he will be the only one tearing his book apart, he changes the topic (12), completely ignoring the request for action.

Chuck's skill lies in his ability to refuse without appearing to refuse. He and Sally are friends and interact very frequently, and Chuck manages to protect his own self-interests without angering her by his refusals to comply with her requests for action. It is precisely this type diplomacy that exemplifies the sophistication in social contexts and relations known as communicative competence.

Requests for Information

The children in this study used a variety of syntactical forms to convey their requests for information to listeners, including the interrogative form of *Wh*-question, (e.g., *How do you do this?*); the yes–no question (e.g., *Did you guys put four ones?*); the tag question (e.g., *That was a simple word, wasn't it?*); or the intonational marker (e.g., *She doesn't even know 'when'?*); the declarative (e.g., *I'm stuck on a word*); and the imperative (e.g., *Tell me what it says*). Declarative forms were used as requests for information on only two occasions in this study and imperatives not at all; the frequencies of the various interrogative forms are given in Table 10.1.

Requests for information vary in directness. The most direct requests for information were expressed through interrogative forms, especially *Wh-* and yes–no questions. Cherry (1978) further distinguished between explicit and inexplicit requests for information; explicit requests for information are those that specify the informant being addressed as well as the information desired. The children's speech in our study revealed varying degrees of directness and explicitness in requests for information. For example, the speech of two female students illustrates both direct and indirect speech: Ann's requests to Judi are direct and explicit (*Judi, what's that word? Mitch, what do you do on this?*), whereas Tammy uses indirect and inexplicit requests for information (*I'm stuck on a word. Stuck on another word.*). In fact, one of Tammy's requests for information is so elliptical that it would probably not have been identified in the transcripts were it not for Mitch, who correctly interprets her nonverbal messages as a request for information:

Tammy: *Umm* (large sigh).	(1)
Mitch: *Ask Michelle this time.*	(2)
Tammy: *No, I'm asking one of you two.*	(3)

Requests for information can be mitigated or aggravated, just like requests for action. Most requests for information were successful, resulting in the listener supplying the information to the speaker. The same rules regarding the need to account for refusals to requests for action appear to hold with requests for information. In the present study the most frequent reason used by listeners when they did not supply the information requested was their inability to respond, that is, "I don't know." There was one occasion when a listener refused to supply the information requested on the grounds that she was not the appropriate person to supply it:

Ann: *Judi, what goes in this?*	(1)
Judi: *You gotta read the directions by yourself.*	(2)

In a few instances, requests for information that did not specify the listener were ignored, but even inexplicit requests received responses in the majority of cases:

Mitch: *Blue, where's blue?*	(1)
Ann: *I got it.*	(2)

If the request for information specified the intended listener by name, the information was almost always either supplied or an accounting given, except in the case of one pair of children in Group C.

Speakers in the present study pursued unsuccessful requests for information more frequently than they did unsuccessful requests for action. Some examples of the strategies used to follow up on unsuccessful requests for information are discussed in what follows. The first example consists of a series of requests for information from one girl to another:

Ann:	*Judi. Judi, what's that word? Judi. Judi. Judi.*	(1)
	Judi, what's that word? Judi, Judi, Judi, Judi.	(2)
	Judi, Judi, Judi, Judi, Judi. What's that word?	(3)
Judi:	*Only.*	(4)

In this example, Ann relies on dogged persistence and repetition of her direct, explicit request for information in attempting to overcome Judi's lack of cooperation. She does use stress and intonation changes to make the later requests sound more urgent, and finally succeeds in getting the information. Apparently undaunted, Ann uses the same strategy again a few minutes later, but fails completely:

Ann:	*Judi, what's that word? Judi, Judi. Please,*	(1)
	please. Right there, right there, right there.	(2)
	Judi, what's that word right there? Judi, Judi.	(3)
	Judi, please Judi what's that word? Judi,	(4)
	Judi, Judi.	(5)
(Judi gives no response)		(6)

Ann's strategy of merely repeating her requests contrasts with the actions taken by Tammy when her requests for information are unsuccessful:

Tammy:	*Stuck on another word.*	(1)
Mitch:	*Well, you help her, Al.*	(2)
Al:	*No.*	(3)
Tammy:	*Yep.*	(4)
Al:	*What word? Ask Mary, I gotta do this. Mary knows*	
	it, she already gots her whole thing done.	(5)
Tammy:	*You did too.*	(6)
Mitch:	*Yeah, Al.*	(7)
Tammy:	*Here, Al, what's the word?*	(8)
Al:	*Don't you know it? Cave.*	(9)

After Tammy makes an initial indirect, inexplicit request for information (1), Mitch delegates the responsibility for answering her to Al (2), who refuses without giving an accounting (3). Tammy is persistent (4) and Al first appears to cooperate, only to refuse again while both accounting for his refusal and suggesting another listener to her (5). Tammy finds his accounting unsatisfactory (6) and is supported by Mitch (7). She then becomes more direct and forceful (8), and Al accedes, although he does so with a deprecating remark suggesting that her ignorance of the word is surprising (9).

Another example of Tammy's reaction to an unsuccessful request is the following.

Tammy: *Umm* (large sigh).   (1)
Mitch: *Ask Mary this time.*   (2)
Tammy: *No, I'm asking one of you two.*   (3)
Al: *No.*   (4)
Mitch: *Okay, me.*   (5)

In this example, Tammy responds to Mitch's refusal (2) not by giving up, but by leaving Mitch and Al the choice as to who will answer her question (3). Although Al refuses without an accounting (4), Mitch backs down and agrees to help her (5).

In examining the differences between the strategies and success of Tammy and Ann in obtaining information, a question naturally arises about the strangeness of the interactions between Ann and Judi. Ann works so hard in producing so many identical requests before Judi acknowledges her and provides information. Information about Ann's and Judi's perception of their relative status in the group would contribute to understanding the factors underlying this communicative interaction. We are currently studying the relationship between students' communicative behavior toward one another and their perceptions of one another on dimensions of popularity, reading competence, and authority, in order to learn more about the determinants of their communicative strategies and success.

Content of the Requests

A question arose regarding the kinds of information being requested by the subjects in this study. We wanted to know whether the children were asking for information that would help them complete their assignments, and we distinguished among four topic categories of requests for information.

The first topic category consisted of requests for information aimed at obtaining a particular answer needed for the completion of the assigned academic task. Approximately half of the subjects asked for at least one answer, and their peers were generally cooperative in supplying the requested information. Examples include:

Hey, what's this word, Kim?
Did you guys put four ones on your sheet?

The second category of requests for information involved requests that were also oriented to the task, but that had to do with general task parameters rather than specific answers to questions about the assignment. These requests included instructions on how to do the task and group members' progress on the task. Examples include:

> *What did the teacher say, after we're done reading, do what?*
> *We're supposed to read our books now, aren't we?*
> *Are you finished?*

The third category was less directly related to the particular tasks assigned to the groups; it consisted of requests for information about the materials used by the groups, including such aspects as possession, location, attributes, and actions associated with these materials. Examples include:

> *Hey, is this yours?*
> *Who wants to trade?*
> *Okay, where's the crayons?*

The fourth category contained requests for information unrelated to the tasks or materials of the groups; the topics of these requests for information were not to be found in the immediate group context. Few instances of this category were found. Examples include:

> *Hey, didja watch Flintstones last night?*
> *Hey, Kim, remember that time we went into my room?*

The frequencies of instances of these categories showed that most requests for information involved topics related to the group context. Occurrences of the first three categories were approximately equal in number. In future research it might be useful to examine the effect of task requirements on the kinds of information requested. On more difficult individual tasks, requests for specific answers might be expected to predominate, whereas easier tasks would be expected to result in more requests for information of the second or third type. Nonchallenging tasks, requiring little attention by the students, might also facilitate the occurrence of requests for information on topics unrelated to the task or group context.

The present study has included a comparison of the children's language production with the adults' and we have seen that the children's system is an incompletely developed version of the adults' system. We have also taken another approach in the present study, in which the children's system is described without reference to the adult system. The description of strategies used by children to issue, mitigage, aggravate, and respond to requests has illustrated their ability to accomplish a variety of ends through the use of language. In addition, the comparison of their strategies to those used by adults have suggested some areas in which the children's system may be incompletely developed (e.g., in accounting for refusals). In a study currently in progress, we are investigating first-grade children's competence with the request function of language in greater detail.

Issue 2: Speaker Preference for Sex of Listener

The second major issue addressed in this study was: Do speakers in first-grade reading groups show a preference for same-sex or cross-sex listeners in directing their requests for action or information? Some anecdotal evidence for a general same-sex preference can be found in statements by the children such as the following:

Sally:	*At last I'm sitting by a girl.*	(1)
Chuck:	*So wowie.*	(2)

Joanie:	*Who wants to trade? Who wants to trade?* (holding puppet)	(1)
Tim:	*I do* (raising hand).	(2)
Evan:	*I do* (raising hand).	(3)
Kim:	*I do.*	(4)
Joanie:	*Kim* (gives puppet to her).	(5)
Tim:	*Guy, you always pick the girls.*	(6)
Joanie:	*Boys pick boys and girls pick girls.*	(7)

The next section of the chapter includes a summary and discussion of a quantitative analysis of sex of listener choice. The children's raw same-sex and cross-sex scores (with Group A adjusted for its longer duration) are presented in Table 10.2, along with the scores that resulted from an adjustment for differences in group sex composition. An examination of the adjusted raw scores provides insight into the children's same-sex and cross-sex preferences, but the results can be represented even more clearly by computing the percentage of each child's requests which were addressed to cross-sex listeners. These percentages are presented in Figure 10.1. Note that same-sex percentages are the complement of the cross-sex percentages. The reader can compare these percentages to the percentages expected if the probability of making a request of a cross-sex listener were equal to 50% (i.e., if no cross-sex or same-sex preference existed). The data show that there does not appear to be a clear-cut trend toward either a same-sex or a cross-sex preference in the scores of individual children. Figure 10.1 also shows the distribution of individual percentages, group mean percentages, and the grand mean percentages for requests for information and action or object. These plots of the percentage scores are based on the raw scores adjusted for duration and group sex composition. Only requests for information and requests for action or object that were directed to another student were included in this analysis. Subjects who produced no requests were not included in this figure. It is apparent that the mean percentage of requests for information and requests for action or object varied greatly from group to group. The percentage of cross-sex requests for information ranged from

TABLE 10.2

Raw and Adjusted Scores for Individual Subjects' Requests to Cross-Sex and Same-Sex Listeners

Sex of Subject	Requests for action				Requests for information			
	Raw scores		Scores adjusted for group sex composition		Raw scores		Scores adjusted for group sex composition	
	Cross-sex	Same-sex	Cross-sex	Same-sex	Cross-sex	Same-sex	Cross-sex	Same-sex
Group A								
Male	3	1	1.5	1.0	7	2	3.5	2.0
Male	3	1	1.5	1.0	0	0	0	0
Female	5	1	2.5	1.0	3	1	1.5	1.0
Female	0	0	0	0	0	1	0	1.0
Group B								
Male	6	3	3.0	1.5	1	0	.5	0
Male	8	1	4.0	.5	1	1	.5	.5
Male	3	3	1.5	1.5	2	0	1.0	0
Female	15	0	5.0	0	2	0	.67	0
Female	3	4	1.0	4.0	3	0	1.0	0
Group C								
Male	2	7	.5	7.0	2	13	.5	13.0
Male	5	5	1.25	5.0	0	3	0	3.0
Female	2	0	1.0	0	5	0	2.5	0
Female	1	2	.5	.67	1	16	.5	5.33
Female	0	0	0	0	0	1	0	.33
Female	0	0	0	0	0	0	0	0

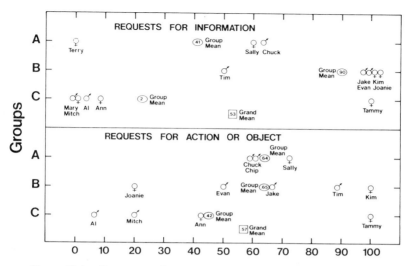

Figure 10.1.   Percentage of requests to cross-sex listeners.

90% in Group B to 23% in Group C, whereas the percentage of cross-sex requests for action and object ranged from 65% in Group B to 42% in Group C.

One of the most striking aspects of these data is the wide variation that existed in the proportion of cross-sex and same-sex requests produced by these children. Inspection of Figure 10.1 provides an important insight that can be drawn from exploratory data analysis (Tukey, 1977), where little is known about expected values and the samples are small. The mean number of cross-sex requests for information for all subjects is 53%; however, as can be seen, not one child in the study actually obtained this mean score. This fact in itself would not be important if there was a cluster of scores around the mean, but in this case, examination of the actual distribution of the data reveals that the mean score of 53% is not due to a clustering of scores in the middle of the range, but rather to a bimodal pattern of two clusters of scores at the extreme ends of the distribution. It would be very misleading to report the mean of 53% as though it actually represented the most common tendency for the children to make cross-sex requests. Instead, it appears that many of the children in this study showed an all-or-none pattern, that is, some subjects tended to address their requests for information only to same-sex listeners (0% cross-sex), whereas others addressed requests for information only to cross-sex listeners (100% cross-sex). This suggests a very different interpretation than that which could be made from inspection of the mean. Rather than interpreting the data as showing an equal probability that requests for information will be made to cross-sex and same-sex listeners, it appears that individual differences in same-sex and cross-sex listener preference are marked and make it difficult to talk about "typical" patterns of listener sex preference in first-graders in this context.

The unusual bimodal pattern found in the requests for information deserves closer inspection. Sex of speaker does not explain the two modes, for we can see that speakers of both sexes can be found at both ends of the listener preference scale. Two of three boys in Group B always preferred to address requests for information to girls, whereas neither of the boys in Group C ever did so.

It can be seen, however, that the two extreme modes are accounted for nearly perfectly by two different groups. Four out of five of Group B's students preferred cross-sex listeners 100% of the time in making requests for information, whereas four of five students in Group C showed the opposite preference, addressing 10% or fewer of their requests for information to cross-sex listeners.

Although the different patterns shown by these groups cannot be explained by the limited information available, speculation is possible. Group C, with its high percentage of same-sex interaction, contained three children (one male, two female) who consistently addressed questions to only one other group member of the same sex. The group interaction might best be characterized as a collection of dyads, usually consisting of same-sex partners. Children in Group B, on the other hand, showed more diversity in choosing listeners for their requests for information; they appeared to behave more like a true group and less like a series of same-sex dyads. An interesting question for future research involves the factors responsible for these two contrasting group structures.

There is yet another factor that might account for the bimodal pattern of listener sex preference in requests for information. In the previous section it was noted that requests for information in the reading group context frequently concerned requests about the assignment. If children in these groups are aware of a hierarchy of academic competence among group members, the primary factor underlying choice of listener may not be sex, but rather the speaker's perception of the listener's competence in performing academic tasks. Information on the children's perceptions of status hierarchies is not available in this study, but we are currently conducting a study that uses sociometric techniques to determine the relationship of such social factors as perceived academic competence, authority, and affiliation to the communication patterns observed in classrooms. This is one example of the way in which a detailed visual inspection of quantitative data can suggest fruitful avenues for future research.

The analyses of requests for action or object showed that individual and group percentages directed to cross-sex listeners were more normally distributed patterns of scores. The extremes of cross-sex preference do not account for a disproportionate number of scores; in fact, there were no children who chose only same-sex listeners, whereas only two chose only cross-sex listeners for their requests for action. The other children's scores are distributed fairly evenly along the scale, although Groups B and C do show tendencies similar to those shown in their requests for information. Members of Group C tended to prefer same-sex listeners whereas Group B members tended to be found on the cross-sex end of the scale. The reasons that preference for sex of listener is less marked in requests for action than in requests for information is not known. A relevant area for future research on this question is the issue of the perception of power and dominance hierarchies by group members.

The data presented in this study, although preliminary, seem to demonstrate that the same-sex preference which has been found in previous research in play contexts, and which was verbalized by some of the children in this study, does not occur in actual communication patterns in the reading group context. Individual children showed cross-sex or same-sex preferences, but no general preference exists for all the subjects in the present study.

There are several possible explanations for the lack of the expected same-sex preference in choice of listener. As discussed earlier in this chapter, previous research has focused on affiliative choices in spontaneously formed play groups. In contrast, the present research focused on previously established mixed-sex reading groups in the classroom. The differences between these two situations may account for the observed variation. The reading groups that were studied here provided an opportunity for cross-sex interaction, and the students in this situation seemed to prefer it. Another possible explanation for the differences found in the present study in comparison with previous research is the current emphasis on sexual equality and the possible effects of changing sex roles for boys and girls.

Future research should examine the consistency of the effects that were observed in the present study. Specifically, further research could include more subjects with more data per subject, as well as more qualitative descriptions. More extensive research would result in useful contributions to our understanding of sex role socialization in young children, and the role of educational institutions in this process. Mixed-sex instructional groups provide for proximity to members of the opposite sex and encourage cross-sex interaction. The consistency of this effect needs to be further investigated, particularly over the course of the school year.

Overall Conclusion

In this chapter we have attempted to address some issues in the sociolinguistic investigation of small reading groups. Several conclusions follow from our work. First of all, it is possible to analyze group structure in first-grade reading groups with a sociolinguistic method, which includes ethnographic description. Ethnography is necessary in order to specify the context within which the data are collected; it is only possible to explore the questions of interest if an ecologically valid study is conducted. The results of the ethnographic analysis provided in this study demonstrate both that we can specify the context from which the data samples are drawn, and that this specification and description is necessary to interpret the data.

A second point is that the accurate and complete collection of data on student–student interaction is possible if we employ methods of videotaping and audiotaping. The sociolinguistic method of analysis requires accurate and complete data.

A third conclusion is that sociolinguistic analysis is applicable to the study of an important dimension of small-group communication in school: same-sex and cross-sex communication patterns. Specifically, it is possible to use measures of communication—in this case, request forms—in an exploratory data analysis (Tukey, 1977) to answer questions about a social variable. Additionally, it may be useful to explore the relationship of the communication patterns observed in the small groups in this study to other social variables, for example, to the social structure. Other measures of language use that could be studied include informatives (Labov & Fanshel, 1977), politeness and indirectness (Labov & Fanshel, 1977; Lakoff, 1973), and the turn-taking structure (Mehan *et al.,* 1976; Sacks, Schegloff, & Jefferson, 1974).

The study presented here exemplifies the use of the sociolinguistic method in exploring educational questions. The school is a social system that functions to encourage children to become competent members of society by providing them with opportunities to develop their skills. Analyses that examine the processes of socialization, such as sociolinguistic analyses, are necessary if we are to understand the process of education and how it differs for individual children. In conclusion, the authors of this chapter believe that the methodology presented here is a very fruitful approach to exploring the processes of classroom communicative interactions.

Acknowledgments

The authors express their thanks to the teachers who allowed us to come into their classrooms, Shari Kuemmel, Iris Othro, and Theresa McCarragher, and to the students of Elvehjem School. The authors gratefully acknowledge the contribution of W. Patrick Dickson for suggestions in exploratory data analysis and the assistance of Mary Brady and Freddy Hiebert in data collection. This research was supported by a grant from the National Institute of Education to the Wisconsin Research and Development Center for Individualized Schooling (Number OB-NIE-G-78-0217).

References

Abelson, R. P. Script processing in attitude formation and decision-making. In J. S. Carroll & J. W. Payne (Eds.), *Cognition and social behavior.* New York: Lawrence Earlbaum, 1976.
Adams, R., & Biddle, B. *Realities of teaching: Explorations with videotape.* New York: Holt, Rinehart, & Winston, 1970.

Bates, E. Peer relations and the acquisition of language. In M. Lewis & L. A. Rosenblum (Eds.), *Friendship and peer relations*. New York: John Wiley & Sons, 1975.

Bronfenbrenner, U. Toward an experimental ecology of human development. *American Psychologist*, 1977, *32*, 513–531.

Brophy, J., & Good, T. *Teacher–student relationships: Causes and consequences*. New York: Holt, Rinehart, & Winston, 1974.

Cahir, S. Activity between and within activities: Transition. In P. Griffin & R. Shuy (Eds.), *Children's functional language and education in the early years* (Final report to the Carnegie Corporation of New York). Rosslyn, Va.: Center for Applied Linguistics, 1978.

Campbell, J. D. Peer relations in childhood. In M. L. Hoffman & L. W. Hoffman (Eds.), *Review of child development research* (Vol. 1). New York: Russell Sage Foundation, 1964.

Cazden, C. The neglected situation in child language research and education. *Journal of Social Issues*, 1970, *26*, 35–60.

Cazden, C. *"You all gonna hafta listen": Peer teaching in the primary classroom*. Paper presented for the Minnesota Symposium on Child Development, October 1977.

Cherry, L. J. *Sex differences in preschool teacher–child interaction*. Unpublished doctoral dissertation, Harvard University, 1974.

Cherry, L. J. The preschool teacher–child dyad: Sex differences in verbal interaction. *Child Development*, 1975, *46*, 532–536.

Cherry, L. J. Teacher–student interaction and teachers' expectations of students' communicative competence. In P. Griffin & R. Shuy (Eds.), *Children's functional language and education in the early years* (Final report to the Carnegie Corporation of New York). Rosslyn, Va.: Center for Applied Linguistics, 1978.

Cherry, L. J. A sociolinguistic approach to language development and its implications for education. In O. Garnica & M. King (Eds.), *Language, children, and society*. New York: Pergamon Press, 1980.

Dunkin, M., & Biddle, B. *The study of teaching*. New York: Holt, Rinehart, & Winston, 1974.

Erickson, F., & Schultz, J. When is a context? Some issues and methods in the analysis of social competence. *Quarterly Newsletter of the Institute for Comparative Human Development*, 1977, *1*(2), 5–10.

Ervin-Tripp, S. *Language acquisition and communicative choice*. Stanford, Calif.: Stanford University Press, 1973.

Ervin-Tripp, S. Is Sybil there: The structure of some American English directives. *Language and Society*, 1976, *5*, 25–66.

Garvey, C. Requests and responses in children's speech. *Journal of Child Language*, 1975, *2*, 41–63.

Goffman, E. *Relations in public*. New York: Basic Books, 1971.

Goffman, E. *Frame analysis*. New York: Basic Books, 1974.

Griffin, M., & Shuy, R. (Eds.). *Children's functional language and education in the early years* (Final report to the Carnegie Corporation of New York). Rosslyn, Va.: Center for Applied Linguistics, 1978.

Groff, P. J. A survey of basal reading grouping practices. *The Reading Teacher*, 1962, *15*, 232–235.

Hare, A. P. *Handbook of small group research*. New York: The Free Press, 1976.

Hartup, W. H. Peer interaction and social organization. In P. H. Mussen (Ed.), *Carmichael's manual of child psychology*. New York: John Wiley & Sons, 1974.

Haskett, G. J. Modification of peer preferences of first grade children. *Developmental Psychology*, 1971, *4*, 429–433.

Hawkins, M. L. Mobility of students in reading groups. *The Reading Teacher*, 1966, *20*, 136–140.

Henley, N. *Body politics: Power, sex, and nonverbal communication*. Englewood Cliffs, N.J.: Prentice-Hall, 1977.

Hymes, D. *Foundations in sociolinguistics*. Philadelphia: University of Pennsylvania, 1974.

Jackson, P. *Life in classrooms.* New York: Holt, Rinehart, & Winston, 1968.

James, S. *The effect of listener and situation on the politeness of preschool children's directive speech.* Unpublished doctoral dissertation, University of Wisconsin–Madison, 1975.

Labov, W. The study of language in its social context. In W. Labov (Ed.), *Sociolinguistic patterns.* Philadelphia: University of Pennsylvania Press, 1972.

Labov, W., & Fanshel, D. *Therapeutic discourse.* New York: Academic Press, 1977.

Lakoff, R. Language and woman's place. *Language in Society,* 1973, *2,* 45–79.

Loban, W. D. *Language development: Kindergarten through grade twelve* (Research Report No. 18). Champaign, Ill.: National Council of Teachers of English, 1976.

Maccoby, E. E., & Jacklin, C. N. *The psychology of sex differences. Stanford, Calif.: Stanford University Press, 1974.*

McGuire, W. J. The yin and yang of progress in social psychology. *Journal of Personality and Social Psychology,* 1973, *26,* 446–456.

Mehan, H. Structuring school structure. *Harvard Educational Review,* 1978, *48,* 32–64.

Mehan, H., Cazden, C., Coles, L., Fisher, S., & Maroules, N. *The social organization of classroom lessons* (CHIP Report). La Jolla: Department of Psychology, University of California, San Diego, 1976.

Miller, J. F. Personal communication, 1978.

Miller, J. F., & Yoder, D. E. The Miller–Yoder Test of Grammatical Comprehension: Experimental Edition, 1975.

Mischel, W. On the future of personality measurement. *American Psychologist,* 1977, *32,* 246–254.

Mishler, E. Meaning in context: Is there any other kind? In *Putting the horse before the cart: Suiting research methods to research purposes.* Symposium presented at the annual meeting of the American Educational Research Association, Toronto, Canada, 1978.

Moore, S., & Updegroff, R. Sociometric status of preschool children related to age, sex, nurturance-giving, and dependency. *Child Development,* 1964, *35,* 519–524.

Moreno, J. L. *Who shall survive? Foundations of sociometry, group psychotherapy, and sociodrama.* Beacon, N.Y.: Beacon House, Inc., 1953.

Parten, M. B. Social play among preschool children. *Journal of Abnormal and Social Psychology,* 1933, *28,* 136–147.

Read, B., & Cherry, L. J. Preschool children's production of directive forms. *Discourse Processes,* 1978, *1,* 233–245.

Sacks, H., Schegloff, E., & Jefferson, G. A simplest systematics for the organization of turn-taking in conversation. *Language,* 1974, *50,* 696–735.

Sinclair, J., & Coulthard, R. *Towards an analysis of discourse: The English used by teachers and pupils.* London: Oxford University Press, 1975.

Smith, H. W. Some developmental interpersonal dynamics through childhood. *American Sociological Review,* 1973, *38,* 543–552.

Soskin, W., & John, V. A study of spontaneous talk. In R. Barker (Ed.), *The stream of behavior.* New York: Appleton, Century, Crofts, 1963.

Tukey, J. W. *Exploratory data analysis.* Reading, Mass.: Addison-Wesley, 1977.

Weinstein, R. S. Reading group membership in first grade: Teacher behaviors and pupil experience over time. *Journal of Educational Psychology,* 1976, *68,* 103–116.

11

Timing and Context in Everyday Discourse: Implications for the Study of Referential and Social Meaning

FREDERICK ERICKSON

In interdisciplinary conferences there is often a problem of communication across research specialties which makes the successive reading of different kinds of papers not so much a dialogue among different research specialties as an exercise in parallel play (cf. Shulman, 1978). During the conference upon which this volume is based, one could see manifested the distinctions that Dickson makes in the introductory chapter between the referential and sociolinguistic approaches to the study of children's oral communicative capacity and its development. The difference between approaches that was most striking to me involved underlying assumptions of semantic theory; specifically, these were differences in the relative weight given to the literal, *referential meaning* of speech versus the more metaphoric *social meaning* of speech. As Olson and Hildyard (this volume) point out, the distinction between these two aspects of meaning is an essential one for sociolinguistics (see also Austin, 1962; Gumperz, 1977; Hymes, 1964); indeed it can be said that it is this distinction that defines the phenomena of interest to sociolinguistics. As a sociolinguist, I assume as a first principle of research that, although it is possible to draw an analytic distinction between

Children's Oral Communication Skills

referential and social aspects of meaning in talk, in the state of nature these two aspects of meaning are never found in separation; in naturally occurring conversation they are always inextricably linked. During the conference it seemed that my assumption was not shared by referential communication researchers. They seemed to make a distinction between referential and social aspects of meaning, but then in the conduct of research, they took that distinction to a different place than would a sociolinguist.

If one pushes the assertion that in nature the social and the referential aspects of meaning in talk are inextricably and nonrandomly linked, then it follows that the construction of experimental task situations to study referential communication in isolation from social aspects is an exercise in utter futility. One can argue this for two reasons. First, because of the inevitable "leakage" of social meaning into the subject's interpretation of the verbal and nonverbal interaction between himself and the experimenter (or machine stimulus source), the degree of "control" required for experimental manipulation of variables is not present. Second, because the experimental task situation is an attempt to arrange conditions so that the referential aspects of communication can be studied in relative isolation from the social aspects, the social situation of the experiment is so unlike anything in nature that it is itself a source of profound alienation and confusion to subjects. Hence, the data derived suffer, not only from intrinsic invalidity, but also from extrinsic invalidity; they are "ecologically invalid."

That is the critique in its classic form. It has been made by psychologists, as well as by linguists, anthropologists, and sociologists. The work of Rosenthal supports the former argument of the intrinsic invalidity of experimental data, especially his most recent research on the leakage of social meaning into experimental situation through the nonverbal channel of communication (Rosenthal, 1979). Bronfenbrenner explicitly makes the latter argument of ecological invalidity (Bronfenbrenner, 1975). Cole's critique of experimental research in cognitive psychology combines the two arguments (Cole, Hood, & McDermott, 1978). Yet to stop there would be simplistic.

There may be middle positions that are more reasonable than those at the extremes. During the conference I realized that, although the stream of referential communication research may have been failing to deal adequately with the role of social meaning in speech, the stream of sociolinguistic research may have been focusing too narrowly on social meaning at the expense of the referential. This is understandable, given the origin of the interdisciplinary sociolinguistics "movement" as a reaction to what was considered the artificial abstraction and "de-sociation" of the notions of *speaking* and *semantics* in linguistics and in analytic philosophy. Nonetheless, it seems that sociolinguists could profit from considering referential aspects of meaning more fully as they study children's speech. If a purpose of sociolinguistic research is to relate to the field of education, and more specifically, to achieve a better understanding of the processes of classroom instruction, then the ways in which speech communicates the information and the logical relations that constitute part of the content of "subject matter instruction" ought to be of greater interest to sociolinguists than they have been. Even as we continue to argue that social meaning is an essential part of the whole meaning package in the language of "academic" instruction in school (and in the language of referential communication tasks in the laboratory), sociolinguists need to account more adequately for the referential contents of talk as well, if we are to construct a more comprehensive theory—just as referential communication researchers need to account more adequately for social meaning in talk. Some synthesis of the two approaches may be desirable.

The Substance of This Chapter

It should be noted that cognitive psychologists are not the only ones to have attempted the research strategy of separating out social from referential meaning. Chomskyan linguistics does this too, as does British analytic philosophy and French structuralist analysis in the anthropology of Levi-Strauss and his followers. But the sociolinguistic critique of Chomsky by Hymes (1974), the critique of analytic philosophy by Wittgenstein together with the growing conception within linguistically oriented philosophy of speech as social action (cf. Searle, 1969), and the current attacks on French structuralism by such critics as Bourdieu (1977) ought to be attended to by students of referential communication. In each case, the critique centers on the attempt to separate the study of referential meaning from that of social meaning and on the attempted analytic abstraction of language from the scene of its use in social life, from its context of practical action. Each of the three lines of criticism argues, using differing "surface structural" terms, that humans do not just talk for the sake of talking. Rather, they talk together in order to accomplish social purposes, making use of the human capacity to transmit social and referential meaning simultaneously, implicitly and explicitly, verbally and nonverbally, and to read off these meanings inferentially against (or better, within) the context of the action itself. This chapter is concerned with the question of what we can learn about these processes of multifunctional encoding and decoding through detailed observational analysis of audiovisual records of children's naturally occurring communication.

Crucial to such work is a theoretical conception of the semantics of the relationship between message form and message context. We know a good deal about how to analyze aspects of form in verbal messages, but we know much less about social contexts and their dimensions; our theoretical understanding of contexts is singularly undifferentiated. One dimension of the context of an utterance, as Olson and Hildyard (this volume) so clearly argue, is the social relationship between speaker and hearer. The aspect of social relationship that Olson and Hildyard consider is relative status: the relation of subordination–superordination, or of equality of status, between speaker and hearer. With different status positions go different attendant communicative rights and obligations between speakers and hearers, such as obligations of politeness and right in giving orders. Directives will be performed by speakers in different "appropriate" forms depending on the rank relationship between speaker and hearer.

For a sociolinguist, the social *appropriateness* of a given message form is of central interest. Apparently, for the referential communication researcher, *ambiguity* of reference is of central interest (see, for example, Markman, this volume, and Robinson, this volume). For speakers and hearers, making judgments of social appropriateness and ambiguity of reference would seem to involve quite different inferential processes. A judgment as to referential ambiguity would seem to involve primarily the processing of lexical and syntactic information; the focus is on the message form itself. A judgment as to social appropriateness, however, may be a more complex process involving not only the decoding of the message form, but in addition a "reading off" of the message form against the backdrop of the social context of its occurrence. Thus the sign–social context relation (what Burke, 1969, pp. 3–7, has called the "act–scene ratio") is a source of semantic content in addition to the form of the sign itself. One aspect of the interpretative competence of a hearer, then, may be the ability to distinguish between "fit" and "lack of fit" in the message form–content relation, an ingredient in the process of decoding social meaning that may be analogous to the "comparison task" ability discussed by Asher (Asher, 1976; Asher & Wigfield, this volume).

Interestingly, lack of fit between message form and social context does not necessarily result in an interpretive judgment of ambiguity of social meaning. A metaphoric transformation may result. People can play upon one another's interpretive capacity to read message form–context incongruity as an implicit signal for irony or other kinds of metaphoric fooling around, as in an exaggeratedly polite request from a surgeon to a nurse during the course of an operation, "If I asked you very nicely, would you give me a scalpel?" (Goffman, 1961). The very exaggeration of politeness by the physician points ironically to the physician's absolutely superordinate position vis-à-vis the nurse—a position from which the physician has the actual communicative right to issue unmasked commands: "Scalpel! Hemostat!" Neither way of asking for the scalpel is read as *ambiguous;* it is just that the first form is interpreted as signaling an ironic key, whereas the second form signals lack of irony.

This playing upon apparent message form–context incongruity may be an adult ability that young children possess only incompletely. Indeed, as Olson and Hildyard note (this volume), for young children, the process of reading the social context of a message is more salient than that of reading its syntactic form. A crucial problem of decoding for children, then, may be, not so much that of ambiguity of message form, but rather that of ambiguity in the message–context relation—a kind of "situational ambiguity" (or message–context incongruity) in contrast to the "message ambiguity" which has been of interest to referential communication researchers.

In everyday interaction, young children may find it adaptive to scan the social context more acutely than the message form. It is possible, then, as Olson and Hildyard (this volume) and Cole *et al.* (1971) suggest, that the apparent inability of young children and other cultural neophytes to attend to fine tuning in the experimental manipulation of variation in message form is not due to children's *egocentricity,* as Flavell argues, following Piaget (see Flavell, Botkin, Fry, Wright, & Jarvis, 1968), but is due rather to children's *sociocentricity*—to the greater salience of message context over message form for them at that age. What may be being acquired at around age 7 is a greater awareness that the school "game" (as well as the laboratory referential communication task "game") involves attending primarily to the form of the message considered apart from its context.

Asking people to attend only to the text of a message runs quite contrary, sociolinguists would argue, to the experience of children and adults with speech in everyday life. In naturally occurring conversation, utterances are not just texts, but are texts shaped by what ethnomethodologists doing conversational analysis call *the principle of recipient design.* This principle refers to the usual tendency of speakers in forming their utterances to take account of the social context—the social identity of their hearers and the practical activity that is occurring at the moment—and to choose among optional ways of saying the same thing referentially (e.g., *gimme that* versus *please*) that which signals the social relationship the speaker intends (cf. Gumperz, 1977). For the speaker, then, a recurring question is "Who [in terms of social identity] is the recipient of my communication and what is it [activity] that's happening now?" For the hearer, a recurring question is "Who is the speaker and what is his/her way of speaking and telling me now about who I am and what's happening?" Interpretive confusion can result when the speaker's speech does not fit the hearer's reading of the social situation. It is reasonable to speculate that many referential communication experiments present children with puzzling relations between an "odd" social situation and "odd" ways of speaking in that situation, and that these puzzlements produce interpretive confusion, which affects the children's task performance.

The problem is further compounded in that, in naturally occurring conversation, the answer to the question "Who is the recipient of my conversation?" is not fixed, but continually changes in subtle ways from moment to moment during the course of the conversation. This is due to two factors: First, a person in everyday life occupies not just one status, but many simultaneously (i.e., that person's social identity is a composite package of many statuses, many attributes of social identity); and, second, at different times in a conversation, different attributes of the social identity package may be being signaled as interactionally relevant (Goffman, 1961, pp. 105–106). For example, in interaction with a child, a teacher or parent may signal differential superordination vis-à-vis the child from one moment to the next. The archaic sense of the term *condescension* refers to the sliding-scale nature of the superordination–subordination relationship. Goldsmith's heroine "stooped to conquer" in differing amounts and in differing ways during the course of the play. The ethnomethodologist Cicourel (1972) points out that, between speaker and listener, status and role (and the attendant distribution of communicative rights and obligations) are not fixed but are continually being renegotiated during the ongoing course of everyday interaction.

Moreover, the cues that listeners and speakers are apparently reading—as to who-is-it-the-other-persons-are-signaling-themselves-to-be-now and what-is-the-activity-that-is-happening-now—are being presented simultaneously by speakers and listeners. It is not as if, while a speaker talked, only those cues in the speaker's speech and nonverbal behavior were available to be read. While the speaker or speakers are doing speaking, the listener or listeners are doing listening. Listeners' ways of listening apparently provide speakers with information about how the spoken message is getting across, and that information is apparently used by speakers in shaping the recipient design features of their speech as they are talking. In explanations, for example, the speaker may continue on from one explanation point to the next, or may recycle an explanation point in successive phrases in which the level of abstraction of the explanation is progressively lowered at each repetition (cf. Erickson, 1979; Erickson & Shultz, in press). What is necessary is a theory of oral communication that is informed by notions of the social organization of face-to-face interaction.

When people are "copresent" to one another in face-to-face interaction (cf. Kendon, 1975), what looks on the surface to be a series of discrete, successive "turns" is actually a process of continuous, simultaneously reflexive behaving and monitoring by the two players. Through such *reflexivity*, the conversation can be said to be *jointly produced* by its participants (cf. Mehan & Wood, 1975, pp. 20–23). From this theoretical perspective, an essential aspect of conversationalists' oral communication skills is a capacity for interactional inference, which would include a capacity to anticipate (predict) the likely state of affairs in subsequent moments, together with an ability to read the current state of affairs in the present moment. Such inferential capacity may be part of what Flavell (this volume) means by "metacognition," as the cognizing subject is engaged in face-to-face interaction.

Some Functions of Timing in the Social Organization of Conversation

All this points to the importance of the *when* of copresence; of the role of time and timing in the social organization of interpersonal coordination in face-to-face conversation. It is the significance of *when* that I want to stress here. In conversation, as McDermott (1976) puts it, "people are environments for each other." They are constantly, actively engaged in telling each other what is happening, by verbal and nonverbal means. To rephrase McDermott's description slightly, people are part of one another's *task environment*, whether in an experimental or a naturally occurring situation of oral communication. The task environment for conversationalists can be seen as a *sociocognitive task environment*, with the simultaneous organization of speaking and listening behavior constituting, continually, part of the "array" for the conversational partners. If the partnership is so interdependent as conversationalists jointly produce social and referential meaning in their conversation, then they must have some means of coordinating their interactional behavior and interactional inference. That means appears to be timing.

Condon and Ogston (1967) first documented the fact that the speaking and listening behavior of conversational partners occurs in synchrony. This finding has since been found to generalize across a wide range of human cultural groups (Byers, 1972) and age levels. The pediatrician Brazelton and subsequent researchers have found interactional synchrony in the behavior of newborn infants and their caretakers (Brazelton, Koslowski, & Main, 1974). Some researchers have in addition investigated the rhythmic patterning of this synchronous organization of verbal and nonverbal behavior (e.g., Byers, 1972; Byers & Byers, 1972; Chapple, 1970; Erickson, 1976). These researchers have found an underlying, metronomic periodicity in the organization of verbal and nonverbal behavior in speaking and listening. It seems that the recurrence of a regular rhythmic interval in interactional behavior enables conversationalists to coordinate their behavior by what Chapple (1970) terms *entrainment*, and that the engagement in entrainment by conversational partners enables them to judge the occurrence in real time of the "next moments" they need to be able to anticipate in order to do the kind of interactional inference required if each is to take action in the context of the action of the other; i.e., action that is *social*. This *real time* (in the sense of clock time) aspect of the organization of behavior in conversation seems to be crucial for its social organization.

There is yet another aspect of time and timing that needs to be considered in a theory of the social organization of conversation. This is a less precise kind of timing, *lived time* as distinct from mechanically measurable time. European phenomenologists deal with this notion of lived time in their introspective accounts of "lived experience" (Merleau-Ponty, 1965). Sudnow (1978) considers the lived aspects of time and timing in an introspective study of the process of learning to play jazz piano in ways that were judged appropriate by other jazz musicians. In so doing, Sudnow learned how to anticipate the appropriate occurrence of chord change and then to perform successive chord changes in a way that went beyond the temporal literalness of the metronome.

Introspective accounts have, of course, been ruled out of bounds by scientific psychology. Yet there has been within psychology a tradition of observational study—Piaget, for example—in which entities just as elusive as the notion of nonmechanically measurable aspects of timing have been studied to bring greater conceptual clarity in theory construction. So, even though lived time cannot be operationally defined, it may be useful to look for in observational studies. The potential importance of the distinction between mechanically measurable time and other kinds of time is underscored by philology; this is precisely the distinction made by the use of two different words for time in the Greek translation of the Hebrew Bible, the Septuagint, and in the Greek New Testament. One term, *chronos,* referred to what we now think of as mechanically measurable duration. The other term, *kairos,* referred to the time and timing of divine action in human history. When the Hebrew prophets predicted the Day of the Lord, they spoke of it as occurring in the domain of *kairos* rather than *chronos.* The psalmist in Psalm 103(104):27 uses *kairos* for the "right time," translated as "in due season" in the Revised Standard Version (see also a similar usage in Matthew 24:45, translated as "the proper time"). The distinction between *chronos* and *kairos* is analogous to that the anthropologist Hall makes between *technical* time (measurable) and *formal* time (Hall, 1959, pp. 63–92).

It is in the sense of *kairos,* as well as of *chronos,* that I want to consider the *when* of social context and of change in social context from moment to moment in a particular conversation. As the context changes, so does the *participation structure* (Erickson & Shultz, 1977; Philips, 1972), that is, the overall pattern of allocation of communicative rights and obligations among the partners.

In summary, I have been making two points: First, naturally occurring talk communicates social, as well as referential, meaning. Conversationalists are constantly relying on one another's capacity to encode and decode social meaning; this is an essential feature of the moment-to-moment steering of one another through a conversation, such that interpersonal discourse has a social organization, as well as a logical organization. Second, conversationalists not only have ways of indicating and interpreting their social intentions from moment to moment; they also have ways of pointing to the broader (temporally longer term) contexts of interpretation against which their indications of momentary intentions are to be read off. They have ways of telling one another—verbally and nonverbally, usually implicitly—what the overall activity context is and how it is changing, when a new sequence of connected action is about to begin, and how their social relationship is changing as the course of the action changes.

The following example illustrating these points comes from a naturally occurring event which is in many ways similar to an experimental referential communication task: a screening test given by an adult to a 5-year-old child. The test is administered in the kindergarten classroom at the beginning of the year by the special education teacher to determine whether children entering kindergarten have any handicaps for which special services are needed. The test is a referential communication task in that the tester is required to attend to the literal meaning of the tested child's answers. But the test is also a social communication task in that, in order to know how to answer correctly, the child must understand the social as well as referential meaning of much of the tester's speech (cf. Mehan, 1978).

On the third day of school, the test was being given to Angie, a 5-year-old entering kindergarten, who had very little prior school experience, and who had no experience with tests of this sort. The social situation of the test was unusual in that a second child, Rita, was also present, seated around the corner of the table from the tester and Angie. The presence of this extra member complicates the social situation, as does Angie's apparent lack of knowledge of the nature of the test as a social occasion. Because of the interactional confusion that results during the course of the test's administration, the test results are invalid as assessment data. Fortunately, in this case, the criterion level of performance was so low that Angie "passed" it.

One can infer from the false starts, seemingly irrelevant remarks, and other interactional breakdowns that appear in the transcript that the tester and the children are having troubles with contextual definition and interpersonal coordination during the enactment of the test. Many of their troubles seem to involve frame definition and maintenance (Goffman, 1974). There is trouble in relation to membership boundaries and to distinctions among member roles—who is "in" the event and who is "outside" it, what the communicative rights and obligations of the various "insiders" are. There is even more fundamental trouble in relation to temporal boundaries—defining the beginning, continuation, and ending of the event; when the opening is being opened, when the closing is being closed.

These are not simple matters. They are never definitively resolved by the tester and the two children. That is not, I think, just because this example is an odd instance of a test, although it is indeed an odd instance. One expects that definition of situation, role, and status is never fully resolved during the course of an event. Because the particular circumstances of any actual event are in some respects unique, it is adaptive for the normative cultural guidelines for appropriate action to be quite general and thus inherently incomplete (cf. Garfinkel & Sacks, 1970), and for the interacting individuals to possess the interpretive capacity to play the encounter by ear, organizing their action as a specific adaptive variation on a more general sociocultural theme for the type of event in which they are engaged. One expects, therefore, that people will be working from moment to moment at definitions of role and situation, relying on some socioculturally shared expectations of how what is happening should happen, yet never able to rely fully on those general expectations.

In the example of the screening test, the interactional partners do not seem to share enough mutual understandings of the nature of the test as a social occasion, nor of one another's ways of communicating social as well as referential meaning, to be able to interact in reciprocal and complementary ways. In the absence of some of the social steering capacity that the participants need in order to coordinate their social action as improvisation, their performance keeps falling apart.

Transcription Notation System

Before presenting the transcript, a note about the transcription conventions is necessary. Sentence terminal pauses (usually indicated in print by a period) are indicated in the transcript by a double slash (//); shorter, clause terminal pauses are indicated by a single slash (/), which is the equivalent of the comma. As will be shown later, the duration of these pauses is usually uniform across instances of them; this stability of duration is part of the underlying rhythmic organization of the discourse.

Speaking turns are indicated by numbers in parentheses. Usually in the transcribed conversation at least one sentence terminal pause separates a prior turn from a succeeding one. Occasionally, however, turns at speaking are exchanged without being separated by a pause. If the successive speaker begins to speak exactly at the point in time in which the previous speaker has stopped, this is indicated by a vertical bar with horizontal flags on it going in opposite directions.

(7)   A: *Wanna play house?*

(8)   T: *Not yet /*

If the successive speaker begins to speak before the previous speaker has stopped speaking, so as to overlap the previous speaker's speech, this is indicated by a vertical bar with horizontal flags going in the same direction:

(32)   T: *You can* *drink milk*

         R: *and JUICE*

Elongation of a syllable is indicated by a succession of double dots (e.g., O::H).

These notation conventions are an adaptation of those of Sacks, Shegloff, and Jefferson (1974) and of the adaptation by Gumperz and his associates (cf. Gumperz, 1979) of the stress, pitch, and pause notation of Trim (1975). Stress (a sudden increase in loudness, independent from a shift in pitch) is indicated in the transcript by capitalization of the letters of the stressed syllable or word (e.g., T: *BEAUtiful*). Additionally, stress is indicated in a slightly more complicated way, through use of a vertical mark preceding the stressed syllable. If the pitch of the stressed syllable is high, the stress mark appears above the line of text (e.g., T: '*Good*). If the stressed syllable is low in pitch, the stress mark appears below the line (e.g., T: ˌ*good*). These marks account for stress in the absence of a pitch shift. When stress is combined with a pitch shift, diagonal marks are used. If the left side of the diagonal is high(\), that indicates a shift from higher to lower pitch during the syllable; if the left side of the diagonal is low (/), that indicates a shift from lower to higher pitch. Placing the diagonal mark above the line of text indicates that the shift (in either direction) starts at a high point, whereas placing the diagonal mark below the line of text indicates that the shift begins at a low point. Thus there are four possible shifts:

1. high falling: ＼*good*
2. high rising: ／*good*
3. low falling: ＼*good*
4. low rising: ／*good*

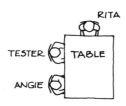

Scene

Screening test in a kindergarten-first grade classroom to identify entering kindergarten children who need special educational or medical help. It is the third day of school. Angie, who has had little school experience and no experience with tests of this type, is being tested. Rita has just taken the test.

Protocol

(1) T: *Angie? // or Teresa.*

(2) A: *Angie.*

(3) T: *Little Angie / OK dear.*   (pause as tester writes notes on the
        //   //   child who has just been tested)

(4) A: *Angie and Brienza*

(5) T: *I'm writing down little things*
        that Rita said to me /   (looking at Angie)
        and I'm gonna write down
        things that YOU say to me //

(6) R: *When are you _____ ? //*   (Rita addresses Angie)

(7) A: *Wanna play house?*   (looking at Rita)

(8) T: *Not yet /*
        not yet /   (rapidly)

(9) R: *After // after / ah / after _____*
        gonna go play with the / um
        things.

(10) A: *What things?*

(11) T: *Angie? //*   (the tester, who up to now has been
                                                      writing notes on what Rita said dur-
                                                      ing the previous test, now turns to
                                                      face Angie and speaks more loudly)

(12) A: *What things?*   (looking at Rita)

(13) T: *Maybe you can play it after*   (the tester looks at Rita and speaks
        'THIS.   with slightly higher volume and
        //   //   with widened intonation contour)
        OK, take this pencil, Angie //   (the tester hands Angie a pencil)
        tell me what THAT is //   (the tester points to the paper)

(14) A: *A circle*

(test questions continue)

(15) T: *OK, Angie / OK //*   (the tester turns page—Angie has
        \NOW /   just finished writing letters of her
                                                      name)

(16)   *Can we go and play now?*

(17) T: *Not yet // After this you and*   (the tester looks at Rita)
        she can go and play house //
        maybe you'd like to play with   (more volume, wider intonation
        a doll over there.   contour, points across room)

(18) R: (remains seated)

(test questions continue)

(19) T: *OK? Listen carefully now //*   (the tester turns to face Angie)
        In the daytime it is /LIGHT /
        what is it at nighttime? // /

(20) R: *DARK*   (loudly, one-half pause-unit "too
                                                      soon")

     T: *O::H! //*   (shakes head at Rita)
     A: *dark*   (softly)

You can't sit here if you
TELL her. // //
What is nighttime?   (turns head to face Angie)

(21) A: *// // ⌈dark*   (Angie says this very softly)
(22) T: *⌊If ˈdaytime is ˌlight /*   (rhythmic singsong)
              ˈnighttime is //
(23) A: *light //*
(24) T: *nighttime is ˌwhat //*
(25) A: *ˌlight*
(26) T: (marks down Angie's answer as wrong)   (a pause of two sentence-terminal
          What do you do at nighttime /   pause units in duration)
          go to bed? //
(27) A: (nods)
(28) T: *What do you do when you're*
          thirsty? //   (Angie shrugs)
(29) A: *// get a glass of water*   (in a "that's obvious" intonation)
(30) T: (writes this answer on paper)   (pause as the tester writes)
(31) R: *Yeah if you're thirsty / huh //*
          or you can drink milk
(32) T: *You can drink water //*   (writing on paper and looking down
          You can ⌈drink milk   at it)
(33) R: *⌊and JUICE! //*   (loudly)
(34) T: *You canˌdrink juice //*
(35) A: *Can I get some water*
          now?⌉
(36) T: *⌊Not now //*   (rapidly)
          What do you need stoves for,
          Angie?   (looks at Angie)
(37) A: *// ˌCook.*   (shrugs, and says *Cook* in a "that's
                                                        obvious" intonation)
(38) T: */ To ˈcook / of ˌcourse //*   (full terminal pause—appropriate
                                                        for turn exchange in the next
                                                        moment)
(39) A: */ What's that door?*   (pointing to tall cupboard)
(40) T: *ˌCloset // The ˈcloset door //*
(41) A: *What's inside it?*
(42) T: *Well ˌmaybe you can ˈlook after*   (exaggerated intonation and stress)
          you ˈfinish here //
          ˈOK / I'm going to say a sentence
          and you repeat after me.

(test questions continue)

(43) T: *Can you skip, Angie? //*
          Go over there to that house /   (points across room to area in
          and skip back to me.   which children are building a house
                                                        of blocks)

(44) A: (skips about five steps over to the
          house and comes part-way back)

(45) T: `BEA Utiful
      A: *I want to go over*   (points to boys listening to record
                     here.   player with headphones on, and
                                                      speaks somewhat more loudly)

(46) T: *You'd have to ask the boys /*
          I don't know if they'll let
          you /   (the test is not finished)
(47) A: *CAN I GO IN THERE?*   (turns back on the tester and shouts
          (starts off to the house area and does   across the room to the girls who are
          not return)   building the house of blocks)
(48) T: (pauses without moving, then shrugs
          shoulders and turns back to the paper,
          bending down as she begins to write
          on it)   (the test has ended)

Discussion of the Text

Beginnings of events, and their endings, must be interpersonally negotiated and interactionally cued (see Cook-Gumperz & Corsaro, 1976, on the negotiation of entry and the beginnings of events in young children's play). The test event begins to begin as the tester establishes that the little girl who has come over for the testing is Angie and not Teresa—Turns (1)–(2), which is the first membership issue. Angie's membership in the test as an "insider" is manifested by the tester's question (1), her repetition of Angie's answer to the question (3), and her comment addressed to Angie (5). The summons issued by a question can be seen as de facto granting of communicative rights (and obligations) to the addressee by the addressor of the question.

The second membership issue begins to arise as Rita addresses a question (6) to Angie. The literal content of that question is unintelligible, but the social significance of it as a summons for a response seems to be clear to Angie, because she responds to it [with a question—Turn (7)—which functions as an acceptance of Rita's apparent invitation]. The content of Angie's question, *Wanna play house?* is inappropriate because it is an invitation to Rita to leave the event itself, whose opening for official business the tester is about to open up. We will return later in the discussion to some issues of the temporal boundaries of the event. For now the salient point is that Angie's response to Rita, Turn (7), acknowledges her right as a member inside the frame of the event to have her question responded to in some way. Rita has been granted by Angie the right to take a turn at speaking in the event that is beginning.

The tester, however, does not immediately grant Rita that communicative right. The way the tester does this leaves ambiguous Rita's status. Is she an outsider? This is an ambiguity of social meaning rather than of referential meaning. The literal meaning—the lexicon and syntax—is clear. It is the distribution of membership rights and duties that is not clear. At first, the tester does not address Rita at all. She responds to Angie's invitation to Rita to play house by saying rapidly to Angie, *Not yet/not yet* (8). That seems to function as an implicit cue to Angie that the tester will soon begin the instrumental business of the event. Simultaneously, it seems also to function as an indirect cue to Rita that she is not "in" this conversation. Rita, undaunted, responds, not to the tester's cues that the test is about to start, but to Angie's invitation to play house. Rita does this by saying *after. . . gonna go play with the/ um things* (9). Referentially, this is ambiguous enough that Angie asks Rita to clarify what "things" she is talking about. I infer from that and from the referential content of the tester's comment, *Maybe you can play it after* `*THIS* (13), that Rita and the tester assume that Rita means "play with the things for playing house," as the house-playing props are located right past where Rita is sitting, in the place where the children usually play house.

Even as Angie's question *What things?* (10) can be interpreted referentially as an attempt to tell Rita that she does not understand what Rita just said, it can also be interpreted socially as reiterating her acknowledgement of one of Rita's fundamental rights as an insider—she can expect response from Angie to her questions. The tester, by next addressing Angie rather than Rita (11), may be implicitly denying Rita's right to get a turn in the conversation. This seems even more clear in Turn (13), after Angie has again acknowledged Rita's response rights by repeating her question to Rita (rather than responding to the tester's opening cue, *Angie?*). At this point the tester says to Rita (rather than to Angie) in an intonationally pointed way, *Maybe you can play it after* `*THIS* (two second pause, in which Rita does nothing, including not getting up and leaving, which she might have done) *OK, take this pencil, Angie.*

Referentially, the tester's comment opens up the possibility of playing house sometime in the future. It also seems to communicate two social messages which are apparently contradictory. The first implicit message of Turn (13) could be glossed, "Wait until I've finished giving Angie the test," or perhaps. "Butt out, kid, `NOW." The intent seems to be a nudge out of the event. Yet the indirectness of the directive is confounded by another implicit message. By addressing Rita at all (except to say explicitly, *Out,* `*NOW*) the tester has left ambiguous whether or not she is acknowledging Rita's membership rights to any turns at speaking.

That this ambiguity is the cuing of social meaning may have been a strategic mistake for the tester is suggested a few turns later, when Rita interjects another question to Angie, *Can we go and play now?* (16). This time the tester responds somewhat more directly (17) but still does not say explicitly *Out, \NOW.* In Turn (18), after the tester has said in an even more intonationally pointed way to Rita, *Maybe you'd like to play with a doll over there* (17), Rita still remains sitting at the table. From Rita's lack of response to Turn (13)—in which there is a 2 second pause after *Maybe you can play it after \THIS*—we can infer that she may not understand the intended directive force of such masked imperatives. The pause seems to be a cue that Rita had better shut up now, but the imperative force of the pause cue seems to have been lost on Rita. In this instance, the tester may be using these indirect command forms because she is being videotaped; but the ubiquity of such masked imperatives in the talk of teachers during lessons is well established in the literature (e.g., Griffin & Shuy, 1978; Gumperz & Herasimchuk, 1972; Mehan, 1979; Sinclair & Coulthard, 1975). Whatever the tester's reasons for using indirect means of control, a consequence is that Rita fails to comply with the directive intentions that the tester is communicating in increasingly more unmasked ways in Turns (13)–(17), but Rita seems unable (or unwilling) to interpret the tester's directive cues in the ways the tester seems to be intending.

A few turns later, Rita raises the ante and so does the tester. In Turn (20), Rita enters the conversation between the tester and Angie, not as she had done before—by addressing a question to Angie—but by giving the answer to the question the tester has just addressed to Angie. The tester responds to Rita's inappropriate taking of a turn by being very explicit (20): *\O::H// You can't sit here if you TELL her* (shakes head). From this point on Rita does not talk during the test, either to provide answers to the questions addressed to Angie or to address questions to her, with but one exception [Turns (31) and (33)] which will be discussed later.

Turns (19)–(26) are of interest in part because they show problems of membership and role definition—with the ground rule finally established, almost in so many words, "You can sit here, Rita, but you can't answer Angie's questions." In addition, this set of turns shows one aspect of the importance of timing in the social organization of conversation. In this instance, the reciprocal timing of successive answer slots and question slots becomes arhythmic momentarily and this interferes with the mutual production by the tester and Angie of an answer by Angie that will be regarded by the tester as referentially "right." Angie does provide the referentially right answer; she does so twice [Turns (20) and (21)], but *says the right answer at the wrong time.* This social interactional mistake in timing results in the tester's apparently not "hearing" Angie's right answers when Angie produces them. The final result of the interchange is that the tester writes down Angie's referentially wrong answer as the official answer to the question. Here the social "rightness" of the temporal placement of the answer relative to the timing of the end of the tester's question seems to be what is salient for the tester. The tester seems to "hear" the answer given at the right time, even though that answer is informationally wrong.

To understand how this may be happening, it is necessary to consider the role that timing seems to be playing as an organizing device for interpersonal coordination in conversation. It is also necessary to consider briefly the communicative means by which people seem to be giving one another cues about the temporal organization of their behavior together as they engage in face-to-face interaction. In English, which is a heavily stressed language, one of the means by which timing cues are given is by patterns of vocal emphasis. Emphasis is achieved by stress (increased loudness) and pitch (rising or falling intonation shifts). Stress may occur without pitch shifts. Usually pitch shifts are accompanied by some stress. By these means certain syllables are more prominent than others in the speech stream. Syllables that receive both stress and pitch shift are termed *tonal nuclei* by some linguists.

Two things about emphasized syllables are especially relevant to this discussion. First, in English, tonal nuclei and other kinds of emphasized syllables often occur at those points in the speech stream at which the speaker is introducing new informational content (cf. Gumperz, 1978). Second, emphasized syllables tend to appear in the speech stream at evenly spaced intervals across time. Thus, in English, tonal nuclei and other prominent syllables mark an underlying, regular cadence in speech rhythm. This rhythmic "beat" is also maintained in patterns of emphasis in nonverbal behavior—the "peaks" of motion in gestures and head nods, the points in time at which people change postural positions while talking. The underlying cadence is also maintained by points of onset in speech after a period of silence, or at the exchange of turns between speakers. This is not to say that every stressed tonal nucleus, or every gestural sweep of the hand, or every other sort of verbal and nonverbal emphasis occurs at a regularly spaced rhythmic interval when people are conversing. Rather, it is that these points of emphasis occur more often than not at a regular interval. That is enough redundancy to make for a discernable, regularly periodic pattern of timing; one that may allow speakers to signal crucial next moments in their speech, and listeners to predict crucial next moments in the speech they are attending to.

One kind of crucial next moment is one in which new information is to be conveyed (see the text examples in Bennet, Erickson, and Gumperz, 1976, and in Gumperz, 1979), another is one at which the current speaker relinquishes a turn at speaking to another speaker. These strategically important next moments in conversation can be signaled by maintaining a regular cadence in speech rhythm. In question–answer sequences of the sort we have been considering in the text from the screening test, both *turn exchange* and *new information* occur at the same moments in time. It is thus reasonable to expect that questions and answers will be rhythmically enacted by the partners in conversations, and that the timing of *answer slots* in relation to the just-previous *question slots* will be of crucial consequence, for both the social and the cognitive organization of an interrogation sequence. The presence of an underlying cadence may enable the answerer to anticipate the next moment in which the answer needs to be said and enable the questioner to anticipate the next moment in which the answer will need to be heard.

In a study of 56 school counseling interviews conducted by speakers of American English (see Erickson, 1975; Erickson & Shultz, in press) we found that routine question–answer sequences were performed in a very rhythmically regular fashion. That same kind of singsong cadence between question and answer also occurs in the kindergarten classroom in lessons with the teacher, and in the example of the screening test we have been considering.

To highlight the rhythmic organization of question–answer alternation in the test, Turns (19)–(26) in the previous test example can be rewritten for illustrative purposes as though the initial syllable of each line occurred in a regular rhythmic cadence. Also on that cadence would normally occur the full sentence terminal pauses between one speaker's turn and that of the next speaker, and so that is the way the pauses appear in the hypothetical rewrite.

The reader should read the text aloud and practice the cadence first before reading the full text. Reading the text aloud in order to hear and feel the rhythmic organization of it is necessary if the subsequent discussion is to make sense to the reader. Practice by reading aloud in succession only the initial syllables of the lines (including the regular spaces for sentence terminal pauses), keeping a metronomic beat going while reading: *day-, light-, what-, night-, pause-, dark-, O.-, pause-, now-, pause-, oth-, pause-, bro-, boy-, what-, sis-*. Reading this string of syllables aloud while looking at the full text one notices that the items placed by themselves at the rightmost end of a line (*in the, at, an-, if, is a*) occur in relation to the emphasized syllables as anticipatory syllables, similar to upbeat notes in music (*in the DAY, at NIGHT, if BROther*). With this in mind, one can read the text aloud, maintaining the cadence of stressed syllables (and "stressed" pauses), and placing the anticipatory syllables in correct rhythmic relationship to the stressed syllables:

1a.		*in the*
1b.	ˈ*day time it is*	
1c.	ˌ*light*	
1d.	ˌ*what is it*	*at*
1e.	ˈ*nighttime*	
1f.	*//*	
2a.	*dark*	
2b.	*//*	
3a.	*O.K.*	

3b.	//	
3c.	*now*	
3d.	//	*an-*
3e.	*other one*	
3f.	//	*if*
3g.	*'brother*	*is a*
3h.	*'boy /*	
3i.	*'what is*	
3j.	*'sister*	

It is apparent that the turn-exchange points between the question and its answer are rhythmically regular. There is a right time for the answer slot, and a right time for the initiation of the next question. Line (1e) contains the last stressed syllable of the question. Line 1f) indicates one sentence-terminal pause duration, which marks the next cadence interval, or beat. The new information of the answer to the question is contained in Turn (2a). It is said on the next beat after the previous pause. Then the next question begins in Turn 3, but the new information of the question begins in Line (3g). It is prepared for by other new information—a rhythmically regular series of framing moves consisting of alternating pauses and clause fragments in Lines (3b)–(3f). The answer (*dark*) comes in the right time and its new information is regarded (apparently "heard") as the answer to the previous question. The next question is then prepared so that its new information can be "heard" by the person to whom the question is addressed.

In the preceeding rewrite, the answer (and the questions) comes at the right time. That is not the case in the actual test (see transcript presented earlier). There in Turns (19)–(26) neither the answers nor the questions are said in their interactionally right rhythmic times. Moreover the first answer—Turn (20)—is given by the wrong person, Rita, who is not the designated answerer, as the test is being given to Angie. Rita's interjection is most interesting analytically because it seems to have thrown the tester's and Angie's mutual timing off, with the result that, as Angie says the referentially right answer twice in the wrong times, the tester apparently does not hear what Angie is saying as *answers*. Rita's interjection comes itself slightly ahead of the full sentence terminal pause which typically separates the last words of a question from the first words of its answer, and that slightly ahead-of-time placement of the answer may have contributed to throwing off the tester's timing. In Turn (20), the tester cooperates in the rhythmic disorganization, by interrupting Rita's slightly arhythmic interruption (i.e., the tester starts to speak slightly ahead of the "right" time). Then, just as the tester has collided with Rita by overlapping Rita's speech, Angie adds to the conversational traffic jam by overlapping what the teacher was saying to Rita (O: :H). What Angie says in that wrong time to be answering, is the informationally correct answer to the question (*dark*). This answer is apparently not "heard" by the tester, who continues with the reprimand to Rita (*You can't sit here if you TELL her*), and then asks the question again to Angie, *What is nighttime?* Angie answers the question correctly in Turn (21), but again does so in the wrong time. In Turn (20) she answers too late—slightly more than two sentence-terminal pause lengths too late—in the temporally correct place for the tester to speak again and initiate a prompt, which is exactly what the tester does. The initial syllable of the tester's speech in Turn (22) overlaps exactly with Angie's production of the one syllable answer, *dark*, and again the tester apparently does not "hear" Angie's speech as an answer to the question. The apparent misinterpretation is compounded at this point in that, as Angie has said *dark*—Turn (21)—a second time, the tester's prompt for an answer [which occurs in Turn (22)], is apparently misinterpreted by Angie as a cue that Angie's previous answers have been incorrect. The tester's prompts seem to be a cue for something—something important. That is suggested by the exaggerated intonationally and rhythmically singsong *If daytime is light, nighttime is / /*. The pause after *is*, in combination with the preceding exaggerated cadence seems to be a cue for an answer slot. As Angie has already answered twice, she seems to interpret the prompt as having a more specific meaning—not just the directive "answer now," but that plus the message "change your answer." I infer this because Angie does in fact change her answer. After the prompt in Turn (22), Angie responds with the referentially wrong answer, *light*. Angie places this wrong answer in the exactly correct rhythmic slot. Having given the referentially right answer twice previously in the interactionally wrong times, now, in Turn (23), Angie has given the wrong answer in the right time. In Turn (24), the tester responds with another prompt (in perfect rhythmic cadence with Angie's previous answer). Seemingly, this prompt in Turn (24) is intended by the tester to function as a cue of the sort Angie may have thought the previous prompt in Turn (22) was intended—as a cue that Angie's answer was referentially wrong. From what the tester says in Turn (24), I infer that the tester "heard" Angie's answer in Turn (23) *as an answer,* whereas I have inferred that the tester did not "hear" Angie's previous two answers as if they were indeed answers. Notice that the tester's prompt in Turn (24) begins exactly one sentence-terminal pause length after Angie's answer to the previous prompt. At this point, Angie apparently does not interpret the tester's prompt as a cue that Angie's previous answer has been wrong, for in Turn (25) she repeats her wrong answer again. Notice that Angie says this answer after a sentence terminal pause, in exactly the right rhythmic place an answer should go. This is now Angie's fourth answer to the tester's initial test question in Turn (19).

By Turn (25), Angie and the tester have reestablished the interactionally correct question–answer cadence, and Angie has given a second wrong answer in the right time. It is this last answer that is finally marked down by the tester as Angie's official answer. The answer has become a piece of test data; a social fact.

In the light of the preceding interpretive analysis, the social fact can be seen to have been interactionally produced, through a process of conversational inferences about referential and social meaning of utterances; inferences by the tester and Angie which are apparently at cross purposes; inferences which seem to depend on the cadential timing of questions and answers as an important source of cues pointing toward the referential and social meanings intended by the speakers. Because this pointing toward meaning is so implicit, depending for communicative success on shared background understandings between the speakers, it is easy for misinterpretations to arise, and difficult for the interactional mistakes that result to be repaired.

My hunch is that interactional troubles continually arise in the administration of assessment tests to young children, and in the conduct of referential communication experiments. What is being tapped when children give wrong answers may not so much be their underlying referential cognitive knowledge and abilities, as it may be their underlying knowledge and abilities in the domain of social and interactional inference.

How to distinguish between these two domains and how to devise ways of studying each without confounding either with the other, seems to be an important problem for future research and theory construction. Both referential cognition and what I have been calling interactional inference are kinds of thinking. In what ways are they the same, and in what ways different? How are they involved in children's and adult's interactional production and interpretation of communication in assessment tests and in classroom lessons? These are questions that deserve some new kinds of answers.

Larger Scale Matters of Timing in the Test

In considering patterns of timing within utterances and across connected sets of conversational turns, such as sequences of question–answer pairs, we have been dealing with time in both of the senses discussed earlier—*kairos* and *chronos*. At the micro level of social organization of communicative behavior in discourse, these two aspects of time intersect. The rhythmic cadences in speech which seem to enable conversational partners to predict crucial next moments in communication involve the *kairos* dimension of timing, times of appropriateness for action. *Chronos* is also involved, for the cadences of speech and nonverbal communication rhythms we have been discussing are measurable in terms of clock time.

The discussion turns now mainly to aspects of *kairos* considered by itself; to some of the functions of *kairos* in the social organization of the test as an interactional event. Here we are not considering technically measurable time, but chunks of time that are both longer and more loosely defined in terms of their duration. Within the test there is an overall sequence of constituent parts; each part being a set of questions taken from a standardized test. At the beginning of the test there is a beginning time, which separates the test as an event from the time that has preceded it. At the end of the test there is an ending time, which separates the test as an event from the time that follows it. Yet because this is everyday life, not artificially organized life, the beginning and ending of the event, and the transitions from one constituent part to the next within it, are not signaled unambiguously, as in the ringing of a bell to signal the end of a round in a boxing match. That would be organization of beginnings and endings according to *chronos*. Rather, the organization at this level of the testing event is according to *kairos*. Both the tester and testee need to recognize these times as they happen. One of the recurring problems the tester has with both Angie and Rita seems to involve their understanding of the *kairos* aspects of test time. During the time *continuation of the test*, for example, it is not appropriate for Angie to ask such questions as—Turn (35)—*Can I get me some water now?* The *now* of continuation is no time in which to be asking to do something that would end the event.

The recurring occurrence of the interactional slot, *Angie's answering time*, is another kind of time around which there seems to be recurring confusion during the test. Rita barges into that time right after Angie has answered and the tester is about to go on and ask the next question [Turn (30)]. Then the listing of "things to drink" begins, which ends in Angie's asking *Can I get me some water now?* (35). As we saw earlier, Rita also seems confused about Angie's answering time in turns (19)–(26), in which Rita jumps in and answers the question about light and darkness that was addressed by the tester to Angie. In the previous discussion of these turns it was noted that, at the micro level of timing measurable by a metronome, Rita's inappropriate answer begins one-half of a full pause length too soon. This is an instance in which *chronos* and *kairos* intersect at the micro level of the timing of exchange of turns at speaking. But even if Rita's answer had been given in the correct place in terms of the rhythmic cadence of discourse, *this was still Angie's answering time*, not Rita's. Rita was wrong, then, in terms of *kairos*, as well as wrong in terms of *chronos*.

We can see in Turns (19)–(26), at Turn (35), and at Turns (15)–(16)—points in the *kairos* organization at which the tester is about to begin another question to Angie, or a whole new sequence of questions—that Rita and Angie have recurring trouble with what we earlier called membership boundary definition. Is it time for the children to go off and play, or for Angie to keep on taking the test? Is it time for Rita to be in the conversation, or out? This kind of role confusion was also seen at the very beginning of the conversation—Turns (6)–(13)—in which Angie and Rita get so involved in their discussion of plans for playing house after the test that the tester has considerable trouble opening up the time of the official beginning of the test.

Just as there was ambiguity at the beginning of the test about the time of its opening, so there is ambiguity at the end of the test about the time of its closing. At Turn (43), the tester introduces a set of test items to check Angie's gross motor skills. The tester begins this test sequence by asking Angie to skip over to the section of the room in which girls are building a house out of "big blocks." There are a number of items in this motor skills question series, but the tester is able to administer only the first item in the series. After having skipped "over there" for the tester Angie does not return back "here" to where the tester is sitting. Angie says [Turn (45)] that she wants to go play with the boys listening with headphones to the "scary" record. The tester [Turn (46)] says indirectly that this is inappropriate, using the conditional construction, *You'd have to ask the boys/I don't know if they'd let you.* Angie apparently takes this literally, rather than figuratively as an implicit directive telling her to come back, the test is not over yet. (There is some sense in Angie's taking the tester's comment literally, for the boys have headphones on, and it is therefore counterfactual to propose asking them anything. Angie thus misses the irony in the tester's comment.) Angie then asks the girls playing with the big blocks, *Can I go in there?* (They do not have headphones on.) The girls assent, and Angie walks off to join them. The tester apparently decides not to call Angie back (as evidenced by shrugged shoulders) and so the test has ended. The ending, like so many of the internal transitions, was interactionally produced. The conjoint production of the ending involved apparent misunderstanding by Angie of the tester's interactional intentions in terms of what and whose time it is.

A final example of Angie's apparent confusion as to *kairos* time in the test is found in Turns (39)–(42). This segment begins just after Angie's inappropriate request to get a glass of water [Turn (35)]. The tester has been asking obvious questions, for example, in Turn (28), *What do you do when you're thirsty?* Notice that after Turn (28) Angie pauses and shrugs and then answers *Get a glass of water* in a "that's obvious" intonation. After the next question, in Turn (36), *What do you need stoves for, Angie?* Angie again pauses, shrugs and says, in a "that's obvious" intonation, *|Cook* [Turn (37)]. The tester may be acknowledging the intonation by saying in Turn (38), *To \cook, of |course.*

At this point Angie exchanges roles with the tester. The little girl becomes the questioner and the adult becomes the answerer. Angie points and asks *What's that door?* (39). The tester answers, *Closet, the closet door.* Angie then asks, *What's inside it?* and the tester replies with intonational emphasis *Well, maybe you can look AFTER YOU FINISH HERE.* Then the tester asks the first of a new series of test questions, thus reassuming the role of questioner.

On the face of it, Angie's question seems bizarre. At a literal, referential level of meaning there seems to be no logical connection between stoves used for cooking [Turns (36)–(38)] and closet doors [Turn (39)]. Moreover, in the *kairos* sense, this is not time for Angie to be asking questions; this is the time in which the tester asks the questions and Angie provides the answers. Still, the bizarre makes more sense than what is apparent at first glance. It is a metaphorical rather than literal sort of sense-making. Notice that Angie's question in Turn (39) has a "test-like" quality; it asks about something the answer to which is obvious, as were the answers to the previous questions about thirst and stoves. Also, what is actually behind the closet door is *the play stove used by the children in class for playing house*. The tester has just asked about something to drink (water) and about stoves and cooking. In that context, Angie's question can be interpreted as a way of playing at being the tester, and of doing so by asking her own questions about a topically relevant piece of information—where the play stove is kept, since we have just been talking about actual stoves.

Angie's question about the cupboard door can thus be interpreted as showing she is making sense, on the basis of background understandings about the classroom which are not shared by the tester who is a teacher, but not the classroom teacher in this classroom. In asking that question Angie also reveals once again some of the ways in which she does not share with the tester some fundamentally necessary, taken for granted, and never articulated understandings of the ways in which conversation in tests is to be conducted. Apparently, Angie does not know what and whose time it is. Apparently, she does not know that control over her behavior in that time belongs to the tester, not to Angie. It is not Angie's communicative right to initiate a new conversational topic; that right belongs to the tester alone during test time.

Conclusions

I asserted at the beginning that, from a sociolinguistic perspective, in considering naturally occurring speech it seems impossible to think of referential aspects of meaning as separable from social aspects of meaning. In presenting the example of the screening test, I attempted to show—through interpretive discussion of a transcript of speech, paralinguistic cues, and some nonverbal communicative actions—how people engaged in interaction are communicating social meaning while they communicate referential meaning, and how they seem to be assuming that others engaged in interaction with them are employing strategies for inferring social meaning (or interpersonal intentions of the moment, cf. Goody, 1978, pp. 10–16). When one person's inferences do not match the inferences of others, moments of interactional "stumbling" happen, in which people misinterpret, not only implicitly communicated interactional intentions, but the explicit literal meanings of talk as well.

In one such stumble, the tester and Angie together produced two "wrong" answers to a test question which Angie had twice previously answered referentially correctly. Other stumbles involved trouble over Rita's participation, and Angie's as well. Rita repeatedly seems to have misread the tester's implicit, nonliterally expressed directive for Rita to be quiet. (Alternatively, Rita may have deliberately taken the tester's speech literally, as a way of playing dumb about the implicit imperative force of the tester's remarks. In either case, Rita's actions are situationally inappropriate, as evidenced by the tester's reactions to what Rita is doing.) Angie not only ends up answering a test question wrong, but at one point takes over the role of question asker, and seems unaware, at what becomes the end of the test, of the social meaning of the tester's talk when the tester attempts implicitly to tell Angie that the official test is not over yet. A result is that Angie's overall score on the test is different from what it would have been had she known how to interpret more appropriately the social meaning as well as the referential meaning of the tester's talk.

The example of the test contains only a few instances of apparent miscueing in social as well as referential meaning. What happens there has also been found in other school-testing situations (cf. Cicourel *et al.*, 1974; Mehan, 1978), in classroom lessons (McDermott, 1979), and in academic counseling interviews (Erickson, 1975; Erickson, 1979; Erickson & Shultz, in press). It is apparent that the processes of conversational inference that are employed by the speakers in the example presented here are processes that are used continually in the conduct of everyday discourse. (For an extended discussion, see Gumperz, 1977, and Gumperz, 1979. For discussion of these issues in relation to classroom discourse and other kinds of talk in educational settings, see Gumperz, in press.)

A key aspect of these processes of conversational inference and interpersonal coordination seems to be the timing of interaction itself. Temporal organization was considered at two levels; that of the primary constituent "chunks" of discourse within an event and that of the moment-to-moment timing of speech and nonverbal behavior. As interactional partners go from one major segment of interaction to the next, role relationships are rearranged; who can appropriately say what to whom changes across these segments. Shultz and I, following Philips (1972) have called these patterns of communicative rights and obligations *participation structures* (Erickson & Shultz, 1980).

I have discussed some of the behavioral means—vocal and nonvocal—by which communication is socially and rhythmically organized, by which interactional partners are able to coordinate their activity in reciprocal and complementary ways, and by which they are able to communicate social and referential meaning simultaneously. I have presented a theoretical perspective on communication as socially organized action in real time. This set of perspectives, which can be called those of "interactional sociolinguistics" makes assumptions about the processes of interactional inference which enable interpersonal coordination and which enable people to read the referential and social meanings that are being communicated in and through face-to-face interaction. It is assumed that people's interpretive ability to conduct interactional inference is culturally learned, just as is their capacity to interpret the literal meaning of sentences on the basis of learned knowledge of the sound system and grammar of language.

The emerging approach of interactional sociolinguistics overlaps somewhat with the study of children's referential communication, and with psycholinguistic approaches to the study of children's language acquisition. Interactional sociolinguistics is also discontinuous, in aspects of substance and of method, with these other fields. Substantively, there is an emphasis on social meaning almost to the exclusion of any consideration of referential meaning. Methodologically, there is an emphasis on using audio and audiovisual documents of instances of naturally occurring interaction as a data base, and on interpretive, microethnographic or "constitutive" analysis of the documentary records. These are means of locating the particular organizing features of social action in discourse which are usually not attended to in experimental studies—the interactional processes by which test results and experimental results are produced.

I am not a psychologist and am not used to thinking about thinking. I can only guess at what is involved in children's acquisition of a capacity for socioculturally appropriate interactional inference. Some kinds of underlying cognitive processing must be postulated, it seems to me, in order to account for what we see people doing as they communicate social and referential meaning face-to-face. The interpretive processes that one needs to assume would seem to be of a quite rough-and-ready sort, given that people are able to derive meaning, both social and referential, out of the messiness of naturally occurring conversation, and to do so consistently enough to make everyday communication possible.

If what I have been considering here are some fundamental aspects of what children need to know and be able to do in order to participate in everyday conversation, then somehow this work makes contact with, and needs to be better articulated with, work on referential aspects of children's speech. Such articulation is necessary to advance our understanding of children's oral communication skills; to develop theory that is more clear and more comprehensive than that which presently exists.

References

Asher, S. R. Children's ability to appraise their own and another person's communication performance. *Developmental Psychology*, 1976, *12*, 24–32.

Asher, S. R., & Wigfield, A. Training referential communication skills. In W. P. Dickson (Ed.), *Children's oral communication skills*. New York: Academic Press, 1981.

Austin, J. L. *How to do things with words.* Cambridge, Mass.: Harvard University Press, 1962.

Bennet, A., Erickson, F., & Gumperz, J. J. Coordination of verbal and nonverbal cues in conversation. Unpublished manuscript, University of California, Berkeley, January 1976.

Bourdieu, P. *Outline of a theory of practice.* Cambridge, Mass.: Harvard University Press, 1977.

Brazelton, B. T., Koslowski, B., & Main, M. The origins of reciprocity: The early mother–infant interaction. In M. Lewis & L. Rosenbloom (Eds.), *The effect of the infant on its caretaker.* New York: John Wiley and Sons, 1974.

Bronfenbrenner, U. Reality and research in ecology of human development. *Proceedings of the American Philosophical Society, 1975, 119,* 439–469.

Burke, K. *A grammar of motives.* Berkeley and Los Angeles: University of California Press, 1969.

Byers, P. From biological rhythm to cultural pattern: A study of minimal units. (Doctoral dissertation, Columbia University, 1972). *Dissertation Abstracts International,* 1972. (University Microfilms No. 73-9004)

Byers, P., & Byers, H. Nonverbal communication and the education of children. In C. Cazden, D. Hymes, & V. John, (Eds.), *Functions of language in the classroom.* New York: Teachers College Press, 1972.

Chapple, E. D. *Culture and biological man: Explorations in behavioral anthropology.* New York: Holt, Rinehart and Winston, 1970.

Cicourel, A. V. Basic and normative rules in the negotiation of status and role. In D. Sudnow (Ed.), *Studies in social interaction.* New York: The Free Press, 1972.

Cicourel, A. V., *et al. Language use and school performance.* New York: Academic Press, 1974.

Cole, M., Gay, J., Glick, J. A., & Sharp, D. *The cultural context of learning and thinking: An exploration in experimental anthropology.* New York: Basic Books, 1971.

Cole, M., Hood, L., & McDermott, R. P. *Ecological niche picking: Ecological invalidity as an axiom of experimental cognitive psychology.* Institute for Comparative Human Development, The Rockefeller University, 1978.

Condon, W., & Ogston, W. D. A segmentation of behavior. *Journal of Psychiatric Research, 1967, 5,* 221–235.

Cook-Gumperz, J. Situated instructions: Language socialization of school-age children. In S. Ervin-Tripp, & C. Mitchell-Kernan (Eds.), *Child discourse.* New York: Academic Press, 1977.

Cook-Gumperz, J., & Corsaro, W. A. Social-ecological constraints on children's communicative strategies. In J. Cook-Gumperz, & J. Gumperz, (Eds.), *Papers on language and context.* University of California, Berkeley, 1976.

Erickson, F. Gatekeeping and the melting pot: Interaction in counseling encounters. *Harvard Educational Review, 1975, 45,* 44–70.

Erickson, F. Gatekeeping encounters: A social selection process. In P. R. Sanday (Ed.), *Anthropology and the public interest.* New York: Academic Press, 1976.

Erickson, F. Talking down: some cultural sources of miscommunication in inter-racial interviews. In A. Wolfgang, (Ed.) *Nonverbal communication.* New York: Academic Press, 1979.

Erickson, F., & Shultz, J. When is a context? Some issues and methods in the analysis of social competence. *The Quarterly Newsletter* of the Institute for Comparative Human Development, the Rockefeller University, 1977, *1*(2), 5–10. Also in Green, J., & Wallat, C. (Eds.), *Ethnographic approaches to face to face interaction in educational settings.* Norwood, N.J.: Ablex, 1980.

Erickson, F., & Shultz, J. Talking to the man: Organization of communication in counseling interviews. New York: Academic Press, in press.

Flavell, J. H. *The development of role taking and communication skills in children.* New York: John Wiley and Sons, 1968.

Garfinkel, H., & Sacks, H. On formal structures of practical actions. In J. C. McKinney, & E. A. Tiryakin (Eds.), *Theoretical sociology: Perspectives and developments.* New York: Appleton-Century-Crofts, 1970.

Goffman, E. *Encounters: Two studies in the sociology of interactions.* Indianapolis: Bobbs-Merrill, 1961.

Goffman, E. *Frame analysis: An essay on the organization of experience.* New York: Harper Colophon Books, 1974.

Goody, E. N. *Questions and politeness: Strategies in social interaction.* Cambridge: Cambridge University Press, 1978.

Griffin, P., & Shuy, R. *Children's functional language and education in the early years* (Final technical report to the Carnegie Corporation of America). Arlington, Va.: Center for Applied Linguistics, 1978.

Gumperz, J. Sociocultural knowledge in conversational inference. In M. Saville-Troike, (Ed.), *Linguistics and anthropology* (Georgetown University Roundtable on Language and Linguistics). Washington, D.C.: Georgetown University Press, 1977.

Gumperz, J. Conversational inference and classroom learning. In J. Green & C. Wallat (Eds.), *Ethnographic approaches to face to face interaction in educational settings.* Norwood, N.J.: Ablex, 1980.

Gumperz, J. *The retrieval of sociocultural knowledge in conversation.* Occasional paper, Language-Behavior Research Laboratory, University of California at Berkeley, 1979.

Gumperz, J. J., & Herasimchuk, E. The conversational analysis of social meaning: A study of classroom interaction. In R. Shuy (Ed.), *Sociolinguistics: Current trends and prospects.* Washington, D.C.: Georgetown University Press, 1972.

Hall, E. T. *The silent language.* New York: Fawcett, 1959.

Hymes, D. Introduction: Toward ethnographies of communication. In J. Gumperz & D. Hymes (Eds.), The ethnography of communication. *American Anthropologist,* 1964, *55*(5, Pt. 2, 1–34).

Hymes, D. *Foundations of sociolinguistics: An ethnographic approach.* Philadelphia: University of Pennsylvania Press, 1974.

Kendon, A. Introduction. In A. Kendon, R. M. Yarris, & M. R. Key (Eds.), *Organization of behavior in face-to-face interaction.* The Hague: Mouton; Chicago: Aldine, 1975.

McDermott, R. P. *Kids make sense: An ethnographic account of the interactional management of success and failure in one first grade classroom.* Unpublished doctoral dissertation, Stanford University, 1976.

McDermott, R. P., & Gospodinoff, K. Social contexts for ethnic borders and school failure. In A. Wolfgang (Ed.), *Nonverbal behavior.* New York: Academic Press, 1979.

Mehan, H. Structuring school structure. *Harvard Educational Review,* 1978, *48*, 32–64.

Mehan, H. *Learning lessons: Social organization in the classroom.* Cambridge, Mass.: Harvard University Press, 1979.

Mehan, H., & Wood, H. *The reality of ethnomethodology.* New York: John Wiley and Sons, 1975.

Merleau-Ponty, M. [*The structure of behavior*] (A. L. Fisher, Trans.). London: Methuen, 1965.

Phillips, S. Participant structures and communicative competence: Warm Springs children in community and classroom. In C. Cazden, D. Hymes, & V. John (Eds.), *Functions of language in the classroom.* New York: Teachers College Press, 1972.

Rosenthal, R., Hall, J. A., Archer, D., MiMatteo, M. R., & Rogers, P. L. The PONS test: Measuring sensitivity to nonverbal cues. In S. Weitz, *Nonverbal communication* (Rev. ed.). New York: Oxford University Press, 1979.

Sacks, H., Schegloff, E., & Jefferson, G. A simplest systematics for the organization of twin-taking for conversation. *Language,* 1974, *50*, 696–734.

Searle, J. *Speech acts.* Cambridge: Cambridge University Press, 1969.

Shulman, L. S. *Relating theory to practice* (Occasional Paper #12). Institute for Research on Teaching, Michigan State University, 1978.

Sinclair, J. M., & Coulthard, R. M. *Toward an analysis of discourse: The English used by teachers and pupils.* Oxford: Oxford University Press, 1975.

Sudnow, D. *Ways of the hand: The organization of improvised conduct.* Cambridge, Mass.: Harvard University Press. 1978.

Trim, J. *A system for the notation of English intonation.* Unpublished manuscript, Cambridge University, 1975.

12

What Do They Do at School *Any* Day: Studying Functional Language

ROGER W. SHUY AND PEG GRIFFIN

This chapter grows out of a recently completed study of language use in the early school years.[1] That study, in turn, grew from some concerns about

---

[1] This chapter owes thanks to the researchers and other participants in that study, as well as to those at the conference who were kind enough to suggest improvements on the version presented orally and to our colleagues on both coasts who, as always, provided supportive criticism.

The study, reported in Griffin and Shuy (1978), was funded by the Carnegie Corporation of New York. The report is available from the Center for Applied Linguistics. The project staff included P. Griffin and R. Shuy, Directors; and M. Bruck, S. Cahir, L. Cherry, D. Christian, C. Freeman, J. Greene, F. Humphrey, R. Montes, R. Tripp, M. Wertz, F. Borders, R. Berkemeyer, M. Feldman, P. Good, S. Migdail, J. Ottesen, M. Segall, P. Volkert, and J. Wilhoft. Seven sections in the report are most relevant to the topics presented in this paper: *Methods: Natural and Elicited* (The Staff); *Teachers' Perceptions and Children's Language Use* (Donna Christian and Rosemary Tripp); *Extending a Concept: Functioning Directively* (Rosa Montes); *Teacher–Student Interaction and Teachers' Expectations of Students' Communicative Competence* (Louise Cherry); *A Naturalistic Study of the Directive Control Strategy in Two Kindergarten Classrooms* (Margaret Bruck); *Talk and Task at Lesson Time* (Peg Griffin and Frank Humphrey); *Turn-Taking Processes: Interruptions for Help in the Third Grade* (Majorie Wertz); and *Activity Between and Within Activities: Transition* (Stephen Cahir).

Children's Oral Communication Skills

how to do research on children's language and from observations of children. A very concrete starting point was Joanna, a 5-year-old neighbor of one of the authors.

Joanna knocked on the Shuys' door one evening at seven. Shuy answered and Joanna told him that if he would look across the street he would see that her family's car was gone. Shuy looked and said to her, "Sure enough, Joanna, your car is gone." Then she observed that her mother worried if she missed meals. At this point, Shuy invited her into the house and Joanna said, "You know, I eat almost anything." With three observations about the world, Joanna had gotten herself invited to dinner.

This and other Joanna stories stimulated us to notice the virtuosity of many children as they negotiated events in their everyday life. The ease and expertise with which they used language contrasted sharply with the literature on children's language and our experience with teachers. There were a number of descriptive and evaluative studies of children's phonology, children's syntax, and children's lexicons; but there was little available about language use and what it signified about language development. Teachers told us in workshops that this aspect of language development was a problem for them; they were not sure that their students could use language effectively, and they had intuitions that this was just as important as knowing about the children's sounds and grammar.

One school in particular offered to work with us to find out more about children's functional language. They invited us and our sound and video equipment into their school. They shared with us the children (preschoolers to third-graders) and our concern about finding out how children use language. The variety of events during the school day provided us with ample opportunity to record children interacting with each other and with adults, while they were learning, playing, arguing, and growing.

The literature on very early functional language in naturalistic situations and in experimental situations entered into our work, but we relied most extensively on studies of classroom language. The primary school classroom has been the focus of a great deal of research for several decades, but only within the past years has the naturalistic language of the actual situation been studied carefully. Before this, the basis of most investigation has been the researcher's impressionistic coding of classroom interaction and language (see Dunkin & Biddle, 1974). Most related to our work were major studies that were based on transcriptions of actual school lessons. Sinclair and Coulthard (1975) developed a coding system which presents a hierarchically ordered structure (from macro- to micro-level: lesson–transaction–exchange–move–act). The "teaching exchange" is the basis of their system. The teacher initiates the exchange by asking the child a question, the child replies to that question, and then the teacher evaluates the child's reply. This is an example of the ways in which language use in lessons differs from language use in everyday conversation, which is more likely to be organized in two parts (e.g., question and answer) than in three parts. Mehan (1979) describes lesson talk in a similar fashion and draws attention to the ways in which the talk in the context of schools differs from talk in other contexts.

With this basic understanding of the kind of language involved in educational settings, we felt that we had a good chance to develop understandings of what children's functional language was like.

The Assumptions of the Research

Studies of school language are guided by the researchers' assumptions. Our research grows out of the assumption that language data, in this case school language, should be as naturalistic as possible. We do not object to experimental research, but we view studies of language in its natural setting as a necessary part of making decisions on how to plan an experiment and how to interpret its results. A preference for naturalistic contexts is not shared by all linguists, although sociolinguists tend to value this approach, as do anthropologists and many others.

Naturalistic data involves us in ethical and practical concerns regarding the relationship between researchers and participants in their research, as well as potential uses of the language data pool generated by the study. For expository purposes, we can list six major assumptions, although they are not truly separable in theoretical or heuristic terms.

Context

For years, linguistic work has focused on the universals that characterize language. Within the past decade, however, linguists have begun to examine the context of language in order to understand the variability of language use (see Hymes, 1974). Linguists realized that this variability brought richness to language expression, alternative ways of understanding and producing nuances, and that, however important the universals are, our humanity is clearly revealed through our variability. The use of this variability allows for individual expression, apt phrasing, and even poetry. Without understanding variability and the contextual constraints on it and the contextual opportunities for it, our understanding of universals is incomplete. For instance, the observation that the *p* sound in *pot* differs from the *p* sound in *top* is incomplete without the further explanation based on contextual variability, in this case simply word position.

Examinations of the system of language use bring into play a larger and less well determined notion of context. Beyond the word, beyond the sentence, beyond the discourse event, even, we find the institutional context, the issues of speaker role, and the nonlanguage aspects of the environment of an utterance—these are the fuzzy aspects of context necessary for studies of functional language. The development of sociolinguistics in the past decade has been evidence of the growing concern for context. We have always known that context contributes heavily to children's development. Only recently, however, have we begun to specify the dimensions of context enough to begin to see how it actually works.

As Bloom (1974) has pointed out, we cannot decide between alternative interpretations of the same behavior without a systematic analysis of context. Gumperz and Herasimchuk (1975), in their study of teacher–student interactions, show that children make use of a number of variables, such as task expectancy, role differences, and previous utterances in the conversation, to formulate interpretations and, thereby, to learn. This list can be extended to include factors related to classroom placement, size, competing or simultaneous activities, accounterments, equipment, and so forth.

A comprehensive analysis of the possible perspectives called context has not been made, although Erickson and Schultz (1977) provide one operational and theoretical discussion. Some relationships between context and children's language and learning will be direct. Others will be indirect. Some will affect some children but not others and not always in the same ways. Such variables are difficult to control, and, even when such control is attempted, one is left with the "observer's paradox"—that by controlling variables, the researcher distorts the phenomenon, possibly invalidating the research.

Setting is one part of a larger category of influences that can be referred to as context. Four different types of context have been recognized: physical, situational, social, and linguistic. These categories are not mutually exclusive (Scollon, 1976). Context is not a fixed set of properties of the world which children take into account as they talk or learn. Cook-Gumperz shows context to be a part of the communication and learning process, a set of variables that are constantly being reevaluated by all participants during the interaction (Cook-Gumperz, & Corsaro, 1976).

Involving the Participants

A second assumption underlying this work is that school research must involve in significant ways the research setting, in view of the importance of context. Our understanding of the contextual aspects of functional language is so rudimentary that we need to learn from the setting what contextual variables might be relevant. We need to learn from people involved in the daily life of elementary education what the relevant issues might be. We need to gain a participant's perspective in the particular setting in order to use contextual information in our analysis in the way that the participants rely on it for their language use (McDermott, Gospodinoff, & Aron, 1978). Far from being unobtrusive and in that way not disturbing the setting or the educational process, we found it necessary to become regular fixtures with a place in the setting and a role in the process. Further, we found it valuable to have the adult participants take a role in the research process by assisting in planning data collection, interpreting videotapes and transcripts, and in formulating research issues.

The emphasis on involving the setting is also related to the question of how researchers can give to the lives and work of the participants something equivalent to what they have given the researchers. What we did has been called action research; this sort of research is essential if participants in research are not to feel exploited. Anthropologists have been criticized for such exploitation and the effect is now being felt in school research. We guarded against this by keeping the teachers, administration, and parents fully aware of our work, conducting an inservice program, and assisting individual teachers in specified projects broadly related to classroom language.

The Importance of Functional Language

The intuitions and concerns of the teachers and administrators involved in our study identified functional language as a focal point. Getting things done with language is what gives the sound, grammar, vocabulary, and meaning relations value, yet phonology, syntax, lexicon, and reference have been studied more frequently than function. Studies of language and language development are important, but studies of language use are more rare and less available for use by educators.

Shuy has used an iceberg metaphor to describe the state of affairs in research and practice related to language, with sounds, vocabulary, and grammar being the visible tip of the iceberg, and meaning relations and use being its large submerged base. The focus on the language of children has been on that which is highly visible and, especially for purposes of assessment, countable. This principle obtains in foreign language teaching as well as reading and the language arts. These above-the-surface phenomena have the virtue of accessibility but, when we ask ourselves what matters most, they tend to come out lower than understanding or the ability to get things done with language. For example, the New York Puerto Rican who can successfully contrast the words *shoes* and *choose* but who cannot seek clarification effectively is less able to function in many situations than the New York Puerto Rican who confuses *shoes* and *choose* but who *can* seek clarification effectively. Similarly, a child who can phonetically decode but not comprehend is a less competent reader than one who can comprehend but not decode. Two serious errors are often made in measuring language success in education: We tend to measure only those items that can be counted, and we measure weaknesses rather than strengths. The ability to get things done with language, although difficult to quantify, is the fundamental characteristic of an effective language user.

Multiple Disciplines

A fourth assumption of our research is that effective research on functional language requires multiple perspectives, including those of sociology, anthropology, psychology, education, and linguistics.

Achieving an adequate interdisciplinary perspective is difficult. The training of academics requires them to work alone and from the perspective of their training; this often leads to false notions of topic ownership. Some psychologists and some linguists would claim sole rights of their discipline to discourse. Our approach was to start out with an interdisciplinary staff to ensure a variety of data collection procedures, select staff members who had participated previously in work that involved multiple perspectives, team a researcher from one discipline with research assistants from another, and assemble a consultant group to provide input from various disciplines. The process emphasized understanding on an issue-by-issue basis why certain claims needed to be modified, why certain evidence was needed, how two terms meant almost the same thing, and how one term meant very different things to different disciplines. Our mutual concern was to maintain the strengths from our various disciplinary trainings while illuminating our procedures and results with an understanding of those perspectives on the organization of behavior that other disciplines could offer.

Educators, psychologists, anthropologists, sociolinguists, and linguists wrote the chapters in the final report (Griffin & Shuy, 1978). These chapters reflect the process but also show that it is not yet complete and, perhaps, should never be "completed." Our goal is to understand how children participate in language events like those that take place in school. It is a multifaceted problem, and the complementary perspectives of multiple disciplinary investigations may be more valuable than a single-focussed interdisciplinary approach.

The Incompleteness of Discourse Theory

The fifth assumption of our research is that current knowledge and theory of discourse are incomplete. All of the disciplines have contradictions, confusions, and incompleteness in their methods and theory. Yet the examination of language use without a notion of discourse (with say, the limits of a sentence or a turn as a unit) is not fruitful. The lack of a complete or adequate view of discourse means that the researcher cannot analyze new data through an accepted model. If we knew all of the important language functions our task would seem simple enough. We would simply collect new data and then find those functions in operation and note the ages of the speakers as they were acquired and the contexts in which they are required. We would then be able to infer notions of development and of the degree of fit between what children can do and what school talk demands. However, not only do we not know what all the functions are, but we do not know what strategies people have to carry them out. Our work in children's use of directives, for example, revealed a number of strategies used by children to get back an object which another person had borrowed, including *Please give it back to me. Let me have my baseball glove back. Can you give me my glove back?* and *It's my glove.*

Even more problematic is the question of whether a list of functions and a set of strategies associated with each is an adequate reflection of functional language. Such a mode owes much to speech act theory and is reminiscent of syntactic models, but may not capture key aspects of functional language. In addition to practical problems of locating the alternate strategies, there are theoretical problems. Even if enough "round holes" were found (i.e., categories of functions and strategies), attempting to fit "square pegs" (i.e., utterances) into them might lead to the belief that square was round (i.e., that functional language was hierarchical and taxonomic) as all of the pegs fit into holes.

These problems prevented us from following some common school research strategies. From our point of view, classroom interaction checklists or questionnaires mask much of the richness of the discourse, fail to account for the appropriate constraints, and tend to yield misleading results. Our approach emphasized working from data to theory rather than from theory to data.

Education

The final assumption is that work in a setting must have some utility for that setting, not simply out of altruism, but also as a means of evaluating the results of analyses. Language research in naturalistic contexts has, as an object of study, not something that simply happens to occur in that context, but rather something—language—that to a large degree assembles the context (Mehan, 1979). The case is clearest when functional language is the object of study. Research can be evaluated in part by how much it resonates with issues of significance to others who view that context, in this case educators. We feel that the data—in this case, videotapes—have value to educators if properly selected, edited, and packaged. This assumption is influenced by protocol materials projects, begun by B. Othaniel Smith. One tenet concerning protocol materials is that certain concepts are better shown than read about: The six protocol videotapes produced in our project display instances of such concepts. Protocol materials are especially appropriate for children's language.

The protocols embrace a number of the more important principles growing out of the research. They are like other protocol materials in that their primary task is to instance a specific feature. This isolation of a feature, or "instancing" (as it is referred to in the protocol literature), makes the protocol unlike usual television programming in that it does not result in a well-framed story or classroom unit. On the other hand, it offers marvelous opportunities for inductive learning and flexible development of ideas. Educators can use them to evaluate the analysis we provide of children's language use in schools, and to see more clearly significant behavior of the children in their classrooms.

Data Bank and a Test

Videotapes, audiotapes, fieldnotes, and questionnaires documenting the activities of the school participants were collected during one school year. We concentrated on two classrooms (of about 20 children each) from each of the five grade levels in the school (preschool to third-grade). Five times in the course of the year, we videotaped the children and teachers going about their normal activities, which included whole group lessons and small group lessons with the classroom teacher or a subject matter specialist, small groups of children apart from adults, teacher–child dyads, free play, and lunch sessions. For most of the events, we have two views and three sound sources, as well as field observation notes.

Forty children were identified as focal subjects; there were equal numbers chosen from each classroom, of each sex, and of children viewed by the teachers as high, low, and average in their language abilities. No particular emphasis was placed on these children except to make a decision about which of several small groups we should focus on when we had to make a choice.

However, two additional activities involved these children more often than their classmates: instruction chains and corpus extension interviews. Instruction chains are quasi-natural situations in which the teacher instructs a child who, in turn, instructs classmates. We borrowed the technique from Mehan's project, as it seemed likely that the ''peer tutor'' situation might elicit language variation that would not be elicited otherwise.

The corpus extension interviews were designed to elicit utterances that the children might use to accomplish a goal under different conditions of contextual variation. The elicitation frames yield the same range of data from a number of different subjects, although the uniformity among subjects may fail to elicit from a child the language he is able to use, because the frame is divorced from the everyday aspects of his life (Cicourel, Jennings, Jennings, Leiter, MacKay, Mehan, & Roth, 1974). In order to reduce the amount of decontextualization, we devised a series of elicitation frames that included slots to be filled in with reference to objects, people, and events that were meaningful to the individual child being interviewed. Observations of and conversation with the child give information about what to fill in. In order to investigate ''directives,'' we devised a situation in which the subject owned an object that was being held by another person who twice declines to return it, even though the subject has a legitimate right and immediate need. We fleshed out the situation with details from the child's life by mentioning an activity the child enjoyed that would cause him to put aside some prized possession and by mentioning someone that the child knew as the person who had to be ordered to return the prized possession. We were particularly interested in the variations that the frame would elicit from the subject in relation to the status of the other person and in relation to whether it was a first, second, or third attempt to get the person to comply. The situation is developed as a narrative dialogue with the child; he is encouraged to cooperate in developing this story about himself and his acquaintances; then the interviewer stops at the point in the story when the owner (the subject) needs his object back and says, "So, what're you gonna say or do to get your *X* back from *Y*," again filling in the name of the object and the person. The utterances collected from the children in many of these interviews seemed not to differ in any respect that we could determine from utterances in the naturalistic corpus.

As a data-gathering device, these frames proved useful: They were contextualized, the utterances elicited were like naturalistic ones, and the children (even the 4-year-olds) found them pleasant to do. The procedure gets around the major analytic problem of how to attribute intentions to the speaker. Much of the analysis of language assumes that the form reveals the intention of the speaker. In fact, any language use makes the same assumption: One interlocutor can figure out what the other is doing with his language on the basis of the sounds, words, and grammar that can be heard. But speakers can be indirect and the route from form to intention can be circuitous both for an interlocutor and for an analyst. Understanding, say, a question uttered by a superior assumes that we are able to deduce the intention of the questioner, yet there can be mysteries involved (Does she want information? Is it a test? Is it a hint for me to act?). It is difficult to attribute intentions to a speaker, particularly one who is remote in status. The elicitation procedures overcome the problem by providing the intention as part of the frame of reference; the form of utterance can be assumed to be related to an intention of getting the addressee to return the object. Further, since the elicited utterances are like those in the naturalistic corpus, the procedures help us to attribute intentions to utterances there. That is, within the utterances elicited by the frame, we found a number of types of utterances that we would not otherwise have had any strong reasons for grouping together in an analysis. For example, Montes (in Griffin & Shuy, 1978) reports that "directives" include utterances like the following: "There are some other balls in the closet." "You can use the *blue* ball." "Ask Mrs. B. to give you one." and "Get another ball." Montes found reasons based on the patterns of occurrence to group these together as examples of a strategy for directives that she called "there exist alternatives." Although some of these kinds of utterances (e.g., the last two) might have been included in a study of directives, others (e.g., the first two) would not have been noticed as directives in the naturalistic corpus unless we were looking for them because they had occurred in the elicited extension corpus. Once located in the corpus, the context of the utterance verified that they were functioning as directives. Furthermore, these "there-exist-alternatives" utterances were a part of a group of directives based on "reasonableness" that tended to be related to the age of the speaker: Older children more often used them than did younger children. Montes's discussion also shows that they are adaptive to a value important to the culture: Sharing is valued; taking your possession back can be seen as violating the sharing principle; pointing out that there are other objects the other person can just as well use is a way to avoid being accused of "hogging" a resource as, in fact, it is not a scarce resource.

Other Results

The productivity of the entire project is best illustrated by discussing a few of the results in some detail. In addition to the work of Montes just discussed, we will now discuss three other analyses from the project. Complete reports of all aspects of the project are available in Griffin and Shuy (1978).

Donna Christian worked extensively with children's language use in request for clarification sequences. Analyses based on experimental contexts (particularly Garvey, 1975), did not seem adequate for our data, so Christian developed a new set of categories for this function (Table 12.1).

Christian chose to examine the area of requests for clarification

> because it possibly gains in importance for a child once school is begun, and the data under consideration involves school-age children. . . . In other words, it was thought that requesting clarification might be an aspect of a child's developing communicative competence that would be crucial to successful participation in interactions within the school setting [Griffin & Shuy, 1978, p. 11].

Christian found that when the phenomena were looked at carefully, in naturalistic contexts, with her theoretically justified categorizations, there was little that correlated with teachers' perceptions of children's effectiveness in using language. Children rated as above average and older children tend to address their requests for clarification to other children rather than to the teacher. Christian went on to examine how the children responded to requests for clarification. Older children tended to respond with more elaborations, whereas younger ones responded with repetitions. However, the teacher perception rating was not consistently related to differences in ways of responding to clarification questions. Christian applied Loban's (1976) measures of complexity and again found no clear correlates of the teacher's judgements.

TABLE 12.1
Categories of Requests for Clarification

Whole repetition—nonconfirmation

Teacher:	*And how are they gonna know which set you're talking about?*
Andy:	**What?**
Teacher:	*How are they gonna know which set you're talking about, Andy?*
Andy:	*By pointing.*

Whole repetition—confirmation

Paul:	*One, one, zero, zero*
Ashley:	**One, one, zero, zero?**
Paul:	*Yeah.*
Ashley:	*It's only eleven hundred.*

Partial repetition—nonconfirmation

Teacher:	*All my other classes have always called it the Ed and Edna game.*
Ashley:	**The what?**
Teacher:	*The Ed and Edna game.*
Ashley:	*Oh.*

Partial repetition—confirmation

Melissa:	*Adam, do you know where my paper is?*
Adam:	**Your paper?**
Melissa:	*Umhmm.*
Adam:	*No.*

Specification—nonconfirmation

Catherine:	*Let's pretend that she didn't know that this girl put on one of her ballet slippers, OK?*
Ingrid:	**Which girl?**
Catherine:	*This one.*
Ingrid:	*And she was angry with her.*

Specification—confirmation

Charles:	*I think that would be a good diagram to follow.*
John:	**The troop at rest?**
Charles:	*The troop on the move.*
John:	*That's what we're doing.*

Elaboration—nonconfirmation

Joyce:	*You get to put the chapstick on.*
Mary:	**On what?**
Joyce:	*On her lips.*
Mary:	*O.K.*

Elaboration—confirmation

Teacher:	*But everyone was sorta pushed back.*
Jennifer:	**By the white men?**
Teacher:	*Uh-huh. Pushed back.*

Montes's study of directives verified some notions in the literature and brought others into question. Among the categories of directives she discusses are

1. *Nonverbal directives* (e.g., the child grabs the object or points to it)
2. *Direct imperative form,* which includes an action type (*Hand over my ball*) and an outcome type (*Let me have my ball*)
3. *Indirect modal questions,* which includes an action type (*Will you give me my ball?*) and an outcome type (*Can I have my ball?*)
4. *Inferred directives or hints,* which includes those based on "righteousness," concerning who should have the right to perform an action or possess an object (*It's not your ball, you know*), and those based on "reasonableness," concerning why the following of the directive is a simple, easy, or natural thing to do (*There are some other balls*)

Montes compared the responses of the children when issuing directive under different degrees of urgency and to different kinds of people. Assuming that high-urgency contexts would call for less polite language and that politeness is also called for when the addressee is an adult or a child seen as highly respected, Montes investigated what kinds of politeness strategies the children used and concluded

> Our study verified the general understanding of indirect directives as "polite" on the urgency dimension, but found no warrant for seeing direct directives as particularly polite *or* impolite; and we found that the "rights" type of inferred directive could be seen as polite, but not the "reasons" type. Sharing, rather than issuing any directive, was the most polite tack to take but was never taken with a teacher or with a child of low status. . . . Teachers were treated differently and one special strategy, "countering objections" was used exclusively on them.
>
> [Children's characteristics were related to] the relative frequency of responses but no responses were limited to any age group, or sex, or group based on the teachers' perception of the child's language use ability. Girls and older children gave more functional directives; more verbal directive strategies were used by the older children. The use of adjuncts (e.g., *please*) is a function of higher grade level, as are the use of "reason" type of inferred directives. Bribes, including covert ones issued as threats, are not much relied upon by older children [Griffin & Shuy, 1978, pp. 40–52].

Montes's work points to a possible problem in the developmental literature on directives. Cross-sectional or longitudinal studies that report on different acquisition times for *indirect* as opposed to *direct* forms of the directive may be in error by ascribing the difference to form. Both of these categories are crosscut by the *action–outcome* dimension, that is, whether the speaker tells the addressee what to do (action strategy) or what state of events should come about (outcome strategy). Most of the indirect directives in Montes's corpus are outcome strategies, whereas most of the direct directives are action strategies. In the odd cases (the direct–outcome and indirect–action types), the data patterns point to the outcome–action dimension being a better indicator; that is, the direct–outcome strategies more often turn up in situations where we find indirect–outcome types than where we find direct–action types, and indirect–action strategies appear where direct–action types appear, not where indirect–outcome types appear. Developmental statements about indirect and direct directives may be reporting on epiphenomena related to the fact that indirect forms are usually outcome types, and, in fact, the developmental statements might be better stated in terms of action and outcome strategies even for the younger children treated in the literature.

In their section of the report, Griffin and Humphrey focus on the role of talk in lessons. Of particular interest is the detailed description of utterances having multiple functions. Two such cases involve invitations to bid and covert evaluations (Table 12.2). Griffin and Humphrey present arguments and evidence that show that the very ordinary invitation-to-bid sequence is a very interesting use of language. The first teacher turns in invitations to bid functions as a "pre-sequence" to the elicitation sequence which follows it. Other pre-sequences in ordinary language use include questions like "Are you busy Saturday night?" which we all recognize as a "pre" to an invitation. The children's response in the sequence is a summons, but it functions simultaneously as a response to the pre-elicitation. The teacher's next turn is a response in answer to one of the children's summons and at the same time is the elicitation that was "pre-ed" before. Children in kindergarten get taught to wait until the pre-elicitation is finished before they raise their hands and they get taught that when they raise their hands they have not only made

TABLE 12.2
Invitations to Bid and Covert Evaluations

Invitation to bid

Teacher: *Who knows, raise your hand if you do, what the last word says.*
Children: (Raise hands. Call out *Me.*)
Teacher: *Bobby*
Bobby: *Easter*

Covert evaluation: positive

Teacher: *What's the first word, Jane?*
Jane: *Christmas*
Teacher: *What's the second word, Susan?*

Covert evaluation: negative

Teacher: *What's the first word, Jane?*
Jane: *Easter*
Teacher: *What's the first word, Jane?*

---

a summons, but also have made a commitment to the elicitation that follows it. As Griffin and Humphrey note:

> What at first glance appears to be a simple but classroom-specific conversational device turns out, on examination, to be a complex case involving multiple functioning utterances but relying on mechanisms of general conversation—arranged and packaged for the tasks of education. What the children are overtly taught is basically related to the multiple functioning. We can paraphrase the rules as follows: (1) Child, your bid is not just a summons; you have to wait until the conditional relevance demands of the first pair-part of the pre-elicitation sequence are available before you can issue your bid since it also functions as a second pair-part to this pre-elicitation. (2) Child, the teacher utterance is not just an answer to your summons; you have to issue a second pair-part to it since it functions as a first pair-part of an elicitation which you are committed to participate in by virtue of your participation in its pre-sequence. Of course, and luckily, these rules are merely indexed in the teachers' mini-lessons on bids and in their sanctions on the occasions of violations, which are what we are referring to as "overt teaching." The important point is that the children do not get overt teaching about pre's or summons or elicitations—just about their juxtaposition and the corollary multiple functioning.

The ease and expertise that the children usually exhibit when dealing with these sequences, should not be forgotten—the overt teaching is rare, even in kindergarten—nor should it be overlooked as an indication of their ability.

Covert evaluations (Table 12.2) are another case of multiple functioning. In many cases, classroom talk includes an overt utterance by the teacher that comments on an answer given by a child. In fact, very seldom does the teacher use statements to transmit the educational material in the lesson plan. Teachers usually co-construct the academic topic with the children by using elicitation sequences. However, a child's answer can be wrong! In fact, we would question the value of a lesson that covered only what everyone already knew, or, at least, we would question whether we should call it a lesson. The teacher's evaluation utterance serves an important role in these lessons. Yet sometimes such utterances seem to be missing, and they seem to be missing more often when the answer given was wrong, just when we would say they are most crucial. Griffin and Humphrey point out that the evaluation is covertly present. The teacher's question following the answer by the child serves a function as a question but it also works in the evaluation of the answer just preceding it. Going on to a new question with another child is one of the strategies of positive evaluation. Asking the same child the same question is one of the strategies of negative evaluation. There are other strategies for each kind of covert evaluation. Griffin and Humphrey present evidence that, although the children are not producers of these utterances that exhibit multiple functions, they are competent in dealing with them as they are used by teachers in lessons.

Several issues related to theory and method became clear in the course of our project as we developed studies like the three that have been described. The traditional approach to linguistic analysis has been to examine a single sentence. For some things, this is fine. But, for the examination of functional language, it is thoroughly inadequate. Many of the teacher and child utterances in our records of classroom talk clearly indicate the need for analysis at the discourse level rather than the sentence level alone. Most of the examples in this chapter need more than one utterance for use as illustrations, and certainly needed to be analyzed as part of the larger discourse. This point may seem obvious, but it is a new and extremely important one in many fields. Obviously, it is being learned by linguists, but it has a long way to go before it becomes canon in, for example, the field of reading where, for both analysis and assessment, the isolated sentence approach is widely in use.

Conclusion

We still do not understand fully about what it is that is behind the expertise Joanna exhibited when she got herself invited to dinner. But we do know quite a bit more about how to study children's functional language and something more about how children change and about what kind of language use is involved in getting educated. One of the answers to the "What did you do at school today?" asked at dinner tables across the nation could be "I exhibited my competence at using language but nobody noticed because it's so common and, besides, I didn't do it to be noticed but because I have to use language to make it through the day with my friends and teachers and my ideas."

References

Bloom, L. *Language development: Form and function in emerging grammars.* Cambridge, Mass.: MIT Press, 1974.

Cicourel, A., Jennings, K., Jennings, S., Leiter, K., MacKay, R., Mehan, H., & Roth, D. (Eds.), *Language use and school performance.* New York: Academic Press, 1974.

Cook-Gumperz, J. *Situated instructions: Language socialization of school age children.* Unpublished manuscript, University of California, Berkeley, 1978.

Cook-Gumperz, J., & Corsaro, W. A. *Social-ecological constraints on children's communicative strategies.* Language Behavior Research Lab Working Paper #46, University of California, Berkeley, 1976.

Dunkin, M. J., & Biddle, B. J. *The study of teaching.* New York: Holt, Rinehart and Winston, 1974.

Erickson, F., & Shultz, J. When is a context? *Institute for Comparative Human Development Newsletter,* 1977, *1*(2), 5–9.

Garvey, C. The contingent query: A dependent act in conversation. In M. Lewis, & L. Rosenblum (Eds.), *Interaction, conversation, and the development of language: The origins of behavior* (Vol. 5). New York: Wiley and Sons, 1975.

Griffin, P., & Shuy, R. *Children's functional language and education in the early years* (Final report to the Carnegie Corporation of New York). Arlington, Va.: Center for Applied Linguistics, 1978.

Gumperz, J., & Herasimchuk, E. The conversational analysis of social meaning: A study of classroom interaction. In M. Sanchez, & B. Blount (Eds.), *Sociocultural dimensions of language use*. New York: Academic Press, 1975.

Hymes, D. *Foundations in sociolinguistics*. Philadelphia: University of Pennsylvania Press, 1974.

Loban, W. *Language development: Kindergarten through grade twelve*. Urbana, Ill.: National Council of Teachers of English, 1976.

McDermott, R. P., Gospodinoff, K., & Aron, J. Criteria for an ethnographically adequate description of concerted activities and their contexts. *Semiotica*, 1978, *24*, 245–275.

Mehan, H. *Learning lessons*. Cambridge, Mass.: Harvard University Press, 1979.

Scollon, R. *Conversations with a one year old*. Honolulu: University of Hawaii Press, 1976.

Shuy, R., & Larkin, D. Linguistic considerations in the simplification/clarification of insurance policy language. *Discourse Processes*, 1978, *1*, 305–321.

Sinclair, J., & Coulthard, R. *Toward an analysis of discourse*. New York: Oxford University Press, 1975.

IV
Other Aspects of Communication

13

Rules and Roles: The "Communication Game" and Speaker–Listener Processes

E. TORY HIGGINS, ROCCO FONDACARO, AND
C. DOUGLAS MCCANN

Communication development is commonly thought of as the acquisition of a set of necessary and sufficient communication rules which, once acquired, are followed with increasing proficiency. This approach to communication development overlooks an important aspect of communication, namely, conflict resolution and decision making. That is, conflict can occur among communication rules, and learning to resolve such conflicts is an essential aspect of communication development. The perspective on communication taken in this chapter is an elaboration of an approach to communication that has received increasing attention in the fields of speech communication, philosophy, linguistics, and sociology. This approach conceptualizes communication as a "game" in the sense of involving interdependent social roles and purposeful social interaction that occurs within socially defined contexts (e.g., Austin, 1962; Burke, 1962; Cushman & Whiting, 1972; Garfinkel, 1967; Grice, 1975; Gumperz & Hymes, 1972; Lyman & Scott, 1970; Rommetveit, 1974; Ruesch & Bateson, 1968; Wittgenstein, 1953). In contrast to this "communication game" approach, the approach that currently dominates experimental research on communication develop-

Children's Oral Communication Skills

ment emphasizes factors underlying accurate and efficient transmission of information. The communication game approach has intuitive appeal and a wider area of application than this latter "information transmission" approach that it subsumes. More important, perhaps, the communication game approach can also provide new insights about traditional information transmission issues. The purpose of this chapter is to demonstrate the need for and value of the communication game approach for one of these traditional issues—the relation between speaker and listener processes.

The Information Transmission Approach

The *information transmission* approach has been used to investigate communication effectiveness (Glucksberg, Krauss & Higgins, 1975; Mehrabian & Reed, 1968) and the effects of communication on persuasion (Eagly & Himmelfarb, 1978; Hovland, Janis, & Kelley, 1953; McGuire, 1969, 1972). The information transmission approach is based on a mathematical model of communication (Cherry, 1966; Shannon & Weaver, 1949) which involves the following process:

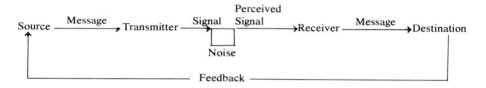

This general approach has inspired a great amount of research in both referential and persuasive communication. The emphasis of this research has been on message accuracy, comprehensibility, and validity, with both the speaker and listener being motivated to transmit or know the "truth" about some stimulus or to transmit or hold the "correct" position on some issue. Research using this approach has typically involved a speaker transmitting information about a stimulus to a listener who, on the basis of the message, is supposed to form an accurate and/or discriminating representation of the stimulus (for reviews, see Glucksberg *et al.,* 1975; Higgins, 1976; Mehrabian & Reed, 1968).

Referential communication models based on an information transmission approach have described the speaking and listening processes in a manner suggesting the presence of "general communication skills" (cf. Flavell, Botkin, Fry, Wright & Jarvis, 1968; Glucksberg & Cohen, 1968; Glucksberg, Krauss & Higgins, 1975; Rosenberg & Cohen, 1966). Two general types of proposals have been offered—the *stochastic* proposal and the *role-taking* proposal.

The stochastic proposal suggests that two basic processes underlie referential communication—the sampling process and the comparison process. In Rosenberg and Cohen's (1966) original version of this proposal, the speaker first samples from his or her repertoire of possible encodings of the referent (the sampling stage), and then compares the extent to which the encoding is true of the referent with the extent to which the encoding is true of the nonreferent(s) (the comparison stage). Subsequent stochastic proposals have suggested that there may also be a perceptual comparison stage prior to any verbal sampling or comparison where the speaker attempts to determine which features of the referent discriminate it from the nonreferents (Glucksberg et al., 1975; Higgins & Akst, 1975). According to these stochastic proposals, the process for the listener also involves perceptual and verbal comparison, but not sampling. Thus, in these proposals, the comparison process is treated as a general communication skill underlying both speakers' and listeners' communicative accuracy.

The role-taking proposal suggests that a basic process underlying communication is the general ability and disposition to take the role of the communicative partner (Piaget, 1926). In Flavell et al.'s (1968) influential version of this proposal, a speaker must first determine the listener's role attributes (e.g., intentions, attitudes, intellectual capacities), and then discriminate those role attributes that appear to be pertinent to the listener's ability to decode the message. The emphasis of Flavell et al.'s role-taking proposal is on the speaker's ability to take into consideration those information needs of the listener that derive from the listener's personal characteristics or attributes—the "individual-related" needs (Higgins, 1977). However, the notion of role-taking can include the speaker's ability to take into consideration those information needs of the listener that derive from the particular characteristics of the communication task—the "task-related" needs (Higgins, 1977). One would expect the same role-taking process to apply to listeners as well. Glucksberg et al. (1975) parenthetically suggest that the listener may also take into account the cognitive, perceptual, and linguistic capacities of the speakers, as when a parent takes into consideration that their child calls all four-legged animals "doggie." Higgins (1978) also extends both individual-related and task-related role-taking to listeners. Thus, taking the characteristics of one's partner and the task into consideration has also been treated as a general communication skill underlying both speakers' and listeners' communicative accuracy.

These information transmission proposals suggest that there would be a positive correlation between speaking and listening skills. Historically, there has also been a common assumption in the area of speech communication that speaking and listening involve very similar, if not basically the same, underlying processes and abilities. For example, both Lashley (1951) and Hockett (1961) argued that speaking and listening involve basically the same operations and problems, and Sarett, Foster, and Sarett (1958) have stated that the skilled speaker is a skilled listener. However, as will be seen, there is little evidence of a positive relation between speaking and listening effectiveness.

The Relation between Speaker and Listener Referential Accuracy

Brilhart (1965) had speakers describe geometric figures to listeners who attempted to draw the figures from the descriptions as accurately as possible. The results showed, if anything, a negative correlation between speaking and listening accuracy. Johnson and Gross (1968) used a multidimensional scaling technique to analyze the results of 16 possible combinations of speaker–listener pairs obtained from four subjects. The subjects were asked to describe Munsell color chips so that listeners, on the basis of a description, could later correctly identify the referent from among a set of color chips. Johnson, & Gross concluded that speaking and listening appeared to form relatively separate and discrete components. In a study of social class differences in communication, Heider (1971) also asked speakers to describe the referent so that listeners could later select it when mixed up with a set of other stimuli. Heider (1971) found no correlation between speaker and listener effectiveness within any one social class.

In a study on the development of communication accuracy, Krauss and Glucksberg (1969) computed correlations between each speaker's score on three lexical measures—type–token ratio, mean of the frequency ranks of words used in relation to the particular lexicon derived from all the subjects' responses, and frequency of use of words common in the language as a whole—and the frequency with which that speaker's message resulted in correct choices by listeners. None of the correlations was significant. Strickler (1975) directly examined whether there is a unitary comparison process underlying both speaking and listening effectiveness. Separate speaker and listener ability scales were constructed in which various communication subtasks were ordered in terms of increasing difficulty. A significant positive correlation between speaking and listening ability was found for kindergartners, but not for either second-graders or fourth-graders. Moreover, on a measure of the total number of correct responses across all subtasks, no significant speaker–listener correlations were found in any grade. A study by Dickson, Miyake, and Muto (1979) appears to be the only study that has found clear evidence of generalizability of speaking and listening skills. Using two different measurement techniques in two different referential tasks, Dickson et al. found significant positive correlations between speaking and listening skills on each task.[1]

In general, the studies discussed do not provide strong support for the

[1] The discrepancy between the results of this study and the other studies could be due to its very different subject population—Japanese college women.

generalizability of speaking and listening skills. In fact, with the exception of Dickson *et al.* (1979), studies have consistently found either little relation between speaking and listening effectiveness, or even a negative relation. A finer analysis of the differential demands on speakers and listeners in the typical referential accuracy task suggests a number of possible reasons for this. In most studies of referential accuracy, the speaker's task has been to provide a message to the listener that will allow the listener to select a designated target item from among a set of alternative items. As has been discussed, this can involve verbal comparison processes for both speakers and listeners. However, the comparison processes of speakers and listeners are not the same. Speakers must focus on the target item while generating messages to distinguish it from the alternative items, whereas listeners must focus on the message received while deciding which item it best describes. Thus, speakers and listeners must focus on different information during the comparison process. The underlying comparison process for speakers and listeners is even less similar if the speaker uses a perceptual comparison process to determine the target's critical features and then simply describes those features, as this need not even involve a verbal comparison process.

More generally, speaking (production) and listening (comprehension) require different types of information processing. For example, although both speaking and listening require retrieving information from long-term memory, speaking requires retrieving verbal schemas whereas listening requires retrieving object or event schemas (Huttenlocher, 1974). In addition, when the referent is not present in the immediate context, speaking requires constructing a mental representation of an item as input to verbal output, whereas listening requires deriving a mental representation from verbal input (Bloom, 1974). Thus, different cognitive demands are placed on speakers and listeners.

Even within the framework of the information transmission approach, therefore, there appear to be a number of reasons why strong positive correlations between speaking and listening accuracy would not be found. Nevertheless, the basic assumptions of previous information transmission proposals implicate a positive relation between speaker and listener effectiveness when, in fact, little evidence of a positive relation has been found. In contrast, the basic assumptions of the communication game approach do not implicate a positive relation between speaker and listener effectiveness. In fact, the communication game notion of distinct speaker and listener roles and goals specifically predicts speaker–listener differences.

The Communication Game Approach

A review of various papers proposing different aspects of a game-like approach to communication suggests the following general assumptions of a communication game approach:

1. Communication involves shared patterns of expectations, rules, or conventions concerning the participants' social roles and the appropriate language to be used, with appropriate language use requiring that both the linguistic and extralinguistic context be taken into account (Austin, 1962; Cushman & Whiting, 1972; Gumperz & Hymes, 1972; Morris, 1938; Peirce, 1940; Rommetveit, 1974; Ruesch & Bateson, 1968; Searle, 1969; Van Dijk, 1977; Watzlawick, Beaven, & Jackson, 1967).

2. Communication requires coorientation and monitoring between the participants, with each participant taking into account the other's characteristics (Cushman & Whiting, 1972; Delia, 1976; Mead, 1934; Muma, 1975; Piaget, 1926; Rommetveit, 1974), and, especially, their communicative intentions (Grice, 1975; Merleau-Ponty, 1962; Searle, 1969; Silverstein, 1976).

3. Communication functions not only to transmit information, but also to create and define a relationship among the participants, with the content and relationship being interdependent (Blumer, 1962; Garfinkel, 1967; Gumperz & Hymes, 1972; Hawes, 1973; Watzlawick *et al.*, 1967).

4. Communication is a simultaneous, interdependent process of social interaction in which the participants intersubjectively and collaboratively determine the purpose and social reality, or "meaning," of the interchange (Blumer, 1962; Bostrom, 1968; Burke, 1962; Garfinkel, 1967; Goffman, 1959; Hawes, 1973; Merleau-Ponty, 1962; Muma, 1975; Rommetveit, 1974; Watzlawick *et al.*, 1967).

Thus, one of the basic assumptions of the communication game approach is that speaking and listening involve different communication roles, with different expectations being associated with each role. The consequences of these different roles for processing stimulus information have been examined in the "cognitive tuning" literature.

Cognitive Tuning and the Relation between Speaker and Listener Roles

Zajonc (1960) hypothesized that *transmitters* (speakers) and *receivers* (listeners) differ in their basic task assignment. The transmitter requires relatively organized, unified, and differentiated cognitive structures for the stimulus information in order that the message be clear, coherent, and comprehensible for the receiver. In contrast, the receiver requires relatively unorganized, nonunified, and undifferentiated cognitive structures in order that the receiver be open to change and prepared for a wide range of possible new information. In order to test whether transmitters' and receivers' cognitive structures do vary in this manner, Zajonc (1960) first had subjects read a letter to form a general impression of the author, and then assigned them to either the transmitter or receiver roles. Transmitters were told that their task was to describe the person who wrote the letter to others "so that they can know him as well as you do now." Receivers were told that other people had detailed information about the stimulus person that they would later transmit to them. Prior to any actual communication, all subjects were given measures of their cognitive structures for the stimulus person. As expected, transmitters had more differentiated, specific, unified, and organized structures for the stimulus person than receivers.

A number of subsequent studies have elaborated and generalized 'Zajonc's distinction between transmitters and receivers. Cohen (1961) gave subjects a contradictory list of traits describing a stimulus person (e.g., "friendly," "cold") after assigning them to either the transmitter or receiver role. Transmitters subsequently described the stimulus person in either positive or negative terms (i.e., "polarization" occurred), whereas receivers tended to provide a more balanced description of the stimulus person. Leventhal (1962) assigned subjects to the role of transmitter or receiver prior to their reading transcripts of interviews with a stimulus person. After reading the transcripts, subjects were given further information about the stimulus person that was discrepant with the original information. In characterizing the stimulus person, transmitters were less likely to include characteristics from both sets of information and produced simpler, more consistent impressions. Powell (1974) found that when subjects were asked to list both positive and negative arguments for attitude issues on which they had positive or negative opinions, expectant transmitters listed significantly more consistent arguments than expectant receivers. Brock and Fromkin (1968) assigned subjects to the transmitter and receiver roles and then gave them a choice of listening to another person's impression that was either consistent or inconsistent with their own impression. Transmitters spent more time than receivers listening to the tape that was consistent with their own impression, and their impressions were more polarized than the impressions of receivers. In a similar study involving automobile characteristics, Mazis (1973) found that when given a choice of listening to novel or familiar information, transmitters spent less time than receivers listening to novel information. Finally, Harvey, Harkins, and Kagehito (1976) and Harkins, Harvey, Keithly, and Rich (1977) found that when presented with stimulus information that was difficult to interpret, transmitters were more willing than receivers to go beyond the information given in making causal attributions to the stimulus person.

The literature thus suggests that, because speakers are supposed to produce clear, concise messages, they polarize and distort stimulus information to a greater extent than listeners who are supposed to be prepared for a wide range of possible message inputs. However, the cognitive-tuning studies have usually involved more than these different normative expectations for the speaker and listener roles. In particular, they have involved different anticipations for speakers and listeners, with the listeners, but not the speakers, expecting to receive additional information about the stimulus person. Subjects are more likely to attempt to integrate and organize information about a stimulus person into a coherent, unified impression if they feel they have all the relevant information than if they know they will later receive additional information. Thus, the difference in expectations about receiving additional information could account for the results of the cognitive-tuning studies. For this reason, we attempted (Higgins, McCann, & Fondacaro, Note 1) to examine independently the effects of the normative expectations associated with the speaker and listener roles as well as the effects of expecting additional information.

University of Western Ontario undergraduates were assigned either the role of speaker or the role of listener. Both speakers and listeners were told they would receive an essay describing another undergraduate. Speakers were told that their task was to summarize their impression of the stimulus person for the listener, and listeners were told their task was to determine their speaker's impression of the stimulus person from the message. Both speakers and listeners were either told that they would later receive additional information about the stimulus person from the experimenter (expectation condition), or were told nothing at all (no-expectation condition). All subjects, in fact, only received the initial essay. After reading the essay, and prior to communication, all subjects were asked to write down their impression of the stimulus person. It is the results of this premessage measure of subjects' impressions that are most comparable to the measure taken by previous cognitive-tuning studies.

All subjects' impressions were scored in terms of whether they contained evaluatively positive or negative trait terms spontaneously labeling the stimulus person. Across all experimental conditions, a strong positivity bias was found, with subjects' impressions containing significantly more positive labels ($M = 2.5$) than negative labels ($M = 1.5$). Thus, in general, subjects' labeling of the stimulus person conveyed a positive impression of the stimulus person that was more coherent and definite than the evaluatively inconsistent stimulus information. However, this positivity bias was not present in every condition. Consistent with the cognitive-tuning literature, there was a significant positivity bias in both the speaker–expectation condition (positive–negative labels, $M = 1.1$) and speaker–no-expectation condition (positive–negative labels, $M = 1.2$), but there was no positivity bias in the listener–expectation condition (positive–negative labels $M = .3$). Thus, in contrast to listeners, speakers positively distorted their impression of the stimulus person even when they expected to receive additional information about the stimulus person. Of course, speakers have to formulate a clear, unified message for the listener even when they expect to receive additional information about the stimulus person. Consistent with this interpretation, speakers' subsequent messages were, indeed, positively polarized, containing significantly more positive labels ($M = 2.3$) than negative labels ($M = 1.7$).

In the listener–no-expectation condition, there was also a significant positivity bias (positive–negative labels, $M = 1.2$). Thus, listeners who did not expect to receive additional information about the stimulus person positively distorted their impression of the stimulus person to the same extent as did the speakers. Therefore, in contrast to the speakers whose positivity bias appears to have been determined by the rules of their communicative role (i.e., be clear, concise, and coherent), the listeners' positivity bias appears to have been determined by whether they expected to receive additional information about the stimulus person.

In sum, the cognitive-tuning literature clearly indicates that the differential demands of the speaker and listener roles can lead to differential processing of stimulus information. In particular, the speaker's concern with producing a clear, concise, and coherent message requires, under certain circumstances, a relatively polarized, incomplete encoding of the referent. There are other aspects of the speaker and listener roles as conceptualized in the communication game approach that suggest still further differences in speaker–listener processes.

Communication Factors and Communication Rules

The factors that mediate the communication game include the processes considered in the information transmission literature: labeling, verbal comparison, perceptual comparison, attention, comprehension, retention, and role-taking. However, the role-taking involved in the communication game consists of more than just taking into consideration the attributes of one's communicative partner; it also includes judging oneself from the perspective of one's communicative partner (Higgins, 1980; in press). In addition to these factors, the communication game includes fulfilling communication roles, defining the communication situation, judging message appropriateness, judging motives and intention, and responding to confirmation or disconfirmation of cultural expectations.

The factors and processes involved in information transmission are an important part of the communication game. Transmitting information about objects and events and advocating particular positions on issues are among the major purposes of communication. Among the rules of communication are those dictating that messages should be accurate, comprehensible, and valid, and that communicators and recipients should take into consideration the attributes of their communicative partner. However, there are other purposes and rules involved in the communication game, some of which are described in what follows. It must be emphasized that the communication game approach at this stage is, at best, a loose, flexible, and preliminary framework for raising new issues and research questions. It is not, therefore, a model in the sense of involving a system of clear, logically interrelated definitions, assumptions, and postulates.

A review of the communication game literature suggests that both the speaker and listener roles involve certain normative expectations.

Speakers should:

1. Take the listener's characteristics into account
2. Convey the truth as they see it
3. Try to be understood (i.e., be coherent and comprehensible)
4. Give neither too much nor too little information
5. Be relevant (i.e., stick to the point)
6. Produce a message that is appropriate to the context and circumstances
7. Produce a message that is appropriate to their communicative intent or purpose

Listeners should:

1. Take the speaker's characteristics into account
2. Determine the speaker's communicative intent or purpose[2]
3. Take the context and circumstances into account
4. Pay attention to the message and be prepared for receiving it
5. Try to understand the message
6. Provide feedback to the speaker about their interpretation or understanding of the message

People's communicative behavior and reactions to others' communicative behavior suggest that these are some of the rules underlying successful communication, but this does not mean either that these are the only rules or that people are consciously aware of these rules. The list of rules is also not meant to suggest that successful communication requires that all of these rules be followed in every communicative interchange. In fact, we will argue that in many cases it is not possible to follow all the rules, and some rules must take precedence over others depending on the circumstances and the purpose of the communicative interaction. Thus, unlike formal games, such as baseball, chess, and bridge, or formal grammars, communicative interaction has no explicit, well-defined set of rules that must all be followed if one is to perform properly.

Still further differences between speaking and listening are apparent from even this preliminary list of speaker and listener rules. For example, to convey the truth as they see it, speakers must create a match between the information conveyed in the message and their own beliefs, attitudes, feelings, *etc.* Listeners, in contrast, do not have to ensure a match between the message content and their private beliefs. Thus, only speakers must produce *internal correspondence* (Brickman, 1978) between the message and their

---

[2] This is not to say that communicators have intentions that recipients actually determine. Rather, recipients believe that communicators have intentions, and, as part of the process of interpreting a communicator's message, recipients do make judgments of intent.

private beliefs. To produce a message that is appropriate to their communicative purpose, speakers must also create a match between the information conveyed in the message and the impact they wish to have on the listener, whereas listeners need not ensure a match between message content and message impact. Thus, speakers, but not listeners, must produce *external correspondence* (Brickman, 1978) between the message and its intended consequences. On the other hand, listeners must provide the speaker with feedback about their understanding of the message (cf. Patterson & Kister this volume), and this can involve very complex processes distinct from those involved in speaking, such as countering a persuasive message.

Even when speaker and listener rules appear to be similar, application of the rules may require different processes for speakers and listeners. For example, although both speakers and listeners must make judgments about the characteristics of their communicative partner, the social judgment processes are different in some respects. Because a major concern of the listener is to explain the purpose behind the speaker's message, making causal attributions is a more important aspect of listening than speaking.

There are other differences between speaking and listening that are not captured in the description of the communication game as a set of speaker and listener rules. In particular, there are conflict and decision-making aspects of interpersonal communication that need to be incorporated into the communication game approach. First, there is the potential for interpersonal conflict between speakers and listeners in their communication goals and orientations, as well as in their attitudes toward the message itself. Second, for both speakers and listeners, there is intrapersonal conflict among different communication goals and different communication rules. In both cases, decisions need to be made to maximize goal attainment and allocate mental resources to different operations and strategies. These aspects of the communication game, and their implications for speaker and listener processes, are considered next.

Goal Interdependence and Speaker–Listener Conflict

People engage in communication in order to achieve certain goals. One of these goals may be to initiate or maintain a social bond with other participants—*social relationship goals*—and another goal may be to achieve a common definition of social reality—*social reality goals*. In fact, a major purpose of social interaction is to achieve consensus about reality, especially when reality is ambiguous, inconsistent, or difficult to interpret (Festinger, 1950; Newcomb, 1953; Schacter, 1959). For example, comments and questions increase when there is disconfirmation of expectations (Stamm & Pearce, 1971) or deviancy from consensus (Schachter, 1951). Other goals include *face goals,* where the communicative interaction is used for impression management, self-presentation, and self-esteem maintenance (Goffman,

1967), and *task goals,* where the communicative interaction is used to achieve particular practical goals, such as group problem-solving (Collins & Raven, 1969). These goals provide extrinsic reasons for engaging in communication. People are also intrinsically motivated to communicate for the simple pleasure of it (Tubbs & Moss, 1977). Exercising communication skills can be fun, like using any of one's symbolic powers (Burke, 1968) or, indeed, practicing any skilled behavior (Piaget, 1951). In fact, people often do not remember what was said in a conversation—only whether the conversation was enjoyable. This *entertainment goal* of communication is, unfortunately, often overlooked in communication models.

These goals can vary as a function of both the individual needs of the participants and the phase of the participants' interpersonal relationship (Schutz, 1960). Indeed, an interesting developmental question is whether one factor underlying developmental differences in communicative performance is developmental change in communication goals. For example, there is evidence suggesting that young children emphasize social relationship goals (Garvey & Hogan, 1973) and that different language functions predominate at different ages (Schachter, Kirshner, Klips, Friedricks, & Sanders, 1974). Thus, it may be inappropriate to judge children's communicative performance solely from the perspective of adult goals.

Both speakers and listeners enter into communication in order to achieve a variety of goals. However, the goal attainment of speakers and listeners is interdependent in the sense that each person can influence but not totally control their own and their partner's goal attainment. For example, in a referential communication task neither the speaker nor listener can alone guarantee success. Typically, some of the speaker's and listener's goals are complementary, such as initiating a social relationship and thereby receiving social stimulation and the opportunity for social comparison. Casual conversation between friends is usually a non-zero-sum game in which both speakers and listeners attain their social relationship, social reality, and entertainment goals. If the participants are good friends who support each other's self-presentations, their face goals will also be attained. Even in casual conversation, however, there is the potential for conflict in goal attainment. One of the more obvious examples concerns the opportunity to talk. For most participants in a conversation, the opportunity to talk is an important factor in achieving both their entertainment goals and their face goals, and, thus, the participants may compete for the opportunity to talk.

For any particular type of goal, such as social relationship goals, there can be conflict between the specific goals the participants wish to achieve. For instance, the participants' needs for affiliation or status may be incompatible (Schutz, 1960). Moreover, certain goals can be mutually incompatible. It is not possible, for example, for both participants to be dominant. Other goals are mutually compatible. For example, if one participant has a high need to be dominant and the other participant has a high need to be submissive, mutual goal attainment is possible. However, conflict could arise if the dominant participant were assigned the role of listener and the submissive participant the role of speaker, as the speaker has greater control over the communicative interaction, especially in referential communication tasks. When feedback is possible, conflict could be removed by the listener controlling the interchange by questioning the speaker.

Another type of conflict occurs when the communicative participants have different types of goals. One participant may wish to form a close relationship whereas the other participant may wish simply to be entertained, as is often found in dating. One participant may wish to solve a problem whereas the other participant simply wishes to maintain self-esteem, as is often found in research collaborations. In fact, the referential communication tasks frequently used in past research on communication development are probably one of the few types of communicative interactions where there is no conflict, as the experimenter gives the participants a common task goal.

How participants handle potential conflict depends in part on the participants' orientation toward goal attainment. The participants could attempt to either maximize their own personal gain (individualism), maximize their relative gain (competition), maximize their joint gain (cooperation), or maximize the other participant's gain (altruism) (McClintock, 1972). Initially, the participants may have different exchange orientations, but over a prolonged interaction a common definition of the interaction is likely to develop, especially if one of the participants takes a competitive orientation (Deutsch, 1949).

The exchange orientation can also be predetermined by the social context. For example, the cross-examination of a prosecution witness by a defense lawyer is socially defined as a competitive situation (a zero-sum game) where each participant seeks to block the other's goal attainment (where the witness' goal is to maintain credibility and the defense lawyer's goal is to undermine the witness' credibility). In many situations, such as the cross-examination, the role of questioner allows more control over goal attainment than the role of respondent. For example, questioners have greater control over presenting themselves as knowledgeable than do respondents (Ross, Amabile, & Steinmetz, 1977). Of course, speakers always have control over the message produced, and this message control has interesting implications for speaker–listener differences in attitudes toward the message. Constructing a message may be similar to constructing any other thing, in that a message is likely to have a special significance to its creator. To the speaker a message is "my product" whereas to the listener the message is "his product." Thus, one would expect the speaker to be more committed to and ego-involved with the message than the listener. Indeed, this could be one of the factors underlying King and Janis's (1956) finding that there is greater self-persuasion when people present their own talk after reading a script than when they simply read the script orally or silently.

This factor could also cause speaker–listener differences in judgments of the message, as commitment and involvement affect social judgments (Sherif & Hovland, 1961). The speaker may be more concerned than the listener that the message succeed, especially when the communicative orientation is competitive or individualistic, given that the message is the speaker's pride and responsibility. Although this is particularly obvious for persuasive communication, it would also be true for referential communication. This could account in part for Robinson and Robinson's (1976) finding that older children and adults blame dyadic communication failure on the speaker (although in their studies the speakers' messages were indeed faulty). Differences between speakers and listeners in their attitude toward the speaker's message could even cause differences in their memory of the message. Because the speaker is often more committed to, and involved with, the message, the speaker is likely to remember the message better (Higgins, 1980; Ross, 1980). Indeed, under some circumstances, such as trading insults, the listener may even be motivated to forget the message.

Although speakers and listeners may often have different attitudes toward the message, there are circumstances where speakers and listeners have the same attitude toward the message. Consider the situation of a female listener attempting to support a nervous male speaker in his pathetic attempt to propose marriage. Both participants are highly ego-involved and committed to the message *Will you marry me?* and both hope that the proposal will succeed. The speaker is motivated to persuade and the listener is just as motivated to be persuaded.

In sum, both speakers and listeners wish to achieve a variety of possible goals through communicative interaction. Since the goal attainment of speakers and listeners is interdependent, interpersonal conflict can occur when the goals are incompatible. For this reason, speakers and listeners need to take into consideration their partner's communication goals and orientations in order to maximize their own goals. This aspect of communicative role-taking has received little attention, and the inferential and decision-making processes underlying such role-taking have yet to be examined. Additional decision-making processes are required to resolve the intrapersonal goal conflict and rule conflict described in the following section.

Goal Conflict, Rule Conflict, and Decision Making

It is not possible for either speakers or listeners to maximally achieve all possible communication goals in the same interaction. Moreover, particular goals can directly conflict with one another. For example, telling the truth can conflict with a speaker's social relationship goals by angering the listener or it can conflict with a speaker's face goals by embarrassing the speaker. Given the limitations of goal attainment, both speakers and listeners must decide how much emphasis to give each goal in the communicative interaction. Of course, the weight assigned to each goal is partly determined by the participants' language community. Communication is part of a cultural system of social action, and its functions necessarily reflect the general culture or subculture (Bernstein, 1970; Cazden, 1970; Higgins, 1976; Scribner & Cole, in press; Silverstein, 1976). For example, in some cultures, communicators are expected to emphasize politeness or decorum above other goals. There are cultural rules of social interaction for the participants as a function of their age, sex, social status, and power that must be reflected in their communicative behavior.

Role obligations can also determine which goals are emphasized. For example, Cazden, Cox, Dickinson, Steinberg, and Stone (1979) describe how teaching requires the management or negotiation of interpersonal relations as well as accurate information transmission. Each teacher, however, must decide how much emphasis to give to management and how much to information transmission. More generally, speakers and listeners cannot simply follow a prescribed set of cultural conventions for assigning specific weights to different communication goals; the emphasis on different goals must vary as a function of the particular circumstances and participants involved in the interaction. Furthermore, the individual needs of a speaker or listener are major determinants of the weights assigned to different goals.

The decision-making processes involved in assigning weights to different communication goals have yet to be investigated. In fact, in most previous studies the experimenter has told the speaker and listener that the purpose of the communication is referential accuracy, thus determining both the communicative purpose and the weight it should receive. It is interesting in this regard that, when speakers are not explicitly told that accuracy should be their goal, as in the cognitive-tuning literature, they give less weight to descriptive accuracy.

Depending on their specific goals and orientations, speakers and listeners should, and do, follow different rules of communication. Speakers, for example, would be more likely to emphasize telling the truth in a referential situation where they had a task goal and a cooperative orientation (e.g., dyadic accuracy) than in a persuasive situation where they had a social reality goal and an individualistic orientation (e.g., obtaining support for their position on an issue). Similarly, listeners would be more likely to emphasize paying close attention to the message in a formal debate situation where they had a task goal and a competitive orientation (e.g., to discover weaknesses in the speaker's argument) than in an informal party situation where they had a social relationship goal and an altruistic orientation (e.g., pretending to enjoy, for the umpteenth time, their spouse's favorite story).

As was mentioned, accuracy has been emphasized by the experimenter in most research on referential communication. In such circumstances, one would expect speakers to emphasize rules concerned with providing the listener with a complete and accurate account of the stimulus material. In other circumstances, however, other rules would receive greater emphasis. For example, when a speaker's goal is to provide the listener with a general impression of a stimulus person, as in the cognitive-tuning literature, coherence and conciseness are emphasized over descriptive accuracy.

Other goals also lead to a decreased emphasis on descriptive accuracy, as evident in studies on audience effects. Participants in a communicative interaction establish a social relationship and some commonality by the very fact of engaging in communication (Rommetveit, 1974). Communication means "to make common or shared," and this involves sharing a social bond and a definition of the relationship, as well as exchanging information (Ruesch & Bateson, 1968). The motivation to maintain the social bond and share a common definition of social reality tends to result in convergence of judgments among the participants (Festinger, 1950; Newcomb, 1953). Manis, Connell, and Moore (1974), Newtson and Czerlinsky (1974), and Higgins and Rholes (1978) have found that communicators will modify their message about an issue or person to suit their listener's attitude toward the issue or person. For example, Higgins and Rholes (1978) found that communicators labeled behavioral descriptions of a target person to be evaluatively consistent with the supposed attitude of their listener toward the person, including many more positive labels and less negative labels in their message when their listener purportedly liked the target person. When the behavioral descriptions were ambiguous, communicators selected a label among the alternatives for a description that was evaluatively consistent with the listener's attitude (e.g., "adventurous" if the listener liked the target person versus "reckless" if the listener disliked the target). When the behavioral descriptions were unambiguous, communicators labeled those descriptions that were evaluatively consistent with the listener's attitude and simply omitted labeling any description that was inconsistent with the listener's attitude. As part of the study mentioned previously (Higgins, McCann, & Fondacaro, Note 1), we also found that communicators were much less likely to distort or delete the behavioral descriptions of a target person when communicating their impression of the person if they believed the listener had received different information about the target person than if they believed the listener had received the same information.

Our studies indicate that communicators will modify their summary of information about a target person to suit the listener's characteristics, and that this message modification can reduce the descriptive accuracy of the summary. These results suggest that descriptive accuracy was not the only goal of these communicators. Communicators in the Higgins and Rholes (1978) study may have produced messages consistent with their listener's opinion in order to avoid conflict with the listener. Communicators in the Higgins, McCann, and Fondacaro (1978) study may have kept to the facts more closely when the listener supposedly had different information because the risk of disagreement was greater. In both studies, therefore, communicators were probably motivated in part by interpersonal considerations, such as avoiding social conflict. This is not to say that communicators were not motivated by information transmission considerations. In the Higgins and Rholes (1978) study, a message consistent with the listener's attitude would likely improve referential accuracy by increasing the probability of the listener selecting the correct stimulus person; and in the Higgins, McCann, and Fondacaro study, communicators should be more concerned with providing a complete, accurate account of the stimulus information when the message provides additional information for the listener.

More generally, studies of audience effects on message production demonstrate how one rule, such as "tell the truth," will receive less emphasis in order for the speaker to follow another rule, such as "take the listener's characteristics into account." The rules that speakers and listeners must emphasize in a communicative interaction depend upon their communication goals. It is not possible for speakers and listeners to emphasize, or even follow, all of their communication rules. This is in part because the organization and integration of techniques or operations necessary to follow all the rules is likely to overload a participant's cognitive capacity. Participants must allocate their limited cognitive resources to those techniques that will maximize goal attainment (Shatz, 1979).

It is also not possible for participants to follow all the rules because different goals can require following rules that are mutually exclusive in application. For example, a girl who emphasizes social relationship goals over task goals may say when asked out on a date by a boy she does not like, "I'm sorry, but my parents are coming and I need to clean my apartment." This message sacrifices accuracy, clarity, and conciseness for the sake of protecting the boy's feelings and avoiding social conflict ("No thank you" would suffice to satisfy the task of refusing the date). A storyteller who emphasizes entertainment goals over task goals may be more concerned with dramatic impact and humor than accuracy or conciseness. A listener who emphasizes social relationship goals over task goals may be more concerned with being polite (let the speaker finish) than with efficiency (interrupt the speaker whenever comprehension has occurred and further elaboration is unnecessary).

From this perspective, it is misleading to discuss communication rules as if they were a set of necessary and sufficient general laws, fundamental principles, or maxims, as to do so would suggest that communicative behavior is not appropriate unless each rule is followed. A *rule,* however, can also mean a standard procedure for obtaining goals that is limited in application to particular circumstances. It is this sense of *rule* that, we suggest, describes the nature of communication rules. Certainly some communication rules have broader application than others, but there are relatively few rules that must be followed in every communicative interaction. Communication rules, then, are general procedures that can be used to accomplish various goals of communicative interaction. Underlying each communication rule are a variety of operations that must be learned to effectively apply the rule. Little is presently known about how children learn the operations underlying the various communication rules. Even less is known about how children learn which rules are most effective for obtaining various goals and goal combinations. The decision processes involved in selecting rules to maximize a particular combination of goals must be very complex, and learning to make such decisions effectively must take a long time. Unfortunately, both the age of the subject samples and the communication tasks have been so restricted in studies of communication development that there is little, if any, evidence concerning the acquisition of such decision processes.

Both speakers and listeners must make decisions about which rules to emphasize in order to maximally achieve their communication goals. To this extent, speaking and listening are similar. Moreover, speaking and listening involve the same general types of communication goals—task goals, social relationship goals, face goals, *etc.* However, the specific goals of speakers and listeners are often different (e.g., a speaker's goal to persuade versus a listener's goal to resist persuasion), as are their conflicts between competing goals, (e.g., a speaker's conflict between coherence and accuracy versus a listener's conflict between interrupting for efficiency and not interrupting for politeness). In addition, because the communication rules of speakers and listeners are not the same, the techniques for satisfying these goals are not the same, nor are the decision processes involved in goal maximization.

Conclusions

Both the review of the empirical literature comparing speaking and listening and the analysis of the factors underlying them suggest that they cannot adequately be described in terms of a common set of skills or processes. From the perspective of the information transmission approach to communication, speaking and listening appear to have some skills in common, such as verbal comparison and taking the characteristics of one's communicative partner into account. However, as we have seen, information transmission generally makes different demands on speakers and listeners, and the actual processes underlying even the supposedly common skills are not, in fact, the same.

Further differences between speaking and listening become apparent when a communication game perspective is taken. The normative expectations of the speaker and listener roles are different, and speaking and listening both involve distinct communication rules. Moreover, the attitudes of speakers and listeners toward the message itself can be different. The general types of communication goals and orientations are basically the same for speakers and listeners, and both speaking and listening can be described as a two-stage process where goal selection and emphasis must precede rule selection and emphasis. However, because the communication rules for speakers and listeners are not the same, the decision-making processes required to resolve conflicts and maximize goal attainment through optimum rule selection are not the same.

The communication game approach to speaking and listening taken in this chapter has a number of implications. From a practical point of view, it suggests the need for separate instruction of speaking and listening skills. It is possible to instruct children in certain skills—such as how to determine the dimensions along which a set of stimuli may be differentiated—which would improve both their speaking and listening on certain communication tasks. However, these skills may not be the most critical skills for effective performance on these tasks, and may be of little importance for other communication tasks. Moreover, it is not clear that instruction of common skills is more economical or effective than training speaker and listener skills separately. In any case, because there are many skills and processes that are not common to speaking and listening, some attention must be given to instruction of each separately.

The importance of goal orientation in rule selection and emphasis also suggests that communication instructors, as well as researchers, should pay greater attention to the possibility that their communication goals differ from those of their students or subjects. There is evidence suggesting that different cultural groups emphasize different communication goals (Cazden, John, & Hymes, 1972) and that different communication goals predominate at different ages (Schachter et al., 1974). Teachers (or experimenters) may judge students to be poor communicators because they do not follow those communication rules that maximize attainment of the teachers' task goals. The students, however, may have the strategies for attaining the teachers' goals, but may choose to allocate their resources to other strategies in order to maximize their own goals. Even when students have not acquired the most effective strategies for attaining the task goals emphasized by the teacher, it would be misleading to characterize the students as poor communicators if they are perfectly capable of maximizing the attainment of their own goals. Because one cannot expect students to be motivated to learn rules and strategies for obtaining communication goals of little value to them, communication instruction becomes as much a matter of modifying communication goals as teaching communication skills. As Hymes (1972) points out, teachers thereby become engaged, not simply in cognitive growth, but also in social change.

Finally, if the goals of speakers and listeners vary with age, researchers must consider whether developmental differences in the relevance of a task for goal attainment contribute to developmental differences in task performance. There is also a need to consider the extent to which developmental differences in performance are due to differences in the ability to resolve goal and rule conflicts and make decisions, rather than differences in knowledge of communication rules per se. In fact, developmental differences in communicative performance may in part reflect a more general developmental difference in decision-making ability that underlies performance differences in various areas, such as selection of optimal memory strategies. Designing studies that will tap the decision-making processes underlying communication and other kinds of performance is a major challenge for developmental researchers.

Acknowledgements

The research by the authors reported in this chapter was supported by Grant R01 MH 31427 from the National Institute of Mental Health to the senior author. We are grateful to Patrick Dickson, Scott Paris, Lorraine Rocissano, and Marilyn Shatz for helpful comments and suggestions.

Reference Notes

1. Higgins, E. T., McCann, D., & Fondacaro, R. The *"communication game": When role-taking and role enactment affect information processing*. Unpublished manuscript, Department of Psychology, The University of Western Ontario, 1980.

References

Austin, J. L. *How to do things with words*. Oxford: Oxford University Press, 1962.
Bernstein, B. A sociolinguistic approach to socialization: With some reference to educability. In F. Williams (Ed.), *Language and poverty: Perspectives on a theme*. Chicago: Markham Publishing Co., 1970.
Bloom, L. Talking, understanding, and thinking. In R. L. Schiefelbusch & L. L. Lloyd (Eds.), *Language perspectives: Acquisition, retardation, and intervention*. Baltimore: University Park Press, 1974.
Blumer, H. Society as symbolic interaction. In A. M. Rose (Ed.), *Human behavior and social processes*. London: Routledge & Kegan Paul, 1962.
Bostrom, R. N. Game theory in communication research. *Journal of Communication, 1968, 18,* 369–388.
Brickman, P. Is it real? In J. H. Harvey, W. Ickes, & R. F. Kidd (Eds.), *New directions in attribution research*, (Vol. 2). Hillsdale, N.J.: Lawrence Erlbaum Associates, 1978.
Brilhart, B. L. The relationship between some aspects of communicative speaking and communicative listening. *Journal of Communication, 1965, 15,* 35–46.
Brock, T. C., & Fromkin, H. L. Cognitive tuning set and behavioral receptivity to discrepant information. *Journal of Personality, 1968, 36,* 108–125.

Burke, R. *A grammar of motives and a rhetoric of motives.* Cleveland: World, 1962.

Burke, K. *Language as symbolic action: Essays on life, literature, and method.* Berkeley: University of California Press, 1968.

Cazden, C. B. The situation: A neglected source of social class differences in language use. *Journal of Social Issues,* 1970, *26,* 35–60.

Cazden, C. B., Cox, M., Dickinson, D., Steinberg, Z., & Stone, C. "You all gonna hafta listen": Peer teaching in a primary classroom. In W. A. Collins (Ed.), *Children's language and communication.* Hillsdale, N.J.: Lawrence Erlbaum Associates, 1979.

Cazden, C. B., John V. P., & Hymes, D. *Functions of language in the classroom.* New York: Teachers College, Columbia University, 1972.

Cherry, C. *On human communication.* Cambridge: MIT Press, 1966.

Cohen, A. R. Cognitive tuning as a factor affecting impression formation. *Journal of Personality,* 1961, *29,* 235–245.

Collins, B. E., & Raven, B. H. Group structure: Attraction, coalitions, communication, and power. In G. Lindzey & E. Aronson (Eds.), *Handbook of social psychology* (2nd ed., Volume 4). Reading, Mass.: Addison-Wesley, 1969.

Cushman, D., & Whiting, G. C. An approach to communication theory: Toward consensus on rules. *Journal of Communication,* 1972, *22,* 217–238.

Delia, J. G. A constructivist analysis of the concept of credibility. *Quarterly Journal of Speech,* 1976, *62,* 361–375.

Deutsch, M. A theory of cooperation and competition. *Human Relations,* 1949, *2,* 129–152.

Dickson, W. P., Miyake, N., & Muto, T. *Generalizability of encoding and decoding skills across two referential communication tasks* (Working Paper No. 261). Madison: Wisconsin Research and Development Center, 1979.

Eagly, A. H., & Himmelfarb, S. Attitudes and opinions. *Annual Review of Psychology,* 1978, *29,* 517–554.

Festinger, L. Informal social communication. *Psychological Review,* 1950, *57,* 271–282.

Flavell, J. H., Botkin, P. T., Fry, C. L., Wright, J. W., & Jarvis, P. E. *The development of role-taking and communication skills in children.* New York: John Wiley & Sons, 1968.

Garfinkel, H. *Studies in ethnomethodology.* Englewood Cliffs, N.J.: Prentice-Hall, 1967.

Garvey, C., & Hogan, R. Social speech and social interaction: Egocentrism revisited. *Child Development,* 1973, *44,* 562–568.

Glucksberg, S., & Cohen, J. A. Speaker processes in referential communication: Message choice as a function of message adequacy. *Proceedings of the 76th Annual Convention of the American Psychological Association,* 1968.

Glucksberg, S., Krauss, R. M., & Higgins, E. T. The development of referential communication skills. In F. Horowitz, E. Hetherington, S. Scarr-Salapatek, & G. Siegel (Eds.), *Review of child development research* (Vol. 4). Chicago: University of Chicago Press, 1975.

Goffman, E. *The presentation of self in everyday life.* Garden City, N.Y.: Doubleday, 1959.

Goffman, E. *Interaction ritual: Essays on face-to-face behavior.* Garden City, N.Y.: Doubleday, 1967.

Grice, H. P. Logic and conversation. The William James Lectures, Harvard University, 1967–1968. In P. Cole & J. Morgan (Eds.), *Syntax and semantics, Vol. 3: Speech acts.* New York: Academic Press, 1975.

Gumperz, J. J., & Hymes, D. (Eds.), *Directions in sociolinguistics: The ethnography of communication.* New York: Holt, Rinehart & Winston, 1972.

Harkins, S. G., Harvey, J. H., Keithly, L., & Rich, M. Cognitive tuning, encoding, and the attribution of causality. *Memory and Cognition,* 1977, *5,* 561–565.

Harvey, J. H., Harkins, S. G., & Kagehiro, D. K. Cognitive tuning and the attribution of causality. *Journal of Personality and Social Psychology,* 1976, *34,* 708–715.

Hawes, L. C. Elements of a model for communication processes. *Quarterly Journal of Speech,* 1973, *59,* 11–21.

Heider, E. R. Style and accuracy of verbal communications within and between social classes. *Journal of Personality and Social Psychology,* 1971, *18*, 33–47.

Higgins, E. T. Social class differences in verbal communicative accuracy: A question of "Which question?" *Psychological Bulletin,* 1976, *83*, 695–714.

Higgins, E. T. Communication development as related to channel, incentive, and social class. *Genetic Psychology Monographs,* 1977, *96*, 75–141.

Higgins, E. T. Written communication as functional literacy: A developmental comparison of oral and written communication. In R. Beach & P. D. Pearson (Eds.), *Perspectives on literacy.* Minneapolis: College of Education, University of Minnesota, 1978.

Higgins, E. T. The "communication game": Implications for social cognition and persuasion. In E. T. Higgins, C. P. Herman, & M. P. Zanna (Eds.), *Social cognition: The Ontario Symposium.* Hillsdale, N.J.: Lawrence Erlbaum Associates, 1980.

Higgins, E. T. Role-taking and social judgment: Alternative developmental perspectives and processes. In J. H. Flavell & L. Ross (Eds.), *New directions in the study of social-cognitive development.* New York: Cambridge University Press, in press.

Higgins, E. T., & Akst, L. Comparison processes in the communication of kindergartners. Paper presented at meetings of the *Society for Research in Child Development,* 1975.

Higgins, E. T., & Rholes, W. S. "Saying is believing": Effects of message modification on memory and liking for the person described. *Journal of Experimental Social Psychology,* 1978, *14*, 363–378.

Hockett, C. F. Grammar for the hearer. In R. Jackobson (Ed.), *Structure of language and its mathematical aspects.* Providence, R.I.: American Mathematical Society, 1961.

Hovland, C. I., Janis, I. L., & Kelley, H. H. *Communication and persuasion: Psychological studies of opinion change.* New Haven: Yale University Press, 1953.

Huttenlocher, J. The origins of language comprehension. In R. L. Solso (Ed.), *Theories in cognitive psychology.* Hillsdale, N.J.: Lawrence Erlbaum Associates, 1974.

Hymes, D. Introduction. In C. B. Cazden, V. P. John, & D. Hymes (Eds.), *Functions of language in the classroom.* New York: Teachers College, Columbia University, 1972.

Johnson, R. L., & Gross, H. S. Some factors in effective communication. *Language and Speech,* 1968, *11*, 259–263.

King, B. T., & Janis, I. L. Comparison of the effectiveness of improvised versus non-improvised role-playing in producing opinion changes. *Human Relations,* 1956, *9*, 177–186.

Krauss, R. M., & Glucksberg, S. The development of communication: Competence as a function of age. *Child Development,* 1969, *40*, 255–256.

Lashley, K. S. The problem of serial order in behavior. In L. A. Jeffress (Ed.), *Cerebral mechanisms in behavior: The Hixon Symposium.* New York: Wiley, 1951.

Leventhal, H. The effects of set and discrepancy on impression change. *Journal of Personality,* 1962, *20*, 1–15.

Lyman, S. M., & Scott, M. B. *A sociology of the absurd.* New York: Appleton-Century-Crofts, 1970.

Manis, M., Cornell, S. D., & Moore, J. C. Transmission of attitude-relevant information through a communication chain. *Journal of Personality and Social Psychology,* 1974, *30*, 81–94.

Mazis, M. B. Cognitive tuning and receptivity to novel information. *Journal of Experimental Social Psychology,* 1973, *9*, 307–319.

McClintock, C. G. Game behavior and social motivation in interpersonal settings. In C. G. McClintock (Ed.), *Experimental social psychology.* New York: Holt, Rinehart, & Winston, 1972.

McGuire, W. J. The nature of attitudes and attitude change. In G. Lindzey, & E. Aronson (Eds.), *The handbook of social psychology.* Reading, Mass.: Addison-Wesley, 1969.

McGuire, W. J. Attitude change: The information-processing paradigm. In C. G. McClintock (Ed.), *Experimental Social Psychology.* New York: Holt, Rinehart, & Winston, 1972.

Mead, G. H. *Mind, self, and society.* Chicago: University of Chicago Press, 1934.

Mehrabian, A., & Reed, H. Some determinants of communication accuracy. *Psychological Bulletin,* 1968, *70,* 365–381.

Merleau-Ponty, M. *Phenomenology of perception.* London: Routledge & Kegan Paul, 1962.

Morris, C. Foundations of the theory of signs. *International Encyclopedia of Unified Science* (Vol. 1, No. 2). Chicago: University of Chicago Press, 1938.

Muma, J. R. The communication game: Dump and play. *Journal of Speech and Hearing Disorders,* 1975, *40,* 296–309.

Newcomb, T. M. An approach to the study of communicative acts. *Psychological Review,* 1953, *60,* 393–404.

Newtson, D., & Czerlinsky, T. Adjustment of attitude communications for contrasts by extreme audiences. *Journal of Personality and Social Psychology,* 1974, *30,* 829–837.

Peirce, C. S. Logic as semiotic: The theory of signs. In J. Buchler (Ed.), *The philosophy of Peirce: Selected writings.* London: Routledge & Kegan Paul, 1940.

Piaget, J. *The language and thought of the child.* New York: Harcourt Brace, 1926.

Piaget, J. *Play, dreams and imitation in childhood.* New York: Norton, 1951.

Powell, F. A. Cognitive tuning and differentiation of arguments in communication. *Human Communication Research,* 1974, *1,* 53–61.

Robinson, E. J., & Robinson, W. P. The young child's understanding of communication. *Developmental Psychology,* 1976, *12,* 328–333.

Rommetveit, R. *On message structure: A framework for the study of language and communication.* New York: Wiley, 1974.

Rosenberg, S., & Cohen, B. D. Referential processes of speakers and listeners. *Psychological Review,* 1966, *73,* 208–231.

Ross, L. D., Amabile, T. M., & Steinmetz, J. L. Social roles, social control, and biases in social-perception processes. *Journal of Personality and Social Psychology,* 1977, *35,* 485–494.

Ross, M. Self-centered biases in attributions of responsibility: Antecedents and consequences. In E. T. Higgins, C. P. Herman, & M. P. Zanna (Eds.), *Social cognition: The Ontario Symposium.* Hillsdale, N.J.: Lawrence Erlbaum Associates, 1980.

Ruesch, J., & Bateson, G. *Communication: The social matrix of psychiatry.* New York: W. W. Norton, 1968.

Sarett, L., Foster, W. T., & Sarett, A. J. *Basic principles of speech.* Boston: Houghton Mifflin, 1958.

Schachter, F. F., Kirshner, K., Klips, B., Friedricks, M., & Sanders, K. Everyday preschool interpersonal speech usage: Methodological, developmental, and sociolinguistic studies. *Monographs of the Society for Research in Child Development,* 1974, (Serial No. 156).

Schachter, S. Deviation, rejection, and communication. *Journal of Abnormal and Social Psychology,* 1951, *46,* 190–207.

Schachter, S. *The psychology of affiliation.* Stanford: Stanford University Press, 1959.

Schutz, W. C. *FIRO: A three-dimensional theory of interpersonal behavior.* New York: Holt, Rinehart & Winston, 1960.

Scribner, S., & Cole, M. Literacy without schooling: Testing for intellectual effects. *Harvard Educational Review,* in press.

Searle, J. R. *Speech Acts: An essay in the philosophy of language.* Cambridge: Cambridge University Press, 1969.

Shannon, C. E., & Weaver, W. *The mathematical theory of communication.* Urbana: University of Illinois Press, 1949.

Shatz, M. The relationship between cognitive processes and the development of communication skills. In C. B. Keasey (Ed.), *Nebraska Symposium on Motivation* (1977). Lincoln: University of Nebraska Press, 1978.

Sherif, M., & Hovland, C. I. *Social judgment: Assimilation and contrast effects in communication and attitude change.* New Haven: Yale University Press, 1961.

Silverstein, M. Shifters, linguistic categories, and cultural description. In H. A. Selby, & K. H. Basso (Eds.), *Meaning in anthropology.* Albuquerque: University of New Mexico, 1976.

Stamm, K. R., & Pearce, W. B. Communicative behavior and co-orientational states. *Journal of Communication,* 1971, *21,* 208–220.

Strickler, R. D. *A developmental study of the relationship between speaker and listener abilities in referential communication.* Unpublished doctoral dissertation, Columbia University, 1975.

Tubbs, S. L., & Moss, S. *Human communication* (2nd ed.). New York: Random House, 1977.

Van Dijk, T. A. Context and cognition: Knowledge frames and speech act comprehension. *Journal of Pragmatics,* 1977, *1,* 211–232.

Watzlawick, P., Beaven, J. H., & Jackson, D. D. *The pragmatics of human communication.* New York: W. W. Norton, 1967.

Wittgenstein, L. *Philosophical investigations.* New York: MacMillan, 1953.

Zajonc, R. B. The process of cognitive tuning and communication. *Journal of Abnormal and Social Psychology,* 1960, *61,* 159–167.

14

Assent and Compliance in Children's Language

DAVID R. OLSON AND ANGELA HILDYARD

Theorists of human cognition have gradually adjusted their accounts of perception and knowledge to accommodate the fact that perception and knowledge are not simple copies of the environmental events that occasion them. Bruner's (1957) "New Look" in perception, which was devoted to showing the role of hypotheses, expectancies, and set on the processes of perceptual recognition, along with Bartlett's (1932/1977) analyses of the role of "schema" in remembering, helped to relativize the accounts of the relation between stimulus and perception or between reality and knowledge.

Now, however, we are asked to make our accounts of human cognition even more relative. Not only must we include innate categories and expectancies based on prior experience, we must also include the social relations in which those knowledge structures are constructed. Theories advanced under the banner of the "sociology of knowledge" have claimed that the structures of knowledge and perception reflect the organizing properties of the social system in which the experiences occur and are assimilated.

This line of argument is usually attributed to Durkheim. According to his biographer Steven Lukes (1973), Durkheim held that cognitive processes

313

Children's Oral Communication Skills

directly reflect the social and political structures of a society. For Durkheim, "conceptual thought [is] social and nothing but an extension of society" and "logical life has its first source in society [Lukes, 1973, pp. 23–24, 441]."

In an admirable collection of essays and monographs, Mary Douglas (1975) takes up and extends the Durkheimian view. With Durkheim, she claims that: "ideas rest on classification. Ultimately any form of knowledge depends on principles of classification. But these principles arise out of social experience, sustain a given social pattern and themselves are sustained by it. If this guideline and base is grossly disturbed, knowledge itself is at risk [p. 245]." Specifically, she argues that the discriminating principles as to what is clean, what is polluted, and what generally is "against nature" are derived from social structure. Nature is classified in such a way as to uphold the social order—thus, in a social order in which men are status-dominant over women and children, it seems only "natural" that women and children be assigned low-status duties, such as taking out the garbage.

Taken in their boldest form, these theories argue that knowledge is socially constructed; there are close ties between the social order and the conceptual order. But how does this social order affect, come to be affected by, or otherwise interact with the conceptual order?

Most of the theories that attempt to relate social structures to cognitive ones have postulated symbols as the mediating link. Symbols are culturally designed, and they are acquired by children for use in communication and for the interpretation of experience. But where in a symbol system, such as language, shall we look for evidence of a relation to social structures?

Theories of symbols have tended to emphasize the semantic, denotative, or referential aspect of meaning at the expense of the social, pragmatic, or interpersonal aspect. In his classical treatment of symbol systems, Nelson Goodman (1968) focused exclusively on the objective, informative, or semantic aspects of symbols, that is, on the relation that exists between the symbol and the event it represents, denotes, expresses, or exemplifies. Chomsky (1972, p. 24), too, focuses on the logical or semantic aspect of meaning—that aspect of meaning which is invariant across the various functions to which a sentence may be put. As a result of this orientation to symbols, most studies of the effects of the social order on language and thought focused on the structure of lexical items and grammatical relations. Durkheim looked at classification systems; Vygotsky (1962) looked at superordinate categories, and "scientific concepts"; Greenfield and Bruner (1966) looked at the use of nouns and adjectives; Cole and Scribner (1974) looked at the structure of logical inferences. And indeed some indications of social differences have shown up in those studies, "the most important forms of cognitive processes—perception, generalization, deduction, reasoning, imagination and analysis of one's own inner life—vary as the conditions of social life change [Luria, 1976, p. 161]." Interestingly, it appears that such differences can be attributed to a single important variable: the ability to reason from the explicitly presented verbal premises rather than from prior factual knowledge (Cole & Scribner, 1974), or, as Olson and Nickerson (1978) state it, the ability to "confine interpretation to the text."

Although it is almost a truism that the conceptual order must reflect and sustain the social order, there are few hypotheses that explicitly link them. Bernstein (1971) and his co-workers have proposed one such hypothesis in their attempt to account for patterns of school failure in working-class British students. They isolated two patterns of speech, an elaborated and a restricted code, which differed in their lexical and grammatical options and which, in turn, characterized middle-class and working-class children. The interesting conjecture was that the linguistic codes were a direct extension of the social structures in which those linguistic codes were employed. In the middle-class family, the social structure was described as person oriented; duties, responsibilities, and privileges were assigned by negotiation and contract with other members of the social group. In working-class families, on the other hand, the social structure was described as positional; there was a fixed hierarchical family structure on the basis of which authority, responsibility, accountability, and privileges were assigned. These social structural differences map directly onto the two linguistic patterns mentioned. The former, relying primarily on negotiation and contract, calls for a high degree of utilization of language for negotiating roles, rights, agreements, and privileges. The latter, relying primarily on position and status, requires sanctions for the violation of status perogatives and a minimum of linguistic negotiation.

Although the evidence for Bernstein's theory has generally outweighed the evidence against it, several critics have claimed that the differences are not necessarily in the linguistic codes to which each subgroup has access. It has been argued, rather, that the use of these forms of language depends on the social relations of the participants and the social-institutional context of the linguistic exchange. If the social relations are asymmetrical, as, for example, when a child is talking to an adult stranger, forms of expression may tend to be more restricted (Labov, 1972). If, on the other hand, the task for which language is to be used becomes more formal, as in narration or explanation, forms of expression may tend to be more elaborated (Edwards, 1976). For example, Labov (1972) found that as occasions of language use changed from casual speech to careful speech, from reading text to reading word lists, New York speakers used with greater frequency such "prestige" phonological features as an explicit -ing word ending or an expressed r (e.g., in guard).

A large number of studies have contributed to our understanding of how the characteristics of the language code are related to characteristics of the speakers (Fishman, 1970; Gumperz & Hymes, 1970). In an exemplary study, Brown and Gilman (1960) examined the social uses of the pronouns tu and vous as expressions of both power (superiors call inferiors by the intimate tu, whereas inferiors call superiors by the more formal vous) and solidarity (familiars will call each other *tu,* whereas unfamiliars will call each other *vous*.). Ervin-Tripp (1971) has extended this analysis to the use of titles, last names, and first names, and has found that it occurs in a variety of languages. Social factors are operative, then, both with respect to terms of address and the elaboration of utterances. Ervin-Tripp concludes:

> It is commonly the case that as one moves from the least deferent speech to the most, from the informal to the ceremonial, there is more elaboration and less abbreviation. Probably this difference is a universal, for two reasons. One is that elaboration is a cost, and is therefore most likely to occur in culturally valued situations or relationships. The other is that a high degree of abbreviation is only possible with in-group communication [p. 41].

But it is not only the lexical and phonological options of language which may be influenced by social factors. Speech act theory, for instance, has shown how social functions may influence the structure of the language. Building upon Austin's (1962) distinction between locutionary meaning and illocutionary force, Searle (1969) and Searle and Vandervekan (Note 1) differentiate the propositional content of a sentence, including reference and predication, from the illocutionary force or social purpose of the sentence, such as asserting or commanding. Every sentence represents some propositional content and some illocutionary force; together they make up such illocutionary acts as assertions (e.g., *I state . . .*), commissives (e.g., *I promise . . .*), directives (e.g., *I command . . .*), and expressives (e.g., *I congratulate . . .*). These illocutionary forces are indicated either by explicit performative verbs, as in the preceding examples; through syntax, for example, *X is . . .*, *Is X . . . ?*, *Do X . . .*; or through mood, indicated by *will, could, etc.*
To illustrate, consider the following three sentences:

1. *The door is closed.*
2. *Open the door!*
3. *Could you open the door?*

The propositional content of (1) is equivalent to the presuppositional content of (2) and (3), and, to that extent, we may say that they have the same logical meaning. The literal illocutionary forces of the three sentences differ somewhat: Sentence (1) is an assertion, (2) is a command directive, and (3) is a request directive. But it is interesting to notice that (1) and (3) may be seen as indirect requests—(1) is indirect indeed—both of which have the same illocutionary force of attempting to get the listener to open the door. They are, in Searle's (1975) terms, indirect speech acts and they vary in their directness and politeness: "Politeness is the most prominent motivation for indirectness in requests . . . [p. 76]." It is here, we may note, that the social work of the language is done, for entirely different social relations between the speakers are assumed by the three sentences. The command directive assumes that the speaker has superior status to the listener, the request directive assumes deference to the listener, and the assertion assumes, perhaps, the equality of the listener. The point to be emphasized is that an utterance is simultaneously doing two things—it is specifying the logical relation between symbol and referent by means of the propositional content, and it is specifying the social relations between the speakers by means of the illocutionary force. Together, these two aspects determine the meaning of the symbol or utterance.

Let us represent this dual structure of meaning by means of a simple diagram. Figure 14.1 shows the set of relations sustained by a symbol. Note that a symbol simultaneously serves two sorts of relations, represented in the diagram by two dimensions of meaning. The horizontal dimension specifies the social relations between speaker–writer and listener–audience; it calls for compliance. The vertical dimension represents the relation between symbol and referent or between signifier and signified; it calls for assent. The first dimension we may call the social or interpersonal meaning of a symbol and the second the logical or propositional meaning of the symbol. Other writers have made much the same point in somewhat similar ways. Halliday (1970, 1973), for instance, has described the contribution of the ideational function and the interpersonal function to the "meaning potential" of the language. Clark and Clark (1977) have stated that, in arriving at an interpretation of an utterance, a listener uses two general principles, the "reality" principle and the "cooperative principle." Goody (1978) has contrasted report functions with command functions and has shown how they interact in the comprehension and production of questions.

It is this horizontal dimension, the social dimension, that until recently has not been given its due. As was mentioned earlier, most tests of hypotheses of the Durkheimian sort, linking cognitive and social forms, have focused on the vertical dimension of meaning, the relation between symbol and referent. This is, of course, the aspect of meaning that most weakly reflects social relations. It is more likely, however, that the two dimensions interact; as Goody (1978) says, "the interpretation of meaning must depend in part on rules governing social relationships [p. 20]." We could, for example, interpret some of the social class and cultural effects on cognition in terms of the interaction of the social and logical dimensions. Thus, it is not so much that working-class children lack phonological, lexical, or syntactic forms, although they may to some degree, but rather that they assign themselves a

Logical
(call for assent)

Social	speaker → symbol → listener
(call for compliance)	↓
	reference

Figure 14.1

social or status position relative to the teacher or other adult which, in their view, calls for deference and compliance. Hence, they may attempt to give the answer or response that they believe the adult wants or expects and they ignore, suppress, or even fail to calculate, an independent answer for themselves.

Greenfield and Bruner (1966) observed just this pattern in some of their studies of classification in traditional Wolof children. We see it too in many experiments with young children: When asked a question, rather than look at the stimulus materials for a clue to the answer, many children will look back at the experimenter as if to say "What would you like me to do (say)?" In general, then, if you have low status, you can expect many utterances to call for compliance; if you have high status, you may take the same utterance as a call for agreement or assent. And these social differences may have cognitive implications. If the social relations call for deference to authority, the calculation of an independent, logical solution is unnecessary; if the social relations call for a measure of responsibility or authority, that calculation *is* necessary.

A number of recent studies have focused on the ways in which social relations (i.e., status differences) influence the production and interpretation of sentences. These studies have focused primarily upon the speech acts called *directives,* including commands and requests (Bruner, 1978; Ervin-Tripp, 1977; Mitchell-Kernan & Kernan, 1977; Gumperz, Note 2), ability requests (Shatz, 1978), and questions (Brown & Levinson, 1978; Goody, 1978). These are all speech acts that either directly or indirectly serve as means of regulating the activities of another person. But the choice of form depends on considerations of status, politeness, rights, and privileges. To illustrate, Gumperz (Note 2) reports a conversation between a husband and wife in which the husband asks "Where's the paper?" and the wife, with some annoyance, replies "I'll get it." The question may be interpreted as either a request for locative information or an indirect request that she get him the paper. The wife took it as the latter and was annoyed that her husband, even if indirectly, would order her about. In our terms, she took it as a call for compliance rather than as a call for information or assent.

Mitchell-Kernan and Kernan (1977) give an example that shows, not only that status considerations may determine the appropriateness of the speech act form, but also that the form of the speech act may be used to test or even to realign status relations. In the course of a group discussion between an experimenter–teacher and a group of children, one child gave an indirect command to the adult, who had her foot on a chair: "I want that chair!" with which the adult complied. Some of the other children gasped and said "O-o-o-o Claudia, you gon' let her talk to you like that?" (p. 205).

To give a command you must have the right or be in a position to give commands, and the child did not have that right. Mitchell-Kernan and Kernan also report that some children would try to command other children simply to see if the listener would comply, thereby establishing a dominant status relation. More often, the child, recognizing the attempt, would reply "Do it yourself." The tie between linguistic form and social structure was shown by the fact that addressees lower in rank than the speaker received over five times as many directives as those of higher rank. Ervin-Tripp (1977), too, found that children varied the form of their directives to honor such factors as age, dominance, and familiarity. James (1978) scaled the politeness of request forms and found that children were more polite when they addressed a higher status individual and when they were requesting a favor rather than a right.

These effects may be summarized in terms of a set of rules of politeness. Lakoff (1977) has set out three such rules: *formality,* that is, use conventional forms, do not impose personal whim on your listener; *deference,* that is, give your listener options; and *camaraderie,* that is, show sympathy, be friendly. Brown and Levinson (1978) have proposed an elaborate set of such rules:

> when formulating a small request one will tend to use language that stresses in-group membership and social similarity. . . . When making a request that is somewhat bigger, one uses the language of formal politeness. . . . And finally, when making the sort of request that it is doubtful one should make at all, one tends to use indirect expressions (implicatures) [p. 62].

Directives are not the only form conditioned by social considerations. Indeed, we suggest that in most conversational language the social aspects of meaning appear to be primary to the logical or propositional aspects of meaning. This point is somewhat misleading in that all speech acts have both a propositional content and an illocutionary force, or, as we have stated it, logical and social aspects of meaning. It is therefore unusual to have an utterance that is only one and not the other. Rather, what we suggest is that either the social or the logical aspect of meaning may be given primary attention. For example, as mentioned earlier, sentences (1) and (2) share the propositional content that the door is shut. That propositional content is expressed in (1) (*The door is closed*) but presupposed in (2) (*Open the door*), hence the propositional content is primary in (1), whereas the social aspects of meaning are primary in (2). On the other hand, the listener has some choice as to what will be taken as primary in the statement or request. Many utterances can be taken as calling attention either to the proposition or to the social meanings "prepared by" or otherwise legitimated by that proposition. If the emphasis in either expression or interpretation falls on the social aspects of meaning, we say that the utterance calls for compliance; if the emphasis falls upon the propositional aspects of meaning, we say that it calls for assent. Several studies, in addition to those mentioned, indicate that differences in status, age, authority, and so on lead to an emphasis on compliance.

Question-forms are particularly interesting because of their ambiguity between being calls for assent as opposed to calls for compliance. Goody (1978), in her study of the use of questions among the Gonja, found that questions were primarily used for reflecting or for challenging status and only secondarily for securing information. Hence, children asked few questions even if they often needed information. Studies of questions in classrooms have indicated a similar bias towards social uses. Bellack, Kliebard, Hyman, and Smith (1966) found that a predominant form of language in the classroom was of the question–answer routine known as the "recitation method"—teachers asked the questions and children provided the answers. Furthermore, the questions were not simply requests for information. The teacher already knew the answer—the point of the question was to see if the child knew the answer. The question serves primarily as a means of holding students accountable for the information acquired from reading a text. Although the utterance specifies true facts, that is, relations between symbols and referents, the form that the sentence takes again reflects the social relations between the interlocutors. This dominance of the control function of teachers' questions is similarly illustrated by Gumperz and Herasimchuk (1975) who point out that only the teacher assumes the right to continue questioning even in the face of no response (cf. Dore, 1978). These asymmetries apply to declarative sentences as well. Sinclair and Coulthard (1975) found that many of the questions and statements used by teachers in fact served as indirect commands. For example, statements such as *Somebody's talking* or *I see chewing gum* were not intended as true descriptions but as indirect commands to stop talking and so on. Such sentences call for compliance rather than assent.

Other studies have shown that these systems are acquired at a very early age. Ervin-Tripp (1977), in asking children to repeat what she said, found that when the statement was "Say, why don't you stand up," the child said "Stand up," and stood up—that is, the child complied. Shatz (1978) found that 2½-year-old children responded to their mother's question directives (e.g., *Can you put the truck over here?*) with an action; only 9% of the children answered the question literally. In other words, these young children responded to the question as an indirect request, that is, a call for compliance, rather than as an information question or call for assent. Again, for these children the social aspect of meaning is primary over the logical aspect of meaning. From such evidence, Shatz (1978), Gelman and Shatz (1977), and Bates (1976) infer that children do not first learn the literal meanings of utterances but rather their social uses.

Note, however, that the majority of Shatz's question directives were in a conventionalized format; such questions are standardly used to communicate requests. Ackerman (1978) has found that children as young as 6 can recover the underlying intention of unconventional directive forms also. In one of the studies to be described in what follows, we have found that kindergarten children's story recall patterns indicate that even declaratives serving as unconventionalized indirect requests are recalled as imperatives.

All of the studies we have reviewed provide a strong indication of the conflation of the social and logical functions of language. As part of our general concerns with literacy and the specialization of the functions of language (Olson, 1977; Olson, & Nickerson, 1978; Hildyard & Olson, 1978) we have begun to examine some of the ways in which these two functions interact in oral language; in subsequent papers we shall examine some evidence for their specialization in written texts. As we have seen, utterances both assert or presuppose a certain propositional content and establish and maintain a social order, a status quo. Stated in another way, a symbol stands simultaneously as part of a logical order and as part of a social order. Both of these dimensions may be invariant across some set of transformations (Searle & Vanderveken, Note 1). Different sentences may represent the same proposition, as, for example, active and passive sentences or declaratives and yes–no questions. Similarly, sentences with different propositional content may be used to construct or maintain the same social relation between speakers; there is more than one way to be obsequious and more than one way to be insubordinate. Furthermore, in using these constructions, a child is simultaneously learning two interrelated pictures of reality, an "objective" reality which is asserted or presupposed in the propositional content, and a social reality—who has the right to command, to request, and even the right to make assertions. To the extent that the logical and the social are conflated, Durkheim is correct in his views regarding the social aspects of cognition.

However, the most interesting test of the Durkheimian claim is to be found, not in the social content of directives, including questions, requests, and commands, but in that of the sentences classed as assertions. The meaning of an assertion is the truth conditions of the proposition asserted by the sentence. However, even in assertions, as long as the social and the logical functions of language are conflated, the truth of the proposition is a function, not simply of the its truth conditions, but *also* of the authority of the speaker. In any social order, some members are "entitled" to make assertions. In a highly specialized society, these persons may be the experts (Putnam, 1975); in a more traditional society, they may be the elders (Gellner, 1973; Horton, 1970). Perhaps it is the case that propositions are asserted, never simply because they are true, but rather because they are also useful, either to uphold a social order—hence the expressions of myth which are taken to be true—or to rationalize commands or requests. Schegloff (personal communication) has pointed out that if a request is followed by even a brief delay, the person making the request will proffer a reason which has the status of an assertion.

Our first concern, then, may be expressed as a set of questions. What are the conditions under which an utterance can be judged simply or exclusively for the truth conditions of its propositional content? And what are the conditions under which an utterance will be judged as a direct or indirect request for action? In the terms we have been using, when will an utterance be taken as a call for *assent* and when will it be taken as a call for *compliance?* Our second concern is more general: What are the social conditions under which a speaker will resort to calls for assent as an alternative to calls for compliance? That is, are there rules for shifting from directives to assertions?

We have addressed our questions in two ways. First, we have examined some transcripts of children's discourse, and, second, we have designed three experiments to follow up and clarify some of the relations we seem to have isolated in the analysis of the transcripts.

Nancy Torrance has recently collected and begun to analyze a series of dialogues between pairs of children as they played with toys. We are interested both in the quality of oral expression (in an attempt to see in what ways oral language competence is related to learning to read) and in the use of statements, questions, and commands in cooperating with, and controlling the behavior of, peers. Although that project is at an early stage, we shall present one analysis of a transcript in terms of the model that has been described. This dialogue occurred between two nursery school children named Jamie and Lisa who had some difficulty arriving at an equitable distribution of a limited resource, namely some dominoes. Let us see how they use language to negotiate this social problem.

> L: *Let's make a domino house out of these.*
> J: *Okay.*

First, by grabs:

> J: *Lookit how many I got. . . . You took a couple of mine!*
> L: *Now **you** took a couple. . . .*

then by commands:

> L: *Now you got to give me three back!*
>
> . . . .
> L: *Now give me just one more and then we got the same.*

and then by requestful declaratives:

> J: *Now, you got more than me-e.*

and denials:

> L: *No-o we got the same.*

by fact collecting and inferencing:

> L: (begins to count her dominoes) *One, two, three, four* . . . *twenty-eight, twenty-nine* (then counts Jamie's dominoes). *One, two, three, four* . . . *eighteen, nineteen* . . . (short pause) *twenty-nine.*
> J: *I got nineteen and you got twenty-nine.* . . . *You got more than me.*
> L: *No-o* (shouting) *I COUNTED.* . . . *You have the same as me.* . . . *We got the same.*
> J: *NO-O-O.*

and when negotiations break down again by grasping:

> (There is a shuffle of dominoes across the floor and now Jamie has more than Lisa.)

and finally by appeal to authority:

> L: *You got much more than me now.*
> J: *No we got the same.*
> (Paul, a volunteer teacher, enters the room.)
> L: *Does he have much more than me?*
> P: *Not too many more!*

Note first that almost all of these quite different utterances are attempts to alter or preserve the social arrangement of two children playing together and sharing the limited supply of dominoes. *Now you got to give me three back,* a command, has the same pragmatic function as *Now, you got more than me,* an assertion standing as an indirect request, spoken by the same person. And both speakers appear to be aware of the social meaning, namely, that the listener should hand over one or more of the dominoes, even if in one case it is the explicit *give me* and in the other, the implicit *you have more.* Why then do they use one device rather than another?

We may see how the logical and the social meanings interact if we score each sentence for both its logical meaning, the assent criterion, and for its social meaning, the compliance criterion (see Table 14.1). For the logical meaning, true may be marked with a " + " and false with a " − ". For the social meaning, the categories are less obvious. We let " + " represent the preservation of any current social arrangement, that is, those statements not requiring compliance and " − " represent the realignment of any social relationship—statements that require compliance and call for revolutionary activity, so to speak. Now let us examine some fragments of this dialogue in this framework.

Note that Jamie tells the truth with the hope of realigning the distribution of dominoes. Lisa, technically speaking, tells a lie. (Recall that she was the one who *counted* them.) But her denial was not merely one of falsehood. She knows that if she agrees to the truth of Jamie's statement, she will have to turn over some of the blocks. She does not want to do that, so she denies the truth of the statement. Our guess is that this is what all lies are—

TABLE 14.1
**The Relationship between Social (Compliance) and Logical (Assent) Criteria
in Indirect Requests and Denials**

		Criterion	
		Assent (Truth-preserving)	Compliance (Status-preserving)
Sentence	Gloss		
L: *You got much more than me now.*	(Give me some)	+	−
J: *No, we got the same.*	(I don't have to)	−	+
P: *Not too many more!*	(It's true he has more but he does not have to give you any)	+	+

tampering with truth value for social or personal ends. Truth, like falsehood, is motivated.

But note also that Lisa is not denying the truth of Jamie's statement simply in the service of social ends. Rather, she does not know any means of simultaneously meeting both the social and logical criteria. Paul, the teacher does. Note his reply when Lisa appeals to him. The presupposition of his sentence is that Jamie has more. Rather than affirm or deny it, he presupposes it and uses his sentence to hold that no redistribution is required, presumably on the premise that possession is nine-tenths of the law.

This example shows that truth conditions are not separated from social utility. Claims of truth appear to be advanced if the gaining of assent may be instrumental in gaining compliance with some social goal. Symmetrically, denials of truth will be offered if the social consequences of assent are perceived to be undesirable.

It is at this point that social relations enter into the language. Micro social orders, small-scale transactions like the one in the example, involve the solution of small-scale interpersonal problems which must be solved either for individual Machiavellian goals or for shared social goals. The main problem is how to secure compliance or agreement, or at least prevent the loss of the status quo. This may be done by several means: direct action, commanding, pleading, or hard negotiation on a common ground. Facts are one such ground, which, as we have seen, are overlooked if they are embarrassing; authority is another such ground, but as we have seen, authority would prefer not to get involved or take sides.

Disputes in the larger social order appear to be solved through somewhat similar means. As Foucault (1971) pointed out, different social orders make use of different criteria for truth and hence different grounds for the legitimation of the social order. Authority, the father in a patriarchical order or the priest in an ecclesiastical order, has the power to decide in the case of disputes, as judges do in our own courts. Hopefully, they have adequate recourse to the truth, but poor judgments carry just as much weight as good ones. The decisions likely to gain the greatest compliance have both truth and authority. It is interesting to recall in this context the wisdom of Solomon. One may wonder if Solomon's judgments were considered to be good because he was so wise or because he happened, as well, to be king. More likely, the stories of his wisdom and justice helped to legitimize the authority that was socially assigned to him.

In our own society, great weight is assigned to "truth," "facts," and "sense data" as objective grounds for making scientific, social, and political decisions. As long as people believe that truth is objective, it serves as an important means of "legitimizing" a social order (Habermas, 1973). Furthermore, the establishment of institutions like universities, devoted to discovering the "truth" independent of its social utility, helps to sustain the view that there are such facts and that those facts can be used to sustain the social order.

A single argument between two 4-year-olds may be insufficient empirical grounds to sustain a general social theory, hence we have attempted to examine further, by experimental means, some of these expressions and their interpretations. In one study, we incorporated statements similar to those in the transcript into a series of six episodes about two children. The stories, which described various social predicaments of the form A has more than B, A has taken something belonging to B, etc., were read to children in kindergarten and second grade. The children were subsequently tested for recall.

Three different speaker–listener relationships were incorporated into the story to take account of the fact that individuals alter the quality of their speech according to both the situation and the audience (Gelman & Shatz, 1977). In two of the episodes, the key statement was expressed by one child to another; in a second pair, the key statement was expressed by a child to an adult; and, in the final pair, the key statement was spoken by an adult to a child. The following is an example of an episode with one child talking to another: "One Saturday morning Susie and Kevin Jones went to the movies. Their mum gave them some money to buy some popcorn. Susie bought a large box and they shared it out. When Kevin looked at Susie's share he didn't feel too happy. 'You've got more than me' he said." Two questions were asked after each episode. The first referred to some story detail (e.g., "Where had the children gone?"); the second referred to the final key statement ("What did Kevin say to Susie?").

The kindergarten and second grade children performed very differently on these final recall questions. Junior kindergarten children (ages 4 and 5 years), when asked what Kevin had said, would frequently answer with a request or a command, "Can I have some?" or "Give me some popcorn."

By the second grade (ages 7 and 8), children tended to recall the statement verbatim: "You have more than me." When further queried as to why he said that, they replied, "Because he wanted more." These results are shown in Figure 14.2. The differences in performance are highly significant $(\chi_3^2 = 34.77, p < .001)$.

The implication of these findings is that almost all of the children interpreted the statement *You have more than me* not simply as a true statement, but also as an indirect request, and that interpretation biased the recall of the younger subjects. Older subjects, on the other hand, remembered both what was intended by the sentence and the means the speaker used, here a declarative, true statement, to achieve it. Thus, the sentence was not interpreted and evaluated strictly or even primarily on truth criteria, but on social criteria. And the younger the children, the stronger the tendency to treat the sentence as a call for compliance and hence to report it as such. These results are similar to those reported by Bates (1976) and Shatz (1978).

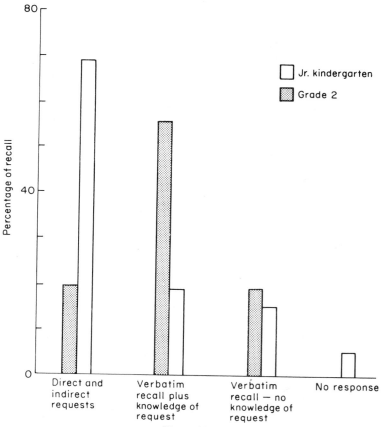

Figure 14.2

The findings were consistent across the three status relations used in the stories. Thus, whether the punch line was initiated by a child and expressed to another child or an adult, or whether the statement originated from an adult, the younger children still recalled the declaratives as requests. However, the status relations did affect the politeness with which the kindergarten children expressed that request. Over 70% of the requests that were directed to an equal or higher status individual were expressed in conventionalized form (*May I . . . ? Can I . . . ?*). Approximately 75% of those utterances directed to a lower status individual were expressed as direct commands (*Give me. . . .*).

In a second study we looked at subjects' open-ended responses rather than their recall. A series of similar stories were composed, but the punch line, which in all cases was to be a request of some form, was omitted. The subjects (16 kindergarters, 16 second-graders, and 16 adults) were asked to imagine what the victim said. As in the previous study, the status relations of the participants in the story were varied. The relations we adopted were as follows: child to child, adult to adult, child to parent/teacher, teacher/parent to child.

A further important factor was also included, that is, whether the request was the addressor's right or favor (cf. James, 1978). The 12 different episodes described in the story included a right and a favor addressed to an equal (child or adult), a higher status (parent or teacher), and a lower status (from parent or teacher) individual. A right was established by having the individual request the return of his or her own property (e.g., Kevin might ask Susie for the return of his sock). In the favor situation, Susie might ask Kevin if she could ride on his new bike, or the teacher might ask Kevin to clean the blackboard, *etc.*

The data are summarized in Table 14.2. The most interesting results were as follows. First, favors were much more likely to be signaled by a conventionalized request than were rights. Over all age levels and status relations, the favor items were marked by conventionalized requests 75% of the time, whereas rights were so marked only 45% of the time. The use of conventionalized requests for favors was particularly clear for kindergarten and second-grade subjects. Although the response pattern of the adults was significantly different ($\chi_8^2 = 37.26$, $p < .001$) from that of the children, the adults did use conventionalized requests to express favors 50% of the time.

How rights were signaled varied with the age of the subject and the status relations involved in the situation. The youngest subjects tended to use direct commands if the request was directed from one child to another, but used mainly conventionalized requests if the request was directed from an adult to a child or vice versa. Kindergarten children, then, considered it appropriate to say *Give me my sock* to a peer, and *May I have my gold star?* (which had been promised) to the teacher. These data are similar to those reported by James (1978).

TABLE 14.2
Percentage of Directive Forms as a Function of the Type of Request, Rights versus Favors[a]

	Kindergarten	Grade 2	Adult	Total
Conventionalized Request "May I have———"				
Favors	87	81	51	75
Rights	59	49	27	45
Commands "Give me———"				
Favors	5	2	16	6
Rights	28	8	14	17
Declaratives and Questions "That's my———," "Where's my———?"				
Favors	7	5	14	9
Rights	11	15	33	20
Legitimized Requests "I need———because———"				
Favors	1	11	11	8
Rights	2	24	19	15
Threats, Negotiations, Appeals "If you give me this———"				
Favors	0	0	7	2
Rights	0	3	6	3

[a] Sixteen children at each grade level responded to four examples of each of the eight types.

For second grade children the incidence of conventionalized requests for rights ranged from 31% (child to child, parent to child) to between 50% and 63% (adult to adult, child to parent/teacher, teacher to child). Like the kindergarten children, the second-graders tended to use direct commands, declaratives (e.g., *That's my sock*), and threats (69%) when the request was from one child to another. Unlike kindergarten children, the second-grade subjects perceived a difference between a parent requesting a right from a child and a teacher requesting a right from a child. Parents were seen as using legitimized requests and declaratives (69%), whereas teachers were seen as using mainly conventionalized requests (63%). If indeed the use of a conventionalized form indicates a higher degree of politeness, as Brown and Levinson (1978), James (1978), and Lakoff (1977) have suggested, then second-grade children consider their teachers to be more polite than their parents!

The adult subjects tended to show a greater variability in their selection of response types for requesting rights. Only 27% of their responses were conventionalized requests, the majority of which occurred in their estimate of how a child would request a right from a teacher. Adult subjects obviously considered it prudent for children to be polite to a teacher. However, adult subjects did not expect children to use the polite form to their parents, as the majority of these requests (63%) were in the form of declaratives and questions which, according to James (1978), rank low on the politeness scale. But as we argued earlier, declaratives and questions can also be regarded as indirect speech acts. The listener can choose to honor the request (comply) or simply respond to the truth of the utterance (assent). Thus although adults may perceive children as being less polite to their parents than to their teachers, they also consider that the parents are given greater optionality in terms of their response.

Adults tended to use each response category equally often for requests directed to the children from another child, a parent, and a teacher. Between adult peers, however, the predominant response category (75%) was that of declaratives and questions. Thus adults consider it preferable to give a peer listener optionality of response. Interestingly, adult subjects tend to use this response category (declaratives and questions) about twice as often as kindergarten or second-grade children.

Note that, in all of these cases, subjects aspired to the same goal, yet the utterance used to express that intention took a different form depending on the social relations between the participants. Primary among those factors is the status relations between them—commands may be issued to lower status individuals, conventionalized requests must be issued to superiors, even if you are only asking for your rights. Second, presumed rights determine the form in which that illocutionary force will be expressed. Favors are largely expressed through conventionalized requests, although adults also frequently add reasons. Rights may be expressed through conventionalized requests (to a high-status listener), commands (to a low-status listener), occasionally through threats or through indirect speech acts, here declaratives and questions.

In a third study, Beverly Wolfus examined how 16 kindergarten and 16 second-grade children responded to a series of direct commands (*Tell me what this is! Put the penny in the glass!*) and ambiguous ability requests (*Can you turn over the cup? Could you tell me the name of this?*), which she made while pointing to the relevant objects. She was particularly interested in whether the children opted for the direct, expressed meaning or the indirect, pragmatic meaning of the ambiguous expressions. Thus *Tell me if you can put the penny in the glass* could be answered by assent, *Yes I can*—the direct meaning—or by compliance, by actually putting the penny in the glass—the indirect, or pragmatic, meaning. The children, who were given four exemplars of each of the eight statement types, responded as follows (see Table 14.3). When issued direct commands, both age groups complied extremely consistently. Told "Open the book," everyone opened the book. To "Tell me what this is" everyone said, "A pen."

TABLE 14.3
**Percentage of Assent versus Compliance in Kindergarten and Grade 2
Children's Interpretation of Sentences**[a]

	Assent	Compliance	Both	χ^2
Put the top on the pen.				
Kindergarten		100		
Grade 2		100		
Tell me what this is.				
Kindergarten		100		
Grade 2		100		
Tell me if you can X.				
Kindergarten	8	83	8	$p < .01$
Grade 2	69	29	2	
Tell me if you know how to X.				
Kindergarten	13	64	8	$p < .01$
Grade 2	66	27	8	
Do you know what this is?				
Kindergarten	5	88	8	$p < .01$
Grade 2	30	67	3	
Can you turn over the cup?				
Kindergarten	8	64	24	$p < .01$
Grade 2	64	19	18	
Do you know how to X.				
Kindergarten	25	11	64	$p < .01$
Grade 2	91	3	5	
The book is closed.				
Kindergarten	73	20	7	n.s.
Grade 2	92	8		

[a] Sixteen children at each grade level responded to four examples of each of the eight types.

The differences in the responses to ambiguous ability requests and statements for the two age groups were striking. These differences occurred for those questions and statements that were ambiguous with respect to a propositional and a pragmatic interpretation, that is ambiguous in their call for assent as opposed to compliance. For two of the statements (*Tell me if you can. . . . ; Tell me if you know how to. . . .*) and one question (*Can you . . . ?*) the second grade children tended to assent, whereas the kindergarten children tended to comply. Thus to the statement *Can you turn over the cup?* older children would say yes, that is, assent; younger children would simply turn over the cup. To the question *Do you know how to . . . ?* again older children simply assented (*Yes, I do*), whereas younger children both assented *and* complied. For only one statement (*Do you know what this is?*) did the majority of both kindergarten and second-grade children comply. Similarly, for only one statement type (e.g., *The book is closed*) did both the second-grade and kindergarten children assent, that is agree to the truth of the statement rather than attempt to treat it as an indirect request.

Overall, these data show that the younger children were more likely to interpret an utterance as a direct or an indirect request for action and to comply with it. These effects are similar to those obtained by Ervin-Tripp (1977) and Shatz (1978). By second-grade, and especially in a context in which the utterances are presented in a game, children have learned that, although in conversations requests and statements of this form call for action, the alternative literal interpretation can also be adopted. Interestingly, only one ambiguous question in this set (*Do you know what this is?*) resulted in compliance from both the kindergarten and the second-grade children. The question *Do you know what this is?* calls indirectly, not for a physical action, but for different *verbal* response. Thus, although the second-grade children were able to interpret literally those utterances with an indirect request for action, that is, they inhibited the action, they were unable to do so if the indirect request called for a verbal response.

Note finally, the children's responses to the simple declarative assertion *The book is closed*. A few of the children in fact treated it as an indirect request to open the book. But, as the sentence did not directly violate any of the conversational maxims (Grice, 1975; Brown & Levinson, 1978), the majority of subjects simply assented to the truth value of the proposition and awaited further instructions.

In sum, these data indicate that, at least for young children, the meaning of a statement is not simply the truth conditions asserted or presupposed by the propositional content of the utterance, although that meaning must be computed as part of its more pragmatic or social meaning. Rather sentences are scanned, as it were, for their social implications. With age or schooling, children begin both to differentiate propositional content from illocutionary force and to be able, for example, to treat an assertion in terms of its truth value (as assent) rather than as an indirect request for action (as compliance). Logical meaning comes to be separated out from a primarily undifferentiated logical–social meaning. The differentiation begins to emerge when, especially in schools, teachers and texts attempt to express ideas that are to be taken as expressions of truth rather than as indirect means of social control. The distinction is not always managed, as in the old antedote:

Teacher: *Who shot Abraham Lincoln?*
Child: *Not me!*

We should point out that our binary classification of calls for assent versus calls for compliance differs somewhat from the primary classifications of speech act theory. In his earlier classification of speech act types, Searle

(1969) treated questions and commands as different speech acts. In his later analysis, he combined questions and commands into the class of directives. Most researchers have adopted the latter system. Dore (1977), for example, adopts this scheme but further differentiates requests for information from requests for action. It is this latter classification that is important to us, so much so that we treat both assertions and requests for information as involving judgments of truth–falsity, that is, as calls for assent. In the first case, the listener simply agrees to the propositional content; in the latter, the listener fills out the propositional content so as to make it true. In requests for action, on the other hand, the propositional content remains secondary: The primary concern is with the action of the listener. Hence, we treat requests for action as calls for compliance. Our distinction is intended to bring into prominence the difference between assent to, and construction of, true propositions and compliance with requests and commands. Except for the questions used by teachers as part of the recitation method, our impression is that requests for information are very similar *socially* to the comprehension and production of assertions, whereas they are quite different *socially* from commands and requests.

Let us return, in conclusion, to the general questions raised at the outset. We have argued that all utterances serve both truth (assent) and social (compliance) functions and that these two functions are conflated in most ordinary language. This is clearly the case for directives, command requests, and many questions. Requests are more likely for privileges and imperatives for rights; requests are more likely when addressed to higher status individuals and imperatives to lower status individuals. And whereas imperatives occur more frequently when children address lower status individuals, rationalized questions, declaratives, and requests are more frequent for adults.

As to our second question, the interpretation of assertions with the putative status of true descriptions also appears to reflect the operation of the social dimension of meaning. As we have suggested, putative true statements call for assent (or falsification), whereas putative imperatives call for compliance (or defiance). But, as we have seen, an individual can respond with compliance even to a true description. Can the criteria of assent and compliance be differentiated and specialized? Can statements ever be constructed such that they call for assent and not compliance? If not, why are there such things as assertions? Merely as polite forms of commanding? Surely not. The fact that it is possible to assent to some statements indicates that truth functions can be isolated, at least somewhat, from the more general social functions. Even in this case, however, true statements can be generated (or denied) when they have social utility, much as Lisa denied Jamie's statement that she had more. And even false statements, or inadequate ones, are less likely to be denied if they are expressed by a superior or an expert. Hence, while the logical and social dimensions of meaning can be differentiated and specialized to some extent, they are, as we have seen, largely interdependent.

Acknowledgements

This chapter is based on an earlier version prepared for Theoretical Issues in Natural Language Processing (TINLAP – 2), Urbana, University of Illinois, July 25–27, 1978. The research reported here is funded by a Canada Council Research Grant to D. R. Olson, A. Hildyard, and N. Torrance. We wish to thank Nancy Torrance for her contribution to several of the issues presented in this chapter, Beverly Wolfus for the use of some of her data, and Robin Chapman for her helpful comments.

Reference Notes

1. Searle, J., & Vandervekan, D. *Foundations of illocutionary logic.* Unpublished manuscript, University of California, Berkeley.
2. Gumperz, J. J. *Language, social knowledge and interpersonal relations.* Unpublished manuscript, Language Behavior Research Laboratory, University of California, Berkeley, 1977.

References

Ackerman, B. P. Children's understanding of speech acts in unconventional directive frames. *Child Development,* 1978, *49,* 311–318.

Austin, J. L. *How to do things with words.* New York: Oxford University Press, 1962.

Bartlett, F. C. *Remembering.* New York: Cambridge University Press, 1977. (Originally published, 1932.)

Bates, E. *Language and context: The acquisition of pragmatics.* New York: Academic Press, 1976.

Bellack, A. A., Kliebard, H. M., Hyman, R. T., & Smith, F. L. *The language of the classroom.* New York: Teacher's College Press, 1966.

Bernstein, B. *Class, codes and control.* London: Routledge & Kegan Paul, 1971.

Brown, P., & Levinson, S. Universals in language usage: Politeness phenomena. In E. N. Goody (Ed.), *Questions and politeness: Strategies in social interaction.* Cambridge: Cambridge University Press, 1978.

Brown, R. W., & Gilman, A. The pronouns of power and solidarity. In T. Sebeok (Ed.), *Style in language.* Cambridge, Mass.: MIT Press, 1960.

Bruner, J. S. On perceptual readiness. *Psychological Review,* 1957, *64,* 123–152.

Bruner, J. S. Introduction. In J. S. Bruner, R. Olver, & P. M. Greenfield (Eds.), *Studies in cognitive growth.* New York: Wiley, 1966.

Bruner, J. S. Learning how to do things with words. In J. S. Bruner & A. Ganton (Eds.), *Human growth and development.* Oxford: Clarendon, 1978.

Chomsky, N. *Problems of knowledge and freedom.* London: Fontana, 1972.

Cole, M., & Scribner, S. *Culture and thought* New York: Wiley, 1974.

Clark, H. H., & Clark, E. V. *Psychology and language.* New York: Harcourt Brace Jovanovich, 1977.

Dore, J. Children's illocutionary acts. In R. Freedle (Ed.), *Discourse comprehension and production.* Hillsdale, N.J.: Lawrence Erlbaum, 1977.

Dore, J. Variation in preschool children's conversational performances. In K. Nelson (Ed.), *Children's language.* New York: Gardner Press, 1978.

Douglas, M. *Implicit meanings.* London: Routledge & Kegan Paul, 1975.

Edwards, A. D. Speech codes and speech variants: Social class and task differences in children's speech. *Journal of Child Language,* 1976, *3,* 247–265.

Ervin-Tripp, S. Sociolinguistics. In J. A. Fishman (Ed.), *Advances in the sociology of language.* The Hague: Mouton, 1971.

Ervin-Tripp, S. Wait for me, Roller-Skate! In S. Ervin-Tripp, & C. Mitchell-Kernan (Eds.), *Child discourse.* New York: Academic Press, 1977.

Fishman, J. A. *Sociolinguistics: A brief introduction.* Rowley, Mass.: Newbury House, 1970.

Foucault, M. *L'ordre du discours.* Paris: Gallimard, 1971.

Gellner, E. The savage and modern mind. In R. Horton & R. Finnegan (Eds.), *Modes of thought.* London: Faber and Faber, 1973.

Gelman, R., & Shatz, M. Appropriate speech adjustments: The operation of conversational constraints on talk to two-year-olds. In M. Lewis & L. Rosenblum (Eds.), *Interaction, conversation, and the development of language.* New York: Wiley, 1977.

Goodman, N. *Languages of art.* Indianapolis: Bobbs-Merrill, 1968.

Goody, E. N. Towards a theory of questions. In E. N. Goody (Ed.), *Questions and politeness: Strategies in social interaction.* Cambridge: Cambridge University Press, 1978.

Greenfield, P. M., & Bruner, J. S. Culture and cognitive growth. *International Journal of Psychology,* 1966, *1,* 89–107.

Grice, H. P. Logic and conversation. In P. Cole & J. L. Morgan (Eds.), *Syntax and semantics, Vol. 3: Speech acts.* New York: Academic Press, 1975.

Gumperz, J. J., & Hymes, D. (Eds.), *Directions in sociolinguistics.* New York: Holt, Rinehart and Winston, 1970.

Gumperz, J. J., & Herasimchuk, E. The conversational analysis of social meaning: A study of classroom interaction. In M. Sanches, & B. G. Blount (Eds.), *Sociocultural dimensions of language use.* New York: Academic Press, 1975.

Habermas, J. *Legitimation crisis.* Boston: Beacon Press, 1973.

Halliday, M. A. K. Language structure and language function. In J. Lyons (Ed.), *New horizons in linguistics.* Harmondsworth: Penguin Books, 1970.

Halliday, M. A. K. *Explorations in the functions of language.* London: Edward Arnold, 1973.

Harré, R. Ethology and early socialization. In M. P. M. Richards (Ed.), *The integration of child into the social world.* Cambridge: Cambridge University Press, 1974.

Hildyard, A., & Olson, D. R. Memory and inference in the comprehension of oral and written discourse. *Discourse Comprehension,* 1978, *1,* 91–117.

Horton, R. African traditional thought and western science. In B. R. Wilson (Ed.), *Rationality.* Oxford: Blackwell, 1970.

James, S. L. Effect of listener age and situation on the politeness of children's directives. *Journal of Psycholinguistic Research,* 1978, *7,* 307–317.

Labov, W. *Language in the inner city.* Oxford: Blackwell, 1972.

Lakoff, R. Language and society. In R. Wardaugh & H. Brown (Eds.), *A survey of applied linguistics.* Ann Arbor: University of Michigan Press, 1977.

Lukes, S. *Emile Durkheim.* Markham, Ontario: Penguin Press, 1973.

Luria, A. R. *Cognitive development: Its cultural and social foundations.* Cambridge: Harvard University Press, 1976.

Mitchell-Kernan, C., & Kernan, K. T. Pragmatics of directive choice among children. In S. Ervin-Tripp & C. Mitchell-Kernan (Eds.), *Child discourse.* New York: Academic Press, 1977.

Olson, D. R. From utterance to text: The bias of language in speech and writing. *Harvard Educational Review,* 1977, *47,* 257–281.

Olson, D. R., & Nickerson, N. Language development through the school years. In K. E. Nelson (Ed.), *Language development.* New York: Gardner Press, 1978.

Putnam, H. Is semantics possible? In H. Putnam (Ed.), *Mind, language and reality: Philosophical papers* (Vol. 2). Cambridge: Cambridge University Press, 1975.

Searle, J. *Speech acts*. Cambridge: Cambridge University Press, 1969.

Searle, J. Indirect speech acts. In P. Cole & J. Morgan (Eds.), *Syntax and semantics, Vol. 3: Speech acts*. New York: Academic Press, 1975.

Shatz, M. Children's comprehension of their mothers' question-directives. *Journal of Child Language*, 1978, *5*, 39–46.

Sinclair, J., & Coulthard, R. M. *Towards an analysis of discourse: The English used by teachers and pupils*. London: Oxford University Press, 1975.

Vygotsky, L. M. *Thought and language*. Cambridge, Mass.: MIT Press, 1962.

Whorf, B. L. *Language, thought and reality*. New York: Wiley, 1956.

15

The Role of Nonverbal Behavior in Children's Communication

VERNON L. ALLEN

Those of us who are concerned with the uses of communication research in everyday life would emphasize the obvious fact that a great deal of communication entails face-to-face social interaction among participants. Face-to-face communication provides the opportunity for involving the sender and receiver in aspects of behavior that far exceed mere consideration of the content of the message itself. Indeed, it is clear that individuals communicate with more than words alone; many other aspects of the behavioral repertoire of both the sender and receiver are also activated during a communicative act. The conclusion clearly conveyed by recent research is that the complex system of nonverbal behavior is not an inconsequential component of the communication process.

The present chapter will discuss the use of nonverbal behavior in communication with specific reference to children's learning in the school. Three contexts account for most of the face-to-face communication in learning situations in the school: communication between a teacher and the class (or to a particular student in the class); communication among peers; and, less often, communication among children across age levels, as in programs of

337

older children tutoring younger children. All these settings provide an opportunity for the employment of nonverbal as well as verbal responses in conjunction with referential communication.

I shall concentrate on reporting our own research, rather than attempting to review all the relevant literature. The first section in this chapter describes types of nonverbal behavior and their functions, and reports research that illustrates the influence of nonverbal responses in communication. In the second section, studies are presented that investigate encoding–decoding ability, characteristics of spontaneous–deliberate behavior, and mutual influence across communication channels. The third section presents research focusing on the influence of characteristics of the encoder and decoder on the communication of nonverbal behavior, and also discusses the important issue of individual differences.

Nature and Function of Nonverbal Behavior

Many classifications of nonverbal behavior have been suggested (Siegman & Feldstein, 1978). The following five general categories seem to be reasonably comprehensive: (a) facial expressions (e.g., smile or frown, brow movement); (b) visual responses (e.g., gaze direction); (c) body movement (e.g., gesture, posture, head nod); (d) proxemics (interpersonal distance); and (e) paralanguage (e.g., tone of voice, tempo). The coding systems used for each of these broad categories depend on the particular investigator; some focus upon very minute responses (Kendon, 1963) and others deal with the pattern and organization of a sequence of responses (Scheflen, 1965). Most previous research on nonverbal behavior has concentrated on emotions or affective responses, to the neglect of the broader role that nonverbal behavior plays in interaction in everyday life. Nonverbal behaviors usually are exhibited concomitantly with ongoing verbal behavior, and this fact greatly increases the complexity of a communicative response.

Several functions of nonverbal behavior can be discerned (Argyle, 1969; Harper, Wiens, & Matarazzo, 1978). First, nonverbal behavior usually supports and illustrates verbal behavior (e.g., by appropriate facial expressions and gestures). A socially skilled individual is usually able to integrate effectively the responses from verbal and nonverbal systems. Second, nonverbal behavior provides cues that contribute to the regulation of speaking and listening. Thus, subtle nonverbal responses can signal turn-taking (i.e., the end of a speech sequence by one person or the desire by the other to initiate speech). A third important function of nonverbal behavior is providing feedback, such as information about attention, interest, agreement, or approval. Fourth, nonverbal behavior serves to reveal underlying attitudes, personality traits, and intentions of a person.

It should be clear that nonverbal behavior serves important functions in the cognitive as well as in the affective area. For instance, whether or not a child understands a lesson can be communicated clearly by nonverbal behavior as well as by a verbal response. Similarly, whether a child's answer to a problem is correct or incorrect can be conveyed as effectively by a nod of the head or a smile as by a verbal response. It can be argued that nonverbal behaviors frequently are even more effective than verbal responses in influencing a person's judgment about the true meaning of an utterance. Most persons believe that nonverbal responses are less easy to control voluntarily than are verbal responses; as a consequence, a listener would be more inclined to accept nonverbal than verbal cues as being veridical indicators of another person's true position (belief, opinion, feeling). Consistent with this assumption, research has shown that nonverbal responses carry substantially more weight than verbal utterances when the two types of cues are in conflict (Argyle, Salter, Nicholson, Williams, & Burgess, 1970).

One way to determine the importance of nonverbal behavior in communication is to eliminate it and measure the outcomes. In one recent study, the value of verbal content and full-channel (verbal plus nonverbal) cues were compared on a series of tasks, each of which had an unambiguous criterion of accuracy (Archer & Akert, 1977). In one condition subjects received a written record of a conversation, and in another condition they observed the full-channel videotape. Results showed that performance was significantly better in the full-channel condition. In fact, subjects in the verbal-only condition performed even worse than chance.

We designed an experiment to study in a more detailed fashion the role of nonverbal behavior of children in a tutor–learner interaction situation (Allen & Plazewski, 1976). The purpose of the study was to examine the accuracy of assessments that tutors and tutees made about each other on cognitive and affective dimensions. A concept formation task was taught to third-grade tutees by sixth-grade tutors. Salience of nonverbal cues was varied across three conditions. In one condition, a physical barrier prevented any (visual) nonverbal communication between tutor and tutee. In a second condition, natural face-to-face nonverbal communication prevailed. And, in a third condition, nonverbal communication was accentuated by instructions that urged both participants to pay careful attention to nonverbal cues from the other person. After a short lesson, tutors gave their own responses and their estimation of the responses given by the other on parallel items assessing task expectations and affective evaluations. The task-related items pertained to expected performance and understanding of the task. Other items asked about teaching ability, student's learning and effort, and an overall evaluation. Accuracy scores on task expectations and affective evaluations (estimates about other minus other's actual response) were used as the dependent measures.

As predicted, results showed that, when visual nonverbal cues were eliminated, the participants' perception of each other was significantly less accurate than in the face-to-face condition. Absence of nonverbal cues was detrimental to communication accuracy for both task-related expectations and affective evaluations. Increasing the subjects' attention to nonverbal cues by instructions did not, however, increase the accuracy of perception. Furthermore, tutees were significantly more accurate than tutors on both task and affective dimensions, although the tutees were 3 years younger than their tutors. A reasonable explanation for the tutor's poorer performance is that the role requires dividing attention between cues indicative of the student's comprehension and cues relevant to evaluation of one's now teaching performance. This division of attention might account for the poorer accuracy of the tutor. Finally, tutors and tutees responded quite differently when nonverbal cues were eliminated. For the tutees, the tutoring situation was viewed most favorably when the nonverbal expressions from the tutor could not be seen, perhaps because of a reduction in the discomfort of being under surveillance. For the tutor, the situation was viewed least favorably when nonverbal cues from the tutee could not be observed: Nonverbal cues seem to play an important role in providing feedback for the tutor even when verbal responses of the tutee are readily available.

Encoding–Decoding Skills

In a teaching situation it is often necessary for the teacher to rely heavily on nonverbal cues to determine how much the student really understands about the material being taught. Little is known, however, about the accuracy of an observer's estimate of the degree of understanding of another person on the basis of nonverbal cues alone. Both peer teachers as well as adult teachers who work with young children need to be adept in decoding nonverbal responses that may serve as indices of the cognitive and affective states of the learner. Although a great deal of interest has been shown recently in research on decoding and encoding of nonverbal behavior, there is still a paucity of evidence concerning children's ability with this type of task.

Dimitrovsky (1964) conducted one of the few studies that directly examined developmental trends in children's skill in decoding emotions. Children ranging in age from 5 to 12 were asked to identify an adult's verbal expression of several emotions (happiness, sadness, anger, and love). Results showed that with increasing age children improved significantly in the ability to identify the emotional content of the adult's response. In another study, Teresa (1972) compared the accuracy of teachers and fourth-, fifth-, and sixth-grade students in decoding the behavior of an actress displaying several different emotions on film. Findings indicated that teachers were slightly more accurate than students, and that differences existed across some grades. In general, though, Teresa's results were inconclusive and inconsistent. Results of an encoding study by Buck (1977) revealed that boys became less expressive as they got older, but girls did not. Most other studies that investigated age trends were concerned primarily with the effect of simultaneously varying verbal, vocal, and visual channels on the evaluative responses of adults and children (e.g., Bugenthal, Kaswan, Love, & Fox, 1970). In sum, only a few studies have investigated age differences in decoding nonverbal behavior, and the available empirical findings are inconsistent. An important limitation of almost all previous research is that the stimuli presented to subjects consist of posed pictures or a role-played sequence of behavior. Any conclusions concerning decoding ability based upon such stimulus conditions are ambiguous at best, as results might be due simply to the sharing of a common norm or stereotype by encoder and decoder.

A study was designed to examine systematically the accuracy of children in decoding the nonverbal behavior of other children, that is, in drawing inferences about underlying cognitive states on the basis of overt nonverbal responses (Allen & Feldman, 1975). A set of 20 silent samples (30-sec. each) were prepared of stimulus persons who had been videotaped while listening to two short lessons. The stimulus persons were 10 third-graders (5 males and 5 females). Two lessons were selected; one was very easy for the children (first-grade level) and the other was very difficult (fifth-grade level). Then the two samples from each of the 10 stimulus persons were placed in random order on a new videotape. Thus, the videotape contained 20 short segments: 10 children listening to an easy and a difficult lesson. These samples of nonverbal behavior were shown to groups of third- and sixth-graders. Observers were told that they would view several short film segments of children listening to an arithmetic lesson. It was explained that each film would be shown without sound, and that, after seeing each 30-sec. film, they would be asked to estimate (on a 6-point scale) how much the student understood about the lesson.

Results showed that both third- and sixth-graders rated the stimulus persons who were listening to the easy lesson as understanding more than stimulus persons listening to the difficult lesson. Thus, it can be concluded that by using only nonverbal cues, third- and sixth-grade children can discern a difference in level of understanding between stimulus children who were listening to an easy and a difficult lesson. It should be noted that, although children were able to differentiate cognitive states on the basis of nonverbal cues, their accuracy in an absolute sense was actually quite poor. According to subjects' self-reports, the decoding task was very difficult for them—due in large part to the small amount of nonverbal behavior exhibited by each stimulus person.

The Allen & Feldman (1975) experiment differs from previous studies in several important respects. First, all the stimulus children displayed natural or spontaneous nonverbal behavior, that is, actors were not used. Frijda (1969) has noted that actors typically tend to exaggerate nonverbal responses, which makes the decoding task much simpler for the observer. In this study, stimulus persons were allowed to respond under completely natural conditions—they were alone and not aware of being filmed. The use of a random sample of several stimulus persons is also atypical. Most experiments have used only one encoder, thereby severely limiting the generalizability of results. In contrast, there were 10 stimulus persons in the present study, which approaches what Brunswik (1956) has called "representative sampling of the social ecology." Finally, this experiment differs from previous studies by focusing on inferences about a single cognitive state (degree of understanding), as opposed to the usual task of discriminating among qualitatively different emotional states such as anger, joy, or fear. Thus, the decoding task presented to the subjects was an extremely difficult one: to determine degree of understanding from a brief sample of spontaneously occurring nonverbal behavior.

The children who served as stimulus persons in the Allen and Feldman (1975) study responded naturally and spontaneously; they were presumably not aware of the nonverbal behavior that they were emitting. Can children also accurately perceive the distinction in cognitive state (understanding or not understanding) when stimulus children make an intentional effort to convey to other persons that they understand or do not understand the material (i.e., role play)? In another experiment children were instructed to try to demonstrate by way of their nonverbal behavior alone that they did or did not understand the lesson they were hearing (Allen & Feldman, 1976), Groups of third-grade children were shown 20 samples (30 sec. each) from the videotapes of third-grade children who had attempted to convey understanding or lack of understanding by role playing. Results showed that, when role playing understanding, children were rated as understanding significantly more than when role playing lack of understanding. Thus, children are able to decode behavioral cues produced intentionally as well as naturally.

In short, children can differentiate between cognitive states of stimulus persons on the basis of nonverbal cues produced either spontaneously or by role play. Since the stimulus films were completely silent, only nonverbal cues were available for the subject to use in drawing inferences about level of understanding of stimulus persons. Therefore, in principle it should be possible to predict the subjects' judgments on the basis of the frequency of occurrence of various categories of nonverbal responses of the stimulus persons. A preliminary analysis exploring this possibility found that the objective frequency of nonverbal responses was significantly correlated with judgments of understanding (Atkinson & Allen, 1978). But there are still other unknown sources of variance in addition to the 18 nonverbal categories that were employed in our analysis. One possibility is that the organization and sequence of nonverbal responses are more important in some conditions than others. These results suggest that it is unlikely that a simple one-to-one relation will be found between nonverbal responses and resulting inferences, particularly when the encoder faces a complex stimulus situation and responds spontaneously (i.e., when intention and self-awareness are low).

An important aspect of communication in teaching settings is the paralinguistic components of speech. Paralinguistic aspects of speech include all noncontent characteristics of speech; that is, paralanguage is *how* things are said rather than *what* is said. Can a child who acts as a tutor intentionally vary the paralinguistic aspects of speech as may be necessary? Such control is often required, for example, when giving reinforcement or attempting to establish a positive relationship. Much of the available empirical research on paralinguistics has been conducted with adults as subjects (Davitz, 1964). Three experiments demonstrated that children can decode accurately the noncontent aspects of speech produced by adults (Dimitrovsky, 1964; Solomon & Ali, 1972; Solomon & Yaeger, 1969). Little is known about children's encoding ability, however.

We designed a study to explore the ability of sixth-grade children intentionally to encode verbal messages with a constant content, but with a variety of vocal intonations. In this study, 40 sixth-grade children were asked to produce verbal responses that tutors typically employ when providing positive and negative sanctions in connection with tutees' performance. Auditory recordings were made of the stimulus children intentionally varying several degrees of positive and negative affect by tone of voice (independently of content). Later, adult judges made assessments about the stimuli on the evaluative scale used in the encoding. The stimulus children were instructed to pretend being a teacher for another student while saying aloud a word ("right" and "wrong") and a sentence ("That was the right answer" and "That was the wrong answer"). Each word and sentence was expressed by the children in five different vocal intonations, as specified on a scale ranging from "extremely unfriendly voice" to "extremely friendly voice."

Analysis of the absolute judgments of vocal friendliness by decoders showed that, across all levels of intonation and for both words and sentences, the decoders significantly differentiated among the five different meanings intended by the encoders. Stated in another way, the children succeeded in producing differences as intended among the five degrees of friendliness–unfriendliness by the use of paralanguage alone. It can be concluded, then, that sixth-grade children have the ability intentionally to modulate their vocal intonations for ordinary sanction words and sentences in such a way as to communicate successfully different degrees of affect to other persons.

Spontaneous and Deliberate Behavior

Like other aspects of behavior, nonverbal behavior may vary along a continuum of degree of awareness and control. As Goffman (1956) has convincingly argued, all behavior partakes to some degree of a dramaturgic or staged character, that is, it is produced for or influenced by other persons or by the demands of the situation. In discussions with school children we have asked explicitly if they ever attempted to mislead the teacher in any way concerning their true understanding of a lesson or on other matters. Most of the children responded affirmatively, citing examples such as trying to convince the teacher that they understood a point in a lesson when they actually did not. Usually, this type of imposture was accomplished by means of nonverbal behaviors. The strategy of the student and the counterstrategy of the teacher can reach quite complex levels, with the teacher's attempt to penetrate behind the mask of nonverbal cues for the true cognitive state leading in turn to the development of still more devious and subtle strategems on the part of the student.

It is of interest for both theoretical and practical reasons to know whether children are able accurately to convey their true level of comprehension by intentionally deploying nonverbal responses. In addition, it would be important to know if children are capable of successfully simulating the understanding or lack of understanding of a lesson. If students can simulate successfully, it would be possible for them to control (to a certain extent) the teacher's perception of their comprehension of material.

In an experiment designed to investigate these questions, third- and sixth-grade children were used (Allen & Feldman, 1976). After responding spontaneously to a very easy and a very difficult lesson, they were told to pretend that they were listening to a very hard and then to a very easy lesson. The children did not speak during the role playing, but tried to indicate by their nonverbal behavior alone that they did or did not understand the lesson. The session was recorded on videotape for later analysis.

Nonverbal behavior was coded into 15 categories, and the data were compared for role play and spontaneous conditions. Results indicated that on each of the 15 categories of nonverbal behavior there was either a significant main effect or interaction involving the spontaneous versus role play conditions. (A multivariate test combining all measures revealed significant main effects for spontaneous versus role play, for easy versus difficult, and for the interaction.) Thus, the data indicated that the deliberate nonverbal responses of the children are quite different from nonverbal responses that occur spontaneously. For example, there was less body fidgeting under difficult than under easy conditions when role playing, but the opposite was found in the spontaneous condition; there was less roaming of the eyes in the difficult than in the easy condition when role playing, but the opposite occurred when nonverbal behavior was natural. In general, under role playing many of the nonverbal responses seemed to be exaggerated and were emitted at a higher rate than when the children were responding spontaneously. It is fair to conclude, therefore, that if children attempt purposely to convey to another person (e.g., teacher or tutor) that they do or do not understand the material, the resulting pattern of nonverbal responses are likely to differ from the nonverbal responses that are emitted naturally.

Why should spontaneous and deliberate (role-played) behavior differ so dramatically? It seems that deliberate nonverbal behavior is likely to be based on a socially learned norm, and not closely related to spontaneous behavior. Deliberate behavior is probably guided primarily by general expectations or stereotypes about the external manifestations of a particular cognitive state; such general expectations or stereotypes are frequently severely discrepant with behavior that occurs spontaneously in a specific situation. Moreover, different circumstances surround the emission of spontaneous and deliberate behavior. Typically, role-played behavior is directed towards an audience, whereas spontaneous behavior may be comparatively private. Also, the degree of conscious involvement in the production of behavior is an important factor. Individuals are generally not aware of their spontaneous behavior, but a high level of conscious involvement and self-monitoring are required in role playing. With deliberate behavior, it is necessary to plan the performance, determine the relevance of particular nonverbal cues, and arrange the desired order among the responses. It is unlikely that most persons (and particularly children) who are untrained in dramatic skills will possess either the knowledge or the experience to create deliberately a convincing performance.

Two questions need to be asked about the deliberate encoding of nonverbal behavior (role playing). First, can observers distinguish between different cognitive states produced by role playing? As mentioned in an earlier section, observers rated understanding as being significantly higher when the stimulus children were role playing understanding as compared to not understanding. Therefore, in spite of the existence of objective differences in the nonverbal responses produced spontaneously and deliberately, children were able accurately to decode comprehension and noncomprehension of a lesson in both cases. Thus, it appears that the sheer frequency of a response does not completely determine an observer's attribution about another person: The structure or organization of the behavior may provide important cues to comprehension. In addition, a certain response may be given greater or less weight depending on the context of other behaviors in which it appears.

A second question deals with the ability of observers to detect whether nonverbal behavior has been encoded deliberately or spontaneously. To answer this question, a study was conducted by Allen and Atkinson (1977) in which adult observers viewed silent videotapes of children who were either actually listening to an easy or a difficult lesson (i.e., their nonverbal behavior was spontaneous) or pretending to understand or not understand a lesson (i.e., their behavior was deliberate). Observers judged whether the child in each videotape was encoding spontaneously or deliberately (and also whether understanding or not understanding the lesson). Results showed that observers did readily distinguish between spontaneous and deliberate nonverbal behavior. Decisions were also faster and more confident when decoding deliberate as compared to spontaneous behavior. In the case of deliberate behavior, the encoder attempts to portray the behavior in the clearest and simplest manner possible. Because a given cue occurs many times in a behavior sequence, the cognitive state that the encoder is trying to convey becomes apparent. This analysis is consistent with an information theory approach (Attneave, 1959). The greater the redundancy (as in deliberate behavior) of any type of information, the easier it is to decode. Deliberate performance does not look like spontaneous behavior to an observer; cues tend to cluster together, specific cues are repeated too frequently, and the behavior does not flow smoothly.

The inference that a given response sequence represents spontaneous or deliberate behavior has important psychological consequences regardless of whether it is a correct conclusion in an objective sense. A great deal of ongoing behavior cannot be categorized easily or unequivocally as being entirely spontaneous or deliberate. Clear-cut indices for a dichotomous decision about the spontaneity or deliberateness of behavior are often not available. Furthermore, an individual is frequently not simply a passive viewer of objective cues provided by someone else; instead, the individual is an active organizer of experience. Any ongoing stream of behavior is susceptible to being analyzed at either a molar (global) or molecular (fine-grained) level (Newtson, 1973). Analyzing behavior at a global-unit level will result in perceiving many component actions as belonging together. By contrast, a fine-unit analysis tends to focus attention on small, discrete elements of action. If a behavior stream were analyzed at a fine-grained level, such close scrutiny should cause one to be more likely to notice novel and repetitive actions than if a global style were used. Deliberate behavior is, of course, objectively novel and repetitive. Therefore, a fine-unit level of analysis should be more likely than a global-unit analysis to result in one's perceiving the behavior as being deliberate.

An experiment was designed to test the hypothesis that behavior organized at a fine-grained level of analysis (as opposed to a global level) is more likely to be perceived as deliberate (Atkinson & Allen, 1979). Subjects observed via videotape the nonverbal behavior of two children listening to a lesson. Each subject received either global-unit or fine-unit instructions that included the words, "break the behavior into the largest (smallest) units that seem meaningful and natural to you." Subjects pressed a button to signal the ending of a meaningful unit. After observing each stimulus child, subjects estimated the probability that the child was acting. Results showed that subjects who unitized the behavior at a fine-grained level (broke the behavior sequence into many units) were more likely to perceive the behavior as being deliberate than subjects who actually employed a global analysis (used fewer units). Thus, the size of the unit of analysis affected the perception of the degree of spontaneity or deliberateness of the sequence of nonverbal behavior. It is clear, then, that an inference about the spontaneity or deliberateness of a behavior sequence depends, not only on the availability of relevant objective cues from the stimulus person, but also on the way in which the observer organizes the behavior.

Multichannel Relationships

There has been an increasing amount of research interest focused on the topic of multichannel communication. That is, investigations have been directed toward studying simultaneously two or more channels, such as verbal–visual or visual–paralinguistic. In face-to-face interaction, verbal and nonverbal behaviors occur concomitantly and are usually congruent in terms of the signals being transmitted. Inconsistency between messages conveyed by different channels will place the receiver in a dilemma. A number of important questions exist in the field of multichannel communication. In this section, I shall briefly report two of our studies that are relevant to this area. One study deals with the relation between visual and verbal channels, and one with verbal and paralinguistic channels.

When children help others (e.g., in tutoring programs), those who act as tutors are frequently instructed uniformly to praise and encourage their tutees. When the learner performs poorly, however, the positive verbal responses given by the tutor are inconsistent with his or her true knowledge about the situation. Under such circumstances, the tutor's true reactions might be revealed through nonverbal cues that are potentially detectable by the learner. That is to say, the interdependence of two channels may cause "leakage" from the nonverbal channel, thereby revealing the tutor's private reactions. Appropriate behavior for the tutor in this situation would be to conceal (if possible) those nonverbal responses that are inconsistent with the content of the verbal channel.

An experiment was designed to investigate the hypothesis of nonverbal leakage in a two-channel communication system (Feldman, Devin-Sheehan, & Allen, 1978). Male and female tutors (ages 8 and 11) were required always to say "good" following the answers of a young child (tutee) on a 20-item concept formation test—regardless of whether the tutee's answers were objectively correct or not. The tutee (a confederate) performed either very well (90% correct answers) or very poorly (90% wrong). Therefore, in one of the conditions, the tutor's verbal responses ("good") were untruthful and, hence, inconsistency existed between the verbal and nonverbal channels.

Videotape recordings were made of the tutoring sessions, and trained coders categorized the tutors' nonverbal responses. Results indicated several significant differences between the successful and unsuccessful performance conditions in terms of frequency of nonverbal responses from the tutor. Tutors in the poor tutee performance condition (inconsistency) exhibited, for example, fewer smiles, more stares, more pauses in speech, and more raising of eyebrows. Thus, nonverbal leakage did occur when the two channels were inconsistent, with the tutor unintentionally revealing the discrepancy between the overt positive verbal responses and the true negative evaluation of the tutee's performance.

Are other children capable of discerning the tutor's underlying reaction to the tutee on the basis of these leaked nonverbal cues? To answer this question, a videotape was constructed showing silent samples of the tutors' nonverbal responses. Fifty-five 8-year-old children observed each of 32 film segments and indicated how "satisfied" the tutor appeared to be with the tutee in each one. Results revealed that other children were able to detect negative reactions of the tutor. Hence, when the tutor gave a nonveridical verbal response, cues indicating dissatisfaction appeared in the nonverbal channel and, furthermore, these cues were decoded accurately by other children.

Recently, we investigated the effect of consistency versus inconsistency between the verbal and paralinguistic channels (Plazewski & Allen, 1978). Forty sixth-grade children were told to pretend they were teaching another student. They were asked to encode intentionally words ("right," "wrong") and sentences ("That was the right answer," "That was the wrong answer") with five different degrees of affect expressed in intonations ranging from "extremely friendly voice" to "extremely unfriendly voice." Thus, the children made statements aloud with an intonation that was sometimes consistent and sometimes inconsistent with the verbal content. (That is, "right" expressed in friendly and "wrong" in unfriendly intonations were consistent communications across channels; "right" expressed in unfriendly and "wrong" in friendly intonations were inconsistent communications across channels.) Accuracy of communication was measured by taking difference scores between the level of intonation the children intended to communicate and judgments made on the same scale by adult decoders.

We hypothesized that the children would intentionally encode paralinguistic cues with greater accuracy under conditions of communicative consistency as compared to inconsistency. Results supported this prediction. It was also predicted that a difference would occur according to the nature of the inconsistency. Specifically, greater accuracy of communication was expected for positive content ("right") expressed with unfriendly intonation than for negative content ("wrong") spoken with friendly intonation. It seems to be more acceptable to express simultaneously positive verbal content and negative paralinguistic cues than the opposite type of inconsistency. As paralinguistic cues can be subtle and unobtrusive, this type of inconsistency is less disruptive than the obverse type (negative verbal content and positive paralinguistic cues—which would seem rather strange and unusual). Greater accuracy should result for the type of inconsistency that an individual has experienced more frequently; that is, positive verbal content and negative paralinguistics. Results of the study supported this prediction. Hence, the particular nature of the inconsistency between verbal and paralinguistic channels will influence the accuracy of communication.

Relationship between the Encoder and Decoder

The nature of nonverbal communication that occurs in interpersonal interaction is affected by the nature of the dyad—the degree of similarity or difference on some dimension between the two persons. Ascribed status characteristics such as age, race, and sex are of particular importance. I shall briefly report two studies dealing with decoding and two concerned with encoding.

Two studies dealing with the racial composition of an interaction have been reported by Feldman and Donohoe (1978). In the first experiment, white undergraduates acted as teachers of white and black third-grade students who were actually confederates of the experimenter. The students were uniformly successful at the task, and the teachers verbally reinforced the students in a standard manner. The nonverbal behavior of teachers was recorded and samples were coded for affective meaning by judges. Results of the analysis indicated a significant difference between teachers with high or low scores on a prejudice scale according to race of student. The high-prejudiced teachers revealed differential nonverbal responses toward the white and black students (favoring whites). A second study was conducted in which 40 white and black teachers taught white and black children (confederates) who performed equally successfully on an analogy-type test. The findings indicated that both white and black teachers behaved more positively toward a student of their own race than of the other race. As an important qualification of this finding, however, the difference in teachers' nonverbal affect as a function of race of student was detected only by the judges who were also of the same race as the teachers that they observed. The Feldman and Donohoe (1978) study indicates that characteristics of the target can influence one's nonverbal responses. It appears that, either unintentionally or intentionally, an encoder takes into account the salient characteristics of the target of communication, and modifies verbal behavior accordingly.

The age differential between an encoder and decoder is another important characteristic on which members of a dyad may be similar or different. Shatz and Gelman (1973) found that other children, when speaking with younger listeners, used simpler and shorter utterances and made a special effort to maintain their interest and attention. We designed a study to investigate the influence of age of target on a person's paralinguistic responses (Plazewski & Allen, 1978). Does a person take into account the age of the listener in terms of the nature of vocalization that is emitted? It seems reasonable to assume that a person will attempt to convey greater positive affect when communicating with a younger child than with a peer. In our experiment undergraduates role played teaching a lesson in mathematics to a same-age student and to a fourth-grade child. The subjects always read a standard lesson aloud in a way they thought was appropriate for a same-age or younger student. An auditory recording was made of the lesson, and two judges coded direction of gaze. Results showed that the subjects' behavior did differ as a function of age of the simulated student. There was a significant difference in amount of time taken to read the lesson—subjects read more slowly for the younger student. Also, there was a significantly greater number of gazes directed toward the younger simulated student. Paralinguistic responses (intonation) were evaluated by judges. Significant differences were found between the young and same-age target in terms of friendliness and warmth of the teacher's tone of voice. Thus, in accordance with whether they are interacting with listeners who are of their own age or of a different age, people modify not only the content and structure of their speech utterances (Shatz & Gelman, 1973) but also the less obvious nonverbal aspects of communication, such as tone of voice and direction of gaze. Consistent with our results are the findings of a recent experiment with children by Ludeke (1978), which varied the age between children in a teaching situation. Results showed that the child who served as teacher made greater efforts at role taking and was more helpful toward the learner when teaching a younger child.

Turning now to the effect of composition of the dyad on the accuracy of decoding, let us first look at age of the decoder. In conjunction with an experiment reported earlier (Allen & Feldman, 1975), we examined the accuracy of adults (most of whom were teachers) and children (third- and sixth-graders) in decoding the nonverbal behavior of third-grade children. Results showed that both third- and sixth-grade children were able accurately to differentiate between level of understanding exhibited by the stimulus children, as reported earlier; but the adults did not significantly differentiate between the two different cognitive states displayed by the stimulus children. It is important to clarify the nature of the lack of significant differentiation in the adults' decoding. Both the children and the adults gave very similar ratings of understanding for the easy lesson; by contrast, adults and children differed in their rating of understanding for the difficult lesson, with adults perceiving a higher level of understanding than the children. Thus, when in reality the stimulus persons did not understand the lesson, the adults judged their understanding as being only slightly less than when they truly did understand.

Perhaps the superior decoding of stimulus children by other children, as compared to adults, is due to the stimulus children and the decoders' sharing a common code concerning the meaning of nonverbal responses. Research on verbal communication has found that persons who are similar on certain cognitive dimensions possess a common code that facilitates effective communication (Triandis, 1960). Because the cognitive structure of a group of children is more similar to that of other children than to that of adults, a common code for nonverbal communication would be more likely to exist for two different groups of children than for a group of children and a group of adults.

An alternative explanation for the Allen and Feldman (1975) results focuses on the familiarity between encoder and decoder. In a relevant study, encoder–decoder familiarity was maximized by employing children as encoders and their parents as decoders (Allen & Brideau, 1977). Parents decoded content (understanding or not understanding) of the nonverbal behavior exhibited by their own and other children. It is assumed that nonverbal behavior consists of stereotypic and idiosyncratic components. When decoding their own child's responses, parents can use information about idiosyncratic responses of a particular child as well as knowledge about stereotypic responses in general. In decoding other children's responses, only the stereotypic component of nonverbal behavior is available to parents. Results showed that with spontaneous behavior parents were more accurate in decoding nonverbal responses of their own than of another child—but only for the female children. Consistent with these results, significantly more help from parents with homework was reported by female than by male children. Helping with homework provides an excellent opportunity for observing nonverbal cues associated with the content of the decoding task—understanding versus not understanding.

Individual Differences

A close examination of available data on nonverbal behavior reveals that an impressive range of difference exists among persons. In our experiments a main effect almost always has been found for the stimulus persons factor. The problem of strikingly large individual differences in the area of nonverbal behavior is a challenge to investigators, and one that has yet to be met satisfactorily.

At first glance it might appear that the question of individual differences in nonverbal communication is a relatively simple and straightforward one: What are the characteristics (personality traits or other factors) that determine whether persons are adept or inept in communicating nonverbal messages? A closer analysis of the situation indicates, however, that this global statement of the problem is too simple; it should be divided into several more specific components about which more detailed questions can be asked. Examination of the components of the nonverbal communication situation suggests several specific questions. To what degree is a person's ability to encode and decode nonverbal behavior consistent (*a*) across different tasks; (*b*) across different types of content; (*c*) across nonverbal channels (e.g., visual, body, paralanguage); (*d*) between encoding and decoding of nonverbal responses; (*e*) between spontaneously and deliberately produced nonverbal behavior? For all these questions, how does the pattern of individual differences change as a function of age and what correlates of individual differences influence the degree of consistency?

These questions should make it obvious to the reader that the problem of individual differences in nonverbal communication is a great deal more complex than might first be assumed. It is clear that differences among individuals may occur on any one of the several specific aspects of the general question. A more precise analysis of the problem will help to organize empirical research and will identify gaps where research is needed. Answering the more specific questions will help us determine whether skill in nonverbal communication depends on a basic general underlying ability or whether there are many specific components of competence.

The first question mentioned is a special case of the problem of the generality or specificity of behavior. There is a paucity of data available on this problem for nonverbal behavior. Studies have reported that the social context exerts a strong influence on decoding (Cline, 1956; Munn, 1940; Watson, 1972), but data are not available for consistency across situations. To explore the generality–specificity problem in connection with the accuracy of child encoders and adult decoders, Atkinson and Allen (1977) analyzed data across four different types of nonverbal behavior (understanding and not understanding, when encoded spontaneously and deliberately). Results of the analysis showed a high degree of specificity of performance across the four conditions for both encoders and decoders—that is, the correlations were near zero. Thus, an individual's ability to encode or decode one type of nonverbal behavior seems to be quite unrelated to performance with another type of nonverbal behavior. The present results suggest that the social and cognitive abilities involved in encoding and decoding nonverbal behavior are highly specific to the type of behavior in question.

Some data are available concerning the relation between encoding and decoding skills. One experiment reported a positive relation between encoding and decoding (Knower, 1945), but two other recent and better designed experiments (Cunningham, 1977; Lanzetta & Kleck, 1970) found a negative relation between ability to encode and decode emotions. Cunningham (1977) suggests that there may be different motivational bases for encoding and decoding (spontaneous expressivity and social vigilance, respectively). The suggestion is supported by his finding that different personality scales correlated with skill in encoding (extraversion and emotional responsiveness) and skill in decoding (neuroticism and female gender).

In attempting to account for individual differences in decoding, certain obvious variables such as sex or achievement come to mind as plausible candidates. A recent extensive review by Hall (1978) examined sex differences in nonverbal decoding ability. It was concluded that the majority of studies found females to be more accurate than males in decoding nonverbal behavior. One must accept this conclusion with caution, however, as a separate analysis of 55 studies by Hall indicated that only 20% found a significant effect for sex of decoder. In our own research, results for sex of decoder have tended to be inconsistent across studies depending on the type of behavior and experimental condition. Almost no data are available concerning decoding skills across different nonverbal channels. One recent study (Cunningham, 1977) reported a positive relation for decoding between different nonverbal channels (i.e., voice, face, and body).

Several studies have explored the personality correlates of encoding ability. Success by children in encoding emotions by visual responses has been found to be correlated with high self-esteem and test anxiety (Buck, Savin, Miller, & Caul, 1972), self-monitoring (Snyder, 1974), and teacher's rating of activity level, impulsiveness, aggressiveness, bossiness, and sociability (Buck, 1975). We found that high-achieving males were more competent encoders than low-achieving males (Allen & Atkinson, 1978). We also constructed several self-report items tapping past experiences and attitudes (e.g., dramatic interests) that might be related to differences in encoding skill among elementary school children. The correlations were uniformly low and almost all were nonsignificant. Previous research on skill in encoding paralinguistic responses found that personality scales did not fare well in predicting individual differences (Davitz, 1964). Research by Davitz (1964) and associates on the correlates of paralinguistic encoding skill is very suggestive. The strongest correlate of encoding skill was sensitivity of the subjects in auditory discrimination, a basic sensory ability that seems closely related to the skill required in encoding. This objective measure was more strongly correlated with accuracy of encoding paralinguistic responses than the personality scales and other self-report measures.

We must conclude, at the present time, that attempts to account for individual differences in nonverbal behavior have met with very limited success. Most of the available research deals with correlates of encoding and decoding skills (mostly of emotional states); data are limited or nonexistent for most of the specific questions we posed earlier. Results often have been ambiguous and contradictory, with no obvious common psychological dimension seeming to underlie the various findings obtained across different studies. Moreover, the magnitude of the obtained correlations is usually low, leaving most of the variance unaccounted for. Perhaps we should closely examine the basic sensory–perceptual, cognitive, or motoric abilities that are involved at each particular phase of the nonverbal communication act. The large variance observed in the existing data in the area of nonverbal communication can simply be acknowledged but can not be explained. Serious attempts to account for the wide range of differences among individuals might contribute significantly toward improving our general understanding of nonverbal communication.

In conclusion, this chapter has presented an overview of research on nonverbal communication, concentrating on a discussion of our own studies. It is hoped that the studies will improve our understanding of the way that cues are utilized in the process of communication among children (or between children and teachers) in typical learning situations. It is obvious that a great deal of research work remains to be done on this problem. Perhaps research in this area will make it possible in the future to devise programs that will enhance children's skills in nonverbal communication in the context of the learning situations that they encounter in school.

References

Allen, V. L., & Atkinson, M. L. *Identifying spontaneous and deliberate behavior from nonverbal responses* (Tech. Rep. 419). Madison: Wisconsin Research and Development Center for Cognitive Learning, 1977.

Allen, V. L., & Atkinson, M. L. The encoding of nonverbal behavior by high- and low-achieving children. *Journal of Educational Psychology*, 1978, *70*, 298–305.

Allen, V. L., & Brideau, L. B. *The ability of parents to decode nonverbal behavior of their own and other children* (Tech. Rep. 444) Madison: Wisconsin Research and Development Center for Cognitive Learning, 1977.

Allen, V. L., & Feldman, R. S. *Decoding of children's nonverbal responses* (Tech. Rep. 365). Madison: Wisconsin Research and Development Center for Cognitive Learning, 1975.

Allen, V. L., & Feldman, R. S. *Nonverbal cues to comprehension: Encoding of nonverbal behaviors naturally and by role-play* (Working Paper 147). Madison: Wisconsin Research and Development Center for Cognitive Learning, 1976.

Allen, V. L., & Plazewski, J. G. *Nonverbal interaction of tutor–tutee dyads: Accuracy of person perception as a function of nonverbal cues and social role* (Working Paper 146). Madison: Wisconsin Research and Development Center for Cognitive Learning, 1976.

Archer, D., & Akert, R. M. Words and everything else: Verbal and nonverbal cues in social interpretation. *Journal of Personality and Social Psychology*, 1977, *35*, 443–449.

Argyle, M. *Social interaction*. Chicago: Aldine-Atherton, 1969.

Argyle, M., Salter, V., Nicholson, H., Williams, M., & Burgess, P. The communication of inferior and superior attitudes by verbal and nonverbal signals. *British Journal of Social and Clinical Psychology*, 1970, *9*, 222–231.

Atkinson, M. L., & Allen, V. L. *The generality–specificity of encoding and decoding skills with spontaneous and deliberate nonverbal behavior* (Tech. Rep. 443). Madison: Wisconsin Research and Development Center for Cognitive Learning, 1977.

Atkinson, M. L., & Allen, V. L. *Predictability of judgments of understanding from objective nonverbal responses*. Unpublished manuscript, University of Wisconsin, Madison, 1978.

Atkinson, M. L., & Allen, V. L. Level of analysis as a determinant of the meaning of nonverbal behavior. *Social Psychology Quarterly*, 1979, *42*, 270–274.

Attneave, F. *Applications of information theory to psychology*. New York: Holt, Rinehart, & Winston, 1959.

Brunswik, E. *Perception and the representative design of psychological experiments*. Berkeley: University of California Press, 1956.

Buck, R. W. Nonverbal communication of affect in children. *Journal of Personality and Social Psychology*, 1975, *31*, 644–653.

Buck, R. W. Nonverbal communication of affect in preschool children: Relationships with personality and skin conductance. *Journal of Personality and Social Psychology*, 1977, *35*, 225–236.

Buck, R. W., Savin, V. J., Miller, R. E., & Caul, W. F. Communication of affect through facial expressions in humans. *Journal of Personality and Social Psychology*, 1972, *23*, 362–371.

Bugental, D. E., Kaswan, J. W., Love, L. R., & Fox, M. N. Perception of contradictory meanings conveyed by verbal and nonverbal channels. *Journal of Personality and Social Psychology*, 1970, *16*, 647–655.

Cline, M. G. The influence of social context on the perception of faces. *Journal of Personality*, 1956, *2*, 142–158.

Cunningham, M. R. Personality and the structure of the nonverbal communication of emotion. *Journal of Personality*, 1977, *45*, 564–584.

Davitz, J. R. *The communication of emotional meaning*. New York: McGraw-Hill, 1964.

Dimitrovsky, L. The ability to identify the emotional meaning of vocal expressions at successive age levels. In J. Davitz (Ed.), *The communication of emotional meaning*. New York: McGraw-Hill, 1964.

Feldman, R. S., Devin-Sheehan, L., & Allen, V. L. Nonverbal cues as indicators of verbal dissembling. *American Educational Research Journal*, 1978, *15*, 217–237.

Feldman, R. S., & Donohoe, L. F. Nonverbal communication of affect in interracial dyads. *Journal of Educational Psychology*, 1978, *70*, 979–987.

Frijda, N. H. Recognition of emotion. In L. Berkowitz (Ed.), *Advances in experimental social psychology* (Vol. 4). New York: Academic Press, 1969.

Goffman, E. *The presentation of self in everyday life*. Edinburgh: University Press, 1956.

Hall, J. A. Gender effects in decoding nonverbal cues. *Psychological Bulletin*, 1978, *85*, 845–857.

Harper, R. G., Wiens, A., & Matarazzo, J. D. *Nonverbal communication: The state of the art*. New York: Wiley, 1978.

Kendon, A. *Temporal aspects of the social performance in two person encounters*. Unpublished doctoral dissertation, Oxford University, 1963.

Knower, F. H. Studies in the symbolism of voice and action: V. The use of behavioral and tonal symbols as tests of speaking achievement. *Journal of Applied Psychology*, 1945, *29*, 229–235.

Lanzetta, J. R., & Kleck, R. E. Encoding and decoding of nonverbal affect in humans. *Journal of Personality and Social Psychology*, 1970, *16*, 12–19.

Ludeke, R. J. *Teaching behaviors of 11-year-old and 9-year-old girls in same-age and mixed age dyads*. Unpublished doctoral dissertation, University of Minnesota, 1978.

Munn, N. L. The effect of knowledge of the situation upon judgment of emotion from facial expressions. *Journal of Abnormal and Social Psychology*, 1940, *35*, 324–338.

Newtson, D. Attribution and the unit of perception in ongoing behavior. *Journal of Personality and Social Psychology*, 1973, *28*, 28–38.

Plazewski, J. G., & Allen, V. L. *The paralinguistic encoding capability of children* (Tech. Rep. 441). Madison: Wisconsin Research and Development Center for Cognitive Learning, 1977.

Plazewski, J. G., & Allen, V. L. *Differential use of paralanguage and nonverbal behavior by tutors as a function of relative age of the student* (Tech. Rep. 491). Madison: Wisconsin Research and Development Center for Individualized Schooling, 1978.

Scheflen, A. E. *Stream and structure of communicational behavior*. Commonwealth of Pennsylvania: Eastern Pennsylvania Psychiatric Institute, 1965.

Shatz, M., & Gelman, R. The development of communication skills: Modifications in the speech of young children as a function of listener. *Monographs of the Society of Research in Child Development*, 1973, *38*, No. 5.

Siegman, A. W., & Feldstein (Eds.). *Nonverbal behavior and communication*. Hillsdale, N.J.: Lawrence Erlbaum Associates, 1978.

Synder, M. Self-monitoring of expressive behavior. *Journal of Personality and Social Psychology,* 1974, *20,* 526–537.

Solomon, D., & Ali, F. A. Age trends in the perception of verbal reinforcers. *Developmental Psychology,* 1972, *7,* 238–243.

Solomon, D., & Yaeger, J. Determinants of boys' perceptions of reinforcers. *Developmental Psychology,* 1969, *1,* 637–645.

Teresa, J. G. The measurement of meaning as interpreted by teachers and students in visuo-gestural channel expressions through nine emotional expressions. Doctoral dissertation, University of Michigan, 1971. *Dissertation Abstracts International,* 1972, *32* (7-A), 3807.

Triandis, H. C. Cognitive similarity and communication in dyad. *Human Relations,* 1960, *13,* 175–183.

Watson, S. G. Judgment of emotion from facial and contextual cue combinations. *Journal of Personality and Social Psychology,* 1972, *24,* 334–342.

16

Problem-Solving Communication and Complex Information Transmission in Groups

JANINE BEAUDICHON

Knowledge about children's communication skills is of great importance for schooling, which is mainly based on the assumption that the child understands what is said to him and is able to express what he wants. Strangely enough, this area of inquiry for a long time received little attention. In fact, if one excludes Piaget's pioneer study (1923) and its continuation in the United States (see McCarthy, 1952), it was only in 1966 that the first publications on child communication appeared. An article by the American psychologists Glucksberg, Krauss, & Weisberg (1966) was published at roughly the same time as a French review of the works of the Rumanian psychologist Slama-Cazacu (1966). Since then it seems that interest in this area continues to grow, if one considers the tremendous increase in the number of publications on this subject every year, as well as its inclusion as a topic of discussion in many of the international scientific meetings.

As fortunate as this may be, it is necessary to point out that the information resulting from these studies—and thus its benefits for teachers and parents alike—is not as substantial as could be hoped for. This is due to the fact that the studies were carried out in two different theoretical

357

frameworks—one traditionally called "referential," the other traditionally referred to as "sociolinguistic" (cf. Dickson's introductory chapter), having little common ground between them with respect to the types of observed behaviors, as well as to the methods employed. As a result, these studies yielded two sets of contradictory conclusions. The reader who tries to form a clear opinion of children's communication skills is left quite bewildered. Thus it is clearly demonstrated, by studies that make up the sociolinguistic tradition (e.g., Garvey, & Hogan, 1973; Mueller, 1972, 1977; Shatz & Gelman, 1974; Slama-Cazacu, 1966, 1978) that development in communication skills and in the ability to adapt to one's partner occur in children as young as 3- to 5-years-old. This justifies a certain optimism with respect to the efficiency of communicative exchanges with the child. But studies in the referential tradition (see Glucksberg, Krauss, & Higgins, 1975, for a review), demonstrate equally clearly that communication skills are quite slow in their development and that even 8-year-olds are poorly equipped in that respect. This leads one to conclude that efforts made in communication with the child are for the most part in vain. So, which view is correct?

The contradiction seems to result from the fact that the authors on the two sides have not considered the same behavioral field. This occurred for two reasons. First, one group studied natural communication behavior as it occurred in the course of a game (Garvey & Hogan, 1973; Mueller, 1972; Slama-Cazacu, 1966, 1978), whereas the other studied communication with unfamiliar and complex referents (e.g., abstract figures), word pairs of variable frequencies, and schematic drawings of faces. The behaviors and motivation required in each circumstance may be of a different nature, as the cognitive activities required to encode and decode the information are not the same. Second, the techniques employed by the two approaches were extremely different. The researchers who studied natural behavior strived as much as possible to protect the subjects from the possible effects of the experimental setting by eliminating all restrictions. The researchers considering communication of specific referents, on the other hand, constrained behaviors through procedural instructions and game rules and limited communication through the use of screens preventing visual contact between the speakers; some required the child to make believe he was speaking to someone in particular when, in fact, he actually spoke for the benefit of the experimenter or to a listener exhibiting pat reactions (Flavell *et al.*, 1968). These restrictions probably rendered even less spontaneous the few behaviors that occurred. At least part of the incompetence exhibited by children in these conditions was due to the fact that they had to *create,* according to the circumstance, novel responses which did not belong to their usual repertoire, in order to adapt to the rather foreign situation with which they were faced. They were not under optimal conditions, moreover, to take the trouble to create these novel responses. To begin with, the motivation to communicate, induced by a complex referent, experimental restriction, or rules, could not have been very high. Second, and this is probably the main reason, the possibilities of interpersonal interaction were extremely limited, if not nonexistent, whereas real life communication takes place in interactional settings, in which speakers do what is necessary to adapt their messages by monitoring their impact on the listeners. (The metaanalysis of referential communication research by Dickson in this volume supports this conclusion.)

To what extent are the behaviors elicited by the particular method employed representative of behaviors naturally occurring in real life situations? Data collected in the sociolinguistic tradition are undoubtedly representative of the child's usual behaviors occurring in the family setting and in peer relationships. These data are uninformative, however, with respect to the extent of specific skills occurring in communication situations employing complex referents, such as in the case of certain explanations a teacher gives to students.

Data collected in the referential tradition are representative of difficult communication situations or ones in which the subject is faced with a communication problem that he encounters, if not for the first time, then at least very rarely. This data is uninformative with regard to the capabilities of the child in communication situations that are common but moderately difficult (e.g., comprehension skills with respect to teacher explanations concerning a wide range of learning situations related to concepts taught in school, the transmission of didactic principles, or peer communication ability vis-à-vis such notions or games of a difficult nature). It is the child's capabilities in precisely these situations that I have sought to clarify in my research.

Purpose and Framework of the Studies

The purpose of the present studies was to examine children's communication with respect to referents characteristic of those that children encounter either in school activities (didactic learning) or during certain intellectual games (storytelling, problems, and puzzles to be solved with fellow classmates). Each of these two areas was examined by a group of studies characterized by significantly different methods. Child communication was observed in 5-year-olds attending the French "maternal school," corresponding to the year just before their entry into elementary school, and in elementary-school children whose ages ranged from 6- to 10-years-old. This was complemented by a limited number of observations of preadolescent communication. These ages were chosen so as to gather information likely to be helpful in distinguishing those teaching methods that enable a normal adaptation in school during the critical first few years.

The rationale behind this research is as follows: In complex communication situations, information transfer occurs primarily through interaction (reciprocal action of the interlocutors on each other). This interaction corresponds to the joint actions effected by the different interlocutors to bring about mutual comprehension. In our opinion, such interaction is necessary in order for the interlocutors to dispense with the illusion that communication goes on automatically (see Piaget, 1923), and to instead exhibit decentration skills and discriminating message exchanges. It seems as if studies carried out in the referential tradition have not allowed for sufficient interaction between children. This explains in part the poor performances witnessed in children faced with communication tasks. It is the present author's hypothesis that interaction exists between children at an early age (even as young as 5-years-old) and that it develops only slightly with respect to its forms. The intelligibility of the messages encoded and the accuracy with which they are decoded do increase, even when the communication remains inefficient.

Our studies, which include approximately 1500 children, are related to those carried out in the referential framework with respect to the choice of the referent and the restrictions imposed on the subjects examined, stemming from the experimental setting. The referent was imposed by the experimenter and was always relatively complex with respect to the cognitive activities required for its comprehension or explanation. In addition, the subjects had to closely follow experimental instructions filled with diverse prohibitions which limited their freedom of initiative and expression. Nevertheless this experimental setting allows for a systematic examination of key variables, in spite of possible artifacts, resulting from the experimental controls. On the other hand the present approach resembles the sociolinguistic tradition in allowing extensive interaction between the participants. As a result, it can be characterized as intermediate between the experimental and sociolinguistic approaches.

Methods and Results of Our Previous Research

Several general principles have guided our approach to children's communication. Situations were constructed to be as different as possible and utilized referents that, although varied, were nevertheless related to those the child encounters in learning situations in school or in the resolution of intellectual puzzles on his own. These referents were chosen for the interest they presented for the child and for their capacity to stimulate and maintain a high motivation to communicate. The possibilities for interindividual interactions were maximally preserved, in spite of the restrictions imposed, by placing the children side by side and allowing them to exchange information through pointing, or, when children were placed on opposite sides of a screen which prevented gesturing, by allowing them to observe their partner's face. In the studies on communication utilizing unfamiliar items or intellectual puzzles, subjects were placed in little houses connected by telephone lines. Subjects were given the impression that the experimenter would be absent at this time. Recording devices were also hidden to enable the children to feel able to do as they wished. These precautions attempt to encourage "natural" interaction in systematically designed contexts. This approach is useful, not so much to enable a systematic comparison between the two methods, but rather because the same method does not always appear to be the most appropriate for each of the two types of communication (social interaction and referential information).

The remainder of the chapter will be structured along the following lines. First, there is a discussion of the results of the studies carried out by me on the exchange of information of the sort the child encounters in school. An attempt is made to point out what effects were due to the interactions between interlocutors. The methods employed will be only briefly mentioned as they can be found elsewhere in greater detail. A study will then be presented that focuses on verbal exchanges with respect to a complex game and the effect of the interaction on message characteristics.

In the first line of research, dealing with the development of communication characteristics and efficiency in referential situations similar to those found at school, the general principle was to have an adult (the experimenter) teach a particular skill to the subject, who was then asked to transmit this knowledge to another naïve subject as a means of examining how information is transmitted, what kinds of information are transmitted, and how efficient the process is. This method is restricting from several viewpoints: Not only is the referent assigned, but the speaker and listener roles are determined beforehand. The message model is provided for the speaker by an adult: The speaker can remember it rather than forming a new message. In addition, the channels of communication were controlled either by separating the interlocutors with a screen, or by preventing them from manipulating the available material. This was necessary to limit the information to the communication itself. The experimenter was always present and might have served as a stimulation to carry out the proposed task. These restrictions did not eliminate all possibility of interpersonal interaction, but they undoubtedly had some effects.

Verbal behavior was recorded on audio-tape and certain nonverbal behaviors were systematically noted. The purpose of the analysis was to reveal the nature and quantity of information in the adult–child and child–child communication. Several levels of comprehension were coded: answers to questions, immediate or deferred execution of the actions mentioned in the messages, and generalization to related ideas. Dialogue characteristics were also considered.

In a first set of experiments, pairs of same-aged children attempted to communicate several principles. Before the communication phase between children, the subject taking the speaker's role learned the notions in question during a communication phase with an adult. The principles to be communicated were the working of a hypodermic syringe (Beaudichon, 1968), weighing (Beaudichon, 1977), and the circulation of air or colored water in a glass maze controlled by the opening and closing of faucets placed along a pathway (Beaudichon, 1969; Beaudichon & Forestier, 1970). In all of these experiments, subjects were placed side by side and could communicate verbally and nonverbally but could not manipulate the materials (except in control groups where the efficiency of gestural communication was examined separately).

In a second set of experiments, pairs of children had to transmit to each other a set of information concerning complex learning situations, including a chemistry experiment where the principle of acid–base differentiation and their reciprocal neutralization was taught (Beaudichon, 1977), the assembly of a complex object from various parts based on different assembly principles (Beaudichon, 1977), and a classification task (Beaudichon & Levasseur, 1972).

In these experiments, children were separated by a screen but encouraged to manipulate the material in order to demonstrate the principles described and to apply the transmitted instructions. Certain aspects will now be extracted from the results of these two sets of studies which argue in favor of the position taken in this chapter.

Practically all the information *transmitted* by the speaker is understood by the listener. Not only does the listener understand practically all the information transmitted, but he adds things. In other words, he seems to understand points of information for which the analyses of the dialogues do not enable one to confirm that the piece of useful knowledge was provided. The personal analysis of the referent is thus woven into the topic of communication. This adjunct depends indeed on the topic of communication, as the situation is such that the possibility of direct knowledge induction is unlikely. Understanding is manifested, not only in answers to questions, but also, for the majority of the referents utilized, in the possibility of generalizing the notion acquired to communication of a similar or logically related notion.

Older children require fewer trials than younger children (i.e., the effort expended is more and more economical). Mutual comprehension occurs more rapidly between older children with an increase in the quantity of information transmitted and comprehended in a given time period, but the rather high level of efficiency attained in communication between children did not occur from the start, especially for younger children and difficult referents. This efficiency is the fruit of an often laborious collaboration. The adjustment does not occur between speaker and listener immediately, but little by little through repeated attempts to understand one another. It is remarkable that even 5-year-olds try to enact these adjustments, even when faced with difficult referents and conditions imposing restrictions. The message initially emitted by the speaker is hardly intelligible and seems to be relied on only as a probe, as evidenced by the speaker's questioning attitude and his lack of self-confidence. He waits until the listener reacts and is very disappointed if his attempt is not greeted by a response. This attempt comprises his temporary coding of information, as is evident in the reactions exhibited on both a verbal and nonverbal level. If the listener makes no response, the speaker asks if his partner has understood, or closely examines his partner's face. In the majority of cases, however, the response does not have to be elicited. It spontaneously follows reception in the form of acknowledgment, approval, interrogation, questioning, or by the corresponding facial expressions, nodding, or blinking. Once this expected reaction occurs, the speaker revises his initial production by making additions, specifying a point, and so on until, in the course of successive communication exchanges, the message improves. Furthermore, the listener is not satisfied with merely signaling that he has received the message, but presents his own knowledge or specific hypotheses as a means of aiding in the transmission of information, encouraging the speaker and asking for specific information. Five-year-olds, as well as older but inhibited children, exhibit these behaviors only in a discrete or sporadic fashion. Certain children appeared to be inhibited by the presence of an observer in the experimental setting.

Effects of Social Interactions on Communication Efficiency

In order to observe more natural behaviors, certain experimental constraints were relaxed in the second line of research. The referent was still assigned and only verbal communication was permitted, but now the experimenter was hidden from the children, who were allowed to act as they wished. They were put into the same individual houses described previously, each containing a complete set of materials necessary for the task. The referents were problems, games, or play activities to be carried out in groups of two to four children.

The purpose of this research using a more natural setting is to elicit behaviors that are as spontaneous as possible in communication about cognitively complex referents. Its goal is to examine the influence of variations in the social situation on message characteristics and communication performance. A second goal is to examine developmental changes in the ability of listeners in these complex tasks.

Three different levels of restriction on channel of communication were studied. The most restricted level compared the speaker's communication with silent versus imaginary listeners, the second level limited communication to bilateral exchanges between speaker–listener pairs, and the least restricted permitted communication to take place among all participants.

The number of speaker's requests was expected to be greater in the less restricted conditions.

The main hypothesis in the study was that variations in social interaction would have a large effect on communication, specifically on message characteristics and the efficiency of verbal exchanges as measured by listener's performance in the task.

The study builds upon an earlier investigation by Flavell *et al.* (1968, pp. 102–122) in which a speaker communicated successively with three imaginary listeners who were supposed to be either able or unable to communicate among themselves. The task required the speaker to communicate the combination of a safe which consisted of eight numbers and information concerning the direction in which the dial was to be turned. Some of the information was known to all three imaginary listeners and some was known only to certain of the imaginary listeners. The speaker's job was to communicate to each imaginary listener *only* that information necessary and sufficient to be able to open the lock. The speaker had to take into account the fact that the imaginary listeners could or could not circulate information among themselves. In the present study, one condition used imaginary listeners similar to Flavell's study, but in a second condition, three real listeners were used who could actually communicate with the speaker. A third condition had the experimenter act as speaker to three real listeners, in order to test listener's ability to carry out a correctly produced message.

Experimental Design

Three experimental conditions were used. In the *speaker–listener* condition, the speaker was a child who communicated with three other children of the same age; during Phase 1 the listeners could not ask questions or interact with each other, whereas during Phase 2 such interaction was permitted. In the *imaginary listener* condition, the speaker was a child who communicated with three imaginary listeners under the same condition as Phase 1 for the speaker–listener condition. In the *experimenter–listener* condition, the experimenter served as speaker and communicated with three children under the same conditions as the speaker–listener condition, except that no dialogue was allowed between experimenter and children: If the children asked questions, the experimenter only repeated the necessary information. The instructions permitted the listeners in half of the groups to exchange information among themselves, whereas, in the other half, the listeners could not exchange information. (In the case of the imaginary listener condition, the speaker was to assume that the listeners could or could not exchange information; in the other two conditions, the listeners were actually permitted or not permitted to exchange information.)

Subjects

The sample consisted of three age levels (6-, 8-, and 10-year-olds). Communication groups consisted of children of the same sex. In the speaker–listener condition, a group consisted of four children (one speaker and three listeners); in the imaginary listener condition, "groups" consisted of only the one speaker; and, in the experimenter–listener condition, the group consisted of three children as listeners. Ten groups were observed in each of the 18 cells in the design, yielding a total of 480 children in all.

Task

The task differed considerably from Flavell's. The speaker gave directions for moving a toy car on a playing board, utilizing landmarks portraying a village so that each listener might arrive at a hidden treasure chest. All information was represented on the playing board by a set of symbols (different colored crosses, arrows, *etc.*). At each junction on the playing board, there were electric sockets beside the two alternative directions. Eight sockets representing the correct path were electrically connected. When eight plugs were inserted in these sockets, a blinking light revealed the location of a treasure.

The speaker and three listeners were located in separate individual houses and were given identical playing boards, as well as a telephone circuit connected either to the experimenter alone or to each of the listeners, depending on the experimental group. The speaker was given a board that contained all the plugs corresponding to the correct path as well as the plugs already placed in each listener's board. Each real listener had a playing board that contained the five plugs corresponding to the five pieces of known information. Each plug was color coded so as to distinguish which plugs belonged to which listener. Two points of information were shared by all three listeners, so the three corresponding color coded plugs were inserted in the same sockets on the speaker's board. The speaker was to communicate the points missing from the total set of eight for each listener. He was, furthermore, to deliver only necessary information, taking into account the possibilities of communication between partners.

Procedure

In the speaker–listener condition, the speaker had to communicate an adequate and efficient message to each listener concerning the route to the treasure. The speaker was to take into account the previous knowledge of each listener, as well as (for half of the groups) the possibility of information exchange among all of the listeners. The speaker–listener condition had two phases. In the first phase the listeners were not allowed to respond and could only apply the information provided by the speaker. In the second phase, which followed immediately after the first, the listeners were free to talk both to the speaker and among themselves if they were in the "listeners interaction" half of the design. In the imaginary listener condition, the speaker's task was identical to the first phase of the speaker–listener condition. In the experimenter–listener condition, the experimenter gave adequate and efficient messages and the three listeners tried to respond to the information given. No true dialogue occurred between the listeners and the experimenter, except that the experimenter would repeat the message each time he was asked.

Each listener's performance was graded on a scale of 0–8, one point being given for each correctly placed plug. In order to compare the results of this study with Flavell's original study, the content of the messages produced in the speaker–listener and imaginary listener conditions were compared, using a detailed coding grid to determine whether the messages were correct or incorrect, taking into account the situation and knowledge of the listeners. Each transcript was coded by two coders and discrepancies resolved through discussion. Results are said to be significant if $p < .05$.

Results

Chi-square analysis of the number of speakers giving adequate and efficient messages in the imaginary listener condition was rather similar to the results found by Flavell et al. (1968, p. 112). In the imaginary listener condition, only 1, 3, and 2 speakers out of 10 speakers at ages 6, 8, and 10, respectively, gave adequate and efficient messages when listeners were assumed to be able to interact with each other, whereas 2, 6, and 8 speakers out of 10 at these age levels gave such messages when the listeners were assumed not to be able to interact. This pattern was essentially the same in Phases 1 and 2 of the speaker–listener condition: No speakers had still given only the necessary information after Phase 2 in which the listeners could interact among themselves and ask questions of the speaker. In other words, across the entire age range, the children showed little ability to say only the necessary information, taking into account the information available to each listener from the other listeners.

Listener Performance

The next analyses were carried out on the success of the real listeners in the speaker–listener and experimenter–listener conditions. Each listener was given a score from 0 to 8 based on the number of correctly placed plugs (including the five already placed on the board, which were sometimes incorrectly moved by the listeners). The data were first analyzed in terms of the number of listeners who achieved perfect solutions, and then analyzed in terms of the mean number of correctly placed plugs. These data are presented in Table 16.1.

Number of Listeners with Perfect Solutions

Of the 180 listeners in each condition, only 18 achieved perfect solutions in Phase 1 in the speaker–listener condition, but this had risen to 73 following Phase 2, in which interaction was permitted between speaker and listener (and among listeners for the half of the groups in which listeners interaction

TABLE 16.1
**Number of Listeners Achieving a Perfect Solution on the
Communication Task by Age and Condition[a]**

| Listeners interaction | Age | Speaker–listener condition | | Experimenter–listener condition |
		Phase 1: no dialogue with speaker	$\rightarrow$ Phase 2: dialogue with speaker	No dialogue with speaker
Listeners could interact among themselves (except in Phase 1)	6	0 (3.60)	1 (3.93)	0 (4.77)
	8	0 (4.40)	15 (6.50)	6 (5.43)
	10	0 (3.83)	13 (5.97)	22 (6.87)
Listeners could *not* interact among themselves	6	4 (4.20)	12 (6.43)	2 (3.47)
	8	5 (5.27)	16 (7.53)	11 (5.50)
	10	9 (5.73)	16 (7.53)	18 (6.60)
Totals		18	73	59

[a] Mean number of correctly placed plugs per listener shown in parentheses; maximum = 8. At each age level there were 10 groups consisting of one speaker and three listeners in the speaker–listener condition and 10 groups consisting of the experimenter as speaker and three children as listeners in the experimenter–listener condition.

was permitted). This improvement is statistically significant for all but the youngest age level. Only 59 listeners in the experimenter–listener condition achieved perfect solutions, indicating that the opportunity to ask questions of the speaker (which was not allowed in the experimenter–listener condition) is significantly related to successful performance, although this difference is not found with the 10-year-old children.

Interestingly, the number of listeners achieving perfect solutions in Phase 2 of the speaker–listener condition is higher in the groups where the listeners were not allowed to interact with each other, although these differences are only statistically significant for the youngest age level. Apparently, the participation of the listeners often leads to confusion.

Mean Number of Correctly Placed Plugs

Analyses were also performed on the mean number of plugs correctly placed by the listeners. These means are shown in Table 16.1 in parentheses. The mean scores increase significantly from Phase 1 to Phase 2 in the speaker–listener condition and tend to increase with age, the largest increase coming between ages 6 and 8. At ages 6 and 8 the mean number of correctly placed plugs is greater with a responsive child speaker than with a nonresponsive adult speaker.

Specific Interpretation and General Conclusion

Several major interpretations and conclusions can be drawn from these results and previous work carried out along the same lines. Having real rather than imaginary listeners noticeably affects 6-year-olds, but the effect is not noticeable in older children. The child becomes progressively capable of addressing an imaginary interlocutor in the way in which he would address a real one. Snow (1972) pointed out differences still existent in mothers with regard to verbal utterances directed toward a child physically present, and those directed toward a child not physically present. We have also reported elsewhere (Beaudichon et al., 1978) that listener's presence has a massive effect on 8-year-old children in a more abstract situation (storytelling). It seems imperative, therefore, to take into account this factor when considering communication in children younger than age 10 who have difficulty cognitively in representing an absent partner.

In the conditions permitting interaction among the children, the 6- and 10-year-olds spoke a great deal, producing complicated effects with both disruptive and positive consequences. The number of parsimonious messages was substantially reduced when the listeners were permitted to interact among themselves, and, similarly, the number of correctly placed plugs was less in the listeners interaction condition, although the effect is less pronounced for listener's performance than for speaker's parsimony.

The possibility of asking questions of the speaker, on the other hand, greatly enhanced the listeners' performance among the 6- and 8-year-olds, as shown by the comparison between the experimenter–listener condition and Phase 2 of the speaker–listener condition. The speakers faced a dilemma between the instruction to the speaker to produce parsimonious messages and the instruction to have the listeners correctly place the plugs. Often the speakers failed to produce parsimonious messages because the listeners would ask for information already available to them or obtainable from one of the other listeners. Typically, the speakers attempted to resolve the dilemma by giving too little information and then systematically compelling the listener to ask the other listeners for other information, but on occasion the listener was still unable to obtain the desired information and would again question the speaker.

The large majority of the messages that included more than the minimum essential information resulted from the difficulty inherent in carrying out a cognitive analysis of a complex referent in the presence of listeners requesting information. Analyses of speech corpora show that speakers provided incomplete messages unless probed by the listeners. This may have resulted from the experimental materials: The speaker's playing board contained all the plugs, which may have prevented him from keeping in mind that the listener did not possess the grey plugs. In many cases, the speaker produced redundant messages in response to the listener's explicit request that he provide the unnecessary information. The information, although unnecessary in the context of the problem's structure, was deemed quite useful, however, to the listener who requested it, as witnessed by his insistence when the speaker hesitated to provide it.

An analysis of the speech corpora also showed the occurrence at all age levels of intense communication activity between listeners and speaker and, when possible, between listeners. This activity will be described and synthesized in the next section. The intensity of this activity—an intensity previously found in other problem-solving situations occurring under comparable conditions (Beaudichon & Melot, 1972)—prevents children from concentrating on the task, even though the topic of conversation deals with problem solving. The incessant requests for information disturb the application of information received and lead to disordered activity. For example, a child requests a piece of information from the speaker. At the same time, he attempts to apply the information contained in the speaker's response to another listener's request. He must either ask for the information again or try to apply the information he was unable to process on the spot the best he can. Occurrences such as these are very frequent. Ten-year-olds, in contrast to 6-year-olds, exhibit signs of having acquired skill in asking their interlocutor to wait, to ask later on, *etc.* At times, they become angry at being bothered in this manner. Younger children, who respond to all requests most willingly and without delay, are thus prevented from accomplishing their own tasks.

The children exhibited an almost continuous intercommunication activity during the entire period of observation. Isolation in separate little houses did not result in the production of a considerable number of monologues; in fact, they were surprisingly scarce. Rather, it resulted in numerous contacts similar to the rituals of adult telephone conversations, as well as numerous exchanges whose purpose was to arrive at a satisfactory level of precision. The verbal activity consisted mainly of speech that attempted to obtain or provide information relative to the problem, or of speech in the form of commentaries, hypotheses, judgments relative to the problem, or to problem-solving strategy, consistent with the positions of Vygotsky (1934/1962) and Luria (1961).

The exchanges, however, were often very laborious in this respect. The children often declared that certain items were not easy to explain and that they were not sure that they always understood everything. A large part of their exchanges consisted of checking their own comprehension with their partner. These behaviors strongly resemble those utilized by adults in similar circumstances. In fact, this experiment shows, as do others carried out in the physical absence of the experimenter (see Beaudichon, 1977), that children often adopt attitudes characteristic of the adult explaining a concept to children in class, for example. This affects all age levels, but with several variations. The 6-year-olds copy adults to the extent of caricaturizing them, often meaninglessly; they ask questions, just as a mother or teacher would, but do it even before supplying the necessary information. Role–copying by the child gives way gradually to adult role-taking which requires one to decompose the information transmitted, to repeat it, and to monitor one's understanding. As funny as its initial clumsiness seems to us at times, role–copying progressively evolves into the role-taking skill found in older children.

It was expected that the interaction between children would be largely manifest in 5-year-olds and develop only slightly as a function of age. In the study just described in detail, the youngest subjects were 6 years-of-age. They engaged in nonstop conversation during the entire observation session as did the older children. Another study was carried out (Beaudichon, 1977) in which general structural aspects of speech utterances produced in the apparent absence of the experimenter were systematically studied in various problem-solving and information transmission tasks. In these situations, children exhibit considerably fewer inhibitions and produce many more utterances than when they know they are being observed. The analysis concerned 26,480 speech utterances, produced by 439 children ranging in age from 5- to 13-years-old; they were placed in the same separate little houses where it was necessary to converse directly aloud or by means of a telephone. It was found that 91% of the utterances were made up of dialogue, whereas only 5% were communications that could not be classified as dialogue and only 4% of the utterances could not be classified as communication at all. No developmental tendancy was found. Simple dialogues made up of a single nucleus (speaker utterance followed by a listener utterance) on a given topic were distinguished from complex dialogues made up of two or more nuclei on a given topic. The results show that single dialogues comprise only 6% and 11% of the total number for 13- and 5-year-olds, respectively, and that, once again, the slight developmental tendency is nonsignificant. This finding leads us to concur with fellow researchers in emphasizing the precocity in communication competency which we found even in situations much more complex than those designed by previous researchers.

These findings do not lead us to conclude that 5-year-olds communicate in the same manner as 13-year-olds, thus discounting any evolution whatsoever. To subscribe to this viewpoint would be contrary to the most current observations. We simply mean to say that the means employed by children remain the same within that age period and that no new behaviors emerge. However, the means utilized do not appear as often, and are less efficient, at younger ages; in addition, they are not applied to the same content and cannot be translated by the same verbal forms. They are utilized, but in various degrees of proficiency.

Discussion

We have introduced behaviors characteristic of complex information transmission: Even if the youngest children ask questions, make judgments, *etc.*, they do so less often than other children, and especially in a more general form (i.e., they analyze to a lesser degree the nature of the subject to which the messages are directed). They process information more slowly and less efficiently, and their messages, as well as the responses they elicit, do not attain the precision and clarity of the older children's productions. Therefore they need to repeat things a number of times and make progressive adjustments in order that the communication succeed. It follows that communication becomes progressively more economical with age in terms of the number of attempts, as well as in effort and in communication time. The result is that, in a given time period, more information is processed. Furthermore, contents that are increasingly abstract become comprehensible to children as they grow older. Also, because children can only communicate that which they have mastered intellectually with a sufficient degree of certainty, one witnesses a growing richness in the topics of communication by virtue of the diversity of the subject matter processed. At the same time, the individual's increasing linguistic tools allow for more precise and fluid exchange, caused only in part by communication development. Our data indicate that interindividual differences at a given age were at least as great, if not greater, than the differences in children two years apart. Thus, communication efficiency improves with age, for reasons owing to cognitive and linguistic development rather than relational capacities (attending to the other person, the desire to successfully communicate, *etc.*) or the qualitative broadening of the means employed in successful communication.

The child communicates what he can in the way that he can; he does so with an obvious determination to succeed even if he ultimately fails in certain instances. He does so at the beginning of a conversation by speaking first "in his own manner," to borrow an expression of Zazzo's (1960), and his speech at that time is clearly egocentric. It is poorly adapted to the needs of the listener; however, in a context allowing for interaction, the listener then informs the speaker of his needs, resulting in a modification of the initial production to a more adapted form of communication. Interaction is the important condition for improving encodings in communication. It is also an important condition for meaningful decoding. It is because of the activities that occur during interaction that the listener, by making sure that he has understood, obtains the additions necessary to his comprehension. This appears to be the basic process in realizing an interpersonal communication exchange between children. Adults have usually first acquired a mental representation of the listener's requirements outside the immediate communication context. Children arrive at this representation little by little, but they are capable of communicating without having acquired this representation if the interlocutor is there to generate information that the speaker is still unable to represent by himself. The speaker, moreover, seeks out the reactions of his partner and is attuned to them. It is through signs and verbal interaction which occur between subjects that the imprecise and poorly constructed initial productions evolve, rather spectacularly, into clearer messages. Therefore we feel that communication is not blocked by egocentrism, but that egocentrism disappears thanks to communication. This model of interaction, which has been presented elsewhere (Beaudichon, 1977; Beaudichon, 1979), leads to information processing on an individual level as well as on a relational level between interlocutors. These two levels are at the same time complementary and inseparable. Children are more or less motivated to try to communicate the subject matter in an efficient manner. The subject matter, portrayed by a referent, is more or less favorable to the realization of the communication as well as its efficiency. The means utilized in this realization are more or less operational. It is at this level that pedagogical action can be enacted. We believe this action is both useful and necessary to compensate for the large individual differences found among children in these tasks.

In order to motivate children to make less entailed and more efficient efforts, several experiments were carried out to show the effects of a learning situation on child communication. Many other experiments approaching the question from a more practical viewpoint (i.e., experiments in real-life situations—the classroom, for example) remain to be carried out. We have carried out a study, with the assistance of a group of school teachers, that directs itself to the first of the three factors mentioned: motivation (Beaudichon, Stindel, Gribet, & Teurlay, 1973). After identifying a group of preschool children characterized by lack of motivation to communicate in the classroom, we tried to awaken in them an interest in communication through enjoyable interactions with children their own age. Adults also helped them rid themselves of their inhibitions through a series of very simple procedures, one of which involved the placement of children in small groups, constituted in such a way as to equalize the verbal fluency of the different speakers present. A communication theme was introduced based on the interest generated from prior observation of a physical representation (operation of a marionette, model assembly, *etc.*). The general goal of this procedure was to make the child feel at ease in a task situation in which his performance was good, so that he would feel at ease speaking about it.

The results of the exploratory study revealed that this procedure can be fruitful. Future studies could help lift the heavy handicap that weighs on the underprivileged child's ability to verbally express himself. This is especially crucial, given the important role verbal expression plays in academic, occupational, and social success. Such research should be one of the objectives of those investigators currently involved in the field of communication.

Acknowledgments

Noëlle Ducroux and Anne-Marie Melot collaborated in the experiment presented in detail in this chapter.

I would like to thank John Porter for his translation of the chapter and Patrick Dickson for his editorial assistance.

References

Alvy, K. T. Relation of age to children's egocentric and cooperative communication. *Journal of Genetic Psychology*, 1968, *112*, 275–286.

Beaudichon, J. La communication entre enfants: Transmission des connaissances relative à un matériel concret. *Psychologie Francaise*, 1968, *13*, 265–280.

Beaudichon, J. La communication entre enfants: Transmission des connaissances relatives à un matériel complexe. *Enfance*, 1969, *1–2*, 87–101.

Beaudichon, J. *Caractéristiques et efficacité de la communication chez l'enfant*. Doctorat d' Etat es Lettres et Sciences Humaines, Paris, Université René Descartes, December 1977.

Beaudichon, J. *Continuity in component processes underlying communicative performance: Presentation of a model*. Paper presented at the biennial meeting of International Society for the Study of Behavioral Development, Lund, Sweden, June 1979.

Beaudichon, J., & Forestier, M. F. Facteurs de l'efficacité de la communication entre enfants: La perceptibilité du stimulus. *Bulletin de Psychologie*, 1970, *23*, 575–582.

Beaudichon, J., & Levasseur, J. Procédés et contenus de la communication entre enfants lors de la résolution d'un problème. *Journal de Psychologie Normale et Pathologique,* 1972, *1,* 69–82.

Beaudichon, J., & Melot, A. M. The influence of interindividual communication on problem-solving. In F. J. Monks, W. W. Hartup, & J. de Wit (Eds.), *Determinants of behavioral development.* New York: Academic Press, 1972.

Beaudichon, J., Sigurdson, T., & Trelles, C. Etude de l'adaptabilité verbale à l'interlocuteur. *Psychologie Francaise,* 1978, *23,* 213–220.

Beaudichon, J., Stindel, Y., Gribet, S., & Teurlay, A. *Essai de validation d'une hypothèse d'action.* Paper read at the Conference of Institut National de la Recherche Pèdagogique, St Germain-en-Laye, December 18, 1973.

Cohen, B. D., & Klein, J. A. Referent communication in school-age children. *Child Development,* 1968, *39,* 597–609.

Flavell, J. H., Botkin, P. T., Fry, C. L., Wright, J. H., & Jarvis, P. E. *The development of role taking and communication skills in children.* New York: Wiley, 1968.

Garvey, C., & Hogan, R. Social speech and social interaction: Egocentrism revisited. *Child Development,* 1973, *44,* 562–568.

Glucksberg, S., Krauss, R. M., & Higgins, E. T. The development of referential communication skills. In F. D. Horowitz (Ed.), *Review of child development research* (Vol. 4). Chicago: University of Chicago Press, 1975.

Glucksberg, S., Krauss, R. M., & Weisberg, R. Referential communication in nursery school children: Method and some preliminary findings. *Journal of Experimental Child Psychology,* 1966, *3,* 333–342.

Luria, A. R. *The role of speech in the regulation of normal and abnormal behavior.* London: Pergamon Press, 1961.

McCarthy, D. [Le développement du language.] In L. Carmichael (Ed.), *Manuel de psychologie de l'enfant* (Vol. 2). Paris: Presses Universitaires de France, 1952.

Mueller, E. The maintenance of verbal exchanges between young children. *Child Development,* 1972, *43,* 930–938.

Mueller, E., Bleier, M., Krakow, J., Hegedus, K., & Cournoyer, P. The development of peer verbal interaction among two-year-old boys. *Child Development,* 1977, *48,* 284–287.

Piaget, J. *Le langage et la pensée chez l'enfant. Etudes sur la logique de l'enfant* (5th ed., 1962). Paris: Delachaux & Niestlé, 1923.

Shatz, M., & Gelman, R. The development of communication skills. Modification in the speech of young children as a function of listener. *Monographs of the Society of Research in Child Development,* 1974, *38* (5, No. 152).

Slama-Cazacu, T. Le dialogue chez les petits enfants. Sa signification et quelques-unes de ses particularités. *Bulletin de Psychologie,* 1966, *19,* 688–697.

Slama-Cazacu, T. *Dialogue in children.* The Hague: Mouton, 1978.

Snow, C. E. Mother's speech to children learning language. *Child Development,* 1972, *43,* 549–565.

Vygotsky, L. S. [*Thought and language*] (E. Haufmann and G. Vakar, trans.). Cambridge, Mass.: MIT Press, 1962 (Originally published, 1934).

Zazzo, R. *Les jumeaux, le couple et la personne* (Vol. 2). Paris: Presses Universitaires de France, 1960.

Author Index

Subject Index

A

Ability
  metalinquist, 78
  roletaking, 89, 90
  speaker, 292
  verbal, 191
Absolutism, 94
Accounting, 226–228
Accuracy
  in communication, 108–109, 124, 304, 348–349
  in comparison training, 117–119
  in decoding, 339, 341
  referential, 106, 162, 292–293
Accustomed skills, 122, 128, 129, 131–133, 138
Acquisition of skill, 106, 127–129
Act theory, speech, 316, 318, 331–332
Action
  analysis, 223–232, 236
  deficit, 156

outcome dimension, 282
request, 214–216, 220–221, 223–228
research, 275
sex preference, 233–236
Activation of scheme, 19, 20, 32
Adult, 106, 144, 328, 329, 372, 373
  response effect on child's message, 175–182
Age difference, 145
  in blame ascription, 170
  in decoding, 341, 349
  in encoding, 349, 350
  in listener skill, 153–155
  in recall performance, 325, 326
  in request, 327
  response, 330
Aggravation, 215, 224–226
Ambiguity
  of message, 244
  of situation, 245
Analysis level, 5
Application, 32, 123